# DETERRENCE AND DENIAL

# DETERRENCE AND DENIAL

The Power of Fleets in Being

EDITED BY **S. C. M. PAINE**

**NAVAL INSTITUTE PRESS**
*Annapolis, Maryland*

Naval Institute Press
291 Wood Road
Annapolis, MD 21402

© 2025 by S. C. M. Paine

All rights reserved. No part of this book may be reproduced or utilized in any form or by any means, electronic or mechanical, including photocopying and recording, or by any information storage and retrieval system, without permission in writing from the publisher.

**Library of Congress Cataloging-in-Publication Data**

Names: Paine, S. C. M., editor
Title: Deterrence and denial : the power of fleets in being / edited by S.C.M. PAINE.
Description: Annapolis, Maryland : Naval Institute Press, [2026] | Includes bibliographical references and index.
Identifiers: LCCN 2026000595 (print) | LCCN 2026000596 (ebook) | ISBN 9781682478868 hardcover | ISBN 9781682478875 ebook
Subjects: LCSH: Combat sustainability (Military science) | Navies—History—20th century | Naval history, Modern—20th century | Deterrence (Strategy) | Sea-power—History—20th century | LCGFT: Case studies
Classification: LCC D436 .D48 2026 (print) | LCC D436 (ebook)
LC record available at https://lccn.loc.gov/2026000595
LC ebook record available at https://lccn.loc.gov/2026000596

♾ Print editions meet the requirements of ANSI/NISO z39.48-1992 (Permanence of Paper). Printed in the United States of America.

9 8 7 6 5 4 3 2 1

The ideas and views expressed by the authors of the various parts of this book are their own and do not represent those of the U.S. government, U.S. Department of Defense, U.S. Navy Department, or the U.S. Naval War College.

*To Milan Vego,*
*distinguished scholar, esteemed colleague,*
*and finest U.S. Naval War College naval theorist*
*since Alfred T. Mahan*

# CONTENTS

*List of Illustrations*   xi
*Editor's Preface*   xiii
*Acknowledgments*   xvii
*List of Abbreviations*   xix

INTRODUCTION: Fleets in Being across Time   1
    S. C. M. Paine

## PART I. THE AGE OF SAIL

CHAPTER 1.   The Anglo-Dutch Fleet in 1690:
A Fleet in Being as Strategy   13
*Andrew Lambert*

CHAPTER 2.   A Fleet in Being? Spanish Naval Strategy
(1783–1820)   32
*Iván Valdez-Bubnov*

CHAPTER 3.   Napoleon's Naval Strategy: "Harassing the British
with expenses and fatigue" (1803–14)   52
*Kenneth G. Johnson*

CHAPTER 4.   The Spanish Fleet in Being and the Wars
for Independence in Spanish America (1810–21)   72
*Jorge Ortiz-Sotelo*

## PART II. THE TWENTIETH CENTURY BEFORE THE WORLD WARS

CHAPTER 5.   "Rediscovering" a Fleet in Being: The Debate in
Britain and the United States before World War I   91
*Kevin D. McCranie*

CHAPTER 6.   The Austro-Hungarian Fleet in Being (1893–1918)   110
*Lawrence Sondhaus*

| CHAPTER 7. | The Port Arthur Squadron as a Fleet in Being in the Russo-Japanese War (1904–5)<br>David R. Stone | 128 |
|---|---|---|
| CHAPTER 8. | Pre–World War I Italian Naval Development<br>Francesco Zampieri | 147 |

## PART III. THE TWENTIETH-CENTURY GLOBAL WARS

| CHAPTER 9. | The High Seas Fleet during World War I: A Fleet in Being Contrary to Its Own Intentions (1914)<br>Michael Epkenhans | 169 |
|---|---|---|
| CHAPTER 10. | The Italian Fleet "*in efficienza*" (1919–43)<br>Fabio De Ninno | 188 |
| CHAPTER 11. | Japan and the Interwar Naval Order (1921–41): Did the Imperial Navy Forgo a Fleet in Being to Contest Naval Dominance?<br>Alessio Patalano | 210 |
| CHAPTER 12. | The British and U.S. Reaction to the Japanese Naval Buildup (1930–41)<br>John T. Kuehn | 231 |
| CHAPTER 13. | German Naval Strategy between 1928 and 1945<br>Jörg Hillmann | 251 |

## PART IV. THE COLD WARS

| CHAPTER 14. | The Soviet Squadron-in-Being and Submarine-in-Being Strategies<br>S. C. M. Paine | 275 |
|---|---|---|
| CHAPTER 15. | A Fleet in Being in the Paracel Islands: Chinese Sea Denial (1974)<br>Bruce A. Elleman | 297 |
| CHAPTER 16. | The Impact of the U.S. Pacific Fleet on Chinese Strategy<br>Joel Wuthnow | 317 |

| CHAPTER 17. | A Fleet-in-Being Strategy through Chinese Eyes<br>*Toshi Yoshihara* | 337 |
| CHAPTER 18. | Combat Stability and the Russian Fleet in Being<br>*Andrew Monaghan* | 354 |
| CONCLUSION: | Possibilities and Problems<br>*S. C. M. Paine* | 375 |

*List of Contributors*   393
*Index*   397

# ILLUSTRATIONS

**FIGURE**

| | | |
|---|---|---|
| 11.1 | A Fleet in Being as a Strategic Posture and an Operational Approach | 215 |

**TABLES**

| | | |
|---|---|---|
| 8.1 | Comparison of Italian and French Battleships, 1880–1900 | 153 |
| 10.1 | Italian Armed Forces Expenditures, 1925–34 | 190 |
| 10.2 | Composition of the French and Italian Fleets, 1934 | 190 |
| 10.3 | Relative Strength of the Regia Marina and Royal Navy, September 1935 | 192 |
| 10.4 | Italian Military Expenditures, 1934–40 | 195 |
| 10.5 | Italian Fleet in the Mediterranean, June 1940 | 195 |
| 10.6 | Allied Losses of Warships and Merchant Ships up to 8 September 1943 | 203 |
| 16.1 | PRC Missile Threats to U.S. Pacific Fleet Bases | 323 |
| 16.2 | Distribution of PLA Navy Capabilities | 327 |
| 17.1 | Combat Power Composition | 340 |

# EDITOR'S PREFACE

This book's case studies on fleets in being make clear the potentially debilitating opportunity costs of buying the wrong naval platforms in peacetime that then perform poorly in wartime. For the many countries whose navies either sat out wars in port or did little to hinder enemies in wartime, the opportunity costs seem not to have been adequately examined prior to purchase. Presumably, the need for such discussions became lost in the interwar interservice infighting over budgets and in political infighting among representatives intent on preserving production in their districts—the tactical problems of either preserving budget allocations or manufacturing revenue streams rather than the strategic problem of defending the homeland. Tactical victories in the budget wars proved fatal for interwar Japan (whose army won the budgetary war and went on an unsustainable land warfare rampage throughout China), for Germany (who bought the wrong naval platforms prior to both world wars), and for the Soviet Union (whose huge military budgets debilitated the civilian economy).

Civilian leaders, who leave the budgetary allocations in the hands of the services and manufacturers may imperil national security. Civilians may claim a lack of expertise to make the necessary calls. As a civilian myself with no prior military background but with a career teaching strategy at the U.S. Naval War College, I offer this and three other books coedited with Bruce A. Elleman that helped me and I hope will help others to educate themselves about what navies can and cannot achieve. Two focus on the preferred strategies of naval powers: *Naval Blockades and Seapower: Strategies and Counter-Strategies 1805–2005* and *Naval Power and Expeditionary Wars: Peripheral Campaigns and New Theaters of Naval Warfare*.[1] Wars involving naval powers often begin with the imposition of naval blockades, and protracted wars often entail the opening of new theaters to overextend the adversary. Reliable oceanic access offers many choices on where to open such second fronts. The third book evaluates the continental counterstrategy to blockades: *Commerce Raiding: Historical Case Studies, 1755–2009*.[2] Continental powers generally lack the oceanic access to blockade a maritime enemy and so resort to commerce raiding as a second-best strategy.

Working on these and other books helped me understand the fundamentally different national security paradigms pursued by continental powers, such as China and Russia today, who remain preoccupied with territorial domination, in contrast to maritime powers, focused on wealth maximization through trade—ideas that I summarized in a short article titled "2022 George C. Marshall Lecture in Military History: Centuries of Security: Chinese, Russian, and U.S. Continental versus Maritime Approaches."[3] I have yet to organize a volume on convoys—the means maritime powers use to protect their trade and troop transports against commerce raiding. I am completing a coedited book on sanctions, the chemotherapy of international finance. Maritime powers often rely on sanctions to suppress their enemies' economic growth so that the economic gap between friends and foes compounds over time, diminishing the size of the threat.

Fleets in being, blockades, peripheral operations, commerce raiding, convoys, and sanctions all deserve careful consideration in peacetime to be ready for wartime. The technology of World War II could not reach the United States, which had sanctuary at home for the war's duration, giving it the time for a two-year, wartime military buildup in which its factories were invulnerable to enemy attack. Those days are over. The main lesson of this book is caveat emptor, buyer beware that the consequences of investing in the wrong things are dire. Imperial Germany, Imperial Russia, Imperial Japan, the Soviet Union, and many other polities no longer exist in part because they botched their military budgets.

As this book makes clear, fleet-in-being strategies have been highly consequential for both dominant and dominated navies. Given the correct geography and platforms, both large and small navies have employed fleet-in-being strategies to great operational and strategic advantage. The case studies in this book show how, when, and why.

*S. C. M. Paine*

A note on terminology and hyphens. "Fleet in being" is the noun and "fleet-in-being" is the adjective, so "fleet-in-being strategy."

## NOTES

1. Bruce A. Elleman and S. C. M. Paine, eds., *Naval Blockades and Seapower: Strategies and Counter-Strategies 1805–2005* (London: Routledge, 2006); and *Naval Power and Expeditionary Wars: Peripheral Campaigns and New Theaters of Naval Warfare* (London: Routledge, 2011).
2. Bruce A. Elleman and S. C. M. Paine, eds. *Commerce Raiding: Historical Case Studies, 1755–2009* (Newport, RI: Naval War College Press, 2013).
3. S. C. M. Paine, "2022 George C. Marshall Lecture in Military History: Centuries of Security: Chinese, Russian, and U.S. Continental versus Maritime Approaches," *Journal of Military History* 86 no. 4 (October 2022): 813–36.

# ACKNOWLEDGMENTS

The Henry A. Kissinger Center for Global Affairs at Johns Hopkins School of Advanced International Studies (SAIS) generously made me a senior fellow and shared its digital library collections, essential for my research. Colleagues Kevin D. McCranie and Anand Toprani provided excellent suggestions for the concluding chapter and my case study, respectively. Milan Vego's encyclopedic knowledge on the Soviet navy and the U.S. Naval War College library collection on the subject were equally important. Unfortunately, much of the library collection is now being de-accessioned to make room for the archives in a space that is inadequate for either, let alone both, and the archives has ceased acquiring new materials. As a result, the insights from the papers of retiring officers and the carefully curated book collection reflecting the recommendations of faculty members writing on maritime topics since the college's founding will be lost to future generations.

At the Naval Institute Press, Adam Kane, Padraic (Pat) Carlin, and Jessica Sparks managed editorial matters; Susan Corrado and Brennan Knight oversaw production; and freelancers Patricia Bower and Matthew Simmons copyedited and designed the cover, respectively. I am grateful to them all for their diverse expertise necessary to transform a manuscript into a book. Should book sales prove promising, I will also be grateful to Claire Noble, Jack Russell, Sam Caggiula, and Elena Pelton, responsible for marketing. If not, the fault is mine alone.

*S. C. M. Paine*

# ABBREVIATIONS

| | |
|---|---|
| A2/AD | anti-access / area denial |
| CID | Committee of Imperial Defence |
| CNO | chief of naval operations |
| ETCN | Eastern Theater Command Navy |
| GRT | gross register tonnage |
| IJN | Imperial Japanese Navy |
| nm | nautical mile |
| NTCN | Northern Theater Command Navy |
| PLA | People's Liberation Army |
| PLAN | People's Liberation Army Navy |
| PRC | People's Republic of China |
| RN | Royal Navy |
| ROC | Republic of China |
| SCIO | State Council Information Office (of the PRC) |
| SLBM | submarine-launched ballistic missile |
| SLOC | sea lines of communication |
| SSBN | nuclear-powered submarine |
| STCN | Southern Theater Command Navy |
| USN | United States Navy |
| USSR | Union of Soviet Socialist Republics |

# INTRODUCTION
## Fleets in Being across Time

S. C. M. Paine

Naval analysts generally emphasize offensive naval missions: blockades shutting down enemy ports for naval and commercial traffic, commerce raiding to sever trade relationships, expeditionary warfare to fight on distant shores, and fleet-on-fleet engagements. Most of these operations primarily concern positive operational objectives (making something happen): shutting down traffic, cutting trade, launching an invasion, or sinking an enemy fleet. The present study examines an essential, often overlooked, and generally poorly understood defensive naval strategy: the peacetime and wartime possibilities for a fleet in being. Unlike offensive naval missions, a fleet-in-being strategy emphasizes negative operational and strategic objectives (preventing something from happening): preventing an enemy attack or fleet deployment. Yet preventing an attack on the homeland or balking an enemy's preferred strategy can be as important as any positive objective.

Fleet-in-being strategies have been used to impose risks on adversaries to deter them in peacetime and to deny them passage in wartime. Determining the efficacy of strategies seeking negative objectives is controversial because of the inherent difficulty of confirming the reasons for a nonoccurrence—perhaps the rival never planned to execute the action supposedly deterred or denied. This does not make negative objectives less important than positive ones, just trickier to evaluate, and well worth a book to examine.

The concept of a fleet in being and its optimal deployment has long been discussed and disputed. During the Cold War, Robert Waring Herrick (1923–2010) served for two years as assistant naval attaché in Moscow and retired as a commander from the U.S. Navy, later publishing some of the finest books on Soviet naval strategy.[1] In his glossary of terms, he distinguished between an active versus a passive fleet in being:

> *Fleet-in-Being Strategy, Active*—A defensive strategy of the potential offensive adopted by a weaker naval power by a fleet whose main naval forces are mainly held in port to avoid any general engagement but whose auxiliary forces (submarines, aircraft, and fast surface-craft) are employed for an "active" (tactically offensive) defense with the aim of holding command of the sea in dispute. This was the strategy for an inferior navy espoused by Sir Phillip Colomb and Sir Julian Corbett and the one seemingly adopted by the Soviet School of naval warfare.[2]
>
> *Fleet-in-Being, Passive*—A defensive strategy of the potential offensive adopted by either a stronger or weaker naval power in which a fleet is held in port or close enough to port not to be cut off. The strategy is employed as a deterrent against amphibious invasion or against attacks on coastal cities or installations. The aim is to persuade a stronger naval adversary to content himself at most with establishing and maintaining a blockade of the fleet in being. Professor [Rear Admiral Vladimir Aleksandrovich] Belli [1887–1981] characterized this strategy as "a fleet in existence, a threat without strikes" because it proscribes accepting battle with the stronger fleet to avoid the risk of its destruction which would leave the country open to seaborne assault or to the imposition of a victor's peace terms.[3]

The following eighteen chapters will put the concept in concrete historical and geographical contexts to see in practice what the strategy could deliver operationally and strategically in wartime and peacetime. The first four chapters concern the age of sail. After Andrew Lambert's chapter on the Anglo-Dutch Wars, two chapters examine the Spanish experience in the late eighteenth and early nineteenth centuries. Chapter 2, by Iván Valdez-Bubnov, focuses on strategic planning in Madrid to protect against rivals in Europe and to defend its empire in the Americas, while chapter 4 by Jorge Ortiz-Sotelo traces Spain's loss of that empire. The intervening chapter 3, by Kenneth G. Johnson, discusses the overarching Napoleonic Wars that ruined Spain and so many other countries.

Andrew Lambert begins the age-of-sail section with a chapter on the man who coined the term "fleet in being," Admiral Arthur Herbert, Lord Torrington, when he laid out the strategy during the War of the League of Augsburg (1689–97). Torrington recommended avoiding a fleet-on-fleet engagement on unfavorable terms with France in order to retain his allied fleet in being to preclude a French amphibious invasion by making such a plan too risky to execute. He argued that the very existence of his fleet would prevent a French invasion in the south of England while England's main force fought in Ireland.

In chapter 2 Iván Valdez-Bubnov examines late eighteenth- and early nineteenth-century Spanish naval planning. Spain faced threats not only in Europe but also from U.S. expansion and colonial revolts in the Americas. Spain developed an active defense strategy of shipbuilding, diplomacy, deterrence, diversion, amphibious operations, localized offensive use of the battle fleet, and trade warfare. A fleet in being was just one component of the overarching plan. It was hoped that a peacetime fleet in being would deter attacks on the homeland by forcing rivals to keep their own fleets close to home to defend their own shores and to shelve plans to invade well-protected Spanish shores.

Napoleon employed a wartime fleet-in-being strategy in many of his early plans, the subject of chapter 3 by Kenneth Johnson. However, a fleet in being did not become central to his naval strategy until the last years of his empire, when he used his smaller fleets to impose costs on Britain by pinning the Royal Navy to specific locations or by dispersing it across theaters. He hoped to buy time while he attempted to overcome France's many resource and port limitations by expanding his empire and then building a navy to rival Britain's. Although he came close to reaching this objective by 1813, Britain used the preceding years to decimate France's overseas commerce and capture all of its colonies by 1810.

Spanish strategy in the waning years of its empire in the Americas is the subject of chapter 4 by Jorge Ortiz-Sotelo. Despite the weakness of the Spanish navy in the Americas, it did not face serious challenges until 1818, when the creation of an opposing Chilean squadron forced its warships based at Callao to adopt a fleet-in-being strategy: Spanish warships avoided a decisive battle, lifted the blockade of the Chilean coast, and concentrated their efforts along the Peruvian coast, awaiting reinforcements that never arrived. Nevertheless, it is amazing how much Spanish authorities accomplished with so little—they retained Callao despite a decade-long, on-and-off blockade and maintained communication among theaters so that independence became a ten-year process.

The second section turns to the period immediately prior to the world wars. With the end of the age of sail, Kevin McCranie's chapter 5 opens the pre–world war section with an overview of how British and U.S. naval theorists addressed a fleet in being. Chapter 6, by Lawrence Sondhaus, then highlights the many achievements of Austria-Hungary's economical fleet-in-being strategy when applied to narrow seas. Chapter 7, by David Stone, then emphasizes Russia's inattention to the possibility of a fleet-in-being strategy in the Russo-Japanese War, while chapter 8, by Francesco Zampieri, shows Italy's unsuccessful attempt to implement the strategy.

In chapter 5, Kevin McCranie provides an overview of the disagreements among nineteenth- and early twentieth-century British and U.S. naval theorists, who reexamined Admiral Torrington's experience and applied his concept of a fleet in being to the First Sino-Japanese, Spanish-American, and Russo-Japanese wars. McCranie compares the divergent assessments of supporters of fleet-in-being strategies, including Philip H. Colomb, James Thursfield, and Julian Corbett, to those who were more critical, such as Spenser Wilkinson, David Hannay, Alfred T. Mahan, John Frederick Maurice, William Laird Clowes, Richard Wainwright, Charles Callwell, and George Aston.

Lawrence Sondhaus turns to Austria-Hungary in chapter 6. He argues that the battle fleet of the Austro-Hungarian navy provides perhaps the best modern example of a fleet in being. Austria-Hungary constructed its fleet not to overpower its rivals but to deter them and to project power regionally, all by its very existence. Despite having the smallest navy among the eight great powers of the era, Austria-Hungary successfully denied regional command of the sea to its rivals and adversaries, and defended its coastline and projected power regionally, forcing its enemies in World War I into expensive Mediterranean convoys to protect against submarine warfare.

If Austria-Hungary is a positive case, Russia in the Russo-Japanese War is a negative case, a point made by David Stone in chapter 7. Given Russia's fundamentally continental nature, its theorists hardly considered the concept at all and even lacked a Russian translation for it. Once engaged in hostilities, when a fleet-in-being strategy might have been applicable, some commanders groped toward fleet-in-being ideas, but the lack of prewar preparations for such a strategy and the objective conditions of naval warfare in the Yellow Sea precluded the strategy. The Japanese army sank the Russian fleet in being at anchor after a long siege of Port Arthur and then destroyed the main fleet that belatedly came to the rescue in the Battle of Tsushima.

In chapter 8, Francesco Zampieri highlights Italy's strategic dilemma and operational trade-offs of defending against both France and Austria-Hungary, adversaries who required large peacetime fleets in being in completely different locations to deter attack and extensive bases in between. Prior to World War I, Italy adopted a fleet-in-being strategy primarily to protect its western coasts from France and, by the beginning of the twentieth century, to contain the Austro-Hungarian fleet in the Adriatic operational theater. At the beginning of the twentieth century the rivalry with France diminished while that with Austria-Hungary grew. Italy's strategy required significant expenditures to build a credible naval force and efficient bases, which proved beyond its financial capabilities.

The chapters on the world wars in the third section detail the experience of Germany (chapter 9, by Michael Epkenhans, for the first world war and chapter 13, by Jörg Hillmann, for the second world war), Italy (chapter 10, by Fabio De Ninno), Japan (chapter 11, by Alessio Patalano), and the United States and Great Britain (chapter 12, by John Kuehn). The geographic constraints facing these countries differed. Germany and Italy bordered on narrow seas, whereas Japan, the United States, and the United Kingdom bordered on open oceans. Fleets in being proved to be major impediments to coastal invasions in narrow seas and to be enablers for submarine commerce-raiding campaigns, but fleets in being were vulnerable targets if far from home.

Michael Epkenhans, in chapter 9, shows how Germany from 1897 onward attempted to build a navy to rival Britain's Royal Navy for an expected war-winning fleet-on-fleet engagement. Yet in World War I, there was only one major fleet-on-fleet engagement, the Battle of Jutland. For the rest of the war the German High Seas Fleet became a fleet in being stuck in port. Nevertheless, it served a key strategic function: the fleet in being, combined with land defenses and sea mines, precluded an enemy invasion over its coastline. It also tied up British ships that otherwise could have served on convoy duty in a commerce war that came perilously close to undermining the British war effort.

Chapter 10, by Fabio De Ninno, turns to Italy, which in the nineteenth century had developed a peacetime deterrent fleet-in-being approach to counter French naval superiority. During the interwar period, this evolved into a wartime doctrine defined as the defensive offense, or fleet *in efficienza* (efficiency). This operational theory sought to inflict naval attrition to compensate for a numerical inferiority in capital ships. Nevertheless, Italian finances again proved insufficient to build up the bases and naval attrition arms—namely, submarines and naval air power—necessary for operational success. During World War II, the fleet in efficiency proved incapable of inflicting the necessary attrition for Italy to dominate its surrounding seas and ineffective in achieving Italy's strategic goals. Defeat at Taranto in 1940 then forced a return to a fleet-in-being strategy, which proved insufficient to counter systematic harassment of Axis communications in the central Mediterranean and, later, to deter an Allied invasion from North Africa.

Alessio Patalano, author of chapter 11, focusing on interwar Japan, distinguishes between the wartime and peacetime variants of a fleet-in-being strategy. The wartime variant, analyzed at length by the naval theorists highlighted by Kevin McCranie in chapter 5, concerns an operationally opportunistic strategy leveraging the latent threat of deployable naval assets. In contrast, the peacetime variant concerns a passive strategic posture intended to avoid war. Japan never intended to use a fleet in being to avoid war. Rather, it envisioned a wartime fleet-in-being strategy made possible by developing the necessary capabilities prior to hostilities to win with an active fleet-in-being strategy in wartime. Japanese naval planners never pursued a fleet that could deter through presence.

Chapter 12, by John Kuehn, compares the U.S. and British responses to Japan's naval buildup in the 1930s. While the U.S. Navy leadership focused on building a battle fleet that would prevail in a Mahanian fleet-on-fleet showdown with Japan, Britain planned to employ an economy-of-force, fleet-in-being strategy centered in Singapore to defend its Asian colonies. The forward-based fleet in Hawaii was never intended to be ready for immediate naval operations, and Britain's fortress-based fleet-in-being in Singapore did not survive the opening hours of the war. The defense of Singapore presumed the ability to hold out until major fleet and air force deployments arrived from Europe, while basing at Pearl Harbor presumed an invulnerability to attack.

Jörg Hillmann shows in chapter 13 how, during the interwar period, Germany's fleet in being initially intended to deter its immediate neighbors expanded with visions of a dominant, offensive fleet. These ambitions reflected the dreams of German naval officers, but their plans never matched the military or geographic realities constraining Germany. Its naval access via narrow seas along the coast of its primary naval enemy required a force structure different from that of Britain, with its unfettered access to the high seas. Had Germany built U-boats instead of capital ships, it might have starved Britain before the United States intervened. The German navy never planned to use a fleet-in-being strategy of deterrence but always wanted to match British warships and use large battleships to cut their sea lines of communication.

The final section analyzes the cold wars of the twentieth and twenty-first centuries. The two twentieth-century Cold War chapters are S. C. M. Paine's chapter 14, examining the Soviet far seas squadron in being and its home-water submarine fleet in being, and Bruce Elleman's chapter 15 on the Sino-Soviet experience in Vietnam with a fleet in being deployed to the Paracels. The contemporary chapters keep the focus on Russia and China. In chapter 17 Toshi Yoshihara outlines China's fleet-in-being possibilities vis-à-vis the United States, while in chapter 16 Joel Wuthnow analyzes U.S. possibilities in dealing with China. In chapter 18 Andrew Monaghan turns to Russia's naval buildup.

Chapter 14, by S. C. M. Paine, focuses on Soviet operational solutions to the geographic constraints of surrounding narrow seas and the technological constraints of countering technologically superior adversaries. To overcome the former, Russia pursued a far seas squadron-in-being strategy, requiring overseas basing and overflight rights, to acquire a veto-player role in the Middle East and Africa. To overcome the latter, it pursued a near seas submarine fleet-in-being strategy to ensure a second-strike nuclear capability as a guarantee for homeland security. The squadron-in-being strategy did constrain and impose costs on the U.S. and Israeli strategy in the Middle East, but the effectiveness of submarine fleet-in-being to deter a NATO nuclear attack remains unclear since the West never intended to launch a preemptive nuclear attack on the USSR. Either way, by the 1980s the combined costs of two types of fleets in being helped bankrupt the Soviet Union.

In the 1979 Sino-Vietnamese War, examined in chapter 15, Bruce A. Elleman shows that China's fleet in being stationed at the Paracels off the main Vietnamese port of Haiphong precluded Soviet military aid from reaching Vietnam. Given that China suffered enormous casualties, one can speculate that timely Soviet military aid would, at minimum, have increased casualties. Elleman shows how the United States, in the waning days of South Vietnam, failed to support its ally but allowed China to wrest control of the Paracel Islands, creating an enduring territorial dispute after the reunification of Vietnam and ceding a strategic location for China to exert continuing pressure on Vietnam.

Joel Wuthnow highlights the elevated risk to fleets in being in the era of precision strike. In chapter 16 he suggests that a modified fleet-in-being strategy could help the United States to deter or respond effectively to Chinese aggression against Taiwan in three ways. First, U.S. naval reliance on Japanese ports would force Beijing to decide whether to attack Japan and risk bringing another major power into the conflict. Second, U.S. naval support for other Asian allies requires China's navy to disperse its capabilities along its maritime frontier and train for multiple contingencies, reducing its ability to focus on Taiwan. Third, the possibility of a U.S. distant blockade of Chinese imports in a crisis could require China's navy to dispatch assets to Southeast Asia or the Indian Ocean region, reducing its capacity to support an invasion. These three counters to China strengthen deterrence by presenting Beijing with the risk of a conflict that expands in number of participants and geographic scope.

Chapter 17, by Toshi Yoshihara, lays out China's offensive version of a fleet-in-being strategy. In a war at sea, China's naval strategy calls for aggressive tactics and counterattacks to achieve its aims in home waters and distant theaters. Near seas defense remains central to the strategy for as long as disputes in the maritime direction remain unresolved and the prospect of third-party intervention over those disputes is probable, if not certain. Yet China also intends to project naval power far from home as its global interests and associated vulnerabilities proliferate. Although a global sea control force remains a distant goal, the force structure reveals the contours of a world-class navy. In the meantime, China's near seas and far seas strategies can be viewed as an aggressive variety of a fleet in being posing significant operational challenges to the United States, should it choose to intervene against Chinese aggression. China's fleet in being and other military capabilities could buy China enough time to achieve territorial objectives before the United States could assemble enough power to respond.

The final case study, in chapter 18 by Andrew Monaghan, reveals a distinctively Russian version of a fleet in being. Although the Russian navy does not use the fleet-in-being concept, aspects of it can be found in Russia's concepts of strategic deterrence, combat stability (survivability), and active defense, in which the Russian navy seeks not to engage in fleet-on-fleet action in a war-winning battle but instead to engage in fleet-against-shore action to assist the overall war effort. Rather than the concept of a fleet in being, Russian planners think in terms of "fleet against shore," "combat stability" and "active defense," which together represent "fleet survivability" and a more dynamic form of war fighting.

The concluding chapter relies on the historical data from the preceding chapters to answer the following questions: Under what circumstances is a fleet in being most and least likely to be successful? It turns out that the relevance of naval theories depends on the specific geography of the theater—open or narrow seas and the presence or absence of threatened landward borders. Given such geographic constraints, for what strategic and operational objectives is a fleet in being most likely to be useful? In practice, peacetime fleets in being have been used for deterrence while wartime fleets in being have been used for denial. Both deterrence and denial are negative objectives, whose success is evaluated not in measurable, tangible results but in the prevention of undesirable actions. This precludes definitive assessments of the efficacy of the strategy. Given this uncertainty, can only dominant navies get cost-effective denial effects? It turns out that dominated navies can impose high costs and preclude promising operations for dominant navies. Finally, what are the best ways to neutralize a fleet in being? Answer: preemptive attack in peacetime or the destruction of naval bases in wartime. The concluding chapter presents the evidence for these findings.

## NOTES

1. Robert Waring Herrick's monographs include *Soviet Naval Strategy: Fifty Years of Theory and Practice* (Annapolis, MD: Naval Institute Press, 1968); *Soviet Naval Theory and Policy: Gorshkov's Inheritance* (Newport, RI: Naval War College Press, 1986); and *Soviet Naval Doctrine and Policy 1956–1986*, 3 vols. (Lewiston, NY: Edward Mellen Press, 2003).
2. Herrick, *Soviet Naval Theory and Policy*, 280.
3. Herrick, 280–1.

# PART I
# THE AGE OF SAIL

CHAPTER 1

# THE ANGLO-DUTCH FLEET IN 1690
## A Fleet in Being as Strategy

*Andrew Lambert*

The essence of a fleet in being is the use of a defensive posture to prevent a superior enemy fleet from exploiting command of the sea; it can be used to delay specific offensive operations—notably, an invasion or a commercial blockade—or cover the assembly of additional naval resources to enable the fleet to challenge for command. It is especially important in the wider context of grand strategy, where the power with an inferior fleet may be superior in another aspect of the conflict where it seeks to secure a decision. It is also an effective strategy for a dominant navy to use in a secondary theater, enabling it to concentrate resources to seek a decision in the primary theater. In 1690 Admiral Arthur Herbert, Lord Torrington (1648–1718) advised this was best achieved by avoiding battle at Beachy Head. He coined the term "fleet in being" when defending his defeat after his superiors rejected his advice and forced him to fight.

### THE CAMPAIGN OF 1690

The Battle of Beachy Head occurred during the War of the League of Augsburg (1689–97) fought by a grand coalition that included the Dutch Republic, the Holy Roman Empire, England, and Spain to prevent Louis XIV's France from securing control of Western Europe. English concerns focused on the strategic region around the Scheldt Estuary, the obvious base for a French invasion of England. The coalition was led by the Dutch stadtholder and English king William III, who controlled the economic, naval, and military resources of both states. In 1690 William launched a military campaign to secure control in Ireland, to stabilize England, and to release its resources to support the coalition. The French deployed their battle fleet, and a small military force in Ireland, to pin William on the defensive while advancing in Europe. The French had not planned to invade England that year—nor deployed the necessary troops. They were at a serious disadvantage in the Channel: without a single deep water naval base.

The critical strategic move of 1690 would be an Anglo-Dutch offensive to secure control of Ireland. However, the allies made a late start mobilizing their navies and detached significant forces to the Mediterranean and Irish waters, leaving the main fleet in the English Channel significantly weaker than the combined French fleets. The allied commander, Admiral Lord Torrington, advised the English ministers that he would withdraw from the English Channel if necessary, keeping his fleet "in being," ready to counterattack if the French attempted to invade, attacked allied merchant shipping, or threatened William's communications with Ireland.

Having commanded the Dutch fleet that invaded England in 1688, Herbert became Lord Torrington and sat on the Privy Council, the royal advisory body that developed national and alliance strategy. This prominent political role influenced his strategic choices in 1690. He had commanded the main allied fleet in 1689 and recognized that the French had secured their strategic objectives in Ireland through an inconclusive combat in Bantry Bay. He saw no reason to rush into battle with a superior force.

The Channel campaign of 1690 had begun the previous summer, when French admiral Anne-Hilarion de Tourville and twenty major warships sailed from the Mediterranean to form and command a combined fleet of sixty-two ships of the line at Brest. The allies had too few ships at sea to intercept or even observe this movement. Pressure from the City of London apparently led William to escort the Mediterranean trade, detaching Admiral Sir Francis Killigrew with thirteen ships of the line, while Admiral Sir Edward Russell escorted the new bride of the Spanish king from Ostend to la Coruna before detaching most of his squadron to join Killigrew, who had orders to observe the French and engage or pursue them if they attempted to leave the Mediterranean. While Killigrew intercepted the enemy in the Straits of Gibraltar on 10 May with a superior force, he lost contact. This tactical setback became a strategic problem when he waited to refit his ships and convoy the trade rather than pursue the enemy. Killigrew's ships would have balanced the two fleets but arrived at Plymouth after Torrington had been defeated at Beachy Head.[1] In addition six ships of the line under Rear Admiral Sir Cloudesley Shovell were escorting William and his army across the Irish Sea.

These detachments were deliberate strategic choices to be judged at the highest level of the war. William had to secure Ireland before he could use English resources in European campaigns, while exerting allied influence in the Mediterranean was critical to the grand alliance against Louis XIV.[2] In William's mind, the naval component of allied strategy was necessarily subordinated to the terrestrial, where Louis XIV posed the greatest threat. It appears William knew the French had not assembled an army on the Channel coast to invade England.[3] Sending a few thousand French troops to Ireland did not indicate an ability to invade England. That said, when William sailed from Chester for Carrickfergus with 288 transports, escorted by a mere six warships, he was taking a serious strategic risk since the location of the French battle fleet was unknown.

The weakness of the allied position in 1690 flowed from the late mobilization of their fleets, reflecting political instability in England, economic difficulties, and the uncertain outcome of the 1688 revolution, which hardly seemed "glorious" at the time. William's new regime was only one first-class disaster away from utter ruin. The silent majority was uncommitted. William left London for Ireland, relying on Daniel Finch, Earl of Nottingham, a politician with Admiralty experience, to direct the English government. Nottingham relied on Admiral Sir Edward Russell, an old enemy of Torrington, for professional input. Russell and Nottingham assumed Killigrew would detain the French Mediterranean squadron in the Straits of Gibraltar and, along with Shovell's small squadron, rejoin the main fleet before a major action. Such optimism proved unfounded. The French combined their fleets while the allies remained dispersed, leaving Torrington with fifty-six ships of the line to face Tourville's sixty-eight or seventy. Further pressure on allied fleet strength came from English and Dutch merchants, men with real political power, unlike their French counterparts.

The naval members of the Admiralty Board, including Torrington, had resigned in January 1690, complaining of inadequate preparations for the forthcoming campaign. By early May 1690 the situation was so bad that Torrington, waiting for more ships at the Nore, threatened to resign. He finally sailed for Portsmouth, the base for Channel operations, on 23 May, where ships began to assemble in June. During the king's absence in Ireland, the Queen's Council was headed by Nottingham, who remained optimistic. On 17 June he advised the king that the allied fleet was "stronger than any the French can set out from Brest," a claim Tourville had proven false four days earlier. When forced to accept reality, Nottingham and the Queen's Council rushed into action, issuing futile orders for Killigrew and Shovell to join Torrington "immediately" and urging ships be completed for sea at Portsmouth while maintaining a facade of optimism when corresponding with the king. By this time it must have been obvious to Nottingham and his fellow councillors, including Admiral Russell, that their only hope of avoiding blame for a potential disaster lay in making a scapegoat of Torrington. Torrington reported almost eighty French ships of the line, but Nottingham told the king there were only sixty, both to avoid his culpability for the late mobilization and to justify ordering the admiral to fight.[4]

Tourville sailed from Brest on 13 June, when the Mediterranean squadron commanded by François Louis Rousselet de Châteaurenault arrived. He commanded seventy-eight ships, sixty-eight to seventy of them ships of the line, with twenty-two fire ships. The following day William sailed from Chester for Ireland. The French were aware of the weakness of the allied fleet, ordering Tourville to attack Portsmouth, the key English naval base, and then blockade the Thames to prevent the English and Dutch fleets combining.[5] These missions were at the outer limits of what was possible for a seventeenth-century battle fleet without a significant military force. Torrington's smaller fleet lay at Spithead, hurriedly preparing for sea, along with his Dutch allies.

Torrington put to sea on 24 and 25 June with fifty-six ships of the line to conduct essential tactical training. No sooner had the allied fleet begun to anchor on the afternoon of 25 June than the French came into view from the west. Torrington immediately weighed anchor and moved to attack but changed his mind when he realized he was heavily outnumbered. Despite superior numbers, Tourville evinced no enthusiasm for battle, perhaps shocked by the realization that the allied fleets had united. He had expected to defeat the English fleet and destroy Portsmouth before the Dutch arrived.[6]

Both fleets anchored for the night. The next morning Torrington assembled his admirals for a Council of War on board the 100-gun flagship *Royal Sovereign* and reported their collective decision to Nottingham. While noting the enemy's reluctance to fight, the council concluded that the allied fleet was too weak to have any hope of success. The enemy had 20 percent more ships and guns. Torrington planned to retreat eastward and, if necessary, shelter behind the Gunfleet shoal in the Thames Estuary, where he could protect Chatham, attacked by the Dutch in 1667, as well as London and the Dockyards at Woolwich and Deptford, concluding: "I shall not think myself very unhappy if I can get rid of them without fighting." While waiting for a reply he sailed east, placing the weak Dutch squadron in the van, furthest from the advancing French.[7] His fleet should avoid battle, denying the French the effective command of the sea needed to attempt an invasion.[8]

Despite Torrington's considered explanation and the unanimous decision of the Council of War, Queen Mary ordered him to fight "rather than retreat further than the South Foreland": "It is impossible for us here to be able to make a judgement of what ought to be done and we do not doubt but your conduct will be such in this important affair as this is not to lose any fair opportunity of doing service on the enemy, but as to that matter of retiring to Gunfleet the thought of the last ill consequences and so fatal that we apprehend your retiring and being beaten the same thing." The queen's letter to Torrington of 28 June demanded he engage the enemy, if the wind allowed; retreating to the Gunfleet would be worse than a defeat. He was at liberty to head westward, but must remain in sight of the enemy.[9] The Queen's Council detached the Duke of Monmouth to Portsmouth. He arrived on 29 June to find Torrington had sailed east, reporting "the Gunfleet design is put into execution." The reasons why were obvious from the state of the dockyard, where the few remaining ships were without cables and sailors.[10]

On 29 June the Queen's Council decided to remove Torrington from command if he refused to fight.[11] Nottingham claimed Torrington had exaggerated French numbers and interpreted his advice that it might, in the worst case, be necessary to retreat all the way to the Gunfleet as a statement of intent, confusing a fleet in being with a fortress fleet, a fleet that was subordinated to the fortress in which it sheltered. Alfred Thayer Mahan linked this concept with Russian navies.[12] The Queen's Council was alarmed by the precedent that the English fleet had been wind-bound in the Gunfleet when William invaded England two years before.[13] Edward Russell set off for Dover to assume command.

The queen's order to engage reached Torrington late on 29 June. He lost no time replying to Nottingham, stressing his willingness to engage but casting doubt on the assumptions that informed the order, remaining confident the merchant ships and detached squadrons would be safe if he kept the enemy in sight: "Whilst we observe the French, they cannot make any attempt either up ships or shore, without running a great hazard; and if we are beaten, all is exposed to their mercy." This ended any thought of removing Torrington: Russell was recalled from his mission to Dover.[14] Nevertheless, since the Queen's Council in London had rejected the Council of War's fleet-in-being strategy, Torrington accepted that he must fight. To ensure he did not lose the fleet, Torrington decided to engage at long range, to avoid serious damage to his rigging, while massing the ships of his center squadron to threaten a portion of the enemy line. Cornelis Evertsen's Dutch squadron did not follow these plans.

The next morning, 30 June, Torrington bore down on the French to fight ten miles south of the white cliffs of Beachy Head. The Dutch in the van had not understood Torrington's determination to avoid action at close quarters. They were the first to engage and were overpowered.[15] One ship was captured, two sank. The main problem for the allies was numerical. As each squadron was numerically weaker than its opposite number, they risked having ships overpowered by multiple opponents. The three close-ordered allied squadrons drifted apart, unable to prolong their formation to match the more numerous French. The first two divisions of the French center attacked the already hard-pressed Dutch.

Torrington rescued the situation, ordering the fleet to anchor with all sails set, and then towed his imposing flagship, the 100-gun three decker *Royal Sovereign*, into position to defend the crippled ships against a French attack. His seamanship caught the French by surprise: they had been rushing to launch boats to tow their ships into action. By the time the French could anchor, they were three miles beyond the allies and, significantly, to the west.[16] The battle was over. With no secure anchorages between Spithead and the Gunfleet, Torrington had no option but to continue his retreat to the Thames. The allied losses of ships of the line were *Anne* (70 guns) for the English and *Wapen van Utrecht* (64 guns), *Maagd van Enkhuizen* (72 guns), *Tholen* (60 guns), *Elswout* (50 guns), and several expendable fireships for the Dutch.

Contemporary and late-nineteenth century judgments of Beachy Head focused on the battle. Torrington's outnumbered fleet fought well for five to six hours and broke off the action before the enemy had an opportunity to inflict catastrophic losses. The French reported over a thousand casualties.[17] Torrington's seamanship saved the day, taking the French by surprise. Although the allies avoided further damage, they had been heavily and unnecessarily defeated due to political interference from London and unthinking aggression on the part of the Dutch. More ships were scuttled during the remaining stages of the retreat, which ended at the Nore, a more exposed anchorage than the Gunfleet but closer to the base at Sheerness. Tourville did not pursue the allies with any vigor: desperately short of gunpowder and without pilots for the dangerous sandbanks at the Downs, he abandoned the pursuit off Dover. There is no evidence he sought to destroy the allies.[18] The overcrowded French fleet, hampered by weather and disease, lacked the army and transport shipping to exploit their success.[19] Torrington reached the Thames Estuary undisturbed.

Torrington reported the battle to Nottingham on 1 July, castigating the Queen's Council for ordering him to fight: "Had I been left to my liberty, I had prevented any attempt upon the land, and secured the western ships, Killigrew and the merchantmen. . . . Had I undertaken this [action] of my own head, I should not well know what to say; but its' being done by command will, I hope, free me from blame."[20] This backfired. The Queen's Council had no intention of admitting responsibility; it needed him to be the scapegoat. When some Dutch officers, although not Admiral Cornelis Evertsen, accused Torrington of cowardice and desertion, the queen and council apologized profusely to the States General, happy to join them in blaming Torrington, promising to punish those responsible.

Well aware of his own culpability for the disaster, Nottingham shifted attention to Torrington, linking hints of treachery with the inflammatory claim that the admiral had abandoned the Dutch to their fate. He wrote to the king of "the base treachery or cowardice of my Lord Torrington, . . . tho' as yet there are no formal proofs of it the fleet being not come in." He claimed the admiral had "deserted the Dutch so shamefully that the whole squadron had been lost, if some of our ships had not rescued them." Although his only coherent complaint was that Torrington had not engaged closely, Nottingham insisted he should be removed from command "before he destroys the whole fleet."[21] The order was issued on the same day.[22] Recognizing a serious threat to the cohesion of the Grand Alliance, William echoed the Queen's Council, promising the States General that Torrington would be punished without troubling to check if there had been any malfeasance.

Having judged the admiral without evidence, Nottingham soon discovered the fleet did not share the hostile opinions of Edward Russell, nor did it wish their admiral removed to appease the Dutch.[23] The following day Nottingham shifted his focus to the negative outcomes of a battle he had ordered Torrington to fight against the publicly expressed professional opinion of an allied Council of War. Now the Queen's Council advised the king that the French would not have come into the Channel if they did not intend an invasion, an argument no doubt influenced by Edward Russell. Three days later Nottingham reported it was thought the French, last seen off the Ness (Dungeness), were "going to meet their galleys and going to make some attempt on our ships at the Buoy of the Nore and Chatham, or on Portsmouth or Plymouth."[24] While this was pure speculation and without foundation, it had become by default the only basis for scapegoating Torrington.

The most important outcome of the action was that the allied fleet escaped further punishment. The French pursuit was, as Torrington had anticipated, halfhearted and brief. Tourville abandoned the task off Dover on 9 July. French admirals found the straits a serious physical and psychological barrier. However, Torrington could not exploit that decision for want of a suitable harbor, dockyard, and supplies to refit his ships between Portsmouth and Sheerness. Having failed to annihilate an inferior opponent, Tourville dropped back down the Channel, anchoring off Le Havre to land his wounded and replenish his powder and shot, of which a prodigious quantity had been expended. Tourville left the Channel on 5 August with an alarming sick list.[25]

While Torrington had lost a battle he never wished to fight, his cautious tactics and orderly retreat ensured that the allied fleet remained sufficiently powerful to prevent an invasion. The hysterical invasion panic that followed the battle reflected the overwrought anxieties of the year, rather than the strategic situation. A cautious strategist, William would not have gone to Ireland if he had expected a major French operation against England.[26] His victory at the Boyne the day after Beachy Head and subsequent rapid advance through Ireland effectively silenced the anxiety, rendering Beachy Head strategically irrelevant. Although a small French contingent remained in Ireland, the Stuart cause was lost from "the want of a squadron of French men of war in the St. George's Channel," while the French had no plans to reinforce the Irish army or invade England.[27] As is often the case, a great sea battle bore little strategic fruit.[28] Both admirals would be dismissed—as Torrington wryly observed.

Torrington became the scapegoat for the failures of others, notably a council that had given Queen Mary bad advice. He was not a traitor or a fool. The wisdom of his conduct was acknowledged by Nottingham when he ordered the allied fleet back to sea in early August. He endorsed the fleet-in-being concept, directing the admirals to cruise between the South Foreland and the Ness, "but on intelligence the French fleet are drawing that way to retire to the Gunfleet and on no account to engage the enemy if their strength be not inferior to his." Another squadron of heavier ships would assemble at the Gunfleet.[29] At the end of the month Nottingham investigated the invasion risk, dispatching an agent to France for intelligence of the enemy fleet and the ex-king.[30]

Torrington had been sent to the Tower of London on 10 July, joining suspected Jacobites. The ministers were anxious to convict him, but the choice of a suitable legal process was complicated, while naval opinion rapidly hardened against the attempt to appease the Dutch and exculpate the Queen's Council. Although the Admiralty realized an acquittal would raise awkward questions about the level of preparation before the battle, a court-martial was finally ordered for the want of any alternative: Torrington was charged with holding back and not aiding the Dutch. These were serious charges; if found guilty, he faced execution. Admiral Sir Ralph Delaval, who had commanded the rear squadron, was appointed president, with a panel of twenty-seven English captains, all of whom had been present at the action, as the judges.[31] Torrington marshaled his defense with the same attention to detail he had displayed on 30 June. A stout defense of his conduct was backed by the argument that the queen had been misled. It was in this context that he first used the phrase "fleet in being."

> That our fighting upon so great a disadvantage as we did was of the last consequence to the kingdom, is as certain as that the Queen would not have been prevailed upon to sign an order for it, had not both our weakness, and the strength of the enemy, been disguised to her.
>
> It is true, the French made no great advantage of their victory, tho' they put us to a great charge in keeping up the militia, but had I fought otherwise, our fleet had been totally lost, and the kingdom had lain open to an invasion. What then would have become of us in the absence of His Majesty and most of the land forces? As it was; most men were in fear that the French would invade; but I was always of another opinion; for I always said, that whilst we had a fleet in being, they would not dare to make an attempt.
>
> In my letter of the 29th, the matter is stated pretty plain; whilst we observe the French they can make no attempt either on sea or ashore, but with great disadvantages; and if we are beaten all is exposed to their mercy. This I dare be bold to say, that is the management of the fleet had been left to the discretion of the Council of War, there would have been no need of the excessive charge the kingdom was put to in keeping up the militia, nor would the French have gone off so much at their ease.[32]

Delaval reported how the incoherent rage of a Dutch witness confirmed the panel's suspicions that the trial was a politically motivated witch-hunt. The Royal Navy consistently refused to bow to political pressure from the government.[33] The seamen took a similar view, blaming Dutch losses on their impetuosity. Within hours Torrington had been acquitted and rowed up the river to London, saluted by gunfire and loud cheers. William, desperate to preserve the alliance, was furious. He dismissed Torrington from the honorary post of vice admiral of England two days later and removed him from the Privy Council in 1692. Despite these slights, Torrington remained on the Navy List and was considered for employment later in the war.

## PRECEDENT

While many strategists have credited Torrington with the fleet-in-being strategy, there were precedents—notably, England's last major naval conflict, the Third Anglo-Dutch War of 1672–74. Dutch admiral Michiel de Ruyter had used a strikingly similar approach to secure the coast of the republic against an Anglo-French invasion.

In May 1672 French armies conquered approximately half the republic, leaving the Dutch fighting for survival. The initial naval battle at Solebay on 7 June 1672, a Dutch stalling attack, took place after the English fleet had cruised along the Dutch coast but retired without attempting to force a battle. In essence, de Ruyter exploited the allied withdrawal to stage a bold fleet-in-being operation on the grandest scale. The Dutch had 91 ships of the line; the allies, 101 generally larger, more heavily armed ships. Both sides had numerous fireships. To compensate for his numerical inferiority at the tactical level, de Ruyter contained the French squadron with a smaller force, concentrating his attack on the English fleet, the core of naval threat. The battle was drawn, de Ruyter withdrew, but the battered allied fleet was unable to pursue him, delaying an amphibious landing intended to outflank the Dutch land defenses for a year.

Solebay did not save the Dutch regime, which was overthrown on 8 July, with Stadtholder William III restored to political and military authority, just as other major European powers recognized that the destruction of the republic would make France dominant in Europe.

The Dutch war effort was necessarily dominated by military operations, restricting the navy to a supporting role, and preventing the enemy from using amphibious power projection to outflank the land defenses. In 1673 de Ruyter fought three additional fleet-in-being battles to deny the enemy control of Dutch coastal waters. The two battles of the Schooenveldt, on 7 and 14 June, and the Battle of the Texel on 21 August, demonstrated a mastery of strategy and tactics that frustrated and then fractured the hostile coalition. In all three actions, de Ruyter attacked at a time of his choosing and retired as soon he had achieved the desired strategic effect—forcing the enemy to withdraw. Keeping his fleet "in being" was the key.

In two of these battles, de Ruyter obliged the enemy to come to him, basing his fleet in the Schooenveldt passage, an anchorage secured by dangerous sandbanks. The Anglo-French fleet of eighty-one ships of the line under Prince Rupert and Admiral Jean d'Estrées was superior in force. Observing fifty-five Dutch ships of the line at anchor, Rupert sent a squadron to draw them out, a challenge de Ruyter accepted with alacrity, bringing the allies to action before they had formed a line of battle. In these actions, shoal water and limited local knowledge hampered the larger, deeper-draft allied ships. While the action petered out without any significant losses on either side, as did a second action in the same area a week later, they obliged the allied fleet to return to England to refit, replenish ammunition and food stocks, and land the sick and wounded. When the allies returned to the Dutch coast, they brought troops with them, suggesting they thought they had achieved some degree of control. This time the Dutch fleet was encountered off the coast between the Texel and the river Meuse. Once again the Dutch were outnumbered, by ninety to seventy ships; that additional ships became available after the Schooenveldt battles demonstrated an obvious advantage of the fleet-in-being position.

Once again de Ruyter deployed a small force to preoccupy the French while he concentrated on the English squadrons. The French obliged him by falling out of the action at an early stage, leading to considerable acrimony between the allied commanders. Rupert tried to draw de Ruyter out to sea to prevent him regaining his anchorage, but this plan was disrupted by the commander of the rear squadron,

Sir Edward Spragge, who focused on the Dutch rear squadron, leaving Rupert to fight the other two Dutch squadrons. Spragge's death obliged Rupert to rescue the battered, leaderless squadron before a second phase of the battle saw the entire Dutch fleet attack the English. The belated return of the French squadron prompted de Ruyter to withdraw. While the Dutch fought to a coherent plan, d'Estrées and Spragge ignored Rupert's orders and the strategic context.

Although de Ruyter abandoned the battlefield, the allies were in no condition to follow his fleet into Dutch coastal waters. Much like his political master, the Dutch stadtholder, de Ruyter, knew how to fight a battle that would deny the enemy any strategic advantage without unnecessary risk. William III lost many battles at the tactical level, but he always preserved his army to deny the French any strategic advantage. In the seventeenth century, victory in battles on land or sea between roughly equal forces proved strikingly hard to exploit if the enemy retired in good order. Recognizing the danger of French hegemony, England left the war in 1674.

Torrington took part in all four battles of the Third Anglo-Dutch War, commanding ships of the line in the thick of the action. While he did not reference that experience in 1690, the parallels were obvious. At the Texel, Herbert's ship was stationed in a place of honor, directly astern of Spragge's flagship, the focal point of enemy fire.[34] He was also involved in the next major example of a fleet in being. In 1688 James II, facing a Dutch invasion, positioned his fleet in the Gunfleet, a secure, defensible anchorage behind a sandbank in the Thames Estuary. Herbert had commanded the invading fleet and later had access to the king's orders. James had been a successful admiral before he became king. These two examples, responding to the existential threat posed by amphibious armies, may have shaped Torrington's strategy in 1690.

## THE CONCEPT

Alfred Thayer Mahan emphasized the distinctive nature of the operations of the Third Anglo-Dutch War of 1672–74 and the 1690 campaign in *The Influence of Sea Power upon History, 1660–1783*, published in 1890. Mahan's assessment of the concept of a fleet in being began with de Ruyter's campaigns, citing eighteenth-century British naval historian John

Campbell's assessment: "The consequences which the Dutch, through the prudence of their admiral, drew from this battle were exceedingly great; for they opened their ports, which were entirely blocked up, and put an end to all thoughts, by removing the threat of an invasion."[35] For Mahan, the lesson of 1672–74 and 1690 was that a fleet in being could serve the wider contexts of campaign and conflict.

Mahan recognized that 1672–74 differed from the two previous Anglo-Dutch conflicts of 1652–64 and 1664–67 in that it was fought for the survival of the Dutch Republic rather than command of maritime commerce. After the preemptive strike at Solebay, the Dutch made "strategic use of their dangerous coast and shoals upon which were based their sea operations." However, "they did not use their shoals as a mere shelter"—they attacked to secure defensive ends. When the wind was fair for the allies to attack, de Ruyter exploited the Schooenveldt shoals to protect his fleet, but when the wind enabled him to "attack in his own way, he turned and fell upon them."[36]

Admiral Philip Colomb, lecturer on naval strategy and tactics at the Royal Naval College at Greenwich, first examined the issue in a paper delivered at the Royal United Services Institution in 1888 titled "The Naval Defence of the United Kingdom." He was responding to claims by the British army that the country could be defended more cheaply by fortifying ports and harbors than by building battle fleets. He observed: "We had also had experience that the enemy's fleet in possession of the Channel after beating but not destroying or seriously crippling our own, was incapable of executing any important service against us—held in check by our still capable ships."[37] The following year Colomb developed his argument in a second lecture, making good use of documents hack author John Entick had published in the 1750s, another period when invasion was topical. He had been directed to Entick by John Laughton, an old colleague and the pioneer of modern naval history.[38] In 1889 Laughton published contemporary evidence that argued Torrington's force at the Gunfleet had possessed "such a power in observation as to paralyse the action of an apparently victorious fleet either against sea or shore."[39] Colomb made another critical point when he cited seventeenth-century sea officer Sir William Monson's strategic assessment of Queen Elizabeth's war with Spain: "Whilst the Spaniards were employed at home by our yearly fleets, they never had an opportunity nor leisure either to make an attempt on us or to divert the war from themselves; by which means we were secured from any attempt of theirs." He paraphrased Torrington's defense: "The mere neighbourhood of an inferior naval force which was free to attack was an absolute bar to any operations of the enemy against our shore," stressing that "no conceivable arrangement of fortifications could have strengthened Torrington."[40]

Colomb's Naval College lectures, which addressed the fleet in being, appeared in 1891 as *Naval Warfare: Its Ruling Principles and Practice Historically Treated*. His argument attracted the attention of Mahan and Laughton, while the eminent historian Sir Charles Firth approved the historical analysis.[41] Mahan altered his view, accepting that Torrington had acted correctly: "My treatment of Torrington excited more adverse comment than any point in my first book which certainly did not do him justice." That said, Mahan did not believe a fleet in being would have prevented Tourville from crossing the Channel with an army, although he thought the French admiral risk averse and unlikely to exploit the opportunity.[42] Two decades later he attributed Tourville's failure to exploit Beachy Head to indecision and the lack of transports.[43]

In *Some Principles of Maritime Strategy*, his quasi-official doctrine primer of 1911, Julian Corbett, lecturer on strategy and history at the Royal Naval College Greenwich, stressed that a defensive maritime strategy should not assume the static character so familiar on land. He emphasized Carl von Clausewitz's argument that a true defense includes the capacity for a counterattack. For Corbett, this meant exploiting the mobility of naval forces to harass the enemy and deny them the opportunity to concentrate for offensive operations while attempting to reduce or reverse their superiority of force and reinforce the fleet. Mobility was of the essence. This might involve retreating into waters that were difficult for the enemy to enter (Dutch coastal waters or the Gunfleet), but withdrawal should only be temporary, as it necessarily ceded control of the sea to the enemy. "For a maritime Power, then, a naval defensive means nothing but keeping the fleet actively in being—not merely in existence but in active and vigorous life."[44] Torrington's campaign plan of 1690, once he knew his fleet was inferior to that of the French, conformed to this concept. However, it had been misunderstood, in all probability deliberately, by the Queen's Council in London, where it was treated it as purely defensive. Corbett emphasized the link between Torrington's fleet and William III's Irish campaign. While the Anglo-Dutch fleet remained active, the critical difference between a fortress fleet and a fleet in being, the French could not detach a squadron to attack English communications with Ireland. Torrington was well aware of the link between his fleet and Ireland. Tourville had used a fleet-in-being approach in 1691 and 1693, when his fleet was significantly inferior to the allies. In the American War of Independence, Admiral Richard Kempenfelt developed the concept to enable a numerically inferior British Home Fleet to conduct local offensives.[45]

An alternative strategic perspective was provided by French admiral Raoul Castex (1878–1968), a major contributor to the development of strategic theory. A continental strategist with an affinity for Mahan's focus on battle, Castex thought victory in fleet battle was the only "complete" result.[46] Having summarized the arguments advanced by Colomb, Mahan, and Corbett, Castex criticized Colomb's claim that the fleet in being had "paralysed" Tourville. He concluded that a fleet in being would be ineffective if the enemy was prepared to ignore it and take positive action. While he might have given many examples of the Royal Navy ignoring the inferior French fleet, he chose to explain the principle without such awkward illustrations.[47]

Castex believed a naval offensive should never lose sight of the enemy fleet; indeed, he implied the first role of such action was to bring the enemy to battle and defeat them before imposing an economic blockade. His disagreement with the English theorists reflected the continental perspective he shared with Mahan, both being raised in the French strategic tradition of Antoine-Henri Jomini. He thought Torrington, Colomb, and Corbett claimed too much for an essentially passive defense. The only way a fleet in being could exert significant influence was by remaining active and, as Clausewitz and Corbett stressed, by preparing for counterattacks as soon as the enemy tried to exploit their temporary advantage. While Colomb's 1891 argument had been incomplete, part of an evolving debate with the army over the roles of fleets and forts in national defense, Corbett took the issue to a higher level in *Some Principles*, which contained a section dealing with "methods of disputing command." Corbett had already established that the naval defensive was only truly effective if it contained the capacity for counterattacks, taking care to stress that this had been the basis of Torrington's plan.[48]

A fleet in being is an instrument of strategy and, as the campaigns of 1690–93 demonstrated, individual states had strikingly different views of how to use "inferior" fleets, depending on whether they have been maritime or continental powers.[49] For sea powers, the imperative need to secure trade limited their ability to withhold their fleet from action, while England's insular security and weak army reinforced the imperative to command the sea. It was the need to secure Mediterranean trade and complete a strategic offensive in Ireland that left Torrington outnumbered, not a lack of ships. By contrast, Tourville's 1691 and 1693 campaigns made effective use of an inferior fleet in being because he could focus on attacking allied merchant shipping, an asymmetric weakness, because France was significantly less dependent on oceanic trade. However, like most continental powers with large fleets, France also tended to see warships as a capital asset to be massed as a diplomatic counter, rather than a consumable store to employ in combat to secure strategic ends by direct means. Ultimately, as Castex implied, France was predisposed to a fleet-in-being posture while England was not.

## NOTES

1. William Laird Clowes, ed., *The Royal Navy: A History from the Earliest Times* (London: Sampson, Low 1898), 2:330–44.
2. Julian Corbett, *England in the Mediterranean*, vol. 2 (London: Longman 1904), 161–62; and John Ehrman, *The Navy in the War of William III, 1689–1697* (Cambridge: Cambridge University Press 1953), 517n1.
3. Ehrman, *Navy in the War of William III*, 353, citing Winston S. Churchill, *Marlborough: His Life and Times* (London, 1930), 325.
4. Ehrman, 341–48.
5. Ehrman, 344, citing Charles de la Roncière, *Histoire de la Marine Française, Vol. 6: Le Crépuscule du Grand Règne; L'Apogée de la Guerre de Course* (E. Plon, Nourrit, 1932), 64.

6. Philip Colomb, *Naval Warfare: Its Ruling Principles and Practice Historically Treated*, 2nd ed. (London: W. H. Allen, 1895), 317.
7. Ehrman, *Navy in the War of William III*, 345.
8. Colomb, *Naval Warfare*, 122, citing John Entick, *A New Naval History* (London, 1757), 548.
9. Colomb, 126.
10. Monmouth to Nottingham, 29 June 1690, in Francis Bickley, ed, *Report on the Manuscripts of Daniel Finch, Earl of Nottingham* (London: Historical Manuscripts Commission, 1957), 2:440. Henceforth, Finch.
11. Finch, 2:318, 322.
12. Alfred Mahan, *Naval Strategy* (London: Sampson, Low, 1911), 335, 385, 391–416, 441.
13. Minutes of the Cabinet Committee, 29 June 1690, Finch, 3:385; and Colomb, *Naval Warfare*, 115.
14. Queen Mary to Torrington, 29 June 1690; Queen Mary to Russell, 29 June 1690; and Nottingham to King, 3 July 1690, Finch, 2:318, 322, 331, respectively.
15. Peter le Fevre, "'Meer Laziness' or Incompetence," *Mariner's Mirror* 80, no. 3 (1994): 94.
16. Clowes, *Royal Navy*, 2:340.
17. Ehrman, *Navy in the War of William III*, 350.
18. N. A. M. Rodger, *The Command of the Ocean*, vol. 2 of *A Naval History of Britain* (London: Allen Lane, 2004), 145–48; and W. C. B. Tunstall, *Naval Warfare in the Age of Sail: One Evolution of Fighting Tactics, 1650–1815*, edited by Nicholas Tracy (London: Conway Maritime Press, 1990), 52–55.
19. Geoffrey Symcox, *The Crisis of French Sea Power, 1688–1691* (Den Hague: Brill, 1974), 99–100.
20. Clowes, *Royal Navy*, 2:340.
21. Nottingham to King, 3 July 1690, Finch, 2:333–34.
22. Queen to Torrington, 3 July 1690, Finch 2:355.
23. Nottingham to King, 6 July 1690, Finch, 2:342–43.
24. Nottingham to the King, 10 and 15 July 1690, Finch, 2:352.
25. Ehrman, *Navy in the War of William III*, 353; and Finch, 2:373.
26. Ehrman, *Navy in the War of William III*, 353, citing Winston S. Churchill, *Marlborough: His Life and Times* (1930), 1:325n.
27. Quoting James II's Irish minister, the Earl of Tyrconnell, two weeks after Beachy Head and the Boyne. Rodger, *Command of the Ocean*, 147.
28. Andrew Lambert, "Writing the Battle: Jutland in Sir Julian Corbett's Naval Operations," *Mariner's Mirror* 103, no. 2 (2017): 175–95.
29. Nottingham to Admiral Delaval and Admiral Ashby, 4 August 1690, Finch, 3:441–42.

30. Nottingham, 29 August 1690, Finch, 3:445.
31. Delaval to Nottingham, 7 and 10 December 1690, Finch, 2:493–93.
32. Colomb, *Naval Warfare*, 122, citing Entick, *New Naval History*, 549.
33. For another such court martial, see Andrew Lambert, "Sir William Cornwallis, 1744–1819," in *Precursors of Nelson: British Admirals of the Eighteenth Century*, edited by Peter le Fevre and Richard Harding (London: Chatham, 2000), 362–64.
34. Peter le Fevre, "Arthur Herbert Lord Torrington," in le Fevre and Harding, *Precursors of Nelson*, 9–41.
35. John Campbell, *Lives of the Admirals*, cited in Alfred Thayer Mahan, *The Influence of Sea Power upon History, 1660–1783* (London: Sampson, Low, 1890), 154.
36. Mahan, *Influence of Sea Power*, 144–58.
37. Philip Colomb, *Essays on Naval Defence*, 2nd ed. (London: W. H. Allen, 1896), 131–32.
38. Andrew Lambert, *The Foundations of Naval History* (London: Chatham, 1998), 108, 125, 130–31.
39. John Laughton, ed., *Memoirs Relating to Lord Torrington* (London: Camden Society, 1889), 46, 47.
40. Colomb, *Essays on Naval Defence*, 172–74.
41. Sir Charles Firth, *A Commentary on Macaulay's History of England* (London: Macmillan, 1938), 176.
42. Cited in Laughton, *Memoirs Relating to Lord Torrington*, 95–97.
43. Mahan, *Naval Strategy*, 90, 218, 267; and Raoul Castex, *Strategic Theories*, edited and translated by Eugenia Kiesling (Annapolis, MD: Naval Institute Press, 1994), 340.
44. Julian Corbett, *Some Principles of Maritime Strategy* (London: Longmans, 1911), 214.
45. Corbett, 217–24.
46. Castex, *Strategic Theories*, 318.
47. Castex, 343.
48. Corbett, *Some Principles*, 29.
49. Andrew Lambert, *Seapower States: Maritime Culture, Continental Empires, and the Conflict That Made the Modern World* (London: Yale University Press, 2018), 1–16.

CHAPTER 2

# A FLEET IN BEING?
## Spanish Naval Strategy (1783–1820)

*Iván Valdez-Bubnov*

Is the concept of "fleet in being," originally attributed to Admiral Torrington after the Battle of Beachy Head and developed as an indirect strategy by later naval theorists, relevant to the late eighteenth- and early nineteenth-century Spanish navy?[1] The answer entails consideration of the concept's development throughout the eighteenth century, the purposes for which it was built, and whether these aims reflected any changes during the French revolutionary and Napoleonic Wars (1792–1815). During that period, Spain simultaneously faced a series of conflicts that differed significantly from the great power struggle taking place in Europe: the expansion of the United States and, after 1810, the uprisings that erupted in the rest of Spanish America. This parallel line of conflict had a distinctively naval dimension, which must be considered to avoid oversimplification. This study aims at considering both spheres simultaneously to reflect on the nature of the challenges faced by the Spanish naval system, how they were approached by Spanish naval thinkers, and the impingement of logistical and budgetary constraints on concrete naval operations affecting the implementation of naval strategy at different levels.

### UZTÁRIZ'S NAVAL STRATEGY

The first explicit strategic doctrine of the eighteenth-century Spanish navy was defined in 1724 by Gerónimo de Uztáriz, in his *Theórica y práctica de comercio y de marina* (Theory and practice of commerce and the navy).[2] This complex discourse on grand strategy encompassed fiscal, industrial, and trade policy, paired with a foreign policy based on diplomacy and the development of military and naval power.[3] Uztáriz advocated reducing land forces to make the navy Spain's main defensive expedient since it could transport troops while distracting enemy naval forces elsewhere, thus forcing rivals to concentrate their armies for homeland defense and deterring attacks against Spanish America. This was the principal objective of the navy created by Philip V in 1714, maintained as a permanent establishment in peacetime with a relatively small land force in constant readiness for amphibious attacks.

The Spanish navy's equally important second objective was to deter rivals from attacking the merchant fleets connecting the monarchy's possessions in the Mediterranean and the Atlantic, particularly the New Spain Fleet and the Tierra Firme galleons. On a third level, the navy would execute amphibious attacks in the Mediterranean to further dynastic interests in Italy, to counter the Barbary corsairs, and to prevent the Ottoman Empire from intervening against Spanish interests in Europe.

Deterrence relied on a strong battle fleet core of one three-decked ship of more than 100 guns, supported by two ships of 86 and 90 guns, respectively. These would serve as flagships (*Capitana* and *Almirantas*) of a line-of-battle formed in three divisions—Vanguardia (Vanguard), Cuerpo de Batalla (Battle Corps), and Retaguardia (Rear Guard)—in the French manner, comprising nine 80-gun and eight 70-gun large two-deckers. Ten 60-gun two-deckers would escort the Atlantic merchant fleets, while twenty 54- and 50-gun ships would counter privateers, pirates, and interlopers in the Caribbean and the Mediterranean. Twelve 10- to 40-gun frigates would also support these medium-sized ships of the line.

Deterrence was the purpose of Uztáriz's battle fleet, and the heavy cruiser force was the deterrent. Its core of heavy 70- and 80-gun two-deckers, supported by the three-decked *Capitana* and the two *Almirantas* would discourage aggression and double as a diplomatic tool. None of these ships would remain in permanent service: they would be kept disarmed in the royal dockyards during peacetime, thus maintaining their deterrent value while avoiding high maintenance costs. In wartime, part of the battle fleet would divert enemy naval forces to distant theaters, while the balance of army to navy forces would be adjusted to maintain a credible threat of military invasion. The medium-sized cruisers and frigates, however, would remain in permanent service.

An important offensive element in Uztáriz's view of naval strategy was commerce raiding by royal warships and privateers. Explicitly following the model of the 1689 French *Ordonnance*, he advocated attacking enemy commerce by lending medium-sized warships to private entrepreneurs. This would decentralize the naval effort, reduce overall operational costs, and undermine the enemy's sources of wealth and lines of communication either during peace- or wartime.

Shipbuilding programs over the next thirty years reflected Uztáriz ideas on naval strategy. During the 1730s and the 1740s, warship production concentrated on heavy 70- and 80-gun two-deckers, together with large numbers of 60- and 50-gun ships, frigates, and several minor types. Only one three-decked ship of the line was built, the 114-gun *Real Phelipe*, which served brilliantly in the Battle of Toulon in 1744 but was scrapped in 1755. The first Spanish battle fleet's force structure reflected Uztáriz's opinion concerning three-deckers' limited utility due to their high construction and maintenance costs, the number of hands required to operate them, their lack of maneuverability, the danger of operating them close to shore, and many other drawbacks.

The experience of fighting Britain during the War of Jenkins's Ear (1739–48) led an influential Spanish naval thinker, Juan Joseph Navarro, to propose a more aggressive battle fleet strategy and shipbuilding plan. Consequently, Naval Minister Zenón de Somodevilla hired British shipwrights and increased the size and firepower of the heavy cruisers built during the 1750s. This, however, coincided with a period when neutrality became the main objective of Spanish foreign policy, eventually leading to the navy minister's fall and drastic naval expenditure reductions.[4]

In all, during the first half of the eighteenth century, Spanish shipbuilding policy emphasized the battle fleet's core deterrent purpose as much as its potential for diverting and protecting amphibious operations, the defensive role of heavy cruisers, the offensive role of medium-sized ships of the line and cruisers in commerce raiding, and the relevance of frigates and smaller ships for regional defense and commerce protection in the Mediterranean and the Caribbean. The Mediterranean policy directed against the Muslim privateering enclaves remained important, as the landing and conquest of Oran in 1732 demonstrated. Despite the shift in shipbuilding in the late 1740s and early 1750s based on the increase of size and firepower of the larger two-decked types, Uztáriz's master plan of 1724 remained practically unchanged.

If this can be considered a fleet-in-being strategy, then the concept must be expanded to include this variety of roles. The concept of "active defense" would be more appropriate since the use of the battle fleet as a deterrent or diverting force was only one of the different roles the Spanish naval forces were expected to perform.[5] The idea of a fleet in being was a component of a wider active defense strategy—including localized offensive action, privateering, diplomacy, and deterrence—and shipbuilding policy reflected this complex pattern of objectives well into the reign of Charles III (1759–1788).

## FLORIDABLANCA'S NAVAL STRATEGY

After defeat in the Seven Years' War in 1763, the Bourbon powers envisaged a naval war against Britain. This new coordinated foreign policy attempted to standardize Spanish and French shipbuilding programs. The defensive ideas based on deterrence, commerce protection, and commerce raiding, until then shared by the French navy, were paired with a more aggressive stance against British communications in the Atlantic, the Caribbean, the Indian Ocean, and the southern Pacific.[6] In accordance with Navarro's ideas, the Spanish navy started building new heavy three-decked ships of the line, and hired French shipwrights who increased the size and firepower of the larger two-decked types. This ran parallel to a tougher diplomatic stance, leading to the unfortunate Falklands crisis of 1770. In the Mediterranean, pressure against Muslim privateering was increased, with the naval bombardment of Tétouan (Morocco) in 1764 and an amphibious attack against Algiers in 1775. The battle fleet and the cruisers were crucial for these offensive operations. And tensions with Portugal in South America led to an amphibious expedition capturing the Colonia del Sacramento (Uruguay) in 1776–77. Simultaneously, Spain also attempted to curb the economic development of both West Florida, ceded to the British as part of the peace settlement of 1763, and the Honduran Mosquito Coast, where British logwood cutters from Walix (Belize) antagonized the Spanish settlements and indigenous allies.

The Florida question helped prompt the Spanish Crown to support the American Revolution, despite doubts regarding the reliability of its French ally. When Spain entered the North American war in 1779, Pedro Pablo Abarca de Bolea, the Count of Aranda, then Spanish ambassador in Paris, proposed unleashing a full-scale naval war in the North Atlantic by coordinating American, Spanish, and French privateering with the Bourbon royal navies. He expected that the privateers would force Britain to rely on convoys, vulnerable to attack by the French and Spanish battle fleets. This large mobilization of warships would reduce Britain's available manpower for its own privateers and merchantmen. He also wanted the Bourbon battle fleets to take the offensive in the Mediterranean and the North Atlantic by stationing twenty ships of the line and twelve frigates in American waters. The rest of the battle fleets would protect a landing force amassed on the French coast to force Britain to concentrate its battle fleet there while Gibraltar was besieged. Spanish ships redeployed from the Philippines could reinforce the divisions stationed at Ferrol or Cadiz, and frigates could protect allied Indian Ocean lines of communication.[7]

The head of the Spanish government, the Count of Floridablanca, expanded this general strategy during the 1779–1783 war of the American Revolution to include amphibious operations that secured control of Menorca in the Mediterranean, and Florida, Campeche, and Honduras on the North and Central American mainland. The siege of Gibraltar, however, failed.[8] Operations against Muslim privateering continued, with the blockade and bombardment of Algiers in 1783–1784, and Tangier in 1790.[9] Concurrently, Spain resumed the shipbuilding policy devised after the Seven Years' War, and it continued to launch large and powerful three-deckers, 74- and 64-gun ships, and different types of smaller cruisers. Between 1784 and 1791, seven 112-gun three-deckers were launched, together with ten 74-gun two-deckers, one 70, and three 64s. The Spanish navy thus reached its greatest number of ships in service and the production pace continued until 1798.

In 1787 Floridablanca wrote a grand strategic plan for the newly instituted State Council (Junta de Estado), an institution created to ensure the continuation of the dying Charles III's policies by his successor, the future Charles IV. As in the case of Uztáriz's writings,

Floridablanca's Instrucción reservada (Reserved instruction) contained detailed guidelines on fiscal, industrial, and trade policy, together with precise instructions for the coordination of diplomacy with military and naval power. This extensive document detailed the grand strategy of the Spanish Empire at its apogee, but it has seldom been understood from the perspective of naval strategy.[10]

Its foreign policy guidelines started with North America, prioritizing the preservation of the empire. Floridablanca emphasized the utmost importance of fostering the demographic and economic development of Louisiana, Nuevo México, and the Two Floridas (East and West), to curb the spread of American colonists. The Instrucción made mandatory denial of U.S. use of the Mississippi River to gain access to the Gulf of Mexico, regardless of any agreements made between Britain and the United States.

Next on Floridablanca's list was the island of Trinidad, considered one of the keys to the Spanish Caribbean, which therefore required fortifications and a naval base. Previous experience had shown Cuba's ports and dockyards insufficient to protect and supply Caracas, Cartagena, Tierra, Firme, and the eastern coast of Guatemala, highlighting the necessity of Trinidad as a new naval and military outpost. The same applied to Puerto Rico and Spanish Santo Domingo as well as to Panama and Montevideo, down to the Strait of Magellan. The increased presence of regular armed forces in all these regions would discourage revolutions and help tame its "restless and turbulent" inhabitants. In Central America, gifts, presents, and feasts would buy the loyalty of the indigenous populations of the Mosquito Coast. This, together with increased military presence, would contain the British loggers from Walix.

Friendship and collaboration with Portugal would follow the resolution of frontier questions around the Colonia del Sacramento and the River Plate (Uruguay), and between the Orinoco and the Amazon rivers. The Dutch and French colonies there of Essequibo, Suriname, and Cayenne were not considered dangerous. The Russians, on the other hand, who sailed from Kamchatka in Siberia, threatened Spanish North American possessions, requiring an increased naval presence from the viceroyalty of New Spain.

The Philippines depended on economic development, guided by a recently instituted royal chartered company. The navy would be the mainstay of their defense and would control the flow of Chinese luxury products into the viceroyalties of New Spain and Peru. Meanwhile, the Dutch attempt to prevent the Spanish navy from reaching the Indian Ocean through the Cape of Good Hope elicited Spanish diplomacy and underlined the need to develop naval infrastructure in the South Pacific, both in America and the Philippines. All this amounted to a defensive use of the navy and demonstrated its value in maintaining the whole system of naval ports and coastal fortifications.

The only offensive actions would target the islands of Jamaica, Granada, Tobago, and Curaçao, which would be attacked and seized as soon as the next war was unleashed. In Europe, the only desirable conquest was the Kingdom of Portugal, which would be seized if a succession crisis occurred. Gibraltar, on the other hand, was considered impregnable, but its economic and demographic isolation would impose high costs on Britain and raised hopes of its evacuation, purchase, or exchange for Oran or Santo Domingo. Gibraltar's isolation became the peacetime pretext for permanently stationing a powerful battle fleet core in Cadiz. During wartime, this force could attack enemy convoys and protect amphibious operations, as had been done during the 1779–83 war. This was considered key to wartime naval activity. The offensive stance would also be maintained against the Barbary ports, although peace would be sought with Morocco.

In all, the Instrucción gave a positive appraisal of the naval and military strategy followed during the 1779–83 war and indicated no departure from that model. Several articles concerned army and navy reforms as well as instructions to maintain warship production but no details regarding the fleet's composition.

Sections CCLXXXVIII to CCCII (288–302) of the Instrucción provided specific foreign policy guidelines for different European powers. Sections CCCII to CCCXXXIV (302–334) concerned France and warned against the imposition of French interests upon Spanish policy. France's diplomacy consistently sought to subordinate Spain in order to diminish its wealth and power by excising all possible commercial, industrial, and military advantages. Thus, Spain should avoid commercial treaties and should not grant French shipping equal rights. Above all, Spain must not be dragged into a war to protect French interests, leading to naval and military operations conducted from a subordinate position. The French interpretation of the Bourbon Family Compact (Pacte de Famille) exemplified this situation, and the diplomacy that led to the Bourbon alliance of the 1779–83 war should not be repeated. Likewise, the disastrous results of the Seven Years' War provided another example of subordination to French war aims, acceptable only when British insults had become intolerable. Thus, France was simultaneously Spain's best potential ally and its worst possible enemy.

Chapters CCCXXXV to CCCLXIV (335–364) dealt exclusively with Britain and urged caution and distrust in enforcing existing treaties and preventing a renewed conflict while increasing Spanish maritime power (literally, *nuestro poder marítimo*). The danger posed by France made Britain's total ruin undesirable. These chapters repeated the contents of those on naval strategy, including the positive appraisal of concentrating the battle fleet in Cadiz, in apparent readiness to attack Gibraltar but in reality to attack enemy convoys and to prepare a possible invasion of Jamaica. The League of Armed Neutrality, led by Russia during the last war, could serve as a model to contain the British in the Mediterranean. A commercial treaty based on trade and fiscal reciprocity would be desirable.

## THE WARS OF REVOLUTIONARY AND NAPOLEONIC FRANCE

The optimistic resolve to maintain neutrality with France and Britain vanished quickly. In 1790 the Nootka Sound crisis over trade and navigation at Vancouver Island prompted Floridablanca to plan for what seemed to be an imminent naval conflict with Great Britain. The battle fleet concentrated in Cadiz, to imply amphibious operations against Gibraltar or Rabat-Salé (Morocco), which was then collaborating with Britain. More troops were to be concentrated in the northern naval base of Ferrol to threaten a possible landing on the British Isles. Together this would pin part of the British navy in the Mediterranean and the English Channel, precluding any significant enterprise against Spanish America. Similar actions would occur in Cuba, Puerto Rico, Honduras, and Trinidad to feign an attack against Jamaica. The Philippines would be put on a war footing through communications from the Cape of Good Hope and the Indian Ocean, or directly from Spain through the Strait of Magellan, and from Acapulco and San Blas in Mexico. Spain would seek diplomatic support from Russia, Denmark, and Sweden, and neutrality from Portugal, while it assisted the Dutch Patriot movement to undermine their alliance with Great Britain and Prussia. Key to the whole strategy was the French political and naval support necessary for an amphibious attack against Great Britain, as attempted during the 1779–83 war.[11]

Meanwhile, in Paris the National Assembly disputed Louis XVI's control over foreign policy and eventually declared that France would not go to war in support of its Spanish ally, although the French navy temporarily mobilized. To make the situation worse, Floridablanca concluded that mounting debt precluded financing the war. Consequently, Spain had to resolve the Nootka crisis with conventions signed in 1790, 1793, and 1794. In addition, in late 1790 an earthquake destroyed Oran's fortifications and prompted its evacuation. A peace treaty was signed with the bey of Algiers, thus tacitly recognizing Ottoman sovereignty over the ancient Spanish enclave.

The international situation of the Spanish Empire became progressively more complex after the Nootka crisis. The ideological threat posed by the French Revolution became tangible when the National Assembly declared war on Spain in March 1793. As a result, the new Spanish prime minister, the young favorite Manuel Godoy, having replaced Floridablanca and Aranda, aligned Spain with the First Coalition, led by Great Britain. Spain mobilized a force of twenty-three ships and sailed from Cartagena to counter France's invasion of Sardinia, which it successfully recovered. Spanish and British naval forces also collaborated in the royalist defense of Toulon in late 1793, where France lost fourteen ships captured and fifteen destroyed. After an exhausting land war fought mostly in Catalunya (Catalonia), Gipuzkoa, and Navarre, France and Spain signed the Peace of Basel in July 1795, exchanging territories annexed by France for the eastern part of Hispaniola (Santo Domingo), in the Caribbean. In August 1796 Godoy signed the Second Treaty of San Ildefonso, establishing a military and naval alliance with the French Directory. This not only restored the previous pattern of

Franco-Spanish collaboration but also drastically subordinated Spanish naval policy to French designs. The treaty obliged Spain to provide fifteen ships of the line fully fitted out and 25,000 soldiers.[12] One month later Spain declared war against Britain.

As in previous conflicts, as soon as war was declared, the privateers were unleashed in the Caribbean, especially from Cuban ports, and they received support from cruisers assigned to the naval division based in Havana. Other naval detachments were sent to the South Atlantic to reinforce the naval station at the River Plate, and to the northern Pacific to reinforce the lines of communication between the naval base of San Blas and the Asian squadron based at Manila. During 1796 and early 1797 royal warships escorted merchant traffic and succeeded in delivering royal funds (*situados*) from Veracruz to several ports in the Caribbean. They also launched attacks against British settlements in Terranova (Newfoundland) and destroyed infrastructure in the islands of Saint Pierre and Miquelon and on the coast of Honduras. This was a major financial and logistical effort: a total of forty-four ships were fitted out and deployed, including ten of the heavy three-deckers.[13]

Then disaster came. The main Atlantic squadron, under command of José de Córdoba, joined with the Mediterranean squadron, under Morales de los Ríos, and sailed from Cartagena to Cadiz to protect merchant convoys and seek out the numerically inferior British Mediterranean force, under the command of Admiral John Jervis. This campaign led to the major defeat of 14 February 1797 in the Battle of Cape St. Vincent, leading to the blockade of the decimated Spanish squadrons in Cadiz by Jervis's smaller force.

The British blockade degraded Atlantic communications and impeded the replenishment of the Caribbean and Pacific squadrons, with major consequences. Trinidad fell to a British landing force despite the protection of the squadron under Sebastián Ruiz de Apodaca, and soon Puerto Rico came under attack, but the invaders were repulsed. Britain blockaded Trujillo (Santo Domingo) and reduced the mobility of the Cuban squadron. The expected attack against Manila did not occur, in part due to the presence of the Pacific squadron of José María de Álava. In 1798 Spain repulsed an attack against Tenerife in the Canary Islands but lost Menorca, and a large Franco-Spanish force was blockaded in the French port of Brest, where it remained for the rest of the war, thus precluding an attack against the British Isles. The Cadiz squadron under Joseph de Mazarredo sortied to reach Brest as well but, given the possibility of facing Jervis again, returned to the safety of Cadiz's fortifications. Spain's withdrawal from the Mediterranean facilitated Britain's attack against the French fleet in Aboukir in August 1798, trapping Napoleon Bonaparte's troops in Egypt.[14]

In 1799 Britain's blockade against Cuba became more effective, precluding the transfer of royal funds from Veracruz to the whole Caribbean system. It also diverted the Manila galleons from landing at Acapulco, stopping the transfer of silver to the Philippines until 1801, when royal frigates became regular escorts. The impact on maritime couriers slowed the flow of communication between Madrid and its American squadrons, and shipbuilding operations were soon paralyzed. The absence of silver remittances to pay salaries led to massive workforce desertions in the royal dockyards and impeded even ordinary maintenance and repairs. In 1800 there were successful silver transfers from Spanish America to Spain, undertaken despite British naval presence. In 1800, under the clauses of the Treaty of San Ildefonso, the Spanish navy was forced to cede six ships of the line to France. The end of the war between Lisbon and Madrid then canceled the planned Franco-Spanish attack against Portugal. This led to the Battle of Algeciras in Gibraltar Bay, claimed as a victory by both sides, but Britain attacked the Spanish squadron attempting to escort the French force by limping out of the bay at night, and two Spanish heavy three-deckers were lost to friendly fire. When peace was signed at Amiens in 1802, the Spanish naval system had reached the most complete exhaustion.[15]

## WAR IN THE AMERICAS

It is often overlooked that Spain faced another front not usually considered as part of the French Wars. But as the Instrucción reservada clearly showed, the growing conflict with the United States was a major concern, topping Floridablanca's list of strategic priorities. At the beginning of the War of the First Coalition, when Spain fought the Revolution, the French National Convention sought to gain President George Washington's support. In April 1793 Edmond Charles Genet arrived at Charleston as the first ambassador of the French Republic. Genet aligned with the Girondin faction, representing the maritime elites of Bordeaux, Toulon, and Marseille and deeply committed to free-trade policies, privateering, and the export of revolutionary ideals into the British and Spanish colonies. Genet was commissioned to seek payment of U.S. government debts incurred under the beheaded Louis XVI; to promote the independence of Spanish American colonies, including Louisiana, the Two Floridas, and British Canada; to open the Mississippi River to U.S. navigation; to sign a commercial treaty; and to seek the opening of French and North American ports to privateers of both nations. Moreover, he carried 250 blank military commissions for land operations against Louisiana and Florida to be launched from U.S. territory and immediately began commissioning privateers. The Washington administration ignored Genet, proscribed the privateers, and Congress passed a neutrality act. In 1794 Britain and the United States signed the Treaty of Amity, Commerce and Navigation, or the Jay Treaty, blocking further French overtures.[16]

The Anglo-U.S. rapprochement coincided with the temporary Anglo-Spanish alliance of 1793–95 and led Spain to soften its policies against the United States. Prime Minister Godoy reversed Floridablanca's policies regarding the navigation of the Mississippi and reached an accord on the boundaries of Louisiana and the Two Floridas known as the Treaty of San Lorenzo (1795).

The diplomatic efforts of 1793–95 soon proved counterproductive for Spain. U.S. trade into the Caribbean increased, as did migration into Spanish American territories. There were conspiracies to overthrow the Spanish authorities in Florida, and even a self-proclaimed independent state in Northern Florida, which launched filibustering incursions. This led to a revocation of the recently conceded rights to navigate the Mississippi, which went unheeded. This tougher Spanish diplomacy, however, disregarded the economic consequences of British naval activity in the Caribbean that had almost completely severed intra-imperial Spanish trade. On 18 November 1797 Spain issued its first decree authorizing neutral trade in the ports of Spanish America. The main beneficiary of this formal breach of the Spanish imperial monopoly was the United States, which increased its trade with the Spanish possessions tenfold between 1798 and 1801.¹⁷ Although British ships also participated in this trade, the British Royal Navy also intercepted and captured many merchant ships, declaring them legitimate prizes.

Meanwhile, Franco-U.S. relations deteriorated steadily after Genet's failed mission and the signature of the Jay Treaty. By 1798 the French Directory began to consider trade between Great Britain and the United States as war contraband and unleashed an undeclared privateering war (already raging since 1796) from its possessions in the Caribbean. This conflict, known as the Quasi-War (Quasi-guerre), directly involved the Spanish government because French privateers from Saint-Domingue (Haiti), La Deseada (Cuba), Saint Kitts, and the French Antilles—namely, Martinique, Saint Martin, Saint Barthélemy, and Marie-Galante and Les Saintes in Guadeloupe—collaborated with privateers from Havana, Santiago de Cuba, San Juan de Puerto Rico, and Cartagena de Indias, who made their own captures and allowed their allies to use their resources and ports. The intensity of this privateering campaign arose in part from the slave rebellions and the ratification of the abolition of slavery by the National Convention in 1794 that caused the collapse of the plantation economies of the French Antilles. These events transferred enormous human capital to maritime activities, with officers, crews, and even shipwrights of African and mixed origin, many of them former slaves. By the time hostilities formally ceased in 1800, the French and Spanish American privateers had captured more than two thousand British and U.S. ships.¹⁸

It was in this context that Prime Minister Godoy attempted to leverage France to resolve Spain's issues with the United Sates. In 1800 a complex diplomatic arrangement formalized Spanish cession to France of the large North American territory of Louisiana in exchange for dynastic privileges in Italy. But the 1800 Treaty of Mortefontaine ending the Quasi-War revealed the failure of Napoleon's plans for North America. The collapse of the plantation economies of the French Antilles impeded the development of an outlet for Louisiana's agricultural produce, making unviable the whole idea of a resurrected French American empire. Godoy's miscalculation became evident in 1803, when Napoleon sold Louisiana to the United States, returning Spain to its initial diplomatic position, aggravated by the huge loss of territory.

Now the Two Floridas in the east were physically isolated from the viceroyalty of New Spain in the west and shared a much larger frontier with the United States.

## MacDONNELL'S NAVAL STRATEGY

In 1804, in the interlude after the Peace of Amiens, the Spanish navy made plans for an all-out war against the United States. Again, like Floridablanca's grand strategy, the priority did not lie in Europe but in America. Enrique Reynaldo MacDonnell y de Gondé proposed to resolve the North American question by declaring war against the United States, followed by a swift campaign to close the Mississippi River to U.S. navigation and to prevent any further U.S. expansion into Spanish territory. The attack would take place from February to June, after amassing supplies in San Agustín, East Florida, where an invasion army of 8,000 to 12,000 men would assemble. From there, troops would be transported by sea all the way around Florida to its northwestern coast, to land in San Marcos on the Apalachee Bay. From there they were expected to occupy the state of Georgia and attack New Orleans. A guerrilla campaign was to be simultaneously launched from Nueva Madrid (New Madrid, Missouri) into Indiana, Kentucky, and Tennessee, with the help of local Indian tribes. The land forces were to proceed to attack the Carolinas, thus marking the limits of the land campaign.[19]

The land campaign would be supported by a naval campaign, relying on cruising squadrons sailing from San Juan de Puerto Rico to Havana and from Veracruz to San Agustín de la Florida, where the invading army would establish its base. Other squadrons, composed by one ship of the line and two cruisers, would attack U.S. shipping from New England off Cape Cod, off Boston, between the Delaware River and Chesapeake Bay, and off the Carolinas around Charleston and its adjacent coasts. Other cruisers, based in the Spanish ports of Ferrol, Cadiz, Cartagena, and Algeciras, would patrol the Atlantic and Mediterranean trade routes used by U.S. merchants. Other squadrons would patrol the trade routes from Manila to Canton (Guangzhou), China, and along India's Coromandel Coast and Malabar Coast. Two more cruiser squadrons would operate, one from Havana to the Florida

Keys, and another from Santo Domingo to the port of Baracoa (Cuba). A division composed of two ships of the line and four frigates would attack the enemy frigates deployed against Tripoli and other Barbary nations. In the last phase of the plan, all Spanish naval forces would concentrate and, in three divisions, form a "line of blockade." They would blockade the coasts of New England around Cape Cod, from New York to Cape Henry (off the Chesapeake Bay), and from Cape Fear (off Wilmington) to Savannah. After the blockade had exhausted the local economies, the three divisions would form a "line of attack," uniting to shell enemy ports, land infantry, and burn enemy dockyards and ships. After agreeing to a peace treaty, Spain would close the Mississippi to U.S. navigation from the Ohio River to the Gulf of Mexico, as well as the Pacific from California to Cape Horn, Chile. U.S. whaling in the River Plate would also be forbidden.[20]

Prime Minister Godoy requested to see MacDonnell's plan on three different occasions, but the resumption of war with Great Britain after the attack on Spanish frigates in early October 1804 prevented further consideration of a strategy focused on North America. Once again France set in motion the well-known plan to invade the British Isles that subordinated the Spanish battle fleet to a changing French strategy, while Spanish American ports once again allowed neutral commerce. Napoleon expected to concentrate the still-large Franco-Spanish naval forces on the Channel, including 50,000 troops and twenty-nine Spanish ships, to launch the expected invasion. A diversionary maneuver by French and Spanish forces in the Caribbean would draw British naval forces from the Channel but return rapidly to attack English ports, to land troops in Ireland, and to protect the transit of the troops already gathered in Boulogne. These operations led to the defeats of Cape Finisterre and Trafalgar in July and October 1805, while in late August the French army massed at Boulogne redeployed to face the Austrian and Russian armies and contributed to the Napoleonic triumphs of Ulm and Austerlitz in October and December, respectively.

The successive concentrations of the French and Spanish battle fleets and the maneuvering that led to the Battle of Trafalgar show that, in the minds of Spanish politicians, little had changed regarding the strategic use of naval power.[21] Nevertheless, during this period there were important discussions on tactics: the predominance of the line of battle—still advocated by influential officers like Joseph de Mazarredo—was questioned, and the adoption of melee combat was promoted by Domingo de Grandallana and others. Important developments for cannon design also took place, such as the Rovira chambered gun and Magallanes' conical antipersonnel pieces, both conceived to match the efficacy of the British carronade. A suitable tactical doctrine for these and other inventions was put forward by Cosme Damián Churruca. Strategic doctrine, on the other hand, was developed by MacDonnell, whose detailed plans for the synchronization of land and sea warfare in the form of amphibious landings, blockades, coastal bombardment, *guerre de course*, and battle fleet action demonstrated great operational sophistication. Another important innovation in MacDonnell's thinking concerned his ideas on the total nature of warfare. He envisaged the systematic destruction of enemy civilian infrastructure as one of the means to achieve the political ends required by Spain's complex international situation, and he advocated the understanding of warfare by scientific means, the acceptance of total war, and the integration of military and political objectives in the planning and conduct of naval operations. These ideas foreshadowed military and naval strategic thinkers of later periods.[22]

In 1806 and 1807 the British unsuccessfully attacked Venezuela and Buenos Aires, which were both repulsed, while the navy remained in port due to lack of funding and replacement crews. One of the main concerns of administrators and officers was to prevent the delivery of the battle fleet to the French, as Napoleon had ordered Godoy to do. When French troops occupied Spain in 1808, the officer corps divided between those supporting Joseph Bonaparte's new government and those loyal to the deposed Spanish king, Ferdinand VII, willing to fight alongside Britain once more. Loyalists captured a French squadron stationed in Cadiz in 1808, where the loyalist navy remained for the rest of the war, although the heaviest ships of the line deployed to Havana and Mahón (Menorca). Many ships were cannibalized for the fitting out of these squadrons, and the number of units setting out to sea dwindled rapidly. Their wartime mission was to transfer vital silver remittances from New Spain to Cadiz, often with help from the British Royal Navy. In some cases British warships also helped carry Spanish bullion. A few frigates and other minor units coordinated with Britain in the amphibious operations of the Peninsular War.[23] By 1814, when the conflict ended and the Spanish monarchy returned, twenty-three ships of the line and nine frigates had been lost, most of them due to lack of maintenance, but fifteen ships of the line and sixteen frigates remained.[24] By then, however, the monarchy faced the privateering navies of the nascent independent republics of Spanish America, most of them manned by French and African American crews, as had been the case during the Quasi-War, and unofficially operating with U.S. financial and logistical support.[25]

The connections with the United States of insurgent privateering, along with the war raging in Florida between the Spanish and Anglo-American populations, were the reasons why MacDonnell's plan for a naval war in North America was seriously reconsidered during 1815 and 1816. But Minister of the Navy José Vázquez de Figueroa faced a competing strategy from the Comisión de reemplazos (Replacement commission), a commission of merchants and royal officials charged with finding the troops, supplies, and financial means to reconquer the Americas. They recommended that the remaining ships transfer troops for amphibious operations to secure Spanish American ports.[26] This was the chosen strategy, which left the United States question to diplomacy, which, in the end, could only mean relinquishing the Two Floridas. The purchase of several ships from Russia and France reinforced the navy to follow the plans of the Comisión de reemplazos, although with many financial and logistical problems.[27] To counter insurgent privateering, Spain hired French pirates, who competed for resources and ports, and launched its own effective privateering campaign from Cuba and Puerto Rico, raising the insurance costs of neutral trade and prompting the U.S. government to end its unofficial support for trade warfare. By then, however, the restored Spanish Crown had lost political control of the continent.

In conclusion, the concept of a fleet in being was a component of Spanish naval strategy from the days of Uztáriz, Aranda, and Floridablanca, but it was just one aspect of a much more complex set of ideas regarding the use of naval power that remained unchanged well into the nineteenth century. The concept of an "active defense" comprising diplomacy, deterrence, diversion, amphibious operations, localized offensive use of the battle fleet, and trade warfare is indeed more appropriate and reflects more precisely the diversity and complexity of Spanish strategic thought. The main objective remained the preservation of empire, and this was consistently achieved until the erratic political leadership that followed the fall of Floridablanca. It coincided with the revolutionary turmoil created by the dissolution of the Spanish monarchy, the economic effects of the British blockade, and the expansion of the United States, which together paralyzed the naval system's capacity to respond. Still, there was an important offensive aspect to privateering warfare and counterinsurgency strategies, but this was not sufficient to reverse the effects of political dissent in the larger part of Spanish America.

## NOTES

1. J. B. Hattendorf, "The Idea of a Fleet-in-Being in Historical Perspective," *Naval War College Review* 67, no. 1 (2014): 43–60.
2. G. Uztáriz, *Theórica y práctica de comercio y de marina*, 1724.
3. I. Valdez-Bubnov, "Pensamiento táctico y liderazgo estratégico: La evolución de la doctrina naval española entre los siglos XVII y XVIII," in *Liderazgo estratégico en España, 1475–2018*, edited by A. Guimerá Ravina, 39–63 (Madrid: CSIC/Instituto Universitario General Gutiérrez Mellado, 2019).
4. I. Valdez-Bubnov, *Poder naval y modernización del Estado: política de construcción naval española (siglos XVI-XVIII)* (México-Madrid: Bonilla Artigas/Iberoamericana Vervuert, 2011), 266–67, 273–307.
5. A. Guimerá Ravina, "Naval Leadership and the Art of War: John Jervis and José de Mazarredo Compared (1797–9)," in *Naval Leadership in the Atlantic World*, edited by R. Harding and Agustín Guimerá Ravina, 117–130 (London: University of Westminster, 2012).
6. A. Guimerá Ravina, "The Offensive Strategy of the Spanish Navy 1763–1808," in *Strategy and the Sea: Essays in Honour of John B. Hattendorf*, edited by N. A. M Rodger, J. Ross Dancy, Benjamin Darnell, and Evan Wilson, 98–108 (Woodbridge, UK: Boydell Press, 2016).
7. I. Valdez-Bubnov, "Spanish Naval Strategy and the United States, 1763–1819," *Mariner's Mirror* 101 (2015): 4–20.
8. A. Guimerá Ravina and José María Blanco Núñez, "Spanish Naval Operations," in *The American Revolution*, edited by Allison, David K. and Larrie Ferreiro, 173–223 (Washington, DC: Smithsonian Books, 2018).

9. J. Hernández Franco, *La gestión política y el pensamiento reformista del Conde de Floridablanca* (Murcia, EDITUM, 2008); and A. Guimerá Ravina, "La Marine Espagnole contre la piraterie Nord-Africaine (1750–1785)," in *La piraterie au fil de l'histoire*, edited by Michèle Battesti, 331–45 (Paris: PUPS, 2014).
10. *Gobierno del Señor Rey Don Carlos III ó Instrucción Reservada para la Junta de Estado* (Paris: Girard Hermanos, 1838). The original manuscript differs in some respects; see MSS/7694, Biblioteca Nacional de España, Madrid.
11. J. Marchena and Justo Cuño, *Vientos de guerra: Apogeo y crisis de la Real Armada, 1750–1823* (Seville: Doce Calles, 2018), 2:559–62.
12. *Tratado de alianza defensiva y ofensiva entre Su Magestad Católica y la república francesa; Firmado en San Ildefonso el 18 de agosto de 1796*, in *Tratados de Paz y de comercio desde el año de 1700 hasta el día*, comp. A. del Cantillo, 673–80 (Madrid: Imprenta de Alegría y Charlain, 1843).
13. P. Ortega del Cerro, "Defender los puertos o puertas en aquellas Indias: Despliegue y operatividad de la Real Armada en América durante la guerra de 1796–1802," *Anuario de Estudios Americanos* 79, no. 2 (2022): 673–703; R. E. Vela y Cuadros, "Las divisiones de las escuadras de La Habana durante el conflicto anglo-español (1796–1801)," *Revista de Historia Naval* 157 (2022): 27–62; and Marchena and Cuño, *Vientos de guerra*, vol. 2.
14. M. V. López-Cordón Cortezo, "Entre Francia e Inglaterra," in *Trafalgar y el mundo atlántico*, edited by A. Guimerá Ravina, Alberto Ramos, and Gonzalo Butrón, 19–60 (Madrid: Marcial Pons Historia, 2004).
15. López-Cordón Cortezo.
16. H. M. Ammon, *The Genet Mission* (New York: Norton, 1973).
17. C. Marichal, "El comercio neutral y los consorcios extranjeros en Veracruz, 1805–1808," in *El comercio exterior de México, 1713–1750*, edited by Carmen Yuste López and Matilde Souto Mantecón, 163–192 (México: Instituto Mora, IIH-UNAM/Universidad Veracruzana, 2000).
18. U. Bonnel, *La France, Les États-Unis et la guerre de course (1797–1815)* (París: Nouvelles Éditions Latines, 1959); A. De Conde, *The Quasi-War* (New York: Charles Scribner's Sons, 1966); and P. Crowhurst, *The French War on Trade: Privateering, 1793–1815* (Aldershot, UK: Scholar Press, 1989).
19. Valdez-Bubnov, "Spanish Naval Strategy," 9–13.
20. Valdez-Bubnov, 9–13.
21. J. Cayuela Fernández and Ángel Pozuelo Reina, *Trafalgar* (Madrid: Biblioteca Historia de España, 2004); A. Rodríguez González, *Trafalgar y el conflicto anglo-español del siglo XVIII* (Madrid: Actas, 2005); and A. Guimerá Ravina, "Bloqueos navales y operaciones anfibias: La perspectiva española," in *Guerra Naval en la Revolución y el Imperio*, edited by A. Guimerá Ravina and José María Blanco Núñez (Madrid: Marcial Pons Historia, 2008).

22. I. Valdez-Bubnov, "La representación historiográfica de la guerra en el mar en el largo siglo XVIII: Pensamiento táctico y estratégico, navalismo histórico y metodologías de vanguardia en el siglo XXI," *Cuadernos Dieciochistas* 21 (2020): 235–67.
23. V. Ruiz García, *Las naves de las Cortes (1808–1812)* (Madrid: Sílex, 2013).
24. Marchena and Cuño, *Vientos de guerra*, 2:740–46.
25. C. Laffitte, *Histoire des côtes colombiennes: Navigation, commerce et guerres civiles à l'époque de Bolivar* (Paris: L'Harmattan, 2003); M. MacCarthy, *Privateering, Piracy and British Policy in Spanish America, 1810–1830* (London: Boydell Press, 2013); N. Terrien, *"Des Patriotes sans patrie": Historie des Corsaires Insurgés de l'Amérique Espagnole (1810–1825)* (Mordelles: Les Perséides Éditions, 2015); and E. Pérez Morales, *No Limits to Their Sway. Cartagena's Privateers and the Masterless Caribbean in the Age of Revolutions* (Nashville: Vanderbilt University Press, 2018).
26. E. A. Heredia, *Planes españoles para reconquistar Hispanoamérica, 1810–1818* (Buenos Aires: Editorial Universitaria, 1974); C. Malamud, *Sin marina, sin tesoro y casi sin soldados: La financiación de la reconquista de América* (Santiago: Centro de Estudios Bicentenario, 2007); and J. L. Meige Amézaga, *Los soldados ignorados: Expediciones militares a Indias, 1810–1824* (Madrid: FEHME, 2019).
27. Valdez-Bubnov, "Spanish Naval Strategy," 14–15.

CHAPTER 3

# NAPOLEON'S NAVAL STRATEGY
## "Harassing the British with expenses and fatigue" (1803–14)

*Kenneth G. Johnson*

During the Anglo-French War of 1803–14 and its corollary wars, Napoleon employed a fleet-in-being strategy in many of his early plans. However, it did not become the focal part of his naval strategy until the last years of his empire. He used his smaller fleets to impose costs on Britain by pinning the Royal Navy to specific locations or by dispersing it across theaters while he attempted to overcome France's many resource and port limitations by expanding his empire in order to build a navy to rival Britain. Although he was close to reaching this objective by 1813, Britain had used the preceding years to decimate France's overseas commerce and capture all of its colonies by 1810. Ultimately, Napoleon never engaged in the naval war he sought as his empire collapsed in late 1813, following the failed invasion of Russia.

These wars resulted from the clash of English, French, Russian, Prussian, and Austrian designs for aggrandizement. While the 1802 Treaty of Amiens ended the last remaining war in Europe, it did not endure. Napoleon used it to expand his influence over France's continental neighbors, much to Britain's chagrin. Britain chafed under the disadvantageous peace, concerned with Napoleon's efforts to reestablish France's colonial empire and his refusal to sign a separate commercial treaty. While Napoleon attempted to make concessions to maintain the peace, restoring the colonial economy and protecting France's industry and commerce that had been weakened by years of war were fundamental to his political regime.[1] Having negotiated poorly, Britain believed that the only recourse was to declare war.[2] To strike France's scattered naval assets quickly, Britain declared war on 18 May 1803.

While neither navy was fully prepared for renewed hostilities, the Royal Navy was better situated to do so. Despite having only thirty-two ships of the line and sixty-eight frigates in commission at the start of 1803, the Royal Navy possessed a reserve of another eighty ships and forty frigates laid up or undergoing repairs.[3] Although Admiral John Jervis's crusade against perceived corruption disrupted work in the ports and the stocking of crucial naval stores, the Royal Navy's predominance at sea and its extensive system of dockyards ensured that it could mobilize quickly.[4] Indeed, it quickly expanded to seventy ships of the line by September 1804, then eighty-three ships, and over one hundred frigates by January 1805.[5]

Britain's two primary instruments of power were the Royal Navy and its financial strength. The former, known as the Wooden Walls of Great Britain, was both its primary defense and means of projecting power. The British navy benefited from a massive network of ports and shipyards that spanned the globe. In addition to the seven Royal dockyards of Deptford, Woolwich, Chatham, Sheerness, Portsmouth, Plymouth, and Pembroke (after 1814), the Royal Navy also had contracts with over 110 merchant yards. Furthermore, the British possessed overseas dockyards in Gibraltar, Halifax, and Port Royal, Jamaica, which facilitated maintaining their fleets overseas.[6] The British also benefited from the ports of allies or conquered territory. Having reneged on the promise to evacuate Malta as part of the Treaty of Amiens, its ports facilitated operations in the Mediterranean. When Napoleon turned his sights to Naples in 1805, the British swooped in to secure Sicily to acquire another crucial naval station in the central Mediterranean.[7] The Royal Navy also regained access to Port Mahón on Menorca when Napoleon invaded Spain in 1808.[8] To the east, the Royal Navy had access to the East India Company's dockyard in Bombay, which eventually became a Royal Navy dockyard in 1811.[9] These dockyards and overseas ports were essential to British efforts to blockade Napoleon's growing naval power. While the British army could carry out minor operations, its small size relegated it to a support role in the continental conflict. Instead, Britain relied upon its financial resources to garner continental allies with larger armies, such as Austria, Prussia, and Russia.

Conversely, France's might primarily came from its armies, while its navy struggled through fifteen years of revolutionary turmoil and war.

Its armies saved France from invasion and were the primary means of projecting power to expand its borders and influence over neighboring states. Although Napoleonic France's fiscal situation was more secure than previous governments, it did not enjoy the same level of credit available to England. However, as Napoleon's control over Europe expanded, his primary economic power came from his ability to deprive Britain of its crucial European markets.

## FRENCH CONSTRAINTS

France's insufficient domestic supplies of timber and other naval stores, coupled with its naval ports mostly lacking direct access to Europe's system of rivers and canals, made it difficult to maintain, let alone expand, its navy, especially in the face of Britain's growing dominance of the seas. The French navy, facing a war that it was wholly unprepared to fight, required an enormous effort to refit. In the 1780s it had a target strength of sixty-three ships and sixty-three frigates with sufficient supplies to expand to eighty-one ships and eighty-one frigates in times of war. However, the French navy had suffered from years of political turmoil, disrupted supply chains, and uninterrupted war. Napoleon wore out his navy ferrying troops to colonies across the Caribbean and Indian Ocean rather than using the Peace of Amiens to refit. While nearly 70,000 French prisoners of war, who were mostly sailors, returned to France as part of the peace, nearly 8,000 died from yellow fever. Nominally France possessed forty-eight ships in June 1802, but frequent crossings of the Atlantic Ocean had worn out many.[10] Although Napoleon had forbade the departure of any ships of the line or frigates for the Americas by mid-March 1803, the French navy remained dangerously dispersed, with twenty-five ships and twenty-five frigates out at sea when Britain declared war.[11] In March 1803 Napoleon's minister of the navy, Admiral Denis Decrès, reported that even with the return of most ships from the Caribbean, he would have only twenty-one ships in a state to go to sea by September 1803 because so many ships needed repairs; but with repairs and new construction, he overoptimistically believed that he would have fifty-six ships by September 1804.[12]

Several major logistical difficulties hampered Napoleon's execution of a naval war against Britain. Shipbuilding required a steady supply of timber that France increasingly had difficulty procuring. The increasing demand for oak had outstripped local sources, requiring France to import oak by the 1770s.[13] Similarly, French dockyards had to import fir masts, hemp, and copper. Key naval stores were almost entirely dependent upon secure maritime shipping. Although France's main ports possessed advantageous geographical features that facilitated operations in the Atlantic and the Mediterranean, their locations had serious logistical drawbacks. All were located far from key domestic resources, particularly timber and iron, thereby requiring extensive transportation systems. Except Rochefort, none were located along a major navigable river providing access to the interior. Brest, situated at the far end of the Brittany peninsula, was distant from the Loire and Seine estuaries, two hundred and three hundred kilometers distant, respectively. To the south, Toulon sat nearly one hundred kilometers to the east of the Rhone estuary. Only the secondary port of Rochefort had direct access to a major river, the Charente, which facilitated shipping timber from the Pyrenees mountains.

Therefore, the French navy had to develop an extensive network to supply its dockyards with sufficient naval stores. It needed an auxiliary fleet of fluyts designed to carry large masts, flat-bottom barges, and scows to transport these crucial naval stores.[14] Given Britain's predominance at sea, most had to be shipped slowly along the coast or through an extensive network of canals. To protect the vulnerable coastal shipping, Napoleon used both coastal batteries and mobile flotillas. By July 1810 his empire had more than 900 coastal batteries with more than 3,600 cannons and 13,000 gunners at a cost of 7 million francs a year.[15] To provide a more active defense, Napoleon created small coastal flotillas to patrol the waters around ports and major estuaries with up to 14,000 men serving aboard hundreds of brigs, gunboats, luggers, cutters, and barges.[16] Given the critical nature of key naval stores, France transported most using its secure internal canal network. Once masts, tar, and hemp from the Baltic Sea reached Amsterdam, they were distributed directly to Le Havre, Nantes, and Toulon. From Nantes supplies had to be shipped to Lorient and Brest. While Napoleon initially wanted a canal from Nantes to Brest, in 1811 the difficulty of supplying Brest prompted him to make Antwerp his principal Atlantic port.[17]

Bourbon France had historically relied upon its allies to counter Britain's numerical superiority at sea. The execution of Louis XVI and the French Republic's declaration of war against Spain and the Dutch Republic in 1793 undermined long-standing relationships, but the success of the French revolutionary armies eventually returned some semblance of these naval alliances. Once France and Spain ended their conflict in 1795, they joined a new alliance in 1796. In 1795 France could once again count upon Dutch sea power with the ousting of the pro-British stadtholder, William V, and the creation of a pro-French Batavian Republic. Napoleon eventually reduced the independence of the Batavian Republic by making his brother Louis Bonaparte its king. The resulting Kingdom of Holland lasted only four years until 1810, when Napoleon forced his brother to abdicate, annexed the territory, and controlled its naval assets directly. Meanwhile, after the disasters of Trafalgar and the 1806 naval campaign, Napoleon sought renewed naval strength by commandeering the navies of Denmark, Portugal, and Spain. When these efforts were thwarted, Napoleon fell back to the longer and more expensive recourse of building his own ships.

To facilitate this massive undertaking, Napoleon expanded his system of ports, which grew in tandem with his annexations. To maximize efficiency, he had some ports specialize in shipbuilding and others in repairs and armament.[18] Toulon served as a port of armament. Its basins and slipways would be used only for repairs. Almost all French ships for the Mediterranean would be built eighty kilometers west-northwest of Toulon at Port-de-Bouc, which connected to the major waterways of France through canals. It had the capacity to build several ships of the line at a time.[19] He also used his Italian ports to bolster France's existing maritime facilities as additional ships for the Toulon fleet were built in the Italian port of Genoa, annexed in 1805.[20] Given the exposure of Genoa's facilities, located outside the fortifications, Napoleon found another locale in Italy.[21] A hundred kilometers to the east-southeast of Genoa lay the natural gulf of La Spezia, which he wanted to turn into "a military port like Toulon."[22] This required enormous expenditures that France could not immediately afford. Therefore, he gradually built up La Spezia to spread the expense over a number of years.[23] Meanwhile, he continued to build ships in Genoa to maximize production and to mollify the Genoese with the economic stimulus.[24] The combined production of these ports eventually reestablished the French Mediterranean fleet lost at the Battle of Trafalgar in 1805.

Napoleon reinvigorated the ports of Venice and Ancona on the eastern coast of the Kingdom of Italy to build a fleet to command the Adriatic Sea. Having taken Venice and part of the Dalmatian coast after defeating Austria in December 1805, Napoleon had quickly ordered the construction of "a squadron of six ships and as many frigates" in Venice to "protect commerce from the Levant, either against Turks or Russians, or to leave the Mediterranean." These ships would have shallow drafts to allow them to enter the port of Alexandria, demonstrating Napoleon's continued interest in Egypt.[25] In August 1806 he expanded the construction project to ten 74-gun ships in Venice, with France financing eight of them.[26] Nevertheless, production in Venice remained sluggish. Of the ten ships ordered in August 1806, the first was finally completed in September 1810, followed by two more in 1811 and another two in 1812.

Given the difficulty ships faced leaving the Venetian lagoon, Napoleon needed another base for his future Adriatic fleet. Initially he turned to Ancona, having advocated to the Directory in 1797 that Ancona would "render us masters of the Adriatic Sea."[27] With its open harbor, ships could "enter and leave there under all winds."[28] France occupied the port in 1805 and annexed the region in May 1808. Napoleon had already ordered it dredged and sent engineers to consider building slipways for constructing ships of the line and frigates.[29] Later he ordered the construction of forts to protect it.[30] Without a protected roadstead, Ancona could only safely harbor a few ships or frigates at a time, undercutting its importance.[31] Along with the Venetian port of Cattaro (modern-day Kotor) on the Dalmatian coast, Napoleon possessed a number of Adriatic ports to serve as potential safe havens.

Napoleon also envisioned the satellite Kingdom of Naples augmenting his sea power in the Mediterranean. As Ferdinand had fled to Sicily with most of the small Neapolitan navy in 1806, the French captured only two frigates, four smaller craft, and a score of gunboats as well as the naval facilities surrounding Naples. To the south, Naples also possessed Taranto, whose impressive roadstead had led Napoleon to occupy it since 1803. Heavily fortified, it could shelter a fleet against superior forces.[32] On 15 July 1808 Napoleon's treaty that made his brother-in-law Joachim Murat king of Naples required Murat to fund and build a fleet of two 80-gun ships, four 74-gun ships, six frigates, and six brigs or corvettes to serve as an extension of French naval power.[33] Despite continued prodding, by 1812 Murat had established only a third of this fleet.[34]

Along the Atlantic coast, Napoleon focused on the combined facilities of Antwerp and Vlissingen instead of France's traditional port of Brest. In April 1804 he declared that "it is Antwerp that ought to be our grand dockyard."[35] While most of the ships would be built at Antwerp, Vlissingen would serve as a port of armament where he eventually hoped to have thirty warships.[36] As Vlissingen lay directly across the Channel, the emperor knew that the expanding fleet would become "progressively more worrisome for England."[37] Brest remained an important port of armament, with only limited resources dedicated to shipbuilding, with most ships built at Cherbourg and Lorient. Similarly, the port of Rochefort would serve primarily for repairs, although ships were still built there. Additional dockyards at Bayonne and Le Passage, upriver of Bordeaux, supplemented these facilities.[38]

Although France and its allies nominally had significant ports overseas, the British captured several of them, and years of heavy usage or neglect left the remaining facilities in poor condition to support extensive naval operations. Martinique possessed Fort-de-France, whose bay could accommodate a massive fleet to threaten British possessions in the Caribbean. Its westward-facing harbor nestled within a half-circle of mountains provided the safest anchorage against hurricanes.[39] However, Martinique's service as a hub of the naval campaigns of 1805 and 1806 denuded its limited naval stores. Admiral Louis Thomas Villaret de Joyeuse, the *capitaine-general* of the island, complained in 1808 that "if one of these ships is damaged, I will be obliged to disarm it completely, not having a morsel of proper wood to make a mast or a yard."[40]

While the Mascarene Islands were ideally located along the major shipping routes of the Indian Ocean, they also lacked sufficient resources to sustain a large naval presence. Although Grand Port of Île de France could accommodate several hundred commercial ships, the governor reported in 1804 that "the port is in the worst state," lacking proper dredging and repairs for the last twelve years.[41] It was "extremely denuded" of key naval stores.[42] The British capture of the Dutch Cape Colony in January 1806 exacerbated the precarious position of the Mascarene Islands.

Most importantly, France's overseas ports lacked facilities to undertake major repairs of ships of the line. Insufficient supplies and facilities overseas limited French fleets to the North Atlantic and the Mediterranean. When Napoleon submitted plans for extensive overseas expeditions in December 1806, Decrès begged a postponement, highlighting that "the difficulties of maritime operations have never been as great as on this occasion! The enemy has never had as many ships available and we have never had fewer ports of call and greater shortages in our distant ports." In these conditions, naval commanders could sail only with "extreme precaution," stripping the French fleets of "one of their essential abilities: to chase or to flee at all-out speeds."[43] So Napoleon relied upon his frigates and other smaller craft to resupply his beleaguered colonies and conduct *guerre de course* operations.

## FRENCH NAVAL STRATEGY

All of these constraints in fleet size, naval stores, and safe ports limited French naval strategy. During the early years of the renewed war with England, Napoleon occasionally used a fleet-in-being strategy in support of key operations. In his initial invasion plan for England, the Toulon fleet would rendezvous with the Rochefort fleet and sneak into the Channel. To facilitate their passage, the Brest fleet would remain prepared to invade Ireland, thereby forcing the blockading British fleet to remain close to shore to prevent its departure.[44] Napoleon understood that a fleet in being required activity. In May 1804 he dismissed Admiral Laurent Jean François Truguet as commander of the Brest fleet due to its "immobility," which left "the enemy neither contained nor harassed."[45] Needing "an active admiral who was familiar with movements at sea," Napoleon selected Admiral Honoré Joseph Antoine Ganteaume.[46] With growing agitation in Ireland, British First Lord of the Admiralty Lord Melville instructed the commander of the Channel fleet, Admiral William Cornwallis, to keep at least sixteen ships off Brest, while another seven to ten ships remained off Cork under Admiral Alan Gardner.[47] Although later plans shifted the Brest fleet to a more active role, weather and a vigilant British blockade kept Ganteaume in port, frustrating Napoleon's main objective of seizing command of the English Channel to facilitate the crossing of the invasion flotilla.

After the drastic losses of 1805 and 1806, Napoleon increasingly incorporated a fleet-in-being strategy in his operational and strategic planning. As he acquired additional ships through construction or conquest, he kept his fleets armed and ready to sail, thereby forcing Britain to keep its fleets at sea. Napoleon sought to drain British coffers by forcing it to maintain an expensive and extensive naval presence across the globe and by embargoing British products through the Continental System. In addition to his fleets being built across European ports, Napoleon dispatched frigates to the Indian Ocean to wage a commerce-raiding campaign to divert British forces far from Europe.

Convinced by Decrès' dire assessment in December 1806, Napoleon ceased planning any future commerce-raiding expeditions with his ships of the line and shifted his attention to the Mediterranean. Based on Decrès' recommendation, he directed his fleets at Rochefort and Cadiz to Toulon to create a fleet of eighteen ships in the Mediterranean. By threatening Sicily, Britain's main Mediterranean naval base, or possibly sailing into the Adriatic or to Constantinople to support the Ottomans, he hoped to draw the British fleet to Toulon, thereby freeing up the passage from Naples for an invasion of Sicily.[48] To support this deception, he wanted to name Ganteaume as commander of the Toulon fleet to make the British believe he would sail for Egypt or Constantinople.[49] Orders were issued to the Rochefort and Cadiz fleets, but persistent British blockades prohibited their departure.[50] However, the constant blockading duty slowly wore out British ships. For example, by August 1806 Vice Admiral Cuthbert Collingwood's fleet blockading Cadiz dwindled from fifteen ships to only seven ships as damaged vessels had to return to port for repairs.[51]

The Eylau Campaign against Russia preoccupied Napoleon, who did not return to naval affairs until the end of March 1807. After learning about a failed British attack on the Ottoman fleet in the Dardanelles in mid-March, he wanted the Toulon fleet increased to ten ships and sent to Naples to "give the enemy trouble off of Sardinia and Sicily."[52] A few days later he canceled these plans as the season for naval operations had ended. Instead Decrès was to prepare for the next season (September 1807) with plans to gather thirty ships in the Mediterranean or send an expedition to resupply the Caribbean islands.[53] To find thirty ships, Napoleon pushed Decrès to accelerate naval construction, claiming that "there is not a moment to lose."[54] In order to maintain the blockade and defend against the threat of these expeditions, British had to maintain twenty-seven ships of the line in the Mediterranean.[55]

Although Napoleon tentatively adjourned naval operations until September, he did not wish to give the British any respite as he slowly shifted to a fleet-in-being strategy over the summer of 1807. He sought to use deception to force the British to maintain large fleets on station. While the Brest fleet prepared openly for an expedition to Ireland, the Rochefort fleet was "to do everything possible" to make the British believe that it was heading for the Cape of Good Hope. Napoleon also wanted Decrès publicly to refer to three other "secret expeditions."[56] However, this did not mean that his fleets should remain passive. Upon receiving reports that only three British ships were monitoring the Toulon fleet's five ships in June 1807, Napoleon instructed them to attack under such favorable circumstances, even if this required stripping sailors from the frigates.[57] To the north, the progress of construction pleased Napoleon, as the Franco-Dutch fleet continued to grow. "The English cannot help but be worried by this squadron," he noted.[58]

As shipwrights around Europe labored to expand the navies of France and its satellite states in hopes of rivaling Britain, Napoleon used his port-bound ships and transports for economic warfare in support of his Continental System. Initially conceived as a means of seizing British goods with the Berlin Decree of 1806, his system evolved into a direct attack on British commerce. In November and December 1807 he issued the Milan Decrees to broaden confiscatory measures to include neutral ships carrying British goods. While supervising the invasion of Spain from Bayonne, he laid out his naval strategy. More ships would be armed across Europe, thereby forcing "the English to spend a lot and disseminate their forces, because they are obliged to have ships in the seas around Spain, Portugal, America, the Baltic, etc."[59] Upon learning of attacks on coastal shipping, Napoleon ordered the fleets to "sail frequently, to head out and present combat to [enemy cruisers] who are inferior to them, and to keep themselves in a state of continual mobility." According to his calculations, the British had to rotate their ships on station, which required four ships for every French ship that sat in port ready to sail.[60]

Thus, Napoleon's "system of war" was to "harass [the British] with expenses and fatigue." Aware that an immobilized fleet posed little threat, the emperor ordered small squadrons frequently to set sail to "pass the summer playing tag" with the British.[61] Anticipating that he would secure the Portuguese and Spanish fleets, Napoleon estimated that the British would need 126 ships to blockade his fleets and escort convoys. Therefore, the British would "need to double their navy, leading to the expenditure of money, the pressing of sailors, and increasing risk of disasters."[62] Although Napoleon failed to secure the Iberian fleets, his growing naval power did force Britain to maintain a large navy of over one hundred ships of the line and employ over 140,000 men.[63]

To the east, Napoleon tied up additional Royal Navy vessels by using frigates to threaten British commerce. Dispatching one or two frigates each year between 1805 and 1810, Napoleon sent eight to conduct commerce raiding in the Indian Ocean. While the British intercepted one of them en route, the remaining seven successfully made the long voyage from France. The British quickly took countermeasures. The Admiralty dispatched additional vessels increasing their presence to six ships of the line, twenty frigates, and five smaller vessels by February 1807.[64] The British also captured the Dutch colony on the Cape of Good Hope in January 1806, which eliminated a friendly port of call and threatened the line of communications back to France. Extensive use of convoys also limited the number of isolated ships that French commerce raiders could easily snatch. Furthermore, extended operations in the Indian Ocean put extensive pressure on Île de France's limited resources, which entailed increasingly expensive repairs. While stocks of naval stores ran low, port facilities and workers had to be rented from private owners. An inadequate supply of frigate masts required cannibalizing prizes for replacements. Copper and oil costs increased, and rope became a priceless commodity.[65] Although the *guerre de course* inflicted minimal losses on British merchants, it did force the British to deploy four or five times as many ships and frigates in the Indian Ocean. However, the French could sustain such efforts only for a limited period. Once the British decided to invade the Mascarene Islands, there was little that Napoleon could do to stop them.

Despite this shift to a fleet-in-being naval strategy, Napoleon did not completely abandon launching expeditions. Already contemplating an attack on Sardinia or Sicily in September 1807, he began organizing several major expeditions in the spring of 1808.[66] Possibly inspired by Ganteaume's successful mission to revitalize Corfu, Napoleon and Decrès planned an expedition to Egypt, Tunis, or Algiers in April 1808. The emperor noted that "a foot on this part of Africa will make England think": an expedition to North Africa had the advantage that the British expected an attack on Sicily. In preparation, Napoleon discreetly sent an engineer to conduct reconnaissance in Algeria.[67] Meanwhile, Napoleon expanded his plans for the upcoming winter season to a dual strike to the east. While the Toulon fleet would land 19,000 troops in Egypt, the Brest and Lorient fleets would transport 15,000 troops to the Indian Ocean. To preoccupy the British, the Vlissingen fleet and the flotilla at Boulogne would mobilize to "menace Ireland." Napoleon believed that, together, these operations would strike fear in the British, thereby leaving them with "no means of bothering us [in Europe] or bothering the Americas."[68] Indeed, the operations would "ruin the English colony from top to bottom," thereby striking "a mortal blow to England's affairs."[69] To maintain tight security, Napoleon withheld the destination from his commanders, even asking for reports on different locations in order to spread false rumors.[70]

In response, the British dedicated more forces to blockade Napoleon's fleets. The British fleet off Vlissingen grew from seventeen ships of the line in October 1808 to thirty-four ships the following April.[71] Similarly, the British Mediterranean fleet grew to eighty-four vessels in 1808.[72] In addition to the costs of building and repairing these ships, the Royal Navy also had to feed and supply over 130,000 sailors, many of whom were at sea.[73] Overall, the Royal Navy's budget expanded from £15.4 million in 1806 to £20.8 million in 1809.[74] Thus, Napoleon's growing naval power successfully forced Britain to increase naval spending.

With unexpected popular resistance to the invasion of Spain and growing Austrian hostility, Napoleon considered canceling the expeditions to Egypt and India. Unsure of "detaching such considerable forces from the European continent," he instructed Decrès to continue buying and building ships until he made his ultimate decision in mid-July.[75] With the situation in Spain deteriorating and continual reports of the Austrian army mobilizing, Napoleon eventually called off the expeditions. However, these preparations served as a strategic feint while he shifted additional units to the Iberian front in the fall of 1808. While Murat's Neapolitan troops captured the island of Capri in October 1808 and prepared to invade Sicily, Napoleon maintained the Toulon fleet in a state of preparedness and moved two divisions toward Toulon.[76] The capture of Capri would signal his interest in Sicily, thereby "causing the British to fear for the safety of the latter, which would be very useful."[77] To facilitate this diversion, he had his minister of police, Joseph Fouché, plant indications of plans to invade Sicily in dozens of articles in Dutch, German, and French newspapers.[78] In response to the capture of Capri, the British dispatched three additional ships to Palermo.[79] Yet the invasion of Spain had the adverse effect of freeing up more British ships for blockade duty or offensive operations elsewhere.

As Napoleon awaited the launching of his Venetian ships of the line, he relied on frigates and smaller vessels to contest control of the Adriatic. With the onset of war with Austria in April 1809, he concentrated his naval force in Venice to intercept shipping from Trieste and reinforce the defense of Venice against an Austrian attack. In support of the three frigates and three brigs in the Adriatic, he hoped to send additional corvettes, brigs, and sloops. He even contemplated sending two of his fastest ships of the line into the Adriatic in order to command the sea for two to three weeks, but these never materialized.[80]

The British continued to frustrate French efforts. To facilitate operations in Adriatic, the British seized the island of Lissa, modern-day Vis, in the middle of the Dalmatian coast in 1807. In addition to several frigates, the British occasionally rotated a ship of the line into the Adriatic in anticipation of the launching of French ships from Venice.[81] In March 1810 Napoleon again wanted to reestablish a division of four frigates and other small ships at Ancona, which would either maintain "control of the gulf, or which [would] force the enemy to keep ships of the line there."[82] Thus, Napoleon wanted to enjoy free use of the Adriatic Sea while he could but was content with making the British maintain large forces there. This would divert British ships from his major ports and drain British coffers to maintain a presence on extended logistical lines.

Adjusting his strategy slightly in 1810, Napoleon continued to prepare expeditions across the continent with the intent to drain British resources rather than actually sending these expeditionary forces out to sea. "I am putting everything in movement to keep the English in check," he disclosed to his brother Louis.[83] Admiral Édouard Thomas Burgues de Missiessy was to conduct maneuvers with the fleet at Vlissingen to force the British to maintain a blockading fleet while the Dutch fleet of nine ships moved into the roadstead of Texel to threaten Britain.[84] In Cherbourg, the emperor gathered two ships, two frigates, two corvettes, and a number of transports capable of carrying up to 10,000 soldiers to threaten the Channel Islands with invasion in the hope that this would force the British to maintain a squadron to blockade Cherbourg during the winter and garrison the Channel Islands with many troops.[85] Furthermore, a reduced flotilla in Boulogne capable of carrying 60,000 troops still threatened Britain with invasion. In the Atlantic, the ports of Brest, Lorient, and Rochefort were slowly building ships to create another large fleet in Brest.

In the Mediterranean, the flotilla of transports in Toulon would continue to grow with the eventual goal of providing the capacity to carry 30,000 troops to Egypt, while a Neapolitan flotilla would threaten Sicily with an invasion of 20,000 soldiers.[86] Napoleon continually instructed Murat to expand the Neapolitan navy as "it would force the English to keep an equal force against yours."[87] Napoleon believed that all of these mobilized forces would prohibit the British from deploying any ships to the Adriatic, thereby allowing the combined Franco-Italian fleet to command the sea.[88] Meanwhile, he expanded ship orders to make 140 ships available for campaigns in 1812.[89] Napoleon had finally learned to avoid costly expeditions until he could achieve naval parity with the British. The sole exception to this strategy was his plan to rescue his remaining colonies in the Indian Ocean.

Napoleon remained optimistic about securing control of the Adriatic despite the loss of his frigates at the Battle of Lissa in 1811 and the 74-gun *Rivoli* in 1812. After chastising the Viceroy of Italy, his stepson Eugène de Beauharnais, for deploying *Rivoli* poorly escorted, the emperor spurred him "not to let this loss discourage you" as the French–Italian fleet in the Adriatic would soon have another three ships and a heavy frigate. This force would render them "masters of the Adriatic" or at least force the British to station several ships in these waters.[90] Although he had been well poised to contest British sea power in the Adriatic in 1813, the collapse of the Grande Armée in Russia ended Napoleon's grand designs.

Overall, Napoleon's naval strategy remained constant in 1811. In March he set out his intentions for the 1811 season, stating, "I do not want my squadrons leaving, but that they are provisioned as if they ought to leave." To facilitate the deception, Napoleon planned to fool even his admirals into believing that they would depart by frequently sending couriers with sealed orders to be opened at sea. He wanted 20,000 troops embarked on his fleets at Toulon and the Scheldt for a period of four to six weeks so that "the threat is real."[91] In particular, he wanted to use the fleet at Antwerp, the Boulogne flotilla, and the squadron at Cherbourg to menace Britain with an invasion of Ireland. As these forces steadily grew each year, Napoleon wanted to have these three expeditions ready by September 1813. At that time, he envisioned the Scheldt expedition capable of transporting 36,000 men and 3,000 horses; the Boulogne flotilla, another 40,000 troops; and the Cherbourg expedition, 18,000 men and 1,500 horses.[92] As Napoleon and Decrès organized these expeditions, the former emphasized that "the threat could have an effect only if the operation is planned in a way that everyone believes it and that we can really attempt it." Napoleon did consider invading Sicily or Sardinia from Corsica with forty small boats escorted by one frigate and one corvette in 1811, but this plan never materialized.[93]

If conditions improved, Napoleon envisioned launching these expeditions in 1812 or 1813. While the Toulon fleet would sail either to Sicily or to Egypt, the Scheldt expedition would feign an invasion of Ireland, then head for the Caribbean to retake all of the French and

Dutch colonies. Meanwhile, the Brest fleet would sail with 8,000 men to retake the Cape of Good Hope, thereby spreading "60,000–80,000 men across two worlds."[94] However, the war in Spain stalemated while Russia prepared for war. Although Napoleon started to call on naval personnel to rebuild his army in early 1813, the fleets in Antwerp, Brest, and Toulon were to prepare for expeditions to serve as "veritable diversions."[95] Even though formal relations between France and the United States remained tepid, he wanted to keep the Antwerp fleet armed and ready in order to preoccupy the British navy indirectly to support the Americans.[96] However, as Napoleon faced defeat on the Continent, he never could wage the long-envisioned naval campaign that he had spent so much energy and resources to prepare.

During these later years the Royal Navy was increasingly stretched to blockade Napoleon's ever-growing navy. While the British maintained parity with Napoleon's naval forces, they were at great pains to do so. They had to rely more on untrained sailors to man an ever-increasing number of ships. Even members of the British Admiralty believed it would be impossible to continue to match Napoleon's forces by 1812.[97] In February 1813 the First Lord of the Admiralty reported to the Cabinet that while the French had not gotten out to sea, they were not "inactive in naval preparations." As Napoleon harnessed the resources of Europe, "we may expect him to have advanced to a state of readiness to oppose to us an equal naval force, at least as to the number and magnitude of ships. That period is not very distant." With British ships suffering the wear and tear of blockade duty while Napoleon's sat in the safety of port, the First Lord estimated that Napoleon would achieve naval superiority by 1816.[98] Probably, Napoleon's greatest economic success was his ability to drain the bullion supply of the Bank of England from £6.9 million in 1808 to just £2.2 million in 1814.[99]

Yet Napoleon never got that opportunity as his empire collapsed after the disastrous invasion of Russia in 1812. Although ultimately seeking a traditional naval war upon achieving naval parity, Napoleon had been forced to adopt an interim fleet-in-being strategy. Unable to strike England directly, he developed an indirect strategy targeting its economy. By actively employing his expanding number of ships, he managed to drive up British expenses and pushed the Royal Navy into a major manning crisis. However, Britain's dominance at sea hampered Napoleon's acquisition of naval stores, thereby slowing his naval program. This left him relatively powerless to stop the British from systematically capturing the overseas ports of France and its allies, which greatly diminished his ability to conduct long-range naval operations. Finally, British dominance at sea enabled them to transport men, weapons, and money to support Napoleon's continental adversaries, who ultimately defeated him.

---

Parts of this chapter were originally published in my chapter "Napoleon's War at Sea" in *Napoleon and the Operational Art of War: Essays in Honor of Donald D. Howard*, edited by Michael V. Leggiere (Leiden: Brill, 2016), and are reproduced here with permission from the publisher.

## NOTES

1. Alexander Mikaberidze, *Napoleonic Wars: A Global History* (Oxford: Oxford University Press, 2020), 150.
2. Mikaberidze, 170.
3. William James, *The Naval History of Great Britain* (London: Macmillan, 1902), 1:505.
4. N. A. M. Rodger, *The Command of the Ocean* (New York: Norton, 2006), 477–78.
5. Rodger, 531; and James, *Naval History*, 3:506.
6. James Davey, *In Nelson's Wake* (New Haven, CT: Yale University Press, 2015), 35, 163.
7. Piers Mackesy, *The War in the Mediterranean, 1803–1810* (New York: Longmans, Green, 1957), 27–28, 106.
8. Mackesy, 275, 282.
9. C. Northcote Parkinson, *War in the Eastern Seas, 1793–1815* (London: George Allen & Unwin, 1954), 12.
10. "Reports on the repairs," 11 June 1802, Marine BB4 161, f. 9–11, Service historique de la Defense, Paris.
11. *Correspondance générale* (hereafter, *CG*) (Paris: Fayard, 2004–18), No. 7523, 4:75.
12. Report by Decrès, 25 March 1803, in Édouard Desbrière, *1793–1805: Projets et tentatives de débarquement aux îles Britanniques* (Paris: R. Chapelot, 1900–1902), 3:36–40; and Decrès to Napoleon, 31 March 1803, Archives Nationales de

France (AN), Archives du Pouvoir Exécutif (AF) IV 1900 (hereafter, AN, AF).
13. Paul W. Bamford, *Forests and French Sea Power, 1660–1789* (Toronto: University of Toronto Press, 1956), 107–12, 114–17.
14. Bamford, 49, 62; Decrès to Napoleon, Ventôse XI, AN, AF IV 1190.
15. *CG*, No. 24020, 10:383–85.
16. *Correspondence de Napoleon 1er* (hereafter, *CN*) (Paris: H. Plon, J. Dumaine, 1858–70), No. 13789, 17:45; and *CG*, Nos. 18125 and 23977, 8:649, 10:355–6.
17. Decrès to Napoleon, 10 April 1811, AN, AF IV 1206; *CG*, Nos. 22272, 24430, 25455, 26942, 9:1306, 10:577, 1009–13, 11:279; and *CN*, No. 17200, 21:313–14.
18. *CG*, No. 18190, 8:689.
19. *CG*, No. 22272, 9:1306.
20. *CG*, Nos. 15391, 16472, 7:676–677, 1165–1166.
21. *CG*, No. 29076, 11:1238.
22. *CG*, Nos. 13846, 13848, 14004, 14079, 17:87–89, 217–18, 290–91.
23. *CG*, No. 18208, 8: 695–96; *CN*, No. 13977, 17:193–94.
24. *CG*, No. 29075, 11:1238.
25. *CG*, No. 11353, 6:71–72.
26. *CG*, No. 12720, 6:718.
27. *CG*, No. 1379, 1:839–40.
28. *CG*, No. 23273, 10:42.
29. *CG*, No. 16715, 7:1277.
30. *CG*, No. 17959, 8:564–65.
31. *CG*, No. 20037, 9:60–62.
32. *CG*, No. 16292, 7:1086.
33. Article 12 of the treaty concluded at Bayonne, 15 July 1808, No. 3408, in Paul Le Brethon, *Lettres et documents pour servir a l'histoire de Joachim Murat* (Paris, Librarie Plon, 1912), 6:219–24.
34. *CG*, Nos. 23643, 24452, 24609, 24749, 10:212, 586, 649–50, 715–16.
35. *CG*, No. 8851, 4:695.
36. *CG*, No. 18308, 8:756–57.
37. *CG*, No. 17600, 8:371.
38. *CG*, Nos. 18190, 26181, 8:689, 10:1319–20.
39. Alexandre Moreau de Jonnès, *Aventures de guerre au temps de la République et du Consulat* (Paris: Pagnerre, 1858), 153.
40. Villaret de Joyeuse to Decrès, 2 April 1808, Archives nationales d'outre-mer (ANOM), Colonies C$^{8A}$ 116.
41. Decaen to Decrès, 18 June 1804, ANOM, C 102, quoted in Andre Auzoux, *La derniere campagne de l'amiral de Linois (1803–1806)* (Paris: Librarie Alphonse Picard, [1911]), 32.

42. Linois to Decrès, 4 September 1803, cited in Charles M. I. Decaen, *Memoires et journaux du Généraux Decaen* (Paris: Librairie Plon, 1911), 2:376.
43. Decrès to Napoleon, 23 December 1806, AN, AF IV 1196.
44. *CG*, No. 8388, 4:494.
45. *CG*, No. 8904, 4:720.
46. Decrès to Ganteaume, 31 May 1804, in Desbrière, *1793–1805*, 4:153–54.
47. John Leyland, *Dispatches and Letters Relating to the Blockade of Brest 1803–1805* (London: Navy Records Society, 1899–1902), 2:95–96.
48. *CG*, No. 14043, 7:76.
49. *CG*, No. 14170, 7:131–32.
50. *CG*, Nos. 14167, 14173, 7:130, 134.
51. Davey, *In Nelson's Wake*, 140–41.
52. *CG*, No. 14699, 7:362–63.
53. *CG*, No. 14915, 7:464.
54. *CG*, No. 15391, 7:676–77.
55. Mackesy, *War in the Mediterranean*, 348.
56. *CG*, Nos. 15455, 15514, 15750, 7:706, 736–37, 840.
57. *CG*, No. 15826, 7:873–74.
58. *CG*, No. 15903, 7:908.
59. *CG*, No. 17810, 8:479.
60. *CG*, No. 17850, 8:500.
61. *CG*, No. 17873, 8:512–13.
62. *CG*, No. 18129, 8:651.
63. Rodger, *Command of the Ocean*, 499, 562.
64. Parkinson, *War in the Eastern Seas*, 301–3.
65. Henri Prentout, *L'Île de France sous Decaen, 1803–1810* (Paris: Hachette, 1901), 493–94.
66. *CG*, No. 16292, 7:1086.
67. *CG*, No. 17648, 8:398–99.
68. *CG*, Nos. 17885, 17886, 8:519–21.
69. *CG*, No. 17956, 8:562–63.
70. Maurice Dupont, *L'amiral Willaumez* (Paris: Tallandier, 1987), 320.
71. Davey, *In Nelson's Wake*, 150.
72. Davey, 238.
73. R. J. B. Knight and Martin Wilcox, *Sustaining the Fleet, 1793–1815* (Rochester, NY: Boydell Press, 2010), 29.
74. Rodger, *Command of the Ocean*, 645.
75. *CG*, Nos. 18432, 18496, 8:811, 839–40.
76. *CG*, Nos. 18955, 19133, 19294, 19295, 19297, 8:1092, 1166, 1236–37.
77. *CG*, No. 18955, 8:1092.
78. *CG*, No. 19333, 8:1251.

79. Desmond Gregory, *Sicily: The Insecure Base* (London: Farleigh Dickinson University Press, 1988), 72–73.
80. *CG*, Nos. 20755, 20756, 20764, 9:453–54, 457–58.
81. Davey, *In Nelson's Wake*, 289.
82. *CG*, No. 23273, 10:42.
83. *CG*, No. 23531, 10:157–58.
84. *CG*, Nos. 23531, 23591, 10:157–58, 188.
85. *CG*, Nos. 23500, 23691, 24601, 10:144, 238, 645–46.
86. *CG*, No. 24601, 10: 645–46.
87. *CG*, Nos. 23643, 24452, 10:212, 586.
88. *CG*, No. 24070, 10:412–13.
89. *CG*, No. 24601, 10:645–46.
90. *CG*, No. 30171, 11:347–48.
91. *CG*, Nos. 26134, 28777, 10:1295–96, 11:1103.
92. *CG*, No. 27787, 11:676–78.
93. *CG*, No. 28074, 11:797–98.
94. *CG*, No. 26134, 10:1295–96.
95. *CG*, No. 32772, 13:352–53.
96. *CG*, No. 32732, 13:333–34.
97. Kevin McCranie, "Britain's Royal Navy and the Defeat of Napoleon," in *Napoleon and the Operational Art of War*, ed. Michael Leggiere (Leiden: Brill, 2016), 480–81.
98. Quintin Barry, *Far Distant Ships: The Royal Navy and the Blockade of Brest, 1793–1815* (London: Helion, 2017), 319–20.
99. Mikaberidze, *Napoleonic Wars*, 233–39.

CHAPTER 4

# THE SPANISH FLEET IN BEING AND THE WARS FOR INDEPENDENCE IN SPANISH AMERICA (1810-21)

*Jorge Ortiz-Sotelo*

Spain had naval forces in the Americas based at Havana, Montevideo, Lima's port city of Callao, and Mexico's San Blas. In 1808 most of its colonies began a long fight for independence, but in South America the Peruvian viceroyalty remained a stronghold for the royalist cause. The wars for independence entailed long and bloody land campaigns, which required the use of the sea to transport forces from one place to another. But despite its naval weakness, the Spanish navy was not seriously challenged until 1818, when the creation of an opposing Chilean squadron forced its warships based at Callao to adopt a fleet-in-being strategy: Spanish warships avoided a decisive battle, lifted the blockade of the Chilean coast, and concentrated their efforts along the Peruvian coast, awaiting reinforcements that never arrived. Nevertheless, it is amazing how much Spanish authorities accomplished with so little—they retained Callao despite a decade-long, on-and-off blockade and maintained communication among theaters so that independence became a ten-year process.

In 1808, when Napoleon took control of the Spanish government, a move that was strongly repudiated in Spain and its vast empire, Spanish naval power was far from substantial. Soon after the French invasion, most of Spain's American colonies began their struggle for independence. None of them had the naval forces to challenge the already weakened Spanish military, but this situation began to change in 1814 when the land and naval forces of Buenos Aires gained control of Montevideo, the most important seaport of the Viceroyalty of the Rio de la Plata and a naval base for the protection of the South Atlantic. Despite this loss, the Spanish navy could still exert some control over the Caribbean and the Pacific from its remaining bases at Havana (Spain's largest New World shipyard), San Blas (located on the western coast of modern Mexico), and Callao, which would play a central role in the naval side of the wars for Spanish American independence.

After a long campaign, Chile achieved its independence from Spain in 1818 and established a government headed by Bernardo O'Higgins as supreme director. His government organized a squadron stronger than the Spanish squadron based at Callao. Local naval inferiority forced Spain to adopt a fleet-in-being strategy, waiting for reinforcements to reverse the situation. Even when the Spanish government was able to dispatch two ships of the line and a frigate, only the frigate reached Callao, joining two other frigates and few smaller warships. Brigadier Antonio Vacaro, naval commander at Callao, realized that his only course of action was to avoid a direct confrontation with the Chilean squadron and use his ships to transport troops along the coast. The Chilean squadron was under command of Admiral Thomas Cochrane, formerly a highly successful British captain until his conviction for stock fraud, but now in pursuit of Chilean independence. He very aggressively and almost without opposition transported an expeditionary force, which initiated a long land campaign that finally defeated the last Spanish stronghold in the continent.

## THE IMPACT OF THE NAPOLEONIC WARS ON THE SPANISH EMPIRE

In 1808, when Carlos IV and his son Fernando VII were struggling for the Spanish crown, Napoleon Bonaparte forced them to abdicate in his favor. He immediately appointed his brother Joseph as the new king of Spain, although this change had few supporters. José I (as he was called in Spanish) was disavowed by the great majority of his supposed subjects. Almost immediately, both in Spain and in its American colonies, a number of local councils (called juntas) were established to rule and defend these territories in the name of Fernando VII as their rightful king. With British support, both the Spanish army and the Spanish people fought tenaciously for six years to expel the French in what became known in Spanish historiography as the War of Independence, although the British dubbed it the Peninsular War. During this long struggle, important political reforms supported by much of the Spanish military were introduced to reduce the absolute power of the monarchy. But the war bled the already failing Spanish economy, particularly affecting the navy.[1]

On the other side of the Atlantic, the juntas quickly abandoned their initial allegiance to Fernando VII, removed the local Spanish authorities, and began their fight for independence. The exceptions were Cuba and a few Caribbean islands, where the Spanish rule remain unchallenged, and the viceroyalties of Mexico and Peru. The war for Mexican independence was fought within its own territory and lasted for several years, whereas the Peruvian viceroyalty not only remained stanchly loyal but even acted beyond its jurisdiction, sending troops to restore Spanish rule in present-day Ecuador, Bolivia, Argentina, and Chile.[2]

Only after 1814, after the French were expelled and Fernando VII returned to the throne, could Spain send a considerable number of troops to reinforce the local forces defending the monarchy in the Americas. Obviously, these local forces included some Spanish but mainly consisted of criollos (native-born Spanish), indigenous peoples, enslaved Africans and their descendants, and mixtures of all of these. These forces had to sustain a long campaign against armies raised almost everywhere with a similar composition, including a considerable number of Spaniards who fought for the independence of their adopted homeland. The long war between Spain and the juntas was not an international war but more a civil war in which one side was fighting for independence and willing to make huge sacrifices, whereas the other aimed to cut off subversion almost everywhere, a goal that was far beyond its capacity and therefore could apply only limited means.

The fight took place in several theaters, which Spain considered to be campaigns of the same war but those who fought for independence considered to be different wars.[3] Despite the negotiations that took place in various moments and theaters, both parties were aware that only military victory could achieve their political objectives. But this, as in all wars, required enormous resources, something that both Spanish and the juntas lacked, so both sides took extraordinary measures to sustain the war effort.

Spain also faced serious internal problems when the liberal constitution approved by deputies of the Spanish and American peoples in 1812 was abolished after Fernando VII returned to the throne in 1814. Six years later, the Constitution was reinstated, following a military uprising, only to be abolished again in 1823 when a French expeditionary force invaded Spain to support the absolutist aspirations of Fernando VII. All this created tension within the Spanish military, which largely supported the liberal ideas of the 1812 constitution.[4]

The juntas were not free from political problems, as the process of building new republics entailed the confrontation of different points of view and personal ambitions. General José de San Martín and Bernardo O'Higgins, the former Argentinian and the latter Chilean, emerged as central figures in the naval side of the war in South America.

## THE PERUVIAN VICEROYALTY'S SUCCESSFUL DEFENSE OF THE SOUTH PACIFIC, 1809-18

After several years of war against Britain until 1808 and against France afterward, by 1814 the Spanish navy was in very poor condition. Even so, it managed to keep some control of the Atlantic sea lanes but faced huge difficulties supporting the efforts of the Peruvian viceroyalty in sustaining Spanish rule on South America's West Coast.[5] By this time only part of current-day Argentina and Colombia had become independent, and Spanish rule was challenged in many places in Central and South America.

Although the Spanish fleet officially consisted of two ships of the line, eight frigates, ten brigs, and twenty-one smaller vessels, most of them could not go to sea but awaited repairs. The three maritime departments in Spain—Cadiz, Ferrol, and Cartagena—had been seriously affected during the war, and the overseas departments—Manila, San Blas, Callao, Montevideo, and Havana—had limited resources, mainly due to a lack of funding and workforce. All this prevented a quick recovery of its naval power. Even so, some efforts were made, and in 1815 a frigate and six brigs were purchased from France and used mostly to escort troop convoys to the Americas.[6]

Spanish warships based at Havana, as well some sent from Spain, managed to control the Caribbean. They defeated a small squadron of

Mexican insurgents in 1817, at Soto la Marina in the Gulf of Mexico. However, they suffered some setbacks, such as the loss of the brig *Intrepido* and schooner *Rita*, captured by seven Venezuelan schooners under Captain Luis Brion at Los Frailes early in May 1816.[7] On the South Atlantic, the loss of Montevideo in 1814 was a substantial setback for the Spanish effort to defeat the independent government established at Buenos Aires. The loss also affected its communication lines to the Pacific.

Naval forces based at Callao were sufficient to control the West Coast of South America, given the Chilean junta's failed attempts to create a naval force in 1813. The first real naval threat in that area appeared late in 1815, when a small Buenos Aires squadron rounded Cape Horn under Captain William Brown, capturing a few merchant ships and attacking Callao and Guayaquil (Ecuador's main port) during the first half of 1816. As no naval vessels were available at Callao at that moment, local merchants armed six ships to search for the intruders, returning after several weeks at sea without success.[8]

In September 1816, shortly after Brown left the area, the Spanish 44-gun frigate *Venganza* reached Callao, followed a year later by the 36-gun frigate *Esmeralda* escorting eleven merchant ships with troops destined to reinforce the Alto Peruvian army (Spanish forces at Alto Peru), which had been fighting independence efforts in present-day Bolivia and north of Argentina since 1810. The Spanish navy could not send more as its home fleet remained in very poor condition, with only one seaworthy ship of the line. To improve the situation, negotiations with Russia led to the purchase of five ships of the line and three frigates in August 1817, which reached Cadiz in February 1818, followed in October by other three frigates. Of all of them, only the 44-gun frigate *Reina Maria Isabel* was able to sail for the Pacific escorting a convoy with troops in May 1818.[9]

The Peruvian viceroyalty still controlled almost all the West Coast of South America, Callao being the most important port for Spanish naval forces due to its proximity to Lima, the viceregal capital. North of Callao was Guayaquil, the most important shipyard on the Pacific coast, protected by its location twenty kilometers up the Guayas River and the defenses along its course. Further north, Panama, which was part of the Viceroyalty of New Granada (encompassing much of modern Ecuador, Colombia, Panama, and Venezuela), was a key port for maintaining communications with Spain and the royalist troops who were still fighting at present-day Colombia and Venezuela. Southern Peru had several ports, Arica being the most important to maintain contact with the royalist army at Alto Peru, present-day Bolivia; further south, having lost Valparaiso in 1817, the royalists still controlled the other Chilean ports of Concepcion, Valdivia, and Chiloe.

In February 1817 Argentinian and Chilean forces under San Martín defeated royalist troops at Chacabuco, located in central Chile, and restored an independent Chilean government with O'Higgins as supreme director. Because of this defeat, royalist forces and authorities evacuated central Chile, many of them sailing to Callao from Valparaiso, which also fell into the hands of San Martín's forces. But the royalists still controlled southern Chile, and the Peruvian viceroy reacted by blockading Valparaiso and sending reinforcements to Concepcion to start a new campaign from there. The frigates *Esmeralda* and *Venganza*, the 26-gun corvette *Sebastiana*, the 20-gun brig *Pezuela*, the 16-gun brig *Potrillo*, the 11-gun packet *Aranzazu*, and a number of armed merchant ships—including the frigates *Cleopatra*, *Resolución*, *Presidenta*, *Veloz Pasajera*, *Palafox*, and *Tagle* and brigs *Justiniano* and *Canton*—conducted these missions and transported troops to Arica and to other southern Peruvian ports to reinforce the army fighting in Alto Peru.

O'Higgins had learned from experience when the Peruvian viceroyalty sent three expeditions that finally restored the royalist regime in Chile: he made the great economic effort to create a naval force to oppose the Spanish navy based at Callao. He acquired a few warships to form a small squadron under the flag of Rear-Admiral Manuel Blanco Encalada, which in October 1818 captured *Reina Maria Isabel* and most of the transports under her protection.[10] By the end of that year the Chilean squadron consisted of the 64-gun ship of the line *San Martín*, the 56-gun frigate *Lautaro* and the 44-gun frigate *O'Higgins* (formerly *Reina Maria Isabel*), the 20-gun corvette *Chacabuco*, the 16-gun brig *Puyrredon*, the 6-gun brig *Araucano*, and the 18-gun brig *Galvariño*. To command that force, Vice-Admiral Lord Thomas Alexander Cochrane, a former Royal Navy captain, was hired, bringing with him some former British naval officers.

## THE CHILEAN SQUADRON AND THE NEW NAVAL BALANCE IN 1819

Although small in number, the Chilean squadron was stronger than the Spanish force based at Callao. Brigadier Vacaro as well as Viceroy Joaquin de la Pezuela realized that the balance of power had dramatically changed. Both authorities urged Madrid to send reinforcements. Until they arrived, the available forces had to be preserved, so, along with reinforcing Callao's defenses, the warships were ordered to take refuge there when the Chilean squadron appeared in Peruvian waters.

In response to these insistent requests, in May 1819 two ships of the line, *Alejandro I* and *San Telmo*, as well as the frigate *Prueba*, departed Cadiz for Callao under the flag of Peruvian-born brigadier Rosendo Porlier. As with *Reina Maria Isabel* earlier, this expedition was a failure. *Alejandro I*, in very poor conditions, sailed back to Cadiz from the mid-Atlantic, and *San Telmo* was lost rounding Cape Horn. On 4 October *Prueba* managed to reach Chorrillos, a small port immediately south of Callao and, finding this port under blockade, sailed north, arriving in Guayaquil on 23 October, with almost half of the crew sick and the ship in need of repairs.[11]

This was the second time that the Chilean squadron had blocked Callao, aiming to destroy the Spanish squadron in battle by forcing it to leave the protection of the harbor's defenses. In Cochrane's squadron's first expedition to Peruvian waters in March and April 1819, it had blockaded and repeatedly but unsuccessfully attacked the port. Callao's defenses proved strong enough not only to repulse the attackers but also to attack the Chilean squadron's anchorage on the night of 25 March. As the main goal of the expedition was not achieved, Chilean ships raided other ports, attacking some but mainly encouraging the local population to join the independence cause.

When news of Porlier's expedition reached Chile, O'Higgins realized that once the three warships under Porlier's flag joined the available forces at Callao, the combined force would be stronger than the Chilean squadron, something that had to be avoided at all costs. Given that the long journey and the difficulties of rounding Cape Horn had surely weakened that Spanish squadron, one option would have been to attack it in the southern waters. But instead of adopting this course of action, Cochrane returned to Peruvian waters, aiming to destroy the frigates *Venganza* and *Esmeralda*.

Cochrane's squadron reached Callao in late September, finding the Spanish warships and port defenses ready to fight. In a naive initiative, he proposed that the Spanish squadron abandon the port and engage the Chilean one in a sort of duel, a proposal that Viceroy Pezuela flatly rejected since the Chilean squadron was stronger, and there was no point in losing the advantages of the port defenses. The attacks began on the night of 1 October and were repeated four nights later. Although they caused some damage, they failed to destroy the Spanish frigates.

It was in these circumstances that the Spanish frigate *Prueba*, under the command of Captain Meliton Perez del Camino, reached the bay of Chorrillos on 4 October. Hoisting the British flag, his ship approached the northern point of the bay, where he observed that Callao was under blockade. Given this, Perez del Camino quickly sailed westward to avoid detection by the Chilean squadron. In the following days, *Prueba* got close enough to the coast to send a messenger to Chorrillos to request instructions from Brigadier Vacaro and Viceroy Pezuela as it was clear that *Prueba* could not break the blockade, with almost half of her crew sick after the long passage from Cadiz. Naturally, her presence did not go unnoticed by the blockading squadron, and on 6 October, when *Prueba* approached Chorrillos again, the Chilean ships attempted to intercept her. Somehow Perez del Camino avoided Cochrane's ships and, after a short call at Paita, reached Guayaquil on 19 October in need of repairs and with many sick on board.

Knowing that the Spanish frigate had reached Guayaquil, Cochrane headed to the Gulf of Guayaquil with two frigates and two brigs, ordering the remaining warships to reestablish the blockade of Callao, which occurred on 8 November. Although some merchant vessels were captured in the Gulf of Guayaquil, Cochrane did not attack the port, twenty kilometers upriver. Guayaquil authorities, mindful of Chilean ships in the gulf, had reinforced defenses along the river and in the city itself, with *Prueba* in a central position. Cochrane, unable to capture or destroy this frigate, sailed back to southern waters, capturing Valdivia in southern Chile on 2 February 1820, but failing to do the same at San Carlos de Chiloe (modern-day Ancud in southern Chile). After that he returned to Valparaiso to prepare his squadron to escort a large Argentinian–Chilean expeditionary force that was being assembled to take the war to Peruvian shores.

## ACTIONS OF THE CALLAO SQUADRON

The Callao squadron sometimes hunted enemy ships but mainly transported royalist troops and ammunition from Panama to Callao. The squadron was also employed to reinforce Guayaquil's defenses (then part of the Peruvian viceroyalty) as well as to deliver troops to the southern ports from where they marched inland to join the Alto Peruvian army and to Concepcion, Valdivia, and Chiloe to defend the parts of Chile that remained in Spanish hands.

Since late 1819 the Peruvian viceroy had known that the Argentinian–Chilean expedition was being prepared. Even before the loss of *San Telmo* en route from Spain, it was urgent to ready *Prueba*, *Venganza*, and *Esmeralda* for combat. At Guayaquil, the former remained under repairs and shorthanded, as many crew members had died, deserted, or fallen ill since leaving Cadiz. Even so, *Prueba* left port early in February to join the other two frigates at the island of Puna (located at the mouth of the river leading to Guayaquil). Under the flag of the commanding officer of *Esmeralda*, Captain Luis Coig, the three frigates departed Puna on 23 February 1820 and sailed to Huacho, sixty-one miles north of Callao, where further instructions awaited them. Viceroy Pezuela expected the Chilean expedition to set sail in March with the main military objective to land near Lima. He ordered Coig to proceed to Mollendo, 459 miles south of Callao, and to transport eight hundred men of the reserve army of Arequipa. In accordance with these instructions, the frigates headed south, embarked that force at Mollendo, and returned to anchor at their home port on 14 April.[12]

Eight days later Brigadier Vacaro set sail with *Prueba* and *Maypu*, a captured Chilean privateer, in company with the merchant frigate *Xaviera*. On board were Brigadier José Pascual de Vivero, the new governor of Guayaquil, and a battalion to reinforce that port as well as ammunition and additional troops for Paita (in northern Peru) and Arica (in northern Chile). Having fulfilled his mission at Paita and Guayaquil, Vacaro headed north aboard *Prueba* in search of enemies and on 14 May sighted the Chilean privateer *Rosa de los Andes*. After a long chase, on the following night *Rosa de los Andes* suffered many casualties and severe damage during the engagement off Gorgona Island (modern-day Colombia) before darkness allowed her to break contact. On the following morning the Chilean ship was sighted seeking refuge on the Iscuande River, where she was grounded by her crew. Vacaro proceeded to Arica and landed ammunition for the garrison before heading to Pisco (located 130 south of Callao), where he learned that suspicious ships were approaching Callao. To reach that port as quickly as possible to lead its defense, he landed and proceeded overland. Fortunately, the sails sighted were not from enemy ships, and *Prueba* could anchor at Callao a few days later, on 16 July.

Shortly afterward the other two frigates left Callao for Quilca, a small cove close to Mollendo in southern Peru, to deliver the seven-hundred-man-strong Victoria Battalion. *Maypu* and *Aranzazu* sailed in search of the Chilean schooner *Terrible* (sighted near Pisco), which allegedly landed some enemy agents.

On 20 August, a few days after *Venganza* and *Esmeralda* had returned at Callao, the Chilean squadron departed Valparaiso, escorting fourteen transports with a 4,700-man-strong expeditionary force, with Argentinian general José de San Martín as commander in chief. He would become known as the liberator of Argentina, Chile, and Peru. The expedition reached Paracas, 130 miles south of Callao, on the afternoon of 7 September and began landing troops the next day with very little opposition.[13]

As soon as this news reached Lima, Viceroy Pezuela ordered frigates *Esmeralda* and *Venganza* to approach Pisco to determine whether the landing was a diversion to force him to deploy his army south of Lima. The frigates confirmed it was the main invasion force, and upon their return to Callao on 15 September, the viceroy reinforced the defenses of the capital. As part of these measures, on 10 October frigates *Prueba* and *Venganza* sailed to Arica to bring a 740-man-strong battalion and, having embarked them, departed that port on 19 November.

Meanwhile, after San Martín sent a division to advance north through the central Andes, he reembarked the expeditionary force on 25 October and landed at Ancon, twenty miles north of Callao while the Chilean squadron established a new blockade of this port. Four Spanish warships (*Esmeralda, Maypu, Pezuela,* and *Aranzazu*) along with several armed merchant vessels formed a line linked by chains as a first line of defense, supported by fourteen gunboats. On land, the fortress of Real Felipe, Fort San Miguel, and several batteries covered the anchorage with their guns. Just outside the line of ships was the anchorage for neutral shipping, which included two warships, the U.S. frigate *Macedonian* and HMS *Hyperion*.[14]

Cochrane, having failed to destroy the Spanish frigates in his two previous attacks in 1819, conducted a night raid with the squadron's boats through the neutral anchorage. A first attempt, on the night of 4 November, was aborted when the boats lost their course, but the following night twenty-one boats, with 240 men on board and led by Cochrane himself, reached the sides of *Esmeralda* and *Maypu* and after a fierce fight captured the former. The *Maypu* crew, with the help of some gunboats commanded by Brigadier Vacaro himself, repulsed the attackers, but the loss of *Esmeralda* was a severe blow to the already weakened royalist morale and local Spanish naval power.

A few sailors of the captured frigate jumped overboard and swam to ashore, spreading the news that commands in English were heard among the attackers. As HMS *Hyperion* and the U.S. frigate *Macedonian* were very close to the departure point of the attack, many assumed that they had participated. Indignation soon grew among the population of Callao, many of whom had friends and relatives in the Spanish squadron. Before dawn a mob began to search for and attack English-speaking people in the port. The situation worsened early in the morning when a boat from *Macedonian* came ashore to buy provisions and was attacked by a mob of several hundred men and women, killing two and wounding six of its nine crew members. Only the intervention of troops from the naval arsenal prevented all of them from being killed.[15]

The attackers also seized *Esmeralda*'s naval signals book, which compromised the situation of the other two frigates still sailing to Arica. Four days after departing Arica, the brig-schooner *Inocencia* reached

*Prueba* and *Venganza* to deliver letters from Brigadier Vacaro, making known the loss of *Esmeralda* and the blockade of Callao. Shortly after that, more bad news reached Captain José Villegas and Commander Joaquín Soroa, commanding officers of *Prueba* and *Venganza*, respectively. The important port of Guayaquil had changed sides; pro-independence officers and local citizens had captured the Spanish authorities and proclaimed independence.

## THE FALL OF ACAPULCO AND CALLAO

With Callao under blockade and four Chilean warships searching for the Spanish frigates, Villegas decided to call at Cerro Azul, eighty-one miles south of Callao, to disembark the troops on board and afterward remain off Callao while awaiting further instructions. For two weeks Villegas waited in vain. On 12 December, unable to force the blockade and considering that his original orders prioritized force preservation, he headed to Acapulco, the key port for the Spanish Empire's trade with Asia, calling at Panama (modern-day Panama City) to inform the authorities of his decision, replenish supplies, and land sick crew members. Meanwhile, the remaining Spanish naval forces in Callao were bottled up by the blockading squadron, with little hope of sailing again due to a lack of funds.

Shortly before the frigates reached Acapulco on 28 February, the port came under the control of the newly established Mexican government. But with the frigates' help, the royalists regained control on 15 March. Although under siege, Acapulco remained in Spanish hands until October, when the defenders finally surrendered. During these months the situation on board the frigates became ever more complicated. Some members of the Spanish and criollo-crewed ships supported the restored constitution, others opposed it, and opinions differed over the fate of the frigates. These differences affected discipline in a noticeable way.

Finally, Villegas departed Acapulco for Panama, the last port on the West Coast of America in Spanish hands, but on 28 November the situation changed dramatically when Panama also opted for independence. When the Spanish frigates arrived two days later, both the new local authorities and Villegas found themselves in a predicament since the former feared being attacked while the latter lacked both the forces to do so and the supplies to reach neutral Rio de Janeiro or Manila, the nearest port under Spanish control. On 4 December the two sides agreed that the port would not be attacked in exchange for food, water, and firewood. Several officers and men opposed this agreement and deserted before the frigates departed for Guayaquil, where Villegas thought he could reach a similar agreement and avoid capture by the Chilean squadron. At Guayaquil, negotiations between the local authorities and Peruvian General Francisco Salazar, San Martín's special envoy, culminated on 15 February 1822 with Villegas' agreement to deliver to the Peruvian government both frigates as well as the corvette *Alejandro*, which had joined his flag before reaching port.

In January 1821, while *Prueba* and *Venganza* were still heading to Acapulco, the Spanish army deposed Viceroy Pezuela, accusing him of a lack of aggressiveness, and proclaimed General José de la Serna the new viceroy.[16] To inform Madrid and justify this action, La Serna sent commissioners on *Maypu*, which left Callao in late March, only to be captured off Rio de Janeiro by the Buenos Aires frigate *Heroina* three months later. By mid-July the situation in Lima was increasingly critical. Because of both the threat from San Martín's forces and the growing number of conspiracies within the city, Viceroy La Serna abandoned the capital with most of his troops.

Still under blockade, Callao was to be defended by General José de la Mar and Brigadier Vacaro. It came under almost immediate attack by sea and by land. With no chance of breaking the blockade, the corvette *Sebastiana* and brig *Maypu* were dismantled to arm more gunboats, which now numbered forty. The port suffered several attacks in which five merchant frigates were lost, but as weeks passed it became clear that there was no chance of further resistance, and finally the garrison capitulated on 19 September. Two days later troops of the newly established Peruvian government occupied Callao.

The war for Peruvian independence would continue for three more years, and only in 1824 did the Spanish navy carry out a last attempt to support the efforts of Viceroy La Serna by sending the 64-gun ship of the line *Asia* and the 20-gun brig *Aquiles*. Early that year the Spaniards recovered Callao, which remained in their hands until January 1826. But on 9 December 1824, Viceroy La Serna's army suffered a decisive defeat at Ayacucho, putting an end to the long-running war for Peruvian independence. Generals José Ramon Rodil at Callao and Antonio Quintanilla at Chiloe, refused to surrender and continued resisting until early 1826, but Captain Roque Guruceta, in command of *Asia* and *Aquiles* and at Callao since mid-September 1824, withdrew from Peruvian waters. Rodil and Quintanilla managed to put to sea some privateers, and the former even commissioned as naval vessels the corvette *Victoria de Ica*, the brigs *Moyano* and *Constante*, and eight gunboats. Callao, besieged by land and blockaded by a combined Peruvian, Colombian, and Chilean squadron, managed to resist and only surrendered for lack of food.[17]

To summarize, Spanish naval power had declined substantially by the time its colonies began their struggle for independence but still faced no real challenge until the newly formed republics established their own naval forces. The critical economic situation, aggravated by internal political conditions, reduced Spanish possibilities to regain control over Mexico and Rio de la Plata. Spain could only send substantial reinforcements to the Viceroyalty of New Granada.

On the western coast of South America, since 1809 the Peruvian viceroyalty had successfully fought the independence movements in present-day Chile, Bolivia, and Ecuador. With a few warships—frigates and smaller ships—and armed merchants, the Peruvian viceroy controlled South Pacific waters until 1819, when the newly created Chilean squadron changed the situation, forcing the Spanish squadron to adopt a defensive strategy while waiting for reinforcements to arrive from Spain. In response to repeated requests from the viceroy and the naval commander in Callao, two ships of the line and a frigate were sent to the Pacific to reverse the unfavorable balance of power, but only the latter was able to reach her destination.

By early 1820 it was clear that the Chilean government was preparing an expedition to bring the war to Peru. As the local Spanish squadron had received no reinforcements, strategic options were very limited. The three available frigates were used essentially to transport troops from the Alto Peru and Arequipa reserve armies to Callao to strengthen the defenses around the viceroyalty capital, and when the invasion began, they were to gather at Callao to improve its defenses.

But this strategy could succeed only if adequate reinforcements arrived to contest control of the sea or if the enemy expeditionary force lost a decisive battle. None of these assumptions pertained, so, in practical terms, the Spanish naval squadron could not influence the course of the war.

When San Martín's expeditionary force landed at Paracas in September 1820, two frigates were deployed to bring troops from Arica, dividing the already weakened Spanish squadron into two groups, which were unable to return to Callao and were forced to leave South American waters. At Callao the Chilean squadron bottled up the remaining Spanish warships, a frigate, and the other smaller ships, precluding any possibility of their undertaking a decisive action.

Nevertheless, the fleet-in-being strategy adopted by the Spanish squadron based in Callao was the only realistic option given the unfavorable balance of power vis-à-vis the Chilean naval forces. As no reinforcements arrived from Spain and as the Spanish squadron was not employed aggressively to modify that situation, its military value for the war effort decreased in a noticeable way.

## NOTES

1. There are many works on the Peninsular War, but regarding its impact on the Spanish navy, the first three chapters of Cesáreo Fernández Duro, *Armada Española desde la unión de los reinos de Castilla y Aragón*, vol. 9 (Madrid: Museo Naval, 1973) provide a good overall idea.
2. Among many works on this topic, one of the best remains John Lynch's *The Spanish American Revolutions 1808–1826* (London: Weidenfeld and Nicholson, 1973).
3. For Spanish military efforts to retain its American colonies, see Julio Albi, *Banderas olvidadas: El ejército realista en América* (Madrid: Ediciones de Cultura Hispánica, 1990). Regarding royalist and independentist armies, see Juan Marchena and Manuel Chust, eds., *Por la fuerza de las armas: Ejército e independencias en Iberoamerica* (Castelló de la Plana: Universitat Jaume I, 2007).
4. See Christopher Cornelio, "Los pacificadores de ultramar: La oficialidad expedicionaria durante la guerra de independencia en el Perú, 1816–1821," in *El Perú en revolución: Independencia y guerra, 1780–1826*, edited by Manuel Chust and Claudia Rosas (Lima: Pontificia Universidad Católica del Perú / Castelló de la Plana: Universitat Jaume I / Zamora: El Colegio de Michoacán, 2018), 279–96.

5. Fernández, *Armada Española*, 9:124–27; and José Cervera Pery, *La Marina Española en la emancipación de Hispanoamérica* (Madrid: Mapfre, 1992), 118–27.
6. Cervera, *La Marina Española*, 128–35.
7. Cervera, 145, 165–66.
8. For the final years of the Spanish naval forces based at Callao, see the last chapter of Jorge Ortiz Sotelo, *La Real Armada en el Pacífico Sur: El Apostadero Naval del Callao 1746–1824* (México: Instituto de Investigaciones Históricas / Bonilla Artigas Editores, 2015), 327–87.
9. Fernández, *Armada Española*, 9:136–41; and Gaspar Pérez Turrado, *Las marinas realista y patriota en la independencia de Chile y Perú* (Madrid: Ministerio de Defensa, 1996), 40.
10. On the creation and early actions of the Chilean navy, see Carlos Tromben Corbalán, *La Armada de Chile, una historia de dos siglos* (Valparaíso: Armada de Chile, 2017), 1:153–436.
11. Ortiz, *La Real Armada en el Pacífico Sur*, 365–69.
12. Ortiz, 369–71.
13. See Natalia Sobrevilla Perea, *Independencia: A 200 años de lucha por la libertad* (Lima: Penguin Random House, 2021), 61–83.
14. Ortiz, *La Real Armada en el Pacífico Sur*, 372–75.
15. Edward Baxter Billingsley, *In Defense of Neutral Rights: The United States Navy and the Wars of Independence in Chile and Peru* (Chapel Hill: University of North Carolina Press, 1967), 112–14.
16. On this military coup, see Íñigo Moreno y de Arteaga and Marqués de la Serna, *José de la Serna, último virrey español* (Astorga: Editorial Akrón, 2010), 243–50; and Julio Albi de la Cuesta, *El último virrey* (Madrid: Ollero y Ramos, 2009), 297–317.
17. See José Ramón Rodil, *Memoria del Sitio del Callao* (Sevilla: Escuela de Estudios Hispano-Americanos, 1955).

# PART II
# THE TWENTIETH CENTURY BEFORE THE WORLD WARS

CHAPTER 5

# "REDISCOVERING" A FLEET IN BEING
## The Debate in Britain and the United States before World War I

*Kevin D. McCranie*

The December 1889 issue of *The Illustrated Naval and Military Magazine* included the sixth chapter of Philip H. Colomb's forthcoming book, *Naval Warfare: Its Ruling Principles and Practices Historically Treated*.[1] The chapter discussed events of 1690 during the Nine Years' War (1688–97), where an Anglo-Dutch fleet under Admiral Arthur Herbert, First Earl of Torrington, maneuvered against a larger French fleet. Colomb, a retired British naval officer and author on naval topics, explained that Torrington "was greatly inferior to the French, but they were powerless for mischief as long as his fleet existed." When Torrington received positive orders to fight, he did so at Beachy Head, but as Colomb stated, "There was no hope of winning against ships not only more numerous but of greater individual force, it behoved [sic] him to take care that he ran no risks of being beaten." He then quoted Torrington's own conclusion: "As it was, most men were in fear that the French would invade; but I was always of another opinion; for I always said, that whilst we had a fleet in being, they would not dare to make an attempt."[2] Colomb's description brought "a fleet in being" into the Anglo-American naval strategic lexicon of the late nineteenth century.[3]

Colomb and supporters of "a fleet in being" extolled its potential while others remained skeptical or even hostile. It became the topic of editorials, particularly in *The Times* of London. By the mid-1890s, one explained: "Ten years ago the question 'What is a Fleet in Being?' would probably have provoked the counter-question, 'Is this a conundrum?' To-day we at least know that there is such a thing, or rather let us, for fear of dangerous and hasty concession, say that its existence is asserted.

What, then, is it? How does it act? The phrase does not explain itself."[4] It was referenced in respect to the Sino-Japanese War (1894–95), the Spanish-American War (1898), and the Russo-Japanese War (1904–5), and it fueled strategic discussion in the years before World War I.

## DEFINING A FLEET IN BEING AND THE EXPANDING DEBATE

While Colomb reintroduced a fleet in being into the naval strategic discussion, James Thursfield became his ally. A widely recognized naval authority, Thursfield in 1893 described a fleet in being as a powerful fleet, although weaker than its opponent. It remained in an active state of existence rather than absconded in a protected anchorage or port. It made large-scale invasions impossible because "territorial enterprise . . . is, as we have seen, the one naval operation of all others which requires an undisputed command of the sea as a condition indispensable not merely to its success but even to its inception." As long as the weaker fleet avoided being defeated in a decisive battle, Thursfield explained, "It is more mobile than an army; it is more difficult to reduce than a fortress; its passage from place to place leaves no trace behind; and, except by direct observation . . . its movements cannot be detected." Thursfield then drew analogies to land warfare, describing how "it can operate with equal effect either as a strategical bar to the advance of a hostile fleet, or as an unreduced fortress which threatens its communications and its rear; and it can do this, not at one place only, but wherever the movements and apparent designs of the enemy appear to offer a strategical opportunity or advantage."[5]

Thursfield related a fleet in being to another important concept from naval strategy: command of the sea. He defined command as "the sense of strategic freedom of maritime transit" and claimed, "With it, all things are possible which naval warfare can attain; without it, nothing is attainable." In modern naval war, Thursfield maintained that the Royal Navy must secure command of the sea "or the British Empire must fall to pieces." This required a superior navy capable of defeating its opponents, but if conditions of temporary inferiority existed, "the example of Torrington shows undoubtedly that something less than the command of the sea might for a time suffice for our bare preservation. A 'fleet in being,' undefeated and able to avoid a decisive engagement, is an absolute bar to invasion across the sea."[6]

This description led to a spirited response in *The Times* of London. Spenser Wilkinson, a civilian journalist and widely published commentator on military affairs, countered, maintaining that such a fleet could at most nip at the edges of a larger fleet: he did not believe that Britain should rely on a fleet in being for its naval defense since it could provide nothing more than a temporary defense against invasion. Wilkinson explained, "I think any theory dangerous which regards it as something normal for the weak to win victories over the strong. That is a dream from which war is a grim awakening. War is the employment of force, and in that game, whether by land or sea, the weakest goes to the wall." On land, the weaker side can benefit from using terrain to increase its strength, but at sea, there is no terrain to provide such enhancements to the defense, and thus, "the strongest Power prevails, swiftly, surely, universally." Wilkinson maintained, "England must either become the dependency of another Power holding the mastery of the sea, or she must herself command the sea and lead the world." A fleet in being would not suffice for a sea power such as Britain.[7]

Colomb, having brought a fleet in being into the modern parlance, felt compelled to defend it: "I do not think Torrington meant to say that an inferior fleet was a preventive to invasion, but that it was not safe to invade as long as that inferior fleet was 'in being' and ready to act." Moreover, he admitted that the inferior fleet could only maintain its position for a limited period against an audacious opponent. Colomb explained, "The superior fleet must do what Mr. Spenser Wilkinson says it would do—namely, follow up and beat the inferior fleet—or, at any rate, mask it—before it can proceed with an invasion project."[8] His arguments swayed a core group of supporters.

Others like Wilkinson expressed concern, either unsure what a fleet in being actually meant or fearing the concept would lead to a smaller Royal Navy, incapable of protecting the far-flung British Empire. These arguments tended to be sporadic. Either writers referenced a fleet in being in a publication as Thursfield had done, or commentators applied a fleet in being to real-world events. In both cases, others felt compelled to respond, resulting in bursts of activity with proponents and opponents generally talking past one another, not realizing they had often made similar arguments.

The Sino-Japanese War caused one such flurry of activity. On 29 September 1894 *The Times* of London published an editorial linking a fleet in being to the war. The writer maintained that it only worked against a true invasion attempt: it did not protect against a raid. The editorialist claimed, "What they do assert is what all previous history without any exception proves, and what the recent events off the Yalu in no way disprove viz., that the 'fleet in being' is an absolute bar to hostile expeditions on a great scale and requiring time for execution, such as invasions and sustained attacks on coast positions."[9] This statement drew Spenser Wilkinson back into the fray "because the phrase . . . lends itself to any amount of qualification." He reiterated his less-than-charitable conclusion: a fleet in being only worked against invasion, when the weaker fleet was large enough to be a threat, and it was neither masked nor blockaded. Wilkinson asserted, "Thus in a naval war the power either to prevent or to carry out military operations beyond the sea depends upon the possession of the stronger navy. . . . An inferior fleet cannot, unless the enemy blunders, be very long 'in being'; it will be defeated and contained or blockaded." Wilkinson restated the dangers of a fleet in being because Britain needed more from its navy than invasion defense: it needed to command the sea to protect the vital maritime arteries linking its empire. He worried, "The theory . . . unless its expression is modified, [would] lead to a fatal underestimate of the naval force which the country needs."[10]

Colomb responded with several editorials.[11] In these, he never quite explained that the extended size of the British Empire required expansive naval deployments, and there would never be enough warships to meet every demand. A fleet in being allowed Britain to protect its global position while temporarily accepting inferiority in home waters. Unable to clearly place a fleet in being in the grand strategic context, Colomb continually muddied the waters, leading Spenser Wilkinson to question a fleet in being in even more belligerent terms, calling the concept "a nebulous abstraction. The phrase conveys no more than 'a fleet' except by a quibble which loads the words 'in being' with a whole cargo of strategical theory." Wilkinson only went so far as to admit "the transport of troops on a large scale undertaken by a belligerent not commanding the sea is a dangerous operation. Admiral Colomb's instances prove no more."[12] In response, Colomb quipped, "That Mr. Wilkinson should so completely misapprehend is only another instance of the immense difficulties landsmen have to contend against when they go to sea."[13] Wilkinson then sought the last word: "I am distressed when I am told by a great authority like Admiral Colomb that the vital truth about naval defence is wrapped up in a mystical phrase 'the fleet in being,' which has about as much chance of being understood by the million as the Athanasian creed."[14]

In his second edition of *Naval Warfare* published in 1895, Colomb doubled down. Although the new edition was mainly a reprint of the first edition, the discussion of a fleet in being expanded. Colomb even claimed in the book's preface: "By a powerful body of critics, including, I understand, Captain Mahan, my views have been fully adopted, and Torrington's phrase 'A fleet in being,' has come into general use . . . in naval affairs."[15]

Critics again pounced. One took an in-depth look at the events surrounding the Battle of Beachy Head (1690) that gave rise to the term. This writer claimed, "The mind refuses to accept it without question, and has indeed some difficulty in finding it intelligible." Moreover, proponents of a fleet in being "have committed themselves to the astonishing proposition that a navy defends, not by hard hitting, but by the much easier course of continuing 'in being.'"[16] This proposition was hard for many to accept given the Royal Navy's Nelsonian tradition with its desire for Trafalgar-like battles. Moreover, Britain in the 1890s possessed the largest fleet in the world.

David Hannay, a British naval historian, then claimed, "Why, then, in the name of all that is wonderful, are naval officers found supporting the astounding doctrine. . . . It is so unlike their usual tone. As a rule their cry is for more ships, and their arguments go to show that without a good margin of strength you can do nothing effectual." He continued, "We do not need a new phrase to make us understand that invasion over sea is impossible with a well-handled competent naval force in the way, still unbroken."[17]

Others came to Colomb's defense. They saw the significance of a fleet in being for thwarting attempts to command the sea. As one reviewer put it, "How to establish such a command of the sea, either by destroying the fleet in being or by effectually masking and containing it, is perhaps the most vital problem of modern naval warfare."[18] In this case the reviewer understood that British naval leaders not only needed to know how to employ a fleet in being, but they also needed to know how to defeat an opponent relying on a fleet in being so British naval leaders could secure command of the sea. For only by command of the sea could one conduct major expeditionary operations at a minimum of risk.

Thursfield rejoined the argument: "Command of the sea and a fleet in being are mutually exclusive terms." If one side effectively employed a fleet in being, it would deny command of the sea to its opponent. Successful employment of a fleet in being provided a potent defense against invasion or in fact any other operation that required command of the sea.[19] Thursfield believed that Colomb's argument stood the test from the days of Torrington through the first Sino-Japanese War.

## MAHAN JOINS THE DEBATE ON A FLEET IN BEING

On the other side of the Atlantic, Alfred Thayer Mahan quietly followed the discussion. The author of *The Influence of Sea Power upon History* and *The Influence of Sea Power upon the French Revolution and Empire*, Mahan was in 1894 labeled "the greatest living writer on naval history."[20] His thoughts on a fleet in being received serious consideration. In 1894 he mused in a private letter that something was pushing "English naval thinkers to press the significance beyond its due value." Assessing Torrington's actions in 1690, Mahan claimed, "I have never subscribed to his plea, nor those of his partisans, in thinking that his fleet in being *should* have prevented the descent of the French. It may have done so, but ought not." Mahan understood that risk was endemic in war. Against an opponent willing to accept risk for considerable reward, a fleet in being would likely prove ineffective. Mahan explained, "I think that in the 'fleet in being' you fellows have got hold of a perfectly sound general idea, but by overlooking the necessary qualification they are erecting it into a dogma—a fetish—which involves the danger of becoming 'doctrinaire.' Now of all dangerous conditions a military doctrinaire is one of the worst. He is a quick match and gunpowder." The risk of presenting a fleet in being as incontrovertible truth led

Mahan to caution: "In short my position is that while the principle is sound, much depends upon the application. It is not a panacea."[21] Then, in 1897, Mahan reached out privately to Thursfield to reiterate his conclusion.[22]

Mahan followed his private statements with a public pronouncement in his biography of Nelson where he warned about "the extreme expression now given to that concerning the 'fleet in being.'" Although a fleet in being might work against a timid opponent, Mahan argued that its "effect lies less in the nature of things than in the character of the officer upon whom it is produced."[23] Mahan remained wary when entrusting success of an operation to an apprehensive opponent, for if one encountered a leader who accurately measured risk and reward, a fleet in being offered little prospect of success.

Major General John Frederick Maurice, a noted period British military officer and writer, used Mahan to challenge the concept. Maurice found it troubling that Colomb and Thursfield had contended that, "even if our Navy be temporarily inferior in the Channel, it would be impossible for a foreign invasion to take place as long as we had an inferior 'fleet in being.'" Maurice then used the examples that Mahan had presented in his *Life of Nelson* to counter such claims: "I think I am not the only reader hitherto silent who has been bored to death with this phantom 'fleet in being' which has occupied such reams of print." Maurice then quipped, "Pray heaven that Mahan may have sent it to the bottom never to rise again!" Maurice thought that a fleet in being had received such a "severe a blow, that . . . it no longer affords us such security as to make it patriotic to omit other precautions, lest haply Mahan and Nelson should be right and Colomb and Thursfield wrong."[24]

## APPLYING A FLEET IN BEING TO THE SPANISH-AMERICAN AND RUSSO-JAPANESE WARS

Although important military and naval thinkers including Maurice and Mahan had cautioned against a fleet in being, the concept reached the height of its influence in 1898, the same year that Rudyard Kipling published *A Fleet in Being: Notes of Two Trips with the Channel Squadron*. Although his book lacked strategic and theoretical foundations, the mere fact that Kipling titled the book *A Fleet in Being* signifies how much the concept had become embedded in the contemporary narrative.[25]

More important from the strategic point of view, the Spanish-American War provided commentators another opportunity for application. Initially they questioned whether the Spanish fleet in being could prevent the landing of the U.S. Army in Cuba.[26] One writer even claimed, "If the Spanish admiral adopts the strategy of Torrington, will he succeed in preventing the landing of American troops in Cuba? If he adopts that strategy and fails in the object, then the 'fleet in being' theory ceases to be a principle of importance even to its advocates."[27]

Colomb could not remain silent. In a campaign between Admiral Pascual Cervera y Topete's Spanish squadron and Rear Admiral William Sampson's U.S. squadron, Colomb maintained that "as long as Admiral Cervera's fleet is 'in being,' Admiral Sampson is absolutely paralyzed."[28] Colomb believed that a prudent admiral would not risk moving a large expeditionary army across the water so long as the Spanish fleet denied command of the sea to its American opponent.[29]

Mahan remained unconvinced. He worried that the lack of an agreed-upon definition created ambiguity. Seeking to improve understanding, he explained, "A 'fleet in being,' therefore, is one the existence and maintenance of which, although inferior, on or near the scene of operations, is a perpetual menace to the various more or less exposed interests of the enemy, who cannot tell when a blow may fall, and who is therefore compelled to restrict his operations, otherwise possible, until that fleet can be destroyed or neutralized." Mahan then returned to the arguments he had presented in his *Life of Nelson*: "The probable value of a fleet in being has, in the opinion of the writer, been much overstated; for, even at the best, the game of evasion, which this is, if persisted in, can have but one issue. The superior force will in the end run the inferior to earth."[30] Although Mahan saw value in a fleet in being, it came at high risk. In a protracted campaign, he considered it a recipe for defeat.

Colomb countered: "Open minds will probably comprehend the tremendous power of a 'fleet in being' when they recall the great exertions of the United States to put it 'out of being.'"[31] When it came to a fleet in being, Colomb remained the perpetual optimist. Even though the Americans destroyed the Spanish fleet, he believed even the fleet's destruction had supported his views. As long as the Spanish fleet remained at sea, the Americans did not land in Cuba. Only after the Spanish ships were located and blockaded in Santiago de Cuba did the invasion occur. Colomb downplayed the fact that the U.S. fleet completely overmatched the Spanish fleet; he did not distinguish how much of the timing of the American landing depended on the actions of the Spanish fleet versus other factors; and although improved navigation through steam power was supposed to increase the effectiveness of a fleet in being, the Spanish fleet was intercepted after leaving Santiago.

To his critics Colomb ranted, "To such as are not in the way of thinking like admirals, the thing seems absurd. Yet it is the thought of admirals and not the thought of their critics, that will rule, and naval force retains its power of defence because the thought of admirals . . . will not vary."[32] He had again claimed that only naval leaders could comprehend the effectiveness of a fleet in being.

The Spanish-American War led Colomb to complete the third edition of *Naval Warfare*.[33] He remained absolutely convinced of the effectiveness a fleet in being: "No principle received in the war such extraordinary and unexpected confirmation as this did."[34] Colomb believed that Torrington's concept had become even more relevant in the contemporary environment since a very weak Spanish squadron incapable of defeating the American fleet had caused outsized strategic effects. It was not until the Americans had blockaded the Spanish squadron that their expeditionary force landed in Cuba: "If this evidence is not conclusive on one side of the controversy as to the power of a 'fleet in being' to paralyse all offensive operations against territory, it can only be alleged that the American navy and the American statesmen were unduly timorous."[35] Colomb did not think this the case; rather, he concluded that steam propulsion took much of the chance out of the movement of warships. Because the commander of a fleet in being could now move with certainty, speed, and precision, the strategic effects attainable from a fleet in being had increased. As the third edition of *Naval Warfare* went to print, Colomb died, removing the primary defender of the concept from future debates.

William Laird Clowes, a civilian naval historian, had little sympathy for Colomb's arguments. In the late 1890s, his influence grew considerably as he compiled a multivolume work titled *The Royal Navy: A History from the Earliest Times to 1900*. This project necessitated an authoritative account of Torrington's 1690 campaign. Clowes staked his position first in an 1897 article where he wrote, "As Mahan points out in his 'Nelson' the menace of a 'fleet in being' has been vastly overrated by many recent writers."[36] Clowes stated,

> The position has a lesson for us to-day, since it bears upon the oft-debated question of the possibility of the invasion of this country. If, in wartime, we keep efficient fleets close to the maritime frontiers of our enemies, well and good. We shall not be invaded—at least, until those fleets have been destroyed. But if we trust to a fleet merely "in being"—not necessarily determined to fight, not necessarily in the right place—we may find ourselves deceived. Not only may we be invaded, we may even be invaded while our fleet is still practically intact. The problem becomes one of risk, not of possibility."[37]

The second volume of Clowes's naval history provided a more specific description of Torrington's actions in 1690. He concluded that Torrington's incorrect assessments had inflated the effectiveness of a fleet in being. For Clowes, "a fleet merely 'in being' is not, of necessity, a menace at all. It is not a menace unless it be also 'potential,' and by 'potential' is implied 'able and ready to act up to the limit of its strength at the required moment and at the required point.' "[38] Clowes concluded that risk weighed too heavily on Torrington, thus preventing him from obtaining the greatest reward. French naval leaders suffered similarly. Accepting greater risk might very well have yielded the French tremendous rewards, demonstrating that Torrington's concept of a fleet in being had little chance of success against an aggressive and well-handled opponent.[39] Clowes's deep study of history cast additional doubt on Colomb's conclusions.

An article in the U.S. Naval Institute's *Proceedings* by Richard Wainwright, then a lieutenant commander in the U.S. Navy, struck at the heart of the debate: "Such phrases as 'Sea Power,' 'Command of the Sea,' 'Fleet in Being,' etc., are of great use as serving to crystallize a set of ideas into a few words. But the use of these phrases is not without danger." The risk is "that students . . . are inclined sometimes to enlarge the idea until the facts upon which it rests are lost sight of." Specifically, Wainwright called out a fleet in being that "has at times been so badly misused as to cause much controversy." He explained that "the ruling laws of strategy and tactics are so clouded by collateral events and conflicting narratives that in ascertaining these laws the deductive method is apt to be preferred to the inductive, and the theory is first formed and afterwards the facts are hunted up from many examples. This sometimes leads to a distortion of the facts to fit the theory."[40] Too many involved in discussions about a fleet in being suffered from deductive distortion. Proponents and opponents became less and less willing to budge; rather, they argued more loudly, often using facts more sparingly to support the opinions they had already deduced.

The Russo-Japanese War provided the next real-world opportunity to consider a fleet in being. Early in the war, some looked at the Russian squadron at Port Arthur as a fleet in being. It remained in existence for a long period; it had the potential to become mobile; and its survival forced the Japanese to expend considerable naval resources in masking and eventually capturing that fortified port.[41]

However, the Russian squadron at Port Arthur differed in fundamental ways from how English writers had previously described a fleet in being. It did not prevent the overseas movement of the Japanese army to Korea and Manchuria. This contradicted one of the chief tenets of a fleet in being: it could put command of the sea in enough risk to prevent major overseas expeditions.[42] The Japanese were willing to accept risk; as a result, they disregarded the theory of a fleet in being at the war's start and, as one commentator explained, "were not a penny the worse."[43] Later the Russian squadron lost all attributes of a fleet in being when its naval leaders sacrificed its mobility in the defense of Port Arthur.[44]

## REASSESSING A FLEET IN BEING PRIOR TO WORLD WAR I

The Russo-Japanese War caused many to question a fleet in being. It disappeared from the pages of *The Times*, resulting in the loss of any traction it had with popular audiences. It became confined to the specialist literature on naval and joint strategy. In the aftermath of the Russo-Japanese War, writers such as Mahan, Thursfield, George Aston,

Julian Corbett, and Charles Callwell wrestled with its meaning and its strategic effects. In the process, their arguments became more inductive, driven by evidence instead of preconceived deductions.

In *Military Operations and Maritime Preponderance*, Callwell provided an assessment almost as the Russo-Japanese War came to an end. He grappled with the dissonance between historical precedent from the age of sail and modern conditions. Specifically, he considered how steam-powered warships and new technologies such as the torpedo affected a fleet in being. Callwell explained, "Extreme views are entertained with regard to this question in certain quarters."[45] Rather than let Colomb define the concept, he sought less controversial experts by quoting Clowes, who had described a fleet in being as possessing the "potential" to strike, and Mahan, who described it as "a perpetual menace to the more or less exposed interests of the enemy, who cannot tell when a blow may fall, and who is therefore compelled to retard his operations until that fleet can be destroyed or neutralised."[46] Callwell noted that until the Russo-Japanese War there had been no examples from the age of steam of an army being moved over the sea while a fleet in being existed.[47] Callwell admitted that, in modern conditions, the existence of small torpedo-armed warships added significantly to the risk of expeditionary forces moving overseas. No longer would troopships potentially be captured or turned back: they could now be sunk. If Callwell had published such statements during Colomb's lifetime, the response would certainly have been swift; instead, the next years witnessed a more tempered discussion.

In the final decade before World War I, James Thursfield remained a fleet in being's strongest proponent. Although he had been closely associated with Colomb's views in the 1890s, Thursfield more carefully crafted his arguments. In 1909 Thursfield published *Nelson and Other Naval Studies*, and then in 1913 he published a book on naval strategy. Both volumes drew heavily on his previous articles, including some dating to the 1890s. Thursfield explained, "The fleet in being is merely a definition of the conditions which, so long as they exist, are incompatible with an established command of the sea."[48] He added, "But on the doctrine itself I still insist as the beginning and the end of all sound thinking on naval warfare and its principles. It was because Napoleon never understood it, and Nelson never lost sight of it, that Napoleon's schemes for the invasion of England were brought to naught."[49] In the end, Thursfield remained an unrepentant supporter of the concept, an acolyte of Colomb, and, in the years before World War I, the one British naval commentator who remained under its spell. His 1913 book titled *Naval Strategy* included a full chapter on a fleet in being, likely overemphasizing its significance as a means of disputing command of the sea.[50]

Counterpoints to Thursfield appeared in a pair of books published in 1911, one by Mahan titled *Naval Strategy Compared and Contrasted* and the other by Corbett titled *Some Principles of Maritime Strategy*. Both these general theoretical overviews were the culmination of long study.

Mahan accurately linked Colomb to the modern origin of a fleet in being. "While he cannot be held responsible for every extreme utterance of his disciples," wrote Mahan, "I think it fair presentation to say that he over-rates the proper deterrent effect upon over-sea operations exercised by naval force, when it is strong, though inferior."[51] Mahan held to his previous belief that an audacious commander would not be deterred by the actions of a fleet in being, even one that was actively led. Mahan added, "The possibility is not sufficient reason for stopping transportation; the actual fact is sufficient for taking particular precautions, adjusting dispositions to the new conditions, as was done by ourselves and by the Japanese in the circumstances." The only way truly to deter the movement of an expeditionary army overseas was to possess an equal or preferably superior fleet.[52] Like Callwell, Mahan looked to historical cases for support and found multiple examples from the American Revolution to buttress his argument.[53]

Turning to the contemporary environment, Mahan reflected on the Russo-Japanese War: "The London *Times*, which is, or then was, under the influence of this school, published six weeks before the war began a summary of the situation, by naval and military correspondents, in which appears this statement 'With a hostile fleet behind the guns at Port Arthur, the Japanese could hardly venture to send troops into the Yellow Sea.'"[54] Yet, when war broke out, this was exactly what Japan accomplished. To Mahan, the Russo-Japanese War demonstrated that a fleet in being had reached the level of dogma. Those who bought into the dogma stopped thinking critically. Mahan found this galling because the human element and interaction between belligerents meant that nothing in war reached the level of the absolute.⁵⁵

The Russo-Japanese War did lead Mahan to change one of his views on a fleet in being. At the time of the Spanish-American War, he believed, "The safest, though not the most effective, disposition of an inferior 'fleet in being' is to lock it up in an impregnable port or ports, imposing upon the enemy the intense and continuous strain of watchfulness against escape."⁵⁶ However, Russian actions at Port Arthur led him to espouse a new concept: the "Fortress Fleet" to describe a fleet in the safety of a protected anchorage. He explained, "The phrases, 'Fortress Fleet' and 'Fleet in Being,' are the antipodes of each other.... The one lays all stress on the fortress, making the fleet so far subsidiary as to have no reason for existence save to help the fortress. The other discards the fortress altogether, unless possibly as momentary refuge for the vessels of the fleet while coaling, repairing, or refreshing."⁵⁷ One tied a fleet to a fortress, destroying all advantages it could gain through its mobility, while the other was but a temporary expedient.

Julian Corbett also entered the discussion. A leading naval historian in Britain during the early years of the twentieth century, he became a subject-matter expert for the Royal Navy involved with the education of the next generation of its naval leaders. Until *Some Principles of Maritime Strategy* appeared in 1911, Corbett had written little on a fleet in being.⁵⁸ In *Some Principles*, he recognized the relationship between a fleet in being and invasion defense and particularly the use of a fleet of being to dispute command of the sea.⁵⁹

Studying many historical examples and accounting for the increased lethality of torpedo boats and submarines with their powerful ship-killing armaments pushed Corbett's arguments about a fleet in being in new directions. He concluded that a fleet in being was a necessary component of an active naval defense using counterattacks to break larger opposing forces. The marriage of new technologies with the counterattack led Corbett to assert, "It is a possibility which on the whole tells in favour of naval defence, a new card which, skilfully played in combination with defensive fleet operations, may lend fresh importance to the 'Fleet in being.'"⁶⁰ Under such circumstances, Corbett lamented that a fleet in being was too often applied only to invasion defense when in reality it could be linked to any type of operations designed to dispute command of the sea.[61]

George Aston, a widely published author on naval and defense affairs and an officer of the Royal Marines, provided the following cautionary words about a fleet in being in 1911: "Most people whom I have asked, who do not happen to be students of naval strategy, attribute the invention of the expression to Mr. Rudyard Kipling, at which no doubt he would be much amused." Aston remained skeptical. "I have purposely avoided using the term 'fleet in being' which one comes across so frequently in writings on naval strategy, because I do not know what it means. If 'in being' means 'in existence' the words seem to be redundant and unnecessary."[62] Aston found the concept meant different things to different people: without an agreed-upon definition, it only confused.[63] It is telling that Aston's statement echoed a satirical comment from nearly a decade earlier: "The theory of a fleet in being reminds me of what Calvin said of the Apocalypse—namely, that it either finds you mad or leaves you mad."[64]

The evolution of the fleet-in-being concept in English-language literature in the quarter-century before the outbreak of World War I illuminates important considerations about strategic theory. Throughout the 1890s Philip Colomb cast a long shadow over any discussion. He used his expertise and his notoriety to frame the concept. His arguments had little to do with dispassionate analysis. He and his supporters decided that it was the best means to defend the British Isles from a possible invasion and failed to think critically about it. As Mahan rightly indicated, a fleet in being during the 1890s reached the level of dogma when actually a fleet in being provided no more than a useful implement in the naval commander's toolbox. A combination of Colomb's death and the example of the Russo-Japanese War allowed naval strategists to reassess its possibilities.

The rediscovery of a fleet in being in the years before World War I provides an important example of how the historical context mixes with a contemporary environment. It reveals how human foibles and personality can drive the strategic discourse. From the start, a fleet in being was nothing more than a tool of a weaker naval force. Some hoped for universal applicability in the face of the most existential of threats: an overseas invasion. Others rightly worried about confused meanings and that some were erecting a dogma that rotted the strategic lexicon from within.

## NOTES

1. Philip H. Colomb, "Naval Warfare: Its Principles and Practice Historically Treated," *The Illustrated Naval and Military Magazine: A Monthly Journal Devoted to All Subjects Connected with Her Majesty's Land and Sea Forces* 3, no. 9 (new series, 1889), 1806–27. The first edition of the book with the above title was published in 1891.
2. According to John Hattendorf, "There is some question about the authenticity of the phrase 'fleet in being' in that quotation, as it does not appear in the contemporary manuscript records of Torrington's speech; it is known only from an anonymously prepared pamphlet that purports to be the speech, published twenty years after the event, in 1710." See John Hattendorf, "The Idea of a 'Fleet in Being' in Historical Perspective," *Naval War College Review* 67 (2014): 44.
3. Hattendorf, 43.
4. David Hannay, "The Fleet in Being," *New Review* 77 (October 1895): 411.
5. "The Command of the Sea," *Quarterly Review* (October 1893): 353. The *Quarterly Review* did not include the name of the author of this article, but Thursfield reprinted it in a volume he edited with George Clarke titled *The Navy and the Nation or Naval Warfare and Imperial Defense* (London: John Murray, 1897).
6. "The Command of the Sea," 354.
7. "The Navy, to the editor," by Spenser Wilkinson, *Times*, 20 November 1893; "The Navy, to the editor," Wilkinson, 28 November 1893.
8. "The Navy, to the editor," by Colomb, *Times*, 23 November 1893.
9. "The Yalu and the 'Fleet in Being,'" to the editor, by A Student, *Times*, 29 September 1894.
10. "The Fleet in Being, to the editor," by Wilkinson, *Times*, 6 October 1894.
11. "The Yalu and the 'Fleet in Being,'" to the editor, by Colomb, *Times*, 15 October 1894; and "'The Fleet in Being,'" to the editor, by Colomb, *Times*, 24 October 1894.
12. "The 'Fleet in Being,'" to the editor, by Wilkinson, *Times*, 20 October 1894.
13. "'The Fleet in Being,'" to the editor, by Colomb, *Times*, 24 October 1894.
14. "The 'Fleet in Being,'" to the editor, by Wilkinson, *Times*, 29 October 1894.
15. Philip H. Colomb, *Naval Warfare: Its Ruling Principles and Practice Historically Treated*, 2nd ed. (London: W. H. Allen, 1895), vii–viii.

16. "The Battle of Beachy Head (An Essay in Illustration of the Value of a Fleet in Being)," *MacMillan's Magazine* 72 (May–October 1895), 223, 230.
17. Hannay, "The Fleet in Being," 420–21.
18. "Review of *Naval Warfare*, 2nd ed.," *Times*, 8 November 1895.
19. "The Armada," *Quarterly Review* 182 (July 1895): 6. Published anonymously but later reprinted under Thursfield's authorship in Clarke and Thursfield, *The Navy and the Nation*.
20. *Times*, 11 May 1894.
21. Mahan to George Clarke, 30 September 1894, in Alfred Thayer Mahan, *Letters and Papers of Alfred Thayer Mahan*, vol. 2, edited by Robert Seager II and Doris D. Maguire (Annapolis: Naval Institute Press, 1975), 336–38. Emphasis in the original.
22. Mahan to Thursfield, 21 May 1897, *Letters of Mahan*, 2:509.
23. Alfred Thayer Mahan, *The Life of Nelson and the Embodiment of the Sea Power of Great Britain*, vol. 1 (London: Sampson, Low, Marston, 1897), 137, 198.
24. John Frederick Maurice, *National Defences* (London: Macmillan, 1897), 194–95.
25. Rudyard Kipling, *A Fleet in Being: Notes of Two Trips with the Channel Squadron* (London: Macmillan, 1898).
26. "To the Editor," by Eustace Balfour, *Times*, 26 April 1898.
27. "Probable Lessons of the War, to the Editor," by Balfour, *Times*, 4 May 1898.
28. "Probable Lessons of the War, to the Editor," by Colomb, *Times*, 25 May 1898.
29. Philip H. Colomb, "The Fleet in Being," *United Service Magazine* 17 (July 1898): 360, 368.
30. Alfred Thayer Mahan, *Lessons of the War with Spain and Other Articles* (1899; repr., Boston: Little Brown, 1918), 75–76, 78.
31. Philip H. Colomb, "Second Impressions on the War," *National Review* 186 (August 1898): 841.
32. Colomb, 840.
33. Philip H. Colomb, *Naval Warfare: Its Ruling Principles and Practice Historically Treated*, 3rd ed. (London: W. H. Allen, 1899), xiii.
34. Colomb, appendix, xxxi.
35. Colomb, appendix, xli.
36. William Laird Clowes, "The Battle of Sluis," *Cornhill Magazine* 2 (June 1897): 728.
37. Clowes, 729.
38. William Laird Clowes, *The Royal Navy: A History from Its Earliest Times to the Present*, 7 vols. (London: Sampson, Low, Marston, 1897–1902), 2:341.
39. Clowes, 2:342–44.

40. Richard Wainwright, "Our Naval Power," U.S. Naval Institute *Proceedings* 24 (1898): 57.
41. "The Course of Events in the Far East," *Times*, 1 April 1904.
42. "The Great Naval Lesson of the War," to the editor, by Penrose Fitzgerald, Vice Admiral, *Times*, 20 January 1905; and "Lord Selborne on the Russo-Japanese War," to the editor, by E. M. Lloyd, *Times*, 8 March 1905.
43. "The Blue Water School: A Paper Read before the National Defence Association," 20 November 1906, by the military correspondent of the *Times*, printed in *Times*, 1 December 1906.
44. "The Great Naval Lesson of the War," to the editor, by Cyprian A. G. Bridge, *Times*, 24 January 1905.
45. Charles Callwell, *Military Operations and Maritime Preponderance: Their Relations and Interdependence* (Edinburgh: William Blackwood, 1905), 203.
46. Callwell, 203. Callwell quoted Clowes, *The Royal Navy*, 2:34; and Mahan, *Lessons of the War with Spain*, 76. Please note, Mahan's original used the word "restrict" instead of "retard."
47. Callwell, *Military Operations and Maritime Preponderance*, 205.
48. James Thursfield, *Nelson and Other Naval Studies* (New York: E. P. Dutton, 1909), 109. These words had first appeared in a review of Mahan's *Life of Nelson* in *The Quarterly Review* 187 (January 1898), 145.
49. Thursfield, *Nelson*, 118.
50. James Thursfield, *Naval Warfare* (Cambridge: Cambridge University Press, 1913), 30–48.
51. Alfred Thayer Mahan, *Naval Strategy Compared and Contrasted with the Principles and Practice of Military Operations on Land* (Boston: Little, Brown, 1911), 428.
52. Mahan, 401.
53. Mahan, 209.
54. Mahan, 399.
55. Mahan, 429.
56. Mahan, *Lessons of the War with Spain*, 84.
57. Mahan, *Naval Strategy*, 385.
58. Julian Corbett briefly mentioned a fleet in being in the following: *Drake and the Tudor Navy*, vol. 1 (London: Longmans, Green, 1898), 368; *The Successors of Drake* (London: Longmans, Green, 1900), 142; and *England and the Mediterranean: A Study of the Rise and Influence of British Power within the Strait, 1608–1713* (London: Longmans, Green, 1904), 1:202; and 2:94, 163.
59. Julian Corbett, *Some Principles of Maritime Strategy* (1911; repr., Annapolis, MD: Naval Institute Press, 1988), 224.
60. Corbett, 231.
61. Corbett, 212.

62. George G. Aston, *Letters on Amphibious Warfare* (London: John Murray, 1911), 121–22.
63. George G. Aston, *Sea, Land, and Air Strategy: A Comparison* (Boston: Little, Brown, 1914), 184–85.
64. "The Blue Water School: A Paper Read before the National Defence Association," 20 November 1906, by military correspondent of the *Times*, printed in *Times*, 1 December 1906.

CHAPTER 6

# THE AUSTRO-HUNGARIAN FLEET IN BEING (1893–1918)

*Lawrence Sondhaus*

Austria-Hungary provides a unique and fascinating example of the successful use of a fleet in being. Before and during World War I, the Dual Monarchy employed the strategy not just to deny regional command of the sea to its rivals and adversaries but to defend its coastline in the Adriatic Sea and project power regionally. It managed to do so despite having the smallest navy among the eight great powers of the era. The strategy succeeded remarkably well and remained successful even into the empire's last year of existence. In March 1918, just eight months before its defeat and collapse, a U.S. Navy official wrote that the Adriatic was "practically an Austrian lake, in which no Allied naval operations of importance are undertaken."[1]

The strategic situation in the Adriatic remains one of the most frequently overlooked aspects of the prewar and wartime years prior to 1918, all the more so because Austria-Hungary was such an unlikely naval power. Among the leading states of Europe, none had a less extensive coastline. It was overwhelmingly rural and agricultural, trailing all but Russia in urbanization and all but Russia and Italy in per capita industrialization. No other great power was so dominated by one of its peers, as Austria-Hungary depended on the military and diplomatic support of Germany, which was also its largest prewar trading partner. And in a Europe of nation-states integrated by nationalism, it was a multiethnic empire in which nationalism was a disintegrating factor. The lone attempt at political reform countenanced by the ruling House of Habsburg had come a half-century earlier, when the traditionally dominant German Austrian minority granted constitutional equality to the Hungarians, the most rebellious of the subject nationalities. This Compromise of 1867, which transformed the Austrian Empire into the Dual Monarchy of Austria-Hungary at the expense of the rest of the nationalities, closed the door to further reform as the Hungarians subsequently opposed any revisions that would endanger their hard-won status. In the face of these daunting obstacles, Austro-Hungarian naval leaders managed to build a coalition of special interests from all across the empire to support the creation of a respectable fleet. Given the centrifugal forces of nationalism that ultimately pulled the empire apart, the political coalition and naval-industrial complex supporting the Austro-Hungarian fleet stands out as an intriguing anomaly.

## FOUNDATIONS

Austria acquired its first foothold on the Adriatic in 1382, when Trieste became a Habsburg possession, but its coastline remained insignificant until 1797, when the empire acquired Venetia, Istria, and Dalmatia from the defunct Venetian Republic. For the remainder of the age of wooden sailing ships, Venetians dominated the Austrian navy, and Italian remained its language of command. This untenable situation ended with the Venetian revolution of 1848–49, after which the navy was reborn as a multinational force operating out of bases at Pola (Pula) in Istria and Cattaro (Kotor) in Dalmatia, in which German Austrians eventually provided most of the officers and Croatians accounted for most of the manpower.[2] Emperor Franz Joseph (r. 1848–1916) rarely showed interest in the fleet, but his younger brother, Archduke Ferdinand Max, and his nephew, Archduke Franz Ferdinand, both became strong advocates of naval expansion. Ferdinand Max, better known to history as Emperor Maximilian of Mexico, served as commanding admiral of the navy for the decade prior to his departure for the New World in 1864. In this capacity he orchestrated its transition from sail to steam power and the construction of its first armored warships. Austria's foremost naval hero, Wilhelm von Tegetthoff, then led this underdog force to victory over a larger Italian fleet in the Battle of Lissa (1866), foiling Italian designs on the former Venetian territories of Istria and Dalmatia.[3]

Long after Tegetthoff's premature death (1871), the memory of his decisive victory at Lissa continued to hearten the Habsburg fleet—and haunt its Italian adversary. Ironically, the two navies became partners once the Dual Monarchy joined Italy and Germany in the Triple Alliance (1882), formed because Italy valued German support against France as much as Austria-Hungary valued it against Russia. The two rivals thus tolerated each other for the sake of German friendship, but without the anti-Italian rationale for a stronger fleet, the navy entered a period of decline that continued until Franz Ferdinand took an interest in it. After traveling to Japan in 1892–93 aboard the cruiser *Kaiserin Elisabeth*, the archduke became the leading Austro-Hungarian naval enthusiast. His role as patron of the navy became more significant as Franz Joseph grew older and allowed him a greater influence over the armed forces. While Franz Ferdinand was generally supportive of Austria-Hungary's alliance with Germany, the overall degree of subservience concerned him. He saw overseas trade, and the naval power to support it, as key to the Dual Monarchy's fate as a great power.

## THE NAVAL BUILDUP

The Mediterranean repercussions of an alliance between France and Russia (concluded 1892–94) provided the initial justification for the construction of the fleet which, by its very existence, eventually commanded the Adriatic Sea during World War I. Between 1893 and 1907, Austria-Hungary ordered a dozen battleships in four groups of three—the 5,600-ton *Monarch* class, the 8,300-ton *Habsburg* class, the 10,600-ton *Erzherzog Karl* class, and the 14,500-ton *Radetzky* class—along with three armored cruisers. Thirteen of these ships were built in Trieste by Stabilimento Tecnico Triestino, the remaining pair in the navy's own Pola arsenal. Initially dependent on German guns and armor plate imported from Krupp, the navy soon switched to domestic sources, ordering its armor from the Witkowitz foundry in Moravia from 1895 onward, and its guns from the Skoda Works in Bohemia starting in 1901. That year the navy leadership also promised Hungarian firms a share of naval spending equal to the Hungarian contribution to the joint budget of the Dual Monarchy.[4] These moves brought capital investment and employment to parts of the empire far from the Adriatic and proved crucial to the evolution of a broad pro-navy coalition within a divided domestic political landscape.

For an example of the depth of support that the navy enjoyed, one need look no further than landlocked Bohemia and Moravia, provinces that constitute today's Czech Republic, at the time bitterly divided between a Czech majority asserting itself against a traditionally dominant German minority. In prewar budget debates, Czech leader Karel Kramář admitted "a certain weakness for the navy" and gratitude for the jobs it provided, noting that his party was "happy when Skoda has business."[5] Meanwhile, Bohemian German leader Eduard Stransky supported a stronger fleet because it enhanced "the alliance value of this state for the German Empire."[6] The navy, like the army, was commanded mostly by ethnic Germans but differed from the army fundamentally because the navy was primarily a volunteer service (with its only conscripts coming from coastal districts) in which each warship was a floating microcosm of the multinational empire. The officers bore the burden of effective communication, as the men of their crews were only required to know a bare minimum of words in German, the official language of command. Officers rising to the top of the service tended to know a remarkable number of languages—seven in the case of Admiral Anton Haus, navy commander from 1913 to 1917. In contrast, virtually all soldiers were conscripts, drafted in territorial districts. Many career army officers were fluent only in German and frequently accused of abusive behavior by representatives of the non-German nationalities. Czech politician František Udržal observed that the "national intolerance that reigns within the army" was absent in the navy, where "our people do not complain of nationality troubles."[7] His colleague Josef Kadlčák agreed, remarking that "the officer corps of the navy makes a very favorable impression on all circles of the population."[8] An increasing number of their constituents volunteered for the navy to avoid conscription into their local regiment, even though the navy required an additional (fourth) year of service. By 1910 Czechs accounted for 7.1 percent of the navy's common manpower and 9.2 percent of its officers. Thus, for many Czechs who would soon welcome the demise of Austria-Hungary, the fleet became a cause they could support for the alternative it provided to service in the army as well as for the jobs it created. By 1914 Tomáš Masaryk, future president of Czechoslovakia (1918–35), was one of the few Czech leaders who consistently opposed naval spending.[9]

Under the political leadership of navy commanders Admiral Baron Hermann von Spaun (1897–1904) and Admiral Count Rudolf Montecuccoli (1904–13), spending on the fleet rose steadily until it accounted for 25 percent of the military outlay in the last prewar budget, after averaging just 7 percent in the typical budget of the 1880s. The political necessity of building the fleet in domestic shipyards from domestic resources inflated naval expenditure and made each Austro-Hungarian naval vessel among the most expensive of its type yet built. But in a country with a weak labor movement further divided along ethnic lines, investors in the naval-industrial complex benefited from the naval buildup far more than the workers. While the naval buildup caused shares of stock in Skoda and the Stabilimento Tecnico Triestino to double in value, skilled shipyard laborers in Trieste earned as little as 6 kronen per day (around US$1.25) for a twelve-hour shift. The situation was far worse in the armor plant at Witkowitz, where workers were paid as little as 1.2 kronen per day (around $0.25), likewise for a twelve-hour shift. (In comparison, by 1914 Henry Ford was paying his workers $5.00 for an eight-hour day). Labor costs accounted for just 32 percent of the price of the last prewar battleships constructed in Austria-Hungary, compared to 70 percent for those built in Britain.[10]

The warships they built (at least the larger ones) provided further evidence of the relative status of the ordinary person vis-à-vis his social superiors. Indeed, in the Austro-Hungarian fleet, as in its Russian and German counterparts, the variety of shipboard accommodations reflected the sharp social class divisions within the empire. An American officer touring one of the *Radetzky*-class battleships, observed that they were "constructed with an eye to comfort—for the officers." They featured "large, airy rooms with ports of almost window size for even the junior officers," and the captain's quarters consisted of "a magnificent seven-room suite in the stern of the ship." In contrast, "the crew's quarters were cramped, dark, and stuffy."[11] Such conditions, exacerbated by the uneven distribution of wartime hardships and sacrifices, would make the larger units of the fleet hotbeds of mutiny and revolution in 1917–18. Among the common manpower of the navy, and among the workers who built their ships, social class rather than nationality remained the most divisive factor and the greatest threat to its fleet in being.

The Austro-Hungarian naval buildup was overshadowed by the much greater German naval buildup, authorized in Admiral Alfred von Tirpitz's navy laws of 1898 and 1900, which by 1905 left Germany second only to Britain in naval strength. The German decision to challenge the traditional naval hegemon prompted Britain to resolve its differences with France (1904) and Russia (1907), creating the Triple Entente. Meanwhile, the resulting transformation of the Triple Alliance into an anti-British bloc made the pact far less attractive to Italy, whose leaders began to view Austria-Hungary, rather than France, as their most likely future enemy. Thus, during the last decade of peace before World War I, Europe's greatest naval race outside of the North Sea occurred in the Adriatic between the now-nominal allies. Counting all battleships built since 1880, by 1905 Italy had eighteen to Austria-Hungary's twelve. In his quest to narrow the gap, the navy's commander, Admiral Montecuccoli, continued to enjoy the support of a broad domestic political coalition as well as the patronage of Franz Ferdinand. The Austrian Navy League (1904) helped by lobbying and popularizing the cause; by 1914 it grew to include nearly 45,000 members, making it the second-largest organization of its type in Europe, smaller only than the German Navy League. Thanks to an industrial infrastructure anchored by Skoda, Witkowitz, and the Stabilimento Tecnico Triestino, the Dual Monarchy had the ability to complete major warship projects much faster than Italy. Indeed, during the prewar years, only Britain and Germany could build larger warships faster than Austria-Hungary.[12]

## THE DREADNOUGHT REVOLUTION

In December 1906, just as the Adriatic naval race got underway, Britain revolutionized naval warfare with the 18,110-ton *Dreadnought*, a battleship larger, faster, and more heavily armed than any existing warship. Its commissioning sent the rest of the world's navies scrambling to build "dreadnoughts" of their own. The clean slate created an opportunity for lesser naval powers to catch up with the traditional leaders, if they were willing to pay the price. In Austria-Hungary, Montecuccoli opted to build the three 14,500-ton *Radetzky*-class pre-dreadnoughts, funded in the autumn of 1906, before further straining the budget with dreadnought projects. Italy likewise waited to lay down its first dreadnought until June 1909, after Montecuccoli drafted a plan for a future Habsburg fleet including four 20,000-ton dreadnoughts. Austria-Hungary did not start work on its first dreadnought, *Viribus Unitis*, until July 1910, after a constitutional crisis in Hungary delayed implementation of the new fleet plan but laid down a sister ship in September 1910, *Tegetthoff*, for which the class was named. After Italy began construction of another three dreadnoughts in the summer of 1910, Austria-Hungary funded the third and fourth units of the *Tegetthoff* class in March 1911, giving both navies four of the ships.[13]

For the Austro-Hungarian dreadnought projects, Montecuccoli stuck with the practice of building the navy's ships entirely from domestic resources, despite the exorbitant price. *Viribus Unitis* officially cost 60 million kronen ($12 million), but some estimates range as high as 82 million kronen ($16.4 million). By comparison, the first American dreadnought, USS *Michigan* (commissioned January 1910), cost $7 million, and the first German dreadnought, *Nassau* (commissioned May 1910), cost 37 million marks or $7.4 million. Montecuccoli made no apologies for the price tag. In October 1912, while presenting another record-breaking budget request to the legislators, he made a bold declaration: "We are a Mediterranean power," he asserted, and this fact required "a stronger navy with which we can assume our place among the Mediterranean powers."[14]

By then work was well underway on the last pair of *Tegetthoff*-class dreadnoughts, *Prinz Eugen* at Trieste and *Szent István* at the Danubius shipyard of Fiume (Rijeka), the first major warship to be built in the Hungarian half of the empire. By early 1912 Italy had countered by laying down its fifth and sixth dreadnoughts. In October 1912 Austria-Hungary became the third European power (after Britain and Germany) with a dreadnought in active service when *Viribus Unitis* was commissioned just twenty-seven months after its keel was laid. When Montecuccoli's heir apparent, Admiral Haus, raised his flag in *Viribus Unitis*, he had in his care the most expensive warship in world history. Even the British took notice. Strategists at the Admiralty theorized that once Austria-Hungary had a second dreadnought in service, the two ships plus the three *Radetzkys* would pose a threat to the British Mediterranean Fleet at Malta, which could be cut off or defeated should war break out.¹⁵ Britain thus acknowledged the reality behind Montecuccoli's apparent bravado: Austria-Hungary was indeed a Mediterranean power, or at least a significant strategic factor in the Mediterranean, thanks to the growth of the fleet anchored at Pola. This realization helped drive Anglo-French negotiations that led to Britain further concentrating its fleet in home waters against the German threat. The French subsequently guarded the common interests of the entente in the Mediterranean, supplemented by a British force based at Malta, which, under normal circumstances, consisted of a few battle cruisers backed by older armored cruisers.

Had the war not intervened to cancel its plans, the Austro-Hungarian navy would have become even more formidable. In May 1914 Haus secured approval for a five-year program including a new class of four 24,500-ton dreadnoughts. To ensure Hungarian support, two of the contracts were promised to Danubius of Fiume, while the other two were awarded to the Stabilimento Tecnico Triestino. They were to be laid down following the completion of the last ships of the *Tegetthoff* class. Taking a cue from Tirpitz in Germany, Haus marketed the new ships as replacements for much smaller vessels that had become obsolete—in this case, the three units of the 5,600-ton *Monarch* class and the 8,300-ton *Habsburg*. The legislators took it all in stride, despite the program's price tag of 426.8 million kronen ($85.4 million). A German nationalist politician from Bohemia, Albert von Mühlwerth, reflected the prevailing logic: "If my coat is old and threadbare, I buy myself a new one. . . . It is the same with warships."¹⁶

## THE OUTBREAK OF WAR

At the outbreak of World War I, Austria-Hungary had three dreadnoughts in service and a fourth under construction, while Italy had three in service with another three building. But before then, their naval rivalry took an unexpected turn. After the Italo-Turkish War (1911–12) temporarily strained Italy's relations with the Triple Entente, the Italians agreed in December 1912 to an extension of the Triple Alliance and then, in June 1913, to a Triple Alliance naval convention. In the common war plan for a conflict involving all six European powers, Admiral Haus was to command a fleet of the newest Austro-Hungarian and Italian dreadnoughts, cruisers, and supporting vessels, joined by the ships of the German Mediterranean division. His mission was to engage the French fleet in the western Mediterranean and prevent troop transports from French North Africa from reaching ports in the South of France. After Franz Ferdinand was assassinated at Sarajevo (28 June 1914), Haus began a partial mobilization of the navy to support a limited war against Serbia in the Balkans, for which Austro-Hungarian leaders had secured the backing of the Germans on the assumption that this would keep the Russians neutral. But by late July Russia's decision to stand behind Serbia escalated the conflict into a general war, activating the Triple Alliance naval convention. As a first step in their deployment against the French fleet in the western Mediterranean, the Austro-Hungarian and Italian fleets were to rendezvous at Messina in Sicily.[17]

The German Mediterranean division, consisting of the battle cruiser *Goeben* and light cruiser *Breslau*, was supposed to join them, but on 31 July, while they were en route to Messina and before Haus's warships had left Pola, Italy declared its neutrality. After coaling at Messina, *Goeben* and *Breslau* bombarded two ports on the coast of French Algeria on 4 August, then returned to Messina before making their way, by 10 August, to Constantinople, where they became part of the Ottoman fleet after the Turks joined Germany and Austria-Hungary in their fight against the Triple Entente. While making his escape, the commander of the German division, Rear Admiral Wilhelm Souchon, wired Haus at Pola, asking for Austro-Hungarian help to prevent British warships from blockading him at Messina.[18] The appeal placed Haus in a dilemma because at that point Austria-Hungary was still only at war with Serbia. Hostilities with Russia only became official on 6 August, and with France and Britain on 12 August. Haus also faced sobering realities of geography and relative naval strength. He had sufficient strength to deal with the British forces at Malta—the First Lord of the Admiralty, Winston Churchill, had ordered them not to engage him if he appeared in force—but an Anglo-French combination could easily overwhelm the combination of his own ships plus *Goeben* and *Breslau*. While Souchon's telegram assured Haus that "French forces are not here," on 4 August the Austro-Hungarian consul in Naples had confirmed that the French fleet had left Toulon and at least some French units were already off

Corsica "with orders to intercept Austro-Hungarian and German ships."[19] Thus, Haus knew the French were at sea in force and that they, as well as the British, had much more firepower much closer to Messina than he did, putting him in no position to save the German warships.

Souchon was on his own, unless he made a run for the Adriatic to join the Austro-Hungarian fleet. In that case, Haus was more than happy to help, but the Germans preferred that Souchon take his chances with the Turks. Late on 6 August, when he slipped out of Messina with *Goeben* and *Breslau*, he made a feint toward the mouth of the Adriatic, and to strengthen the ruse, the Germans made another appeal for Austro-Hungarian help, asking Haus to bring his fleet as far as Brindisi, at the mouth of the Adriatic, for a rendezvous with Souchon's ships. Haus responded early on 7 August, putting to sea with a formidable force including his three dreadnoughts, three *Radetzky*-class pre-dreadnoughts, and an armored cruiser. He had steamed halfway down the Adriatic by the time Berlin informed Vienna that Souchon's ships were actually headed for the Dardanelles. The Germans then urged Haus to follow Souchon's lead and deploy his fleet to the Black Sea, where it would better serve the common cause of the Central Powers against Russia.[20] Even though *Goeben* and *Breslau*, as warships, would have little relevance to the broader course of the war, their appearance at Constantinople and subsequent incorporation into the Ottoman navy helped push the Turks to follow through with their decision to enter the conflict on the side of Germany and Austria-Hungary.

Meanwhile, Haus, irritated at the Germans for having scrambled his fleet as a decoy, ignored their unsolicited advice to follow Souchon's ships to the Black Sea. He was back in port by 8 August, but it took him another four days to lay to rest the notion that he should move his base of operations from Pola to Constantinople. Even if the Austro-Hungarian fleet could make it there, through waters soon to be guarded by a superior Allied fleet, he argued that the Ottoman capital was too far from the Russian coast to be a suitable base of operations and, in any event, it lacked the facilities to repair battleships. Worst of all, any Austro-Hungarian ships deployed to the Black Sea would be trapped there for the duration of the war (as *Goeben* would be), leaving the Dual Monarchy's Adriatic coast undefended against the threat from Italy.

Ironically, the Black Sea deployment scheme originated with one of Haus's own subordinates, Rear Admiral Erwin Raisp von Caliga, his liaison to the Austro-Hungarian army high command, who had suggested it to the German naval attaché in Vienna. But Haus made no apologies for his refusal to throw away the fleet in being that his country had built at such great cost. He explained to a subordinate that "so long as the possibility exists that Italy will declare war against us, I consider it my first duty to keep the fleet intact."[21]

The dramatic story of the escape of *Goeben* and *Breslau* is usually told without the context of Britain's prewar concerns about an Austro-Hungarian sortie out of the Adriatic, specifically against Malta, which played a key part in the successful escape of the German ships. In justifying their actions at their courts-martial, Admiral Sir Berkeley Milne, British Mediterranean commander, and Rear Admiral Sir Ernest Troubridge, commander of a squadron of armored cruisers watching the mouth of the Adriatic, both cited standing orders rooted in British respect for the Austro-Hungarian fleet. Troubridge explained that he had declined to pursue *Goeben* because of a directive from Churchill not to engage "superior forces," by which the First Lord contended that he meant the Austro-Hungarian dreadnoughts and *Radetzky*s, whereas Troubridge claimed *Goeben* alone was "superior" to his armored cruisers because of its size, speed, and the range of its guns. Milne, meanwhile, cited word of Haus's sortie down the Adriatic on the night of 6–7 August and a false report on 8 August that the Dual Monarchy had declared war on Britain as reasons for his own decision to focus on the defense of Malta against the Austro-Hungarian threat rather than the pursuit of *Goeben* and *Breslau*. Both admirals were acquitted, but neither ever held a command at sea again.[22]

## COMMAND OF THE SEA IN THE ADRIATIC

In the first months of the war, the Allies shut down the overseas trade of the Central Powers by implementing distant blockades in the North Sea and at the mouth of the Adriatic. While the German High Seas Fleet attempted a few sorties against the British, culminating in the Battle of Dogger Bank (24 January 1915), Haus refused to take his battle fleet out of Pola, even after the French deployed dreadnoughts and pre-dreadnoughts in the southern Adriatic. He reiterated to his critics that the navy of neutral Italy posed the greater potential threat to Austria-Hungary and remained firm in his position that seeking battle with the French made *"absolutely not the least strategic sense."*[23] The fleet's main base at Pola, between Trieste and Fiume, protected the Dual Monarchy's two main ports from attack and was the logical place for it to remain. Nevertheless, while maintaining his fleet in being, he also saw value in keeping the enemy at a distance, even if it took less conventional means to do so. After the Germans, in the first months of the war, used submarines (heretofore conceptualized as harbor defense assets) to sink British warships and even some merchantmen, Haus transferred the small Austro-Hungarian submarine flotilla from Pola to Cattaro, at the southern tip of Dalmatia, and then used it to make the southern Adriatic as inhospitable as possible for the blockaders. After *U12* nearly sank the dreadnought *Jean Bart* in December 1914, the French navy withdrew its capital ships from the Adriatic. After *U5* sank the armored cruiser *Léon Gambetta* in April 1915, the French withdrew every ship larger than a destroyer and subsequently maintained their blockade on a line 300 miles (480 km) south of Cattaro, well below the Otranto Straits.[24]

The loss of *Léon Gambetta* came the day after the Italians signed the Treaty of London (26 April 1915), joining the entente. Their anticipated declaration of war against Austria-Hungary followed on 23 May. At that point the prudence of Haus was vindicated, as he still had his battle fleet intact to fight the Italian navy. On the evening of 23 May, shortly after the onset of hostilities, he sortied from Pola for a bombardment of the enemy coastline. The shelling disrupted the mobilization of Italy's army by damaging several stations and bridges along some 300 miles (480 km) of the Adriatic coastal railway, but the intention was largely punitive, and the operation succeeded mostly in demoralizing the enemy. The attacking force included the dreadnoughts *Viribus Unitis*, *Tegetthoff*, and *Prinz Eugen*, supported by the nine largest pre-dreadnought battleships and a number of smaller units, all of which returned to port safely.[25] In terms of numbers of warships involved, it was by far the largest Austro-Hungarian naval sortie of the war.

Despite being embarrassed on their first day in the war, Italian navy leaders entered the action supremely confident, hoping—like the French before them—to lure Haus out of Pola for a battle somewhere in the southern Adriatic. But having preserved his fleet for the eventuality of Italy entering the war, he did not intend to throw it away in an action fought on the enemy's terms. Amid the standoff, he waged war against the Italians as he had in 1914–15 against the French, harassing the enemy not with the battle fleet but with his submarine force. From May 1915 these Austro-Hungarian U-boats were supplemented by German U-boats, which operated out of Pola and Cattaro during the first round of unrestricted submarine warfare. They remained after Germany suspended the unrestricted campaign that September, and while their main purpose was to attack enemy trade and troopships, their growing presence ensured enemy dreadnoughts and pre-dreadnought battleships would continue to avoid the Adriatic. By the end of 1916 some two dozen German U-boats were operating out of Pola and Cattaro at any given time, supplemented by an expanded Austro-Hungarian undersea force. Together they soon put the entire Mediterranean in play for the Central Powers, forcing the Allies to adopt a conservative posture in the use of their larger warships and to use more expendable, smaller warships for convoy duty. After losing the armored cruisers *Amalfi* and *Garibaldi* to U-boat attacks in July 1915, the Italians became just as cautious as the French. The Italian entry into the war also prompted Haus to establish an office of the Austrian naval intelligence service in neutral Switzerland to coordinate espionage and sabotage efforts throughout Italy but especially against naval targets. The first success came in September 1915, when saboteurs blew up the pre-dreadnought *Benedetto Brin* at Brindisi. Fear of sabotage and submarines deepened the timidity of the Italians, frustrating their allies. The British liaison to the Italian navy lamented that "in spite of inferior naval force . . . the Austrians have command of the sea in the Adriatic."[26]

In November 1915 Austria-Hungary commissioned its fourth dreadnought, *Szent István*, and two months later Italy commissioned its sixth dreadnought, bringing into service the last products of their prewar naval arms race. Despite their numerical superiority, the Italians during 1916 redeployed their dreadnought squadron from Brindisi to the relative safety of Taranto and continued to request more French and British support at the Otranto Straits. The Allies placated the Italians by repeatedly sending more of their own resources to the mouth of the Adriatic. Thus, the perceived threat from the Austro-Hungarian fleet in being continued to tie down an ever-greater number of Allied warships that could have been deployed elsewhere. The loss of the dreadnought *Leonardo da Vinci*, sunk in August 1916 at Taranto by saboteurs, and the pre-dreadnought *Regina Margherita*, mined in December 1916 off the coast of Albania, only made the Italians more timid. Finally, at the end of the year, the Allies attempted to close the Otranto Straits by replicating the Dover Barrage, a line of antisubmarine nets dragged by trawlers and drifters commandeered from fishing fleets and backed by minefields, that had been deployed earlier by the British to block German U-boats from entering the English Channel from the North Sea. They hoped their Otranto Barrage would seal the mouth of the Adriatic without risking larger warships to accomplish the task.[27]

After allowing German U-boats to use Pola and Cattaro as bases during the first round of unrestricted submarine warfare in 1915, Austria-Hungary supported Germany in its fateful resumption of the campaign in 1917. Haus endorsed the policy shortly before his death that February. In the months that followed, his successor, Admiral Maximilian Njegovan, authorized a series of raids by surface warships against the Otranto Barrage, hoping to weaken it enough for more German and Austro-Hungarian submarines to pass through. This effort culminated in the Battle of the Otranto Straits (15 May 1917), a successful strike by light cruisers based at Cattaro, led by Captain Miklós Horthy, which left the straits completely open to U-boats for most of the ensuing summer.[28] During 1917 Italy's greatest victory over Austria-Hungary occurred in Switzerland, of all places, where Italian agents discovered, raided, and shut down the Austrian naval intelligence operation that had coordinated espionage and sabotage efforts throughout Italy since 1915.[29]

## MUTINY AND COLLAPSE

For the Austro-Hungarian navy at Pola and Cattaro, as for the German navy at Wilhelmshaven and Kiel (and the Russian navy at Kronstadt and Sevastopol), the emphasis on operations by light cruisers, destroyers, and submarines left most sailors idle aboard battleships and armored cruisers that remained anchored in port for months, even years at a time. In July

1917 the Austro-Hungarian fleet at Pola experienced its first demonstrations, and in January 1918, when the workers of the Pola arsenal went on strike, the sailors of the fleet joined them. The most serious mutiny followed a month later, on 1–3 February 1918, when an uprising including sailors of all nationalities of the empire temporarily paralyzed the naval forces at Cattaro. The combination of war weariness encouraged by revolutionary politics gave the Cattaro mutiny more in common with the unrest of 1917–18 in the Russian and German navies than with the concurrent unrest in the Austro-Hungarian army and home front, which centered on the nationality question.[30] Four leaders of the Cattaro mutiny were executed and nearly four hundred imprisoned. After an investigation into the broader causes of the mutiny, Emperor Charles (successor to Franz Joseph in December in 1916) sacked Njegovan and restructured the hierarchy of the navy. Horthy received an extraordinary promotion to rear admiral and was appointed fleet commander. The twenty-eight officers outranking him had to either accept posts on land or retire from the navy.[31]

Having assumed command as a result of the mutiny at Cattaro, Horthy sought first and foremost to avoid a mutiny of the battle fleet at Pola, even if it meant breaking with the logic of his predecessors. Within the context of the spring of 1918, he saw the inactivity that was a byproduct of the fleet-in-being strategy as a greater risk to the navy than engaging a superior enemy at sea. But his one bold stroke—a plan to attack the Otranto Barrage with the navy's four dreadnoughts in an attempt to replicate his earlier cruiser action there—came unraveled on 10 June 1918 after an Italian torpedo boat sank *Szent István* off the Dalmatian coast while it was en route from Pola to the barrage. Horthy had hoped that by destroying the barrage he would draw the Allied dreadnoughts out of their base at Taranto for a decisive battle, but the sinking of *Szent István*—the only major warship lost by Austria-Hungary in World War I—forced him to abort the operation. Afterward morale plummeted, and even though Horthy continued to insist that the fleet remained battle-ready, it never left Pola again.[32]

During the last weeks of the war, while Germany belatedly sought peace with the Allies, Austria-Hungary began to fall apart, and all attempts to save it failed. On 30 October, one week after his army on the Italian front disintegrated in the face of an Allied offensive, Charles ordered Horthy to turn over the navy to the Yugoslav national council, a body that by that time included some of the navy's highest-ranking Slovenian and Croatian officers. Horthy formally transferred the fleet to them the next day. But Italy had no intention of agreeing to allow Yugoslavia, a state formed by the union of Serbia with the South Slav lands of Austria-Hungary, to keep the ships, and the rest of the Allied powers ultimately agreed. In the predawn hours of 1 November 1918, the Italian navy launched its own preemptive strike against the newly reflagged fleet, infiltrating the harbor at Pola with saboteurs who sank *Viribus Unitis* (which had been renamed *Jugoslavija* just hours earlier). After the peace treaties were signed, the victorious Allies divided the rest of the former Habsburg warships among themselves and soon scrapped most of them.[33] Trieste, Fiume, and Pola were included in the territories ceded to Italy, which moved quickly to fill the vacuum left by the demise of Austria-Hungary as a regional naval power.

## THE FLEET IN BEING IN CONTEXT

Although it spent nearly all of World War I anchored in Pola, at the head of the Adriatic, the Austro-Hungarian battle fleet served its purpose. The deployment protected the largest and most populous port cities of the Dual Monarchy, Trieste and Fiume, which were threatened only by isolated attacks (and only in the war's last three years) from Italian torpedo boats, submarines, and airships, all of which failed miserably. A weak Italian squadron across the northern Adriatic at Venice had to remain in port for fear of being caught at sea by the superior fleet at Pola. Any move by the entente navies to reinforce Venice with dreadnoughts would have provoked a fleet-scale action in the northern Adriatic on terms very favorable to the Austro-Hungarian navy, something neither the Italians nor French intended to do. The standoff resulted in submarines and smaller surface craft shouldering most of the burden of the campaign in the Adriatic, a campaign in which the outnumbered Austro-Hungarian forces registered the only significant successes, at least until the loss of *Szent István*. The fleet-in-being strategy became untenable for the Dual Monarchy only after the broader factor of war weariness, exacerbated by the pressure of revolutionary politics from the civilian realm, made the risk of operational inactivity too high for it to continue.

Most contemporary observers felt the collapse of Austria-Hungary was inevitable, and most historians have agreed.[34] But speculation over reforms not made and actions not taken to save the Dual Monarchy has overshadowed the initiatives, such as the investment in naval power and development of overseas trade that likely prolonged the life of the empire. It is not unreasonable to conclude that if the Habsburg monarchy had not developed maritime interests in the nineteenth century, it would not have survived into the twentieth, even though the force it constructed remained the smallest among the great power navies. Amid the prewar arms races, and throughout the conflict itself, the maritime position staked out by the Dual Monarchy was defended by a fleet constructed not to overpower its rivals but to have a deterrent effect and to project power regionally, all by its very existence. The battle fleet of the Austro-Hungarian navy thus serves as perhaps the best modern example of a fleet in being.

## NOTES

1. Quoted in Paul Halpern, *The Naval War in the Mediterranean, 1914–1918* (Annapolis, MD: Naval Institute Press, 1987), 439.
2. See Lawrence Sondhaus, *The Habsburg Empire and the Sea: Austrian Naval Policy, 1797–1866* (West Lafayette, IN: Purdue University Press, 1989), 1–171.
3. Sondhaus, 252–58.
4. Lawrence Sondhaus, *The Naval Policy of Austria-Hungary: Navalism, Industrial Development, and the Politics of Dualism, 1867–1918* (West Lafayette, IN: Purdue University Press, 1994), 126, 153.
5. *Stenographische Protokolle der Delegation des Reichsrathes* 44 (17 November 1910): 789; 49 (28 May 1914), 546 (Vienna: k.k. Hof- und Staatsdruckerei, 1868–1918). Cited hereafter as *StPD* with volume number, date, and page.
6. *StPD*, 45 (2 March 1911), 901.
7. *StPD*, 49 (28 May 1914), 541.
8. *StPD*, 49 (28 May 1914), 543.
9. Sondhaus, *Naval Policy of Austria-Hungary*, 196, 202.
10. Sondhaus, 189–91, 196, 200–201.
11. E. E. Hazlett Jr., "The Austro-American Navy," U.S. Naval Institute *Proceedings* 66 (1940): 1759.

12. Sondhaus, *Naval Policy of Austria-Hungary*, 170–84, 194.
13. Sondhaus, 191–95.
14. *StPD*, 46 (15 October 1912), 903.
15. Sondhaus, *Naval Policy of Austria-Hungary*, 233.
16. *StPD*, 48 (16 December 1913), 288–89.
17. Sondhaus, *Naval Policy of Austria-Hungary*, 204–8, 237–47.
18. Halpern, *Naval War in the Mediterranean*, 13–14; and Sondhaus, *Naval Policy of Austria-Hungary*, 248.
19. Souchon to Haus, 5 August 1914, text in Matti E. Mäkelä, *Souchon der Goebenadmiral greift in die Weltgeschichte ein* (Braunschweig: Friedrich Vieweg, 1936), 89; and Egon Pflügl (consul at Naples) to Ministerium des Äussern, August 4, 1914 (cipher telegram), AR, F 44—Marinewesen, Carton 13: Kriegsschiffe Frankreich, Kriegs-Operationen 2, Haus- Hof- und Staatsarchiv (HHStA).
20. Sondhaus, *Naval Policy of Austria-Hungary*, 249.
21. Haus to Rear Admiral Karl Kailer, 6 September 1914, quoted in Halpern, *Naval War in the Mediterranean*, 30.
22. For Churchill's version of these events, see Winston S. Churchill, *The World Crisis*, vol. 1 (New York: Charles Scribner's, 1923), 270–75.
23. Haus to Baron Max von Beck, 31 March 1915, text in Erwin Sieche, "Die diplomatische Aktivitäten rund um das Haus-Memorandum vom März 1915," *Marine—Gestern, Heute* 9 (1982): 95. Emphasis in Haus' original.
24. Lawrence Sondhaus, *The Great War at Sea: A Naval History of the First World War* (Cambridge: Cambridge University Press, 2014), 130–31.
25. Sondhaus, 131–32.
26. Captain Herbert Richmond, quoted in Halpern, *Naval War in the Mediterranean*, 138.
27. Sondhaus, *Great War at Sea*, 165–68, 235.
28. See Paul Halpern, *The Battle of the Otranto Straits* (Bloomington: Indiana University Press, 2004).
29. Sondhaus, *Great War at Sea*, 235.
30. See Richard Plaschka, *Cattaro-Prag: Revolte und Revolution* (Graz: Hermann Böhlau Nachfolger, 1963).
31. Sondhaus, *Naval Policy of Austria-Hungary*, 324–28.
32. Sondhaus, *Great War at Sea*, 316–18.
33. Sondhaus, *Naval Policy of Austria-Hungary*, 348–60.
34. Christopher Clark, *The Sleepwalkers: How Europe Went to War in 1914* (New York: HarperCollins, 2013), 356.

CHAPTER 7

# THE PORT ARTHUR SQUADRON AS A FLEET IN BEING IN THE RUSSO-JAPANESE WAR (1904–5)

*David R. Stone*

The 1904–5 Russo-Japanese War provides the opportunity to place the concept of a fleet in being in Russian naval thought of the period and to examine its application during the war. Given Russia's fundamentally continental nature, its theorists hardly considered the concept at all and even lacked a Russian translation for it. Once engaged in hostilities, when a fleet-in-being strategy might have been applicable, some commanders groped toward fleet-in-being ideas, but the lack of prewar preparations for such a strategy and the objective conditions of naval warfare in the Yellow Sea made the strategy impossible.

**FLEET IN BEING IN RUSSIAN NAVAL THOUGHT**
By 1904 naval theorists P. H. Colomb and Alfred Thayer Mahan had published extensive examinations of fleet-in-being strategies. Russian naval officers could and did read works in foreign languages, and foreign works of theory were translated into Russian. A translation of Mahan's seminal *The Influence of Sea Power upon History, 1660–1783* appeared in 1895 and its sequel on the French Revolutionary and Napoleonic Wars in 1897–98.[1] While those books did not explicitly deal with the concept of a fleet in being, Mahan's subsequent reflections on the Spanish-American War, which discussed the concept at length, appeared in Russian translation in 1899, almost as soon as Mahan completed it.[2]

Despite this, the concept of fleet in being in Russian naval thought at the end of the nineteenth and beginning of the twentieth centuries was conspicuous by its absence. That is, a concept with a substantial place in Anglo-American naval discourse had a far lower profile in Russian. This extends to the lack of a standard Russian term to express the concept, true to the present day. For example, Julian Corbett's history of British naval operations in World War I quoted Admiral Hugo von Pohl as saying that "from the first the German plan had been not to risk the fleet in any large offensive operations . . . . The policy was simply to keep the fleet in being." The 1928 Russian translation of Corbett's work did not attempt to find a Russian equivalent, simply leaving the phrase in untranslated English and in Latin characters.[3] Occasionally the concept appears as *"sushchestvuiushchii flot,"* as in an Imperial Russian translation of Colomb's *Naval Warfare* and a recent Russian edition of Corbett's *Some Principles of Maritime Strategy*.[4] Grammatically, that phrase is a present participle and conveys something like "the fleet currently existing," not quite the sense in which the term is employed in English. Indeed, that Russian phrase is more often actually employed to mean something like "the fleet of ships which we presently happen to possess," with none of the strategic connotations of the English phrase. The term "fleet in being" did not appear in an 1897 *Encyclopedia of Military and Naval Sciences*, and there is no entry for "fleet in being" or an equivalent expression in the standard Soviet reference works *Soviet Military Encyclopedia*, *Military Encyclopedia Dictionary*, or *Military-Naval Dictionary*.[5]

In the era of the Russo-Japanese War, Imperial Russian military thinking paid almost no attention to the idea of a fleet in being. This is not because the Imperial Russian Navy was anti-intellectual; quite the contrary. The briefest acquaintance with *Morskoi sbornik* (*Naval Journal*), the official journal of the Imperial Russian Navy, makes it clear that there was a great deal of interest and attention to technical, scientific, and tactical questions. That said, there was much less attention to questions of naval *strategy*. Indeed, the Nikolaev Academy instituted a naval course in 1895–96 that included naval strategy. Given the poverty of strategy in the Russian navy itself, though, the course was entrusted to General Staff Colonel N. A. Orlov and focused on principles of strategy derived from land warfare.[6]

For one example of the relative poverty of strategy, take Vice-Admiral Stepan Osipovich Makarov, hailed by the Soviets as "the most talented and broadly educated representative of the Russian fleet in the last quarter of the nineteenth and beginning of the twentieth century."[7] Makarov is best known for his short time as commander of Russia's Port Arthur Squadron during the Russo-Japanese War. Appointed to command on 1 February 1904, he arrived at Port Arthur on 8 March.[8] Makarov briefly introduced a vigor and aggressiveness into the squadron's operations before his death on 13 April 1904 when his flagship *Petropavlovsk*, with Makarov on board, struck Japanese mines and sank within minutes.

Well before the war, Makarov had established a reputation as a leading Russian naval thinker. He presented his thoughts in an 1897 series of articles in *Morskoi sbornik*, subsequently reprinted in a number of editions in book form. His interests, however, were largely limited to technical and tactical questions. On issues of strategy and grand strategy, he was silent. He certainly recognized the existence of naval strategy as a sphere distinct from land warfare but did not discuss it. While he spoke often about how a fleet might successfully engage and defeat an opposing fleet, he did not discuss how a fleet might be used to achieve particular political or military objectives, and certainly not how a fleet in being might restrain the actions or effectiveness of an opposing fleet. In discussing tactics, he made it clear that he saw naval tactics as all-encompassing: "a navy exists for war and every element of it [a ship] with its human and material elements is intended successfully to fight a naval battle. Since naval tactics is the science of naval battles, then it encompasses everything on a ship. The point is to win a battle; naval tactics must teach us how to do that." "Naval tactics," he wrote, "standing at the head of all naval sciences, must indicate in each branch the goal to strive for, and sometimes even the means."[9]

While discussions of strategy in Russian naval literature in the late nineteenth and early twentieth century were relatively rare, they were not entirely absent. Discussions of cruiser warfare, for example, often appeared in *Morskoi sbornik*. Simultaneous with Makarov's series on tactics, a Lieutenant Engel'man was writing on the nature of Russia's future fleet. In that context, he specifically discussed the proper structure of a defensive fleet. While he primarily emphasized the right ships for such a mission, he also conceptualized the strategic nature of naval defense. In particular, Engel'man's concept of naval defense is black and white, fundamentally at odds with the elastic and reactive nature of a fleet in being. A fleet in being can counter and parry a potential aggressor landing fleet by taking advantage of moments of vulnerability when the offensive adversary attempts to carry out a landing. While a fleet in being is fundamentally negative in purpose—to constrain or limit the activities of a stronger fleet—it seeks to achieve that objective by the threat, even if implicit, of positive action under particular circumstances.

Engel'man's defensive fleet was quite different. His defensive fleet was not to parry or to counterattack but was instead much more Clausewitzian: to meet force with symmetric but superior counterforce and destroy the enemy fleet or at the very least make its continued presence in hostile waters untenable. That is, "defense must be organized not only to make all important strategic points on the shore invulnerable, but to paralyze any operation of the enemy, no matter how strong the enemy may be, and even render even brief presence in those waters fatal." There is no sense of counterposing weakness against strength at specific moments of particular advantage, but instead should avoid weakness altogether. Engel'man stressed organizing coastal defense "so that the entire length of the shoreline is inviolable, to make the approach of enemy fleets or individual ships impossible and, for the enemy, fatal."[10]

A natural question follows: how to achieve overwhelming superiority to ensure the destruction of any potential landing force? It is easy to say that the key to victory is being stronger; the question is how in fact to *be* stronger. Engel'man's thinking relied on a fundamental assumption about naval design—namely, that purpose-built defensive craft, heavily armed and armored but of limited speed and range, combined with a variety of smaller mine- and torpedo-carrying vessels, would have the advantage over longer-range vessels intended for expeditionary warfare. Sacrificing mobility and cruising range to gain firepower and armored protection, the defensive fleet would shield the coastline by applying force against force. Although Engel'man did not make his logic explicit, his implicit thinking was clear: on approaching a defended coastline, an offensive enemy fleet—superior in abstract terms—would be vulnerable to a swarm of torpedo boats supported by shore artillery and heavier monitors. Engel'man envisaged a network of torpedo boat stations strung out along vulnerable coastlines to raid, harass, and destroy enemy fleets, concentrating multiple squadrons to deal with particularly strong enemy formations.[11]

Despite the general lack of discussion of the concept of a fleet in being in Imperial Russian military thinking, I have found one notable exception—albeit the proverbial exception that proves the rule. In the late 1890s, a Lieutenant A. Shtal' translated a series of articles on naval strategy in *Morskoi sbornik* intended to present foreign naval thinking to Russians. In one he translated the French journal *Revue maritime*'s translation of an original article by Giovanni Sechi in the Italian naval journal *Rivista marittima*. Sechi detailed a clear rationale and justification for a fleet-in-being strategy for a weaker navy in defense.[12]

Without ever using the term "fleet in being," Shtal' laid out in his translation a clear approach to such a strategy. While offensive naval strategy was conceptually simple—concentrate and defeat the enemy fleet—defensive strategy for a weaker fleet was much more complex. Under such circumstances, "in view of qualitative or quantitative insufficiency, [it is] better to avoid a general battle, where there is risk of destruction, limiting oneself instead to attacks on the enemy under well-defined, propitious circumstances and holding the enemy under constant threat of our attack." Should the enemy fleet operate near a friendly shore in predominant force, "the sensible course is to drain it, giving it neither rest nor time while avoiding decisive battles." At the same time, "it is necessary to hold a part of our fleet untouchable, in order that its presence on the sea would make any attempt at a landing irrational."[13]

The article presented five central elements, together providing an able summary of a viable fleet-in-bring strategy for a weaker force:

1. "Oppose individual groupings of the enemy with superior force."
2. "Organize night attacks by torpedo boats [*minonostsy*] and small and medium vessels against intruding enemy vessels."
3. "Organize daytime attack with torpedo boats when circumstances permit."

4. "Disrupt the enemy's efforts to obtain command of the sea, avoiding fleet engagements and conserving in good condition a core of heavy-gunned fast ships, ready to support individual engagements and attack convoyed troops."
5. "Dispatch independent cruisers to sea for pursuit of commercial ships and send scouting vessels to enemy shores as a diversion."[14]

The article's discussion of fleet-in-being concepts produced no further dialogue, and the introduction to the translation is apologetic, noting the unformed nature of the ideas in the original article and their limited applicability.

Why such neglect of the fleet in being in Russian thinking? While it is inherently problematic to explain the nonoccurrence of a phenomenon, the very nature of the article's source helps clarify the problem. The original article was in Italian. At the turn of the century, Italy's membership in the club of European great powers was marginal. It was natural for Italian strategists to focus on managing relative weakness. Tactically and operationally, Sechi's vision for Italy relied heavily on a rich network of ports, observation points, and semaphore stations along a lengthy coastline in order to enable the reactive and parrying strategy he envisaged. Unlike Italy, Russian lacked the populated coastline, let alone the infrastructure.

The very logic of a fleet in being, dating back to Lord Torrington in 1690, militated against the concept's relevance for Russia. It sought to prevent a hostile landing for fear that one's own land forces would prove inadequate to counter it. This approach made sense under Britain's strategic constraints. British strategy for centuries prioritized a strong fleet to acquire and sustain seaborne trade and a maritime empire. For reasons of economy and a political culture alive to the dangers of domestic tyranny created by a standing army, the army remained quite small. Consequently, any invading army could have an outsized effect. Indeed, in the Glorious Revolution of 1688, immediately before Torrington's inauguration of a fleet-in-being strategy, a landing force of only about 20,000 deposed King James II.

For Russian strategists, the logic was entirely different. First, Russian land forces were rarely outnumbered, so there were few fears of inadequate land power. Russian thinkers might worry about their many commitments or their lengthy frontiers, but lack of mass had historically not been a concern. In addition, in the pre–Russo-Japanese War naval literature, Russian naval thinkers emphasized the Baltic and Black Seas, not the Pacific. Surveys of foreign navies focused overwhelmingly on European powers. This reflected Russian centers of gravity, both economic and demographic, which were and are overwhelmingly in the west, and racial dismissiveness about any potential Japanese threat. Russian naval thinkers assumed that they would be fighting in regions, whether the Baltic or Black Sea littoral, thick with population and infrastructure to support land operations against any opponent foolish enough to contemplate landing on Russian shores. They assumed operating against an invasion force from strength, not weakness. An article in *Morskoi sbornik*, translated from a French original by E. Farret in *Revue maritime*, underlined the point. Farret argued that "landings on hostile territory would be in vain and risky to those attempting it, for in view of the size of contemporary armies, an expeditionary corps would be doomed to certain destruction."[15]

As a result, when faced with naval war against Japan in 1904, Russian commanders did not have a fleet-in-being strategy in their conceptual toolkit. Instead, their natural inclination was *not* to imagine a reactive, countering strategy intended to harass landing actions and exploit temporary vulnerabilities. Instead, they prioritized positioning the Russian fleet to defeat the Japanese fleet in battle. From the experience of fighting Japan, some Russian commanders did grope their way toward potential uses of a fleet-in-being strategy but found that a lack of prewar preparation for such an approach, combined with objective obstacles, precluded its implementation. The Russian navy's seven-volume official history of the Russo-Japanese War, relying extensively on original documents, allows a detailed examination of Russian strategic thinking, at times on a day-by-day basis.[16]

## RUSSIAN PLANNING FOR WAR WITH JAPAN

To summarize briefly, the Russo-Japanese War arose over a clash between expanding Russian and Japanese spheres of interest in Manchuria and Korea at the beginning of the twentieth century. Japan proposed a mutual accommodation with Russian predominance in Manchuria in return for Japanese predominance in Korea. When Russia showed no interest in such a settlement, Japan turned to war, launching the conflict with a surprise attack on the Russian fleet in the roadstead outside the Russian base at Port Arthur at the southwestern tip of the Liaodong Peninsula, extending into the Yellow Sea.

Russian naval power in the Far East centered on two bases. Vladivostok, in Russia proper, hosted a squadron of four cruisers. It was at best an imperfect base, as it was distant from the centers of economic and political power in China and frozen for several months of the year. Access from Vladivostok to the open ocean or to the Yellow Sea required passing through one of a number of narrow straits around the Japanese home islands. As a result of Vladivostok's inadequacies, Russia had acquired rights to a base at Port Arthur from the Chinese government in 1896 in the wake of the First Sino-Japanese War (1894–95). Yet Port Arthur also presented numerous difficulties. The base was physically isolated from Russia. Rail access ran six hundred miles north from Port Arthur to the important rail junction of Harbin in central Manchuria, and then an additional six hundred miles west to Russian territory or three hundred miles east to Vladivostok. Naval communications between Port Arthur and Vladivostok required skirting the Korean Peninsula and passing through the Tsushima Strait, providing Japan with a convenient choke point. Finally, access to Port Arthur's protected inner harbor passed through a narrow and shallow passage, making the entrance or exit of any large force a matter of several hours or even days. Nevertheless, by the outbreak of war, it was Russia's main naval base for a force consisting of seven battleships in addition to a number of cruisers and other smaller ships. Russia's fleet in the Pacific was roughly on a par with Japan's fleet of six modern battleships and a substantial number of smaller vessels. Russia's overall navy was much larger, but geography meant that its three main fleets—in the Black Sea, Baltic Sea, and Pacific—were incapable of rapid mutual support.

Despite the rough parity between Russian and Japanese naval forces in the region, prewar Russian naval war plans sought command of the sea by destroying the Japanese fleet in a decisive battle. As late as 1901, war planning had assumed basing the fleet at Vladivostok, but by 1903 the war plan centered around Port Arthur. As of April 1903, that plan accurately assessed that in the event of war, Japan would quickly land troops in Korea and then move them to Manchuria. Given Japan's favorable geographical position, there was no way of preventing Japanese landings on Korea's eastern coast. The Russians were not especially concerned about this possibility: given Korea's hilly terrain and poor roads, any Japanese advance from the eastern coast would take so much time that the Russians could solidify their own position. The danger was Japanese landings on Korea's western coast, whether at Chemulpo (now Inchon), Pyongyang, or as far north at the mouth of the Yalu. Any of those points would allow a quicker advance through easier terrain into Manchuria. This eventuality the Russians must prevent; hence, the war plan envisaged "the necessity of remaining masters of the Yellow Sea and Korean Strait, relying on Port Arthur." Ideally this would prevent Japanese landings altogether. If it did not, Russia would "search out the Japanese fleet in the Yellow Sea and Korean Strait, destroy that fleet, and halt communication by sea to the Japanese army in Korea." Even at risk of losing some of its own ships, the Russian fleet must "remain master of the Yellow Sea."[17] In December 1903 Evgenii Ivanovich Alekseev, newly appointed as Tsar Nicholas II's viceroy in the Russian Far East, led a discussion of potential revisions to the plan as war seemed increasingly imminent; no changes were made.[18]

Thus, even under conditions of relative parity between the opposing fleets, the Russian plan was to halt or reverse Japanese landings by command of the sea, enforced as necessary with a decisive fleet engagement. No part of the discussion envisaged a fleet-in-being strategy as a means to that end.

## PORT ARTHUR AS A FLEET IN BEING?

The Japanese opened the Russo-Japanese War with a surprise attack on Port Arthur by torpedo boats and destroyers on the night of 8–9 February 1904. This brought harsh reality home to the Russian command and made a strategy of decisive fleet engagement temporarily untenable. While Japan's attack on Russian ships anchored unprotected in the port's roadstead did not sink any capital ships, it temporarily disabled two battleships and a cruiser, meaning that any fleet engagement would no longer take place under conditions of rough parity. That attack also apparently had a substantial psychological impact on the Russian naval command. From that initial attack on, the dangers arising from Japan's substantial edge in smaller craft—cruisers, destroyers, and torpedo boats—preoccupied Russian officers. They feared not only capital ship attrition en route to battle but also Japan's advantage in smaller vessels providing a substantial edge in reconnaissance.

The effects were evident in the first days after the Port Arthur attack. On 12 February Alekseev directed his Pacific Ocean Fleet commander Oskar Viktorovich Stark to prepare his ships to sortie as quickly as possible; on 17 February Alekseev made it clear he wanted to attack the ongoing Japanese landings at Chemulpo, provided that the main Japanese fleet would *not* be present. As a result, this sortie required effective reconnaissance to be certain of proper conditions. Lacking this, the Russian battleships stayed at Port Arthur and the attack never happened.[19]

At some level this might be considered an improvised fleet-in-being strategy. That is, Alekseev's concept was to take advantage of the absence of Japanese capital ships to use his weaker force to strike at an ongoing enemy landing. This approach failed on several grounds. The lighter ships required to carry out successful reconnaissance were inadequate and unprepared for the task, and Alekseev's commanders and staff had not thought through the requirements of such a mission. In addition, the real prospect of losing capital ships seems to have sobered Alekseev; his decisions and directives over the next few months stressed preserving Russian battleships, resulting in great passivity by the Port Arthur Squadron. For Japan to achieve its objectives, it had to put substantial military force ashore. The ships at Port Arthur did remarkably little to impede that process.

Despite his status as a naval officer, Alekseev had always felt unprepared for the task of commanding a fleet, and even before the start of hostilities had requested a competent squadron commander to take over his role. He got his wish; Stepan Makarov was appointed to command at Port Arthur. Makarov set out for Port Arthur via the Trans-Siberian Railway on 17 February 1904, arriving on 8 March. While Makarov was en route, Alekseev left Port Arthur for Mukden, several hundred miles inland. Before leaving, Alekseev instructed Stark to preserve the fleet.[20] On 18 March he told Makarov the same thing: Makarov should hold off on efforts to meet the Japanese on an equal footing and conserve the fleet. Only under the most favorable circumstances should he risk battle.[21] While Makarov acquired a posthumous reputation for daring, his initial response on reaching Port Arthur was identical to Alekseev's. On 11 March he found that the squadron was in no conditions to meet the Japanese, although he allowed that, with repair and improved training, that might be a future possibility.[22]

At this point both Alekseev and Makarov had similar views on the danger of trying to meet the Japanese on equal terms, which might be seen as an effort to preserve a fleet in being. For both men, however, the primary goal remained eventually gaining command of the sea through decisive battle, although they did concede some role for counteractions in the meantime. Makarov still intended over the long term, once his capital ships were repaired and his smaller ships were fully prepared for action, to gradually expand his ships' field of operations out from the immediate vicinity of Port Arthur and eventually force a decisive battle. In the meantime, he intended to use both the ships under his direct command and the cruiser squadron at Vladivostok to counter Japanese actions by taking advantage of temporary tactical opportunities and interdicting Japan's seaborne lines of communication to the Asian mainland. In addition, he planned to mine the waters around the Liaoyang Peninsula to prevent Japanese landings.[23] On 23 March Alekseev reiterated to Makarov the importance of preserving the capital ships at Port Arthur by not risking battle. Instead, Alekseev advocated a strategy "in the near term limited to parrying the blows of the enemy" and, "in good time, using the first opportune moment to move to decisive action with the chief goal of destroying the enemy fleet and achieving command of the sea [*ovladanie morem*]."[24] That is, both men—the proverbially bold Makarov and ostensibly timid Alekseev, agreed on the long-term goal of seeking a decisive fleet engagement and on the short-term goal of "parrying" Japanese actions with a weaker force and preying where possible on Japanese communications. This seems, indeed, a consensus on a sort of fleet-in-being strategy to win time for a strategy of decisive fleet engagement.

There were long-term constraints, however, on just how effective a Russian fleet-in-being strategy could be, constraints immediately facing Makarov and his successors at Port Arthur. In the end, contingent events made such a strategy impossible. The first and most obvious constraint was basing and its related question of coal. Coal-burning warships could not function without substantial stocks of coal. Assembling such stocks for a major battle fleet was not a trivial task. While the fuel requirements of a simple escape from Port Arthur to potential safe haven in Vladivostok might have been relatively clear, an open-ended strategy of threat and counter to restrain Japanese actions implied no cap on potential Russian needs for fuel. To make matters worse, the Russian fleet had only two potential bases in the region: Port Arthur and Vladivostok. Chinese ports were neutral and would require substantial effort to assemble and pay for sufficient coal to fuel a battle fleet. They offered only limited opportunity for respite before Russian warships would be interned for violations of neutrality. Russian ships attempting to execute a flexible fleet-in-being strategy faced inflexible basing constraints. A fleet-in-being strategy, predicated on relative weakness, implied being able to avoid confrontation with a stronger enemy. While Russian ships might take refuge in Port Arthur, this would make them simple to track and contain, removing the threat of counteraction that a fleet-in-bring strategy required.

Tactically, Port Arthur presented serious problems for either a fleet-in-being or a decisive-engagement strategy. Perhaps most noteworthy was the time and effort required to move the Port Arthur Squadron into or out of the inner harbor. Ships anchored outside the harbor in the roadstead were vulnerable to bombardment or torpedo attack. Inside the sheltered harbor, ships were protected from direct attack, but the narrow and shallow passage from the inner harbor to the outer roadstead meant that passage of a battle fleet required hours or days, providing ample time for a hostile fleet to respond. While a decisive fleet engagement or breakout to Vladivostok might only require a single instance of braving hostile attack in confined waters, a reactive fleet-in-being strategy of threat and harassment would by contrast potentially require multiple such maneuvers.

As time passed, the problem of entrance and exit became even more acute as both sides engaged in extensive minelaying around Port Arthur.

Even under the best circumstances of carefully recorded mine locations, laying them under combat conditions necessarily meant substantial problems of accuracy. Both sides lost battleships and numerous smaller vessels to mines.

Naval mines finally wrecked any hopes of a Russian fleet-in-being strategy. On arriving at Port Arthur, Makarov had thrown himself and his sailors into a crash program of training and repair to ensure his ships were ready for action. He also increased their operational tempo, probing Japanese responses to local Russian sorties. On 13 April 1904 Makarov personally led a number of his battleships out from Port Arthur to intervene in a destroyer skirmish; on returning to port, his flagship, *Petropavlovsk*, struck mines and sank within minutes, killing Makarov and most of his crew. Loss of the *Petropavlovsk* further reduced the fleet's chance of meeting the Japanese on equal terms.

Makarov's death shattered the morale of the officers and sailors at Port Arthur. Alekseev returned to Port Arthur for three weeks to take direct command of the ships there, but he seemed to have lost whatever ability he previously possessed to think clearly about the role of the fleet. He focused on passive defense. News of potential Japanese landings on the Liaodong Peninsula, threatening to strand him in Port Arthur, led to Alekseev's recall to Mukden. He left on 5 May, handing naval command at Port Arthur to Rear Admiral Wilgelm Karlovich Vitgeft and issuing an astonishing series of contradictory directives in the face of impending Japanese landings and siege of Port Arthur.[25] He left instructions permitting actions only by cruisers, destroyers, and smaller ships and only while avoiding excessive risk. In the event of a Japanese attempt to land on the Liaodong Peninsula itself, Alekseev deemed a Russian naval response "necessary" but "insofar as possible carry out the transfer of destroyers and torpedo boats to the place of attack and their return to Arthur without the danger of being cut off from the port." On the day of his departure, however, on receiving word of potential Japanese landings on the Liaodong Peninsula some sixty miles from Port Arthur, Alekseev telegrammed Vitgeft to attack the landing force with destroyers and torpedo boats, "presenting for your consideration the support of this attack with cruisers and the battleship *Peresvet*, not subjecting the latter to the potential loss." The next day, 6 May, Alekseev told Vitgeft that the top priority was land defense of Port Arthur against Japanese siege, instructing him to "transfer immediately all unnecessary guns, ammunition, and crew" to the Port Arthur garrison troops. The next day, another newly received telegram once again urged an attack by smaller ships against the Japanese landings. The contradictory and vacillating nature of these instructions—to respond decisively but without risking losses while at the same time moving guns, ammunition, and crew to the port's ground defenses—was evident. The first volume of the Russian naval official history closed with the cutting remark: "thus in the achievement of its first and most important task—command of the sea—the First Pacific Ocean Squadron was unsuccessful."[26]

Vitgeft was no more resolute than Alekseev. Upon receiving Alekseev's message just as Japan threatened to cut communications, he pleaded the lack of clarity of the overall situation and called a council of war with his top subordinates on 6 May. This group decided that the danger of mines, the delays required to deploy ships from Port Arthur, and the likely awaiting screen of Japanese destroyers and cruisers suggested that no serious action should be taken.[27]

From the outbreak of war through May 1904, the Russian fleet thus remained largely passive, avoiding both a strategy of decisive engagement with the Japanese navy and a fleet-in-being strategy to threaten and harass Japanese landings in Korea and Manchuria. A perception of weakness drove the reluctance to seek decisive battle: the damage to Russian capital ships in the initial surprise attack on Port Arthur and then the loss of the battleship *Petropavlovsk* had broken the prewar parity. In addition, the realities of Russian basing hampered both strategies. With only two bases in the region, should a ship from Port Arthur be cut off and unable to return, it faced either a long and dangerous run through the Tsushima Strait to Vladivostok or refuge in a neutral port and internment. Both possibilities raised the stakes of leaving Port Arthur. Even the boldest commander—say, Makarov, had he survived—would have faced serious obstacles to executing a coherent strategy.

Japan's siege of Port Arthur in May 1904 changed calculations about how to use the fleet. The Russian army commanders garrisoning Port Arthur considered the fleet's guns and crew vital for its landward defenses. The transfer of the fleet's guns to land defenses further dimmed prospects for either naval strategy. Both army and naval strategists were unsure of the best course. At a general meeting of army and navy leadership on 8 May, the ground commander, Anatolii Mikhailovich Stessel', declared that there was no point in the fleet's leaving Port Arthur; instead, it should defend the fortress. On 2 June, however, the Russian army leadership in Port Arthur almost unanimously recommended that the fleet sortie. A few held that the fleet should escape to Vladivostok, attacking Japanese lines of communication en route. The majority, however, reasoned that the fleet should sortie to attack the Japanese and then return in order to repeat the maneuver because only active naval countermeasures could overcome the siege. If a Russian relief force from the north advanced far enough south, the fleet's ability to bombard Japanese blocking positions on the Liaodong Peninsula might prove key. Stessel' made it clear that his goal was not to preserve the fleet by sending it to Vladivostok but instead to use the fleet to halt the flow of Japanese troops to the mainland.[28] Vitgeft, on the other hand, saw nothing but obstacles. Vitgeft already recognized the enormous difficulties in a sortie either to fight or to reach relative safety at Vladivostok. The fleet had given up a hundred guns from its ships for defense of the fortress, its sailors were losing their skills from confinement to port, and mines choked the exit to the open sea. Without a concrete decision, Vitgeft made halfhearted preparations for a potential exit.[29] This caused tension with Stessel', who grew increasingly frustrated over the fleet's reluctance to sortie in force and confront the Japanese.[30]

On 11 June, further confusing Vitgeft, Alekseev threw his weight behind a fleet sortie. While assuring Vitgeft of his full authority "as a commander completely independent and responsible," Alekseev urged him to "consider the circumstances providing for secure exit and inflicting defeat on the enemy fleet," for "successful outcome of a naval battle may decide the fate of the entire campaign in our favor."[31] Notably, Alekseev put his hope in decisive fleet action. On 16 June Vitgeft received a still different directive from Alekseev to ready the fleet "to go to sea for decisive battle with the enemy, to destroy him and continue on to Vladivostok."[32] Pushed by Alekseev, on 23 June Vitgeft was finally ready to sortie. His order to the fleet noted that, at Alekseev's direction, they were taking the fight to the enemy and assisting in the defense of Port Arthur, leaving unstated whether Vladivostok was the ultimate destination. He explained, "Counting on the enemy fleet's being weaker than ours . . . and scattered around the Yellow Sea . . . we will seek out the enemy and attack him either in full force or in detachments."[33]

The Port Arthur Squadron sortied in force on 23 June, producing precisely nothing. Vitgeft's force encountered the Japanese fleet and found their own torpedo boats and destroyers badly outnumbered. Fearing a night torpedo attack and the loss of valuable assets even before encountering capital ships, Vitgeft returned to port, and the fleet spent the night of 23–24 June in the roadstead outside the harbor. To add insult to injury, the battleship *Sevastopol'* struck a mine. Alekseev subsequently lambasted Vitgeft for failing to take full advantage of his opportunities and particularly for missing a chance for the fleet to escape to Vladivostok.[34] Vitgeft could be forgiven some frustration. Alekseev, who on 11 June had pushed him to seek decisive battle, now criticized him for his failure to make a run to safety to Vladivostok. In any event, Vitgeft's spirit seemed to have broken, and the morale of the fleet's sailors was little better.

For the next month and a half, the fleet's collective leadership found reasons to avoid another sortie. These included the need to preserve capital ships to assist in the ultimate relief of the garrison when Russian troops arrived to break the Japanese siege. A council of war on 17 July unanimously agreed that it was impossible to get out of Port Arthur without risk or to break through to Vladivostok without fighting the Japanese fleet, and if it tried either, the Japanese could whittle away the Russian fleet with torpedo attacks without engaging its capital ships. In sum, the fleet had no choice but to stay and assist the defense.[35]

Alekseev and Tsar Nicholas II found this completely unacceptable. Alekseev insisted that guns be returned from the garrison's defense and remounted on their ships. The same day as Vitgeft's war council, Alekseev informed him that the tsar himself "gave great significance to the fleet's transfer to Vladivostok." As a result, "no matter how difficult the task, no matter what risk is attached to it, it is necessary to exert all strength to gain for yourself a path to the sea. . . . I am certain that you as well as I cannot allow the thought of sinking the fleet in the [Port Arthur harbor] under the guns of enemy land artillery."[36] Vitgeft continued to resist any notion of a sortie, and yet another council of war (increasingly, it seems, a way for Vitgeft to escape responsibility) on 28 July found his subordinates overwhelmingly in favor of remaining at Port Arthur. Alekseev finally made his demand unequivocal. Deeply concerned about the developing Japanese siege of Port Arthur itself, invoking the authority of the tsar, he gave Vitgeft a direct order to lead the fleet out of Port Arthur to Vladivostok, a message Vitgeft received on 7 August.[37]

With enormous trepidation, Vitgeft did just that. On 10 August 1904 the squadron left Port Arthur to break out to Vladivostok. The Japanese fleet met Vitgeft's ships racing southeast toward the exit of the Yellow Sea. The Russian fleet did surprisingly well in the chase, getting the better of the Japanese until a Japanese shell hit the bridge of Vitgeft's flagship, *Tsesarevich*, killing him and sending the ship into an uncontrolled turn. In the subsequent confusion, the Russian fleet lost cohesion and scattered. The bulk of the squadron returned to port, but the damaged *Tsesarevich* went to Qingdao, where the Germans interned it; a number of Russian cruisers and destroyers were likewise interned in neutral ports. The cruiser *Novik* was destroyed in its attempt to reach Vladivostok. After the humiliation of the Battle of the Yellow Sea, no further coherent naval strategy was possible. The Japanese suffered enormous losses taking Port Arthur; a full field army spent another four months reducing it. The overwhelming majority of the time and lives spent, however, came as the Russian fleet had already lost all capacity for independent action. The fleet remained in Port Arthur until the Japanese finally took the port in December 1904 and destroyed the ships at anchor.

Russia's fleet in the Pacific thus did very little to challenge Japanese command of the sea or hinder Japanese landings on the Asian mainland. While the fleet's leadership was generally characterized by irresolution and vacillation, the objective circumstances upon the outbreak of war make it difficult to imagine how it might have successfully employed a fleet-in-being strategy to better effect. Operating from only a single base with difficult access, thus limiting its flexibility, and lacking the necessary complement of smaller scouting vessels to enable it to operate in the face of a stronger enemy, a fleet-in-being strategy was almost impossible to implement once the war began in February 1904.

## NOTES

1. A. T. Mekhen, *Vliianie morskoi sily na istoriiu, 1660–1783* (St. Petersburg: Izd. vel. Kn. Georgiia Aleksandrovicha, 1895); and A. T. Mekhen, *Vlianie morskoi sily na Frantsyzskuiu revoliutsiiu i Imperiiu, 1793–1812* (St. Petersburg: Izd. vel. Kn. Georgiia Aleksandrovicha, 1897).
2. A. T. Mekhen, *Strategichestkii razbor deistvii na more vo vremia Ispano-Amerikanskoi voiny* (St. Petersburg: Morskoe ministerstvo, 1899).
3. Julian Corbett, *Naval Operations*, vol. 2 (London: Longmans, 1921), 399; and Julian Corbett, *Operatsii angliiskogo flota v mirovuiu voinu*, vol. 2 (Leningrad: Upravlenie VMF RKKA, 1928), 379.
4. F. Kh. Kolomb, *Morskaia voina* (St. Petersburg: Tipografiia Morskogo Ministerstva, 1894); and Dzhulian Korbett, *Velikie morskie srazheniia XVI–XIX vekov* (Moscow: Tsentropoligraf, 2009).
5. *Entsiklopediia voennykh i morskikh nauk* (St. Petersburg: Tipografiia Bezobrazova, 1897); *Sovetskaia voennaia entsiklopediia* (Moscow: Voenizdat, 1976–1980); *Voenno entsiklopedicheskii slovar'* (Moscow: Voenizdat, 1986); *Voenno-morskoi slovar'* (Moscow: Voenizdat, 1990).
6. A. A. Koriakovstev and S. L. Tashlykov, "'Krutye provoroty' v razvitii otechestvennoi morskoi strategii," *Voenno-istoricheskii zhurnal*, no. 7 (2020): 4.
7. Introduction to S. O. Makarov, *Rassuzhdeniia po voprosam morskoi taktiki* (Moscow: Gosudstvennoe Voenno-Morskoe Izdatel'stvo, 1942), 3.
8. All dates are converted from the Russian Julian calendar to Western / new-style dates.
9. S. O. Makarov, "Razsuzhdeniia po voprosam morskoi taktiki," *Morskoi sbornik* [hereafter, *MS*], no. 1 (1897): 32; and *MS*, no. 4 (1897): 35.
10. Leitenant Engel'man, "Organizatsiia budushchago flota: Znachenie i organizatsiia oboronitel'nago flota," *MS*, no. 12 (1897): 85, 99–100.
11. Engel'man, 87–104.
12. Leitenant A. Shtal', "Voprosy morskoi strategii," *MS*, no. 12 (1898): 1–14. Translation of M. A. Bunel, "Notes de stratégie naval," *Revue maritime*, no. 135 (October 1897): 139–53; itself a translation of Giovanni Sechi, "Note di strategia navale," *Revista marittima*, no. 30 (January 1897): 5–29.
13. Shtal', "Voprosy morskoi strategii," 2–3.
14. Shtal', 3.

15. A. Shtal', "Voprosy morskoi strategii," *MS*, no. 11 (1897): 12, translating E. Farret, "Questions de Stratégie Navale," *Revue maritime*, no. 131 (1896): 205–36.
16. Both the Imperial Russian Army and Navy official histories bore the same overall title: *Russko-iaponskaia voina*; hereafter *RIaV* followed by a volume number. In this chapter, all references to volumes 1 through 3 refer to the naval history (St. Petersburg: Smirov, 1912–1915); references to volume 8, pt. 1, and volume 8, pt. 2 refer to the army history (St. Petersburg: A. F. Marks, 1910).
17. *RIaV*, 1:62–63, 65–69.
18. *RIaV*, 1:82–3.
19. *RIaV*, 1:373–78.
20. *RIaV*, 1:432.
21. *RIaV*, 1:436.
22. *RIaV*, 1:432–35.
23. *RIaV*, 1:437–38.
24. *RIaV*, 1:438–39.
25. *RIaV*, 1:603–4.
26. *RIaV*, 1:607–9; and *RIaV*, 2:10, 13, 16, 18.
27. *RIaV*, 2:14.
28. *RIaV*, 2:19–21, 99–101.
29. *RIaV*, 8:330–31.
30. *RIaV*, 2:108.
31. *RIaV*, 8, pt. 1:330–34.
32. *RIaV*, 8, pt. 1:355–57.
33. *RIaV*, 2:158–59.
34. *RIaV*, 2:183–85.
35. *RIaV*, 2:207–10, 214–16; and *RIaV*, 3:5ff.
36. *RIaV*, 3:19.
37. *RIaV*, 3:24–25; and *RIaV*, 8:75–76.

CHAPTER 8

# PRE-WORLD WAR I ITALIAN NAVAL DEVELOPMENT

*Francesco Zampieri*

After national unification, the potential enemies of the new Italian kingdom were France and the Habsburg Empire. The Habsburg Empire was a "natural" enemy of Italy because Trento and Trieste were under its control; France was an enemy because its colonial interests in the Mediterranean Sea competed with those of Italy. The Alps protected Italy from a possible ground invasion, but the long and undefended coastline was exposed to threats from the west, east, and south. If the Italian army had remained "in being" in the Po Valley, it could have defeated an enemy that attacked Italy through the Alps, the traditional invasion route. Still, the Italian peninsula's coasts were suitable for amphibious landings. To avoid amphibious landings, Italy needed a navy sufficient to command the Tyrrhenian Sea and destroy enemy transports and their troops on board.[1]

Prior to World War I, Italy adopted a fleet-in-being strategy primarily to protect its western coasts from France and, by the beginning of the twentieth century, to contain the Austro-Hungarian fleet in the Adriatic operational theater. This strategy required significant expenditures to build a credible naval force and efficient bases. Italy chose to develop very capable warships, essentially battleships, which in many cases were at the cutting edge of technology. Unfortunately, industrial and shipbuilding deficiencies eroded the designed capabilities so that the new ships did not alter the balance of power with the French navy in favor of the Regia Marina (the Italian Royal Navy). Despite significant investments in the fortification of key ports and bases—primarily in the Tyrrhenian Sea and secondarily in the Adriatic—the geostrategic disadvantage did not change, and the Regia Marina remained weaker than the French navy.

For thirty years, Italian foreign policy focused on the French threat. Italian fears increased significantly after the Congress of Berlin (1878) and France's occupation of Tunisia (1881). The rivalry with the Austro-Hungarian Empire—most credible from the ideological point of view—remained latent because Italy "forgot" its interests in the Adriatic Sea and the nationalism of Italian citizens of the Austro-Hungarian Empire.[2] To counter France, Italy relied on the alliance with the German Empire and the more unnatural alliance with the Austro-Hungarian Empire (1882), the so-called Triple Alliance. Afterward, Italy also sought naval support in the Mediterranean from Britain, leveraging the latter's periodic clashes with France.[3]

Italian strategists examined public discussion in the French military press of the scenario of a war with Italy; the French debate offered some insights into the possible nature of the conflict and generated fear. Not coincidentally, the same year as the Triple Alliance, the *Journal des sciences militaires* published a detailed French plan to invade Italy that Italian strategists carefully analyzed.[4] One French army would invade through the Cottian Alps and another would land forces on the beaches of Vado while the French navy bombarded the Italian coastline and towns to provoke either a decisive fleet engagement or a blockade of the Italian fleet.[5] To avoid this scenario, Italy negotiated alliances, built a large fleet, and fortified bases in the Tyrrhenian operational theater.

## THE TENSIONS AND THE ALLIANCES

Italy spent the 1880s trying to negotiate alliances with Germany, Austro-Hungary, and Britain to counter France through stable naval cooperation. Even with the Triple Alliance, the Regia Marina remained inferior to the French navy. In the first renewal of the alliance (1887), Germany promised Rome a significant commitment to the Mediterranean Sea. Italy allowed the United Kingdom to use Italian ports as naval facilities but failed in August 1887 to secure an alliance.

Consequently, in February 1888 the expansion of the French Mediterranean Squadron caused a "great naval fear" in Italy. The new French minister of the navy focused on improving French naval capabilities in the Mediterranean. He dispatched to Toulon's naval base two battleships from Atlantic ports, and he increased training for the crews. The Regia Marina feared that this was the prelude to significant French operations in the western Mediterranean and the Tyrrhenian Sea.[6]

Over the next decade the Italian effort to gain an ally would continue, but there would also be a worrisome growing tension between Germany and Britain that had negative repercussions on Italo-British relations. Meanwhile, France and Russia signed a military convention on 18 August 1892, eliciting Italian fears of Franco-Russian deployments from France's new naval base in Bizerte (Tunisia). From here, France would have been able to land its forces on Sicily, to take the island and to gain the command of the western Mediterranean; simultaneously, its Russian ally would have engaged the Austrian and Italian fleets in the eastern Mediterranean. French naval writers—often cited among Italian naval thinkers—had repeatedly speculated about landing French troops in Sicily to provoke an uprising of the poor local population against the Italian government.[7] Given that France already had Tunisia on the southern shore of the Sicilian channel, controlling the northern shore as well would have meant dominating the Mediterranean. Despite Italian pressure, Berlin and Vienna would not sign any naval agreement with Rome, but they did renew the Triple Alliance for the third time. Their refusal was linked to the weakness of the Regia Marina, whose gunners had insufficient training and whose new base at Taranto faced organizational and logistical problems. The naval exercises of 1892 and 1893 were disastrous. During those in April 1893, the firing of the Italian battleships was so inaccurate that the kaiser himself—who was attending the maneuvers—requested them to stop.[8]

A Russian naval buildup greatly affected German, French, and British strategy. From 1883 to 1891 Russia built ten battleships; from 1892 to 1906 it would add twenty-two more. As a result, the Imperial German Navy transitioned from an offensive to a defensive operational strategy. The balance of power in the western Mediterranean and the Tyrrhenian Sea always favored France, which could now expect assistance from the Russian fleet, guaranteed by the 1892 military convention, which evolved into a stable alliance, signed in January 1894 but not announced until June 1895. Britain was pushed to improve its relations with France by its growing competition in the North Sea with Germany, the Franco-Russian alliance, the increasing power of the French fleet, the focus on Suez, and the desire to contain Russia in the Black Sea.

Italy remained ambivalent, maintaining its alliance with Germany and Austro-Hungary, yet aligning with Britain and France during the Crete crisis (1896–98), when Italy supported the Greeks on Crete against the Ottoman Empire in the hopes that weakening Ottoman influence would aid Italian interests in the Levant and its expansion in Libya.[9] Between 1896 and 1905 Franco-Italian relations continued to improve, and in September 1896 Paris and Rome signed an agreement ending fifteen years of rivalry over Tunisia. Italy recognized the French possession, and France gave special rights to Italians in Tunisia. On 21 November 1899 they signed a commercial agreement, ending a ten-year trade war.[10]

After twenty years of diplomatic effort, on 5 December 1900 the powers of the Triple Alliance signed their first naval agreement, a success for Italy. It focused on the Mediterranean and assured cooperation in the Adriatic Sea between the Italian and Austro-Hungarian navies. In the event of hostilities with France and Russia, the Regia Marina still would have borne the brunt of the naval war against the bulk of the French and Russian navies, while the Austro-Hungarian navy's contribution would have been minimal; nevertheless, it was better than nothing. Days after renewing the Triple Alliance and signing the naval convention, Italy signed an agreement with France (16 December 1900): Italy recognized France's ambitions in Morocco, and France renounced any ambitions on Tripolitania, leaving it to Italy.

The "game changer" occurred in June 1902, when Italy renewed, for the fourth time, the Triple Alliance (28 June 1902) and simultaneously signed a neutrality agreement with France. Italy and France agreed on reciprocal neutrality in the event of war between the Triple Alliance and the Franco-Russia alliance. In 1902 Italy also reconfirmed its friendship with Britain and the common will to maintain stability in the Mediterranean Sea. Two years later, on 8 April 1904, France and Britain signed the Entente Cordiale, ending Britain's policy of splendid isolationism. France and Britain recognized their interests in the Mediterranean—respectively, Morocco and Egypt. Thus, two formidable alliances, the Anglo-French alliance in the west and the Franco-Russian alliance in the east, encircled the German Empire.

The Moroccan crisis of 1905–6 revealed the increasing friendship between France and Britain and the isolation of the German and Austro-Hungarian empires. Italy mediated between the two alliances, angering Berlin and Vienna. Germany was becoming the revisionist of the European order, while Balkan nationalism was destabilizing the Austro-Hungarian Empire. Serbia was becoming the primary challenger of the Austro-Hungarian Empire, whose annexation of Bosnia-Herzegovina (1908) had already alienated Italy. Vienna perceived as a threat the increasing Italian interests in Albania. Austro-Hungarian policies in the Balkan region precipitated a "friendship treaty" between Italy and Russia (signed in 1909) and new attention of the Regia Marina to the possibility of fighting the Austro-Hungarian navy in the Adriatic Sea. In a few years the Italian policy in the Mediterranean had shifted from a war with France to a growing rivalry with the Austro-Hungarian Empire in the Adriatic and the Balkans.

In 1911 a second Moroccan crisis strengthened Franco-British relations. A year later they signed a naval agreement that made Britain responsible for the protection of common interests in the eastern Mediterranean (east of Malta), while France would monitor the waters west of Malta. France also signed a naval convention with Russia (16 July 1912) that, although it did not entail combined action in the Mediterranean, was nevertheless sufficient to worry Vienna and Rome that the Turkish straits would be open to Russian ships. The agreement was only a renewal of the convention of 1891 and merely emphasized a willingness of the two fleets to cooperate. Vienna, Rome, and Berlin signed the fifth renewal of the Triple Alliance (5 December 1912), replacing the 1902 version.

Meanwhile, tensions between the opposing alliances increased. Italy shifted its attention to Tripolitania and Cyrenaica (Libya), formally parts of the declining Ottoman Empire. Italy had already obtained permission to occupy them from all the European powers, albeit with different terms. When the Italo-Turkish War broke out, Italian military operations in northern Africa, the eastern Mediterranean, and against the Turkish straits, threatened Ottoman stability.[11] Italy gained Tripoli,

Benghazi, Tobruk, and the Dodecanese Islands. War erupted in the Balkans (the First and Second Balkan Wars) and tensions grew in the Triple Alliance. Despite a shared partnership in Albanian independence, hostility between Italy and the Austro-Hungarian Empire increased.[12]

Nevertheless, the Triple Alliance signatories renewed their naval convention (June 1913), improving that of 1900. The new agreement was more favorable for Italy. The German and Austro-Hungarian navies agreed to subordinate their forces in the Mediterranean to the Regia Marina. The naval strategy would have been offensive: Vienna's navy would have left the Adriatic to join the Italian navy off eastern Sicily. The Habsburg navy would have avoided a blockade by the French navy or Britain's Mediterranean Fleet and exited from the Adriatic before the arrival of the Russian fleet. The two Triple Alliance fleets would have destroyed the French navy in the western Mediterranean and prevented the transshipment of the French army from Algeria to the European front. This plan would have been difficult execute, but it was the only way to defeat French naval power. In August 1914, when World War I erupted, Italy declared neutrality due to the violation of the alliance terms by Vienna, which went on an offensive war without consulting Rome, rendering the plans moot.

Thus, since the beginning of the 1880s, Italian foreign policy successfully contained the French threat in the Mediterranean: Italy encircled France with various alliances and exploited Franco-British rivalries. This foreign policy favored the development of an Italian fleet-in-being strategy. Relative diplomatic security allowed the Italian navy to adopt a quality-oriented shipbuilding policy.

## BUILDING A GREAT FLEET

The first and second naval conventions of the Triple Alliance (1900 and 1913) affected the Mediterranean balance of power, but they were insufficient to contain the French navy. Therefore, from 1881—when France occupied Tunisia, ending its "peaceful coexistence" with Italy—Italy's naval budget generally increased, reaching an average of about 118 million lire between fiscal years 1887/1888 and 1905/1906. Yet compared with the Regio Esercito (the Italian Royal Army), the Regia Marina was underfinanced—between fiscal years 1889 and 1895, naval expenditures decreased continuously—and only by the mid-1890s did naval expenditures again increase.[13] From fiscal year 1896/1897 onward, the increase was constant (except for one brief decline in fiscal year 1901/1902) and sharply accelerated in fiscal year 1906/1907. However, the great leap occurred after the first decade of the 1900s, when, from one fiscal year to the next (1909/1910–1910/1911), the increase was as much as 81.2 million lire. This was not an isolated case; naval appropriations grew by over 85 million lire in 1911/1912, over 77 million in 1913/1914, and over 167.4 in 1914/1915.

At the beginning of the 1880s the French navy had nineteen armored warships: eleven old broadside ironclads of the *Magenta* and *Provence* classes, seven wooden-hulled central battery ships, and one iron-hulled battleship. The Regia Marina was equipped with only five old wooden-hulled battleships, four iron-hulled battleships, and one ram ship. In the 1890s the naval balance between France and Italy changed to seven modern French battleships versus six Italian battleships. Ten years later, the French navy had nineteen modern battleships and Regia Marina only ten. Thus, between 1880 and 1890 there was a rough balance of power between the two navies; one decade later, the situation changed in favor of the French navy.

The last decades of the nineteenth century coincided with the radical and rapid transformation of naval technology. Both Italian and French naval officers debated whether to build a fleet of powerful battleships or a fleet of cruisers and torpedo boats. In France, Admiral Hyacinthe Laurent Théophile Aube, the French navy minister in the 1880s, and the Jeune École (Young School) reduced the battleship focus in favor of more numerous smaller ships. The Jeune École conditioned naval

**TABLE 8.1.** COMPARISON OF ITALIAN AND FRENCH BATTLESHIPS, 1880-1900 (EXCLUDING OLD AND OUTDATED SHIPS)

| Battleships | 1880 | | 1890 | | 1900 | |
|---|---|---|---|---|---|---|
| | Italy | France | Italy | France | Italy | France |
| In service | 1 | 0 | 6 | 7 | 10 | 19 |
| Under construction | 3 | 6 | 4 | 4 | 4 | 3 |

Source: Riccardo Nassigh, "Commento all'opera," in *L'Italia deve essere Potenza Terrestre o marittima?* edited by Cristoforo Manfred (Rome: Edizioni Forum di Relazioni Internazionali, 1996), LIV.

strategy until the end of the nineteenth century. Italy and France both faced the problem of containing and defeating a superior enemy (England for France, and France for Italy), and both were searching for the best solution. According to Aube, future French naval warfare would depend on an integrated force of battleships and torpedo boats to defeat the superior British battleships and of cruisers devoted to commerce raiding (*guerre de course*) to undermine the British economy. In other words, Aube suggested developing a more balanced fleet of battleships, cruisers, and torpedo boats to neutralize the British fleet.[14]

Commander Domenico Bonamico, the leading Italian naval strategist of the late nineteenth century, adopted a similar theory.[15] Bonamico emphasized the importance of cooperation between land and sea defenses, the refusal to fight a decisive fleet-on-fleet engagement, and balanced shipbuilding programs. Bonamico's strategy was a typical defensive strategy emphasizing sea denial over sea control. He argued that the maritime defense of Italy depended on some fortified coastal basing and the construction of a fleet centered on fast, well-armed ships. Bonamico recommended strategically located naval bases able to accommodate a fleet in being. Unfortunately, Italian geography did not support his vision. In the Adriatic Sea, Italy lacked strategic positions to dominate that operational theater; sea control would have required a naval base on the eastern Adriatic coast; in the Ionian Sea, Taranto was the only available naval base, but it was far from both the Adriatic and Sicilian coasts; in the Tyrrhenian Sea, there were some excellent naval bases at Messina, La Maddalena, Elba Island, and Spezia useful to threaten French sea lines of communications (SLOCs) or the French fleet.

Starting in the 1870s Bonamico's thinking played a central role in the Italian debate about shipbuilding policy. Bonamico initially criticized the emphasis on big battleships and the shipbuilding policy of the Regia Marina, advocating the acquisition of smaller but faster and heavily armed warships. Between 1894 and 1899 Bonamico revised his judgment on battleships, writing that they were essential and that strategic qualities (speed, maneuverability) and tactical qualities (armament, protection) needed equal emphasis. He became the advocate of the battle cruiser. He considered torpedo boats essential but not destroyers.

Between 1873 and 1876 and again between 1891 and 1892, when Admiral Simone Antonio Pacoret de Saint-Bon was the navy minister, he advocated big battleships. His preliminary decision was the scrapping of twenty-five old, wooden-hulled warships to obtain sixty million lire and to build new warships. According to Bonamico, this decision was a mistake because a favorable decisive battle between French and Italian battleships was impossible due to French naval superiority. Instead, the Regia Marina should have developed means more suited to coastal defense as part of a joint vision with the Regio Esercito. The Regia Marina's contribution should have been the mobile and wide-ranging protection of the Ligurian and peninsular coasts against any French landings.

The influence of Aube's theories on Bonamico's naval thinking is evident, but it is essential to underline that Bonamico did not reject battleships. Like navy ministers Saint-Bon and Bendetto Brin (1876–78, 1884–91, 1892, 1896–98), Bonamico also believed that the Regia Marina needed powerful ships with tactical (armament and protection) and strategic (speed and maneuverability) characteristics superior to the French warships. Despite this hypothetical convergence of ideas between Bonamico and navy ministers Saint-Bon and Brin, they represented two lines of thinking. Admirals Saint-Bon and Brin were advocates of big battleships with powerful guns and armor; Vice Admiral Ferdinando Acton, navy minister from 1879 to 1883 and a protector of Bonamico, sustained the building of cheap, smaller, and more maneuverable warships.[16] The first two admirals developed the battleships of the *Duilio* and *Italia* classes (1876–83), while Admiral Acton adopted the *Ruggiero di Lauria* class. The three ships of the *Ruggiero di Lauria* class had a displacement inferior to previous ship classes (nominally 10,000 tons) but were equipped with improved seakeeping hulls, breech-loading guns, more efficient armor, and more advanced equipment. The long time required for shipbuilding (seven to nine years per ship) made them obsolete upon commissioning (1888–91). The *Re Umberto* class battleships were laid down in 1884 and 1885 but were commissioned ten years later. They embodied the different ideas of Vice Admiral Ferdinando Acton and Admiral Benedetto Brin, the designer of the new battleships.

Bad relations with France over Tunisia generated these warships: the Regia Marina required heavily armed, fast, and durable battleships. Benedetto Brin designed battleships combining the characteristics of the British *Admiral* class and the *Italia* class to produce these qualities.[17] Once again, the long time for building them was their main limitation, a problem shared with other navies.[18] All Italian battleships were designed to combat the French navy. This task was more manageable than in the past because the quality of French battleships remained inferior to those of the Regia Marina until the beginning of the twentieth century.

In 1889, after the fascination with the theories of Jeune École subsided, the French navy started building new battleships in order to balance British naval power, but they retained old designs and were even less effective. Until 1894–96, the French navy did not build modern pre-dreadnought battleships; only in 1901–2 did it start constructing the modern *République* class. These were capable warships with good armor, powerful armaments, and modern hulls. They became the basis for the design of the *Liberté* class in 1902–3, the French navy's last pre-dreadnoughts.[19] Thus, between 1889 and 1903, the French navy laid down seventeen pre-dreadnoughts, maintaining a numerical superiority over the Regia Marina.

During the 1890s the Regia Marina built fewer battleships than all the other navies. The two battleships of the *Emanuele Filiberto* class were laid down in 1894, commissioned in 1901, and resembled armored cruisers more than battleships. Only from 1898 to 1899 did the Regia Marina start building big battleships, returning to the policy of Saint-Bon and Brin. Focusing on a possible war with the Anglo-French Entente Cordiale, the Regia Marina built the *Regina Margherita* class, four battleships that were well armed and faster than their Anglo-French counterparts. The *Regina Margherita* were the best Italian battleships after the *Duilio* class, characterized by good seakeeping, maneuverability, stability, extensive protection, and excellent guns.[20] The *Regina Margherita* class ended the pre-dreadnought era.

Although France remained the main enemy, at the turn of the nineteenth to the twentieth century, the Regia Marina started to consider the possibility of a war against the Austro-Hungarian Empire. A naval war in the Tyrrhenian Sea or the western Mediterranean remained the most credible and planned scenario. Italian naval strategy to contain the French navy relied on a fleet in being of fast, well-armed, highly maneuverable, and well-protected battleships. The Italian fleet would have tried to prevent both French power projection on the Italian coast and the movement of French 19th Army Corps from Algeria to the European front. However, the Regia Marina needed to fortify and develop strategic positions in the operational theater to ensure the fleet-in-being strategy's effectiveness.

## THE FORTIFICATION OF STRATEGIC CENTERS

In addition to allies and a capable force structure, Italy's fleet-in-being strategy required appropriate basing. In the event of war against France, the Maddalena Archipelago, located in the Strait of Bonifacio separating French Corsica and Italian Sardinia, would be the center of gravity of the Italian maritime defense. This was the opinion of the German allies as well as Italian strategists and statesmen like Bonamico or the long-serving member of Parliament Galeazzo Giacomo Maldini, who focused on defense issues. In 1888 Maldini published an article calling for a powerful navy and fortified positions.[21] He suggested fortifying the three military ports of Spezia, Taranto, and Venice; some secondary ports (Monte Argentario, Syracuse, and Augusta); and other minor ports. Maldini recommended the defense of the Strait of Messina, Elba Island, and the Maddalena Archipelago. The archipelago would be the pivot of naval operations in the northern Tyrrhenian Sea. French strategists of the Jeune École agreed, as did a 1901 article in Germany's *Marine Rundschau* (*Naval Newsletter*).[22]

The Maddalena Archipelago threatened the sea route between Toulon (France) and Bizerte (Tunisia) and, to a limited extent, that between Toulon and Oran (Algeria), thus cutting through the French strategic triangle of Toulon–Oran–Bizerte. Although two hundred miles away from Toulon, the archipelago could serve as a base to undermine this triangular stronghold. The archipelago would have made it possible to monitor the Oran–Bizerte and Gibraltar–Malta SLOCs and would have been an essential base of operations against Spain. In the western Mediterranean, only Cagliari on the southern tip of Sardinia and Port Mahón (Menorca) had equal advantages. Cagliari was a critical offensive position in conjunction with La Spezia (in the northern Gulf of Liguria) and Messina, Sicily. Being much closer to Africa than the Maddalena Archipelago, Cagliari made it possible to cover Sicily and threaten the sea route between Toulon and Bizerte and between Gibraltar and Malta—and, together with Messina, any communication with the eastern Mediterranean. Less advantageous than Maddalena for operations against the French coast, Cagliari was further away from the ports of Corsica and was therefore safer and more accessible.

The island of La Maddalena served as an excellent base to defend the northern Tyrrhenian Sea. The bay of the Maddalena Archipelago was one of the largest and most protected in the western Mediterranean and could accommodate the bulk of the fleet. Surveillance stations, excellent roads, and two telegraph cables to the mainland supported the numerous defensive installations protecting its anchorages from an enemy assault. The exits were defended by quick-firing batteries and patrolled by torpedo boats. Its coal station stored 70,000 tons of coal.

Naval exercises in 1883, 1884, 1885, 1887, and 1899 proved La Maddalena's value. Those in 1883 demonstrated the danger of the French fleet landing troops on the Campanian coast of southwestern Italy.[23] The 1884 exercises tested the Regia Marina's capabilities to attack French SLOCs in the event of an offensive against the Ligurian and Tuscan coasts. *Rivista Marittima* (Maritime magazine), a naval journal published since 1869, described the exercises as focusing on the possibility of a French amphibious landing on Italian beaches of more than 40,000–45,000 men and 5,000 horses using only military transports. With commercial freighters, the French navy could land up to 60,000–70,000 men and 8,000 horses. Due to the supposed vulnerability of the Regia Marina, the French navy might destroy or blockade the Italian fleet in Spezia and take control of Sardinia. The lack of torpedo boats, cruisers, and sloops would have left Italy vulnerable.[24]

The naval exercises of 1885 were more complex and realistic. The Italian fleet was divided into two parts: one simulating the Regia Marina and the other the French navy.[25] For the first time, the naval exercises were planned and conducted with the aim of cutting the French SLOCs from Algiers to Marseille. In the first phase, the squadron simulating the French fleet tried to force the Italian fleet to seek refuge in the

Maddalena Archipelago to gain limited sea control in the area of interest. The second phase entailed a fleet-on-fleet battle: the Italian fleet, leaving from La Maddalena, searched for the French fleet in the northern and southern Tyrrhenian Sea and, having found it, defeated it.[26] These naval exercises confirmed the validity of Bonamico's strategic recommendations: the Maddalena Archipelago was a relevant strategic position and the fleet should follow an active defense strategy combining a fleet in being with an aggressive patrol.

In 1887 the naval exercises simulated the conquest of the Maddalena Archipelago by an enemy fleet and the use of this base as a starting point to attack the Strait of Messina (Sicily).[27] These exercises confirmed the value of the Maddalena Archipelago as an operational base for a national fleet attacking the French SLOCs and its unsuitability as a base for an enemy attack against southern Italy. As a result, the Regia Marina built a state-of-the-art naval base and a naval dockyard in La Maddalena, completed in 1896. In 1910 the naval dockyard, fortifications, signaling towers, barracks, and ammunition depots were completed.

## THE STRATEGY AGAINST THE AUSTRO-HUNGARIAN NAVY

Although Italy considered France to be the main threat and therefore focused on defense of the Tyrrhenian Sea, Italy's security also depended on control of the Adriatic Sea. Diplomatic isolation for a decade (1870–82) had pushed Italy to ally with the German and Austro-Hungarian empires after the French occupation of Tunisia. Despite the young Italian kingdom's vulnerability and worsening relations with France, the decision to build a naval base in Taranto, presented to Parliament in 1871 but funded only in 1882, indicated its abiding interest in the Adriatic Sea. Control of the Adriatic Sea was more achievable for the possessor of the southern gate, represented by Brindisi and the facing Albanian coast, but became progressively harder toward the northern sectors. Taranto and Brindisi were peripheral to operations in the western Mediterranean or the Strait of Sicily but more useful for operations in the Ionian Sea and the southern Adriatic. The Austro-Hungarian Empire considered the two naval bases of Taranto and Brindisi a threat and tried to build a new opposing naval base on the Albanian coast. The Regia Marina envisioned the occupation of Preveza, Vlore, Durazzo, and Corfu (controlled by the Ottoman Empire and the Kingdom of Greece) to form a system of naval bases, but Italian weakness and possible international opposition precluded this plan.[28]

During the following years Italy observed the evolution of the Balkan world and competed increasingly with the Austro-Hungarian Empire to control sea trade to and from the Adriatic Sea. After the conclusion of the Triple Alliance, a cold peace in the Adriatic ensued between Italy and the Austro-Hungarian Empire. In 1887, after the naval exercises in the Tyrrhenian Sea, some Italian parliamentarians asked the minister of the navy why the Regia Marina did not operate in the Adriatic Sea and made no port visits on the Dalmatian coast.[29]

In other words, until the beginning of the twentieth century, Italy forgot its national interests in the Adriatic theater. The Italian membership in the Triple Alliance directed all military energies against France, the more probable enemy until 1896, but did not resolve the strategic imbalance of power in the Adriatic region. Until the first naval convention of the Triple Alliance, the Austro-Hungarian Empire refused to aid the Regia Marina outside the Adriatic Sea or beyond the Santa Maria di Leuca cape. To obtain Austro-Hungarian aid against the French navy, Italy offered to put its fleet under Austro-Hungarian command in the event of hostilities against the French and Russian fleets in the southern Adriatic and Ionian Seas.

After the Italian–French agreements at the end of the nineteenth century, and despite membership in the Triple Alliance and related naval conventions, relations between Italy and the Austro-Hungarian Empire deteriorated as disputes in the Balkans escalated. So planning for a possible naval war in the Adriatic Sea became necessary. In January 1904 the Regia Marina detailed a fleet-in-being strategy from the Taranto and Brindisi naval bases. It required scouting squadrons able to operate in the central and northern Adriatic Sea out of advanced operational bases in Brindisi in the far south and Ancona, midway up Italy's eastern coast. However, Ancona was too small and undefended, while Venice required new fortifications to become militarily valuable in a war against the Austro-Hungarian Empire.

In 1906 the Regia Marina conducted naval exercises in the Ionian Sea that supported the analysis of 1904, among others.[30] The naval exercises revealed, first, the insufficiency and inefficiency of Italy's scouting squadrons; second, the inadequate endurance of its warships; third, the inaccuracy of its naval gunfire due to insufficient training; and fourth, the navy's incomplete operational planning process.[31]

In 1908, after Austro-Hungary's annexation of Bosnia-Herzegovina, relations between Rome and Vienna deteriorated. Consequently, Italy accelerated the improvement of its Adriatic naval defenses, building new batteries to protect the Venetian lagoon and basing torpedo boats at Ancona. Simultaneously, the Regio Esercito redeployed forces from Italy's western to the eastern coast and fortified the entrances to the Valtellina and Isonzo valleys.

In January 1909 two Regio Esercito officers completed a study about joint warfare in the Adriatic Sea affirming the importance of joint army–navy operations and the need to occupy some strategic position on the Dalmatian coast. The Regio Esercito officers disparaged the Regia Marina's ability to blockade or contain the enemy fleet or to prevent enemy's amphibious landings on Italy's eastern coast. That same year, at the army's request, the Regia Marina completed a study analyzing the feasibility of a landing near Trieste or on the Dalmatian coast.[32] It concluded that an amphibious landing close to Trieste required joint action by the Regio Esercito on the Isonzo River. The navy would protect the right flank of the advancing army and deploy its assault force in the Gulf of Trieste. An Italian landing on the Dalmatian coast, assuming Serbian cooperation, required a credible fleet-in-being strategy or an effective blockade of the Austro-Hungarian navy in its home ports. If Italy failed to land ground forces at Trieste or on the Dalmatian coast, the Austro-Hungarian navy, in the first three to four days of the war, could land troops on the Italian peninsula. These troops could occupy some of the Apennine regions, positioning them to march on Rome or attack the Regio Esercito from behind.

During the First Balkan War (1912–13), a new crisis in Italian-Austro-Hungarian relations arose when Vienna considered occupying Scutari and Durazzo on the Albanian coast; the crisis was resolved only with the birth of the Albanian state. Contemporarily, relations between the Italian kingdom and the Kingdom of Greece deteriorated as Athens extended its influence over southern Albania and the Straits of Corfu, where Italy feared that Greece would offer France naval bases facing the Italian coastline and the Brindisi naval base. Turmoil in Albania between 1913 and 1914 erupted into a civil war, which created new tensions between Rome and Vienna. This pushed Italy to limit Habsburg control over the region by supporting Serbia against the Austro-Hungarian Empire. Serbian and Montenegrin revanchism worried the Austro-Hungarian Empire, particularly regarding the defense of its naval base at Kotor. Montenegrin control of Mount Lovćen, overlooking Kotor, threatened the Austrian naval base.[33] In the Italian view, the Austro-Hungarian naval base at Kotor posed a deadly threat, so Italy supported Serbia against Vienna. Italy even offered the British government an exit from the Triple Alliance and studied a possible military intervention in Albania to occupy Vlore and Saseno Bay. In the event of war, control of Vlore, Saseno Bay, and Brindisi would have allowed the Regia Marina to blockade the Austro-Hungarian fleet in its bases and to close the Adriatic to the Franco-Russian alliance.

When World War I erupted, Italy occupied Saseno Bay (30 October 1914) and Vlore (25 December 1914).[34] Berlin and Vienna did not interfere because they were engaged in the war; London, Paris, and Petrograd (formerly St. Petersburg) believed that Italy would soon abandon the Triple Alliance, so the control of Vlore and Saseno would be helpful for the Triple Entente and would disentangle the alliance between the Central Powers and the Ottoman Empire.

Independent of the geostrategic disadvantages, the Regia Marina was always superior to the Austro-Hungarian navy in terms of ship quality and quantity. Vienna's surface fleet could not exit the Adriatic Sea, and the only possible action of the fleet would have been bombarding the enemy's coast or a sortie to challenge the Italian fleet to accept a decisive battle. New weapons, such as submarines and aircraft, would change the prewar theories. During World War I, Italian control of both sides of the gateway to the Adriatic gave an enormous advantage: the ability to bottle up the Austro-Hungarian fleet. Despite the Italian navy's superiority, Italian admirals had no intention of risking their ships by provoking the sortie of the enemy fleet. So the Regia Marina conducted no battle fleet operations, no significant amphibious landings, and ceded the British and French fleets primacy in naval operations outside the Adriatic.

To summarize, Italian naval strategy from 1882 to the beginning of the twentieth century focused on building a credible fleet and not engaging but deterring the French navy. The Regia Marina built not only a powerful battleship fleet but also numerous torpedo boats, adapting the lessons of France's Jeune École naval strategy.[35] At the beginning of the twentieth century the rivalry with France diminished while that with Vienna grew. The Austro-Hungarian navy was a coastal navy but had a geostrategic advantage in the Adriatic Sea. The Regia Marina "discovered" the Adriatic Sea only after 1902 and, against the "new" enemy, chose a naval strategy combining a fleet in being with sea denial to blockade the Austro-Hungarian navy in port.

According to Alfred T. Mahan and other strategists, including Italians, Italy remained conditioned by its geography: it was a peninsula with a strong link to the continent through remarkably undefended land borders both in the Ligurian and northern Adriatic frontiers. It maintained fortifications defending the Alpine passes and an army in being in the Po Valley, projectible by railway along the peninsula. At the beginning of the twentieth century, the enormous progress in mountain warfare, demonstrating the possibility of fighting on the mountain peaks, decreased the strategic relevance of a Po Valley army in being.

Until World War I, coastal defenses remained the task for a powerful navy, which served as a deterrent. Alliances were part of the Italian deterrence strategy, but the feasibility of aid from the Central Powers in the event of a war with France remained doubtful. In such a war, the primary mission of the Regia Marina would have been sea denial in the Tyrrhenian Sea. The Regia Marina would have cut the French SLOCs from Algeria to Provence and countered French power projection against the Italian peninsula. A powerful fleet in being would have prevented French sea control of the western Mediterranean and precluded combined Anglo-Franco-Russian naval operations in the Mediterranean. After thwarting the strategic plans of the French fleet, the Regia Marina would have allowed the Austro-Hungarian navy to exit the Adriatic and avoid the arrival of the Russian fleet. A combined Austro-Italian fleet with the aid of the German cruisers would have fought Britain's Mediterranean Fleet and cut British SLOCs.

In the event of war against the Austro-Hungarian Empire, a powerful fleet in being in Taranto and a scouting force in Brindisi would have contained the enemy fleet in the Adriatic Sea. A fleet in being in Taranto could not guarantee either the protection of the northern Adriatic coasts or action in support of the right flank of the Regio Esercito. This problem required new ideas. The development of warfare with quick motorized torpedo boats built in the shipyards of Società Veneziana Automobili Navali and naval aviation was an answer to this strategic problem, but this solution awaited World War I.[36]

## NOTES

1. F. Zampieri, "Italy, 1861–1914: Did the Sea Build a State and an Empire?" in *The Sea in History: The Modern World*, edited by N. A. M. Rodger and C. Buchet, 210–219 (London: Boydell & Brewer, 2017).
2. F. Chabod, *Storia della politica estera italiana dal 1870 al 1896* (Rome: Laterza, 1962).
3. M. Gabriele, "Il Mediterraneo prima e dopo l'apertura del Canale di Suez, 1869," in *Il Mediterraneo quale elemento del potere marittimo*, edited by P. Alberini, Proceedings of Military History Symposium of Venice 1996 (Roma: USMM, 1998), 32–33.
4. P. C. "I nostri obbiettivi navali e la stampa francese," *Nuova Antologia* 41, ser. 2, no. 19 (1 October 1883): 501–24.
5. *Défense de l'Italie contre une invasion française*, Extrait du *Journal des sciences militaires*, August–September 1882, Librairie Militaire de J. Dumaine, Paris.
6. A. J. Marder, *The Anatomy of British Sea Power: A History of British Naval Policy in the Pre-Dreadnought Era, 1880–1905* (New York: Frank Kass, 1940), 177–78.
7. Commandant Z. and H. Montéchant, *Les guerres navales de demain* (Paris: Librairie Militaire, Berger-Lévrault, 1891), 108–14; and C. Manfredi, *L'Italia deve essere potenza terrestre o marittima?* (Rome: Edizioni Forum di Relazioni Internazionali, 1996), 55.
8. M. Gabriele, *Benedetto Brin* (Rome: USMM, 1998), 89.
9. E. Alberini, *La Marina italiana a Creta: Il potere marittimo in funzione della politica estera (1896–1899)* (Rome: USMM, 1998), 63–64. For the relevance of Suez on the Italian naval strategy, see F. De Ninno, "Italian Sea Power and Suez—From Opportunity to Obsession (1861–1943)," in *Italy and the Suez Canal, from the Mid-Nineteenth Century to the Cold War*, edited by B. Curli, ed., 227–46 (London: Palgrave Macmillan, 2022).

10. F. Micali Baratelli, *La Marina militare italiana nella vita nazionale (1860–1914)* (Milan: Mursia, 1983), 336.
11. M. Gabriele, *La Marina nella guerra italo-turca: Il potere marittimo strumento militare e politico (1911–12)* (Rome: USMM, 1998).
12. V. Mantegazza, *Il Mediterraneo e il suo equilibrio* (Milan: F.lli Treves Editori, 1914).
13. Gabriele, *Benedetto Brin*, 84–85.
14. T. Aube, "La guerra marittima e i porti militari della Francia," *Rivista Marittima*, November–December, 1882, 483–84.
15. D. Bonamico, *Scritti sul potere marittimo (1894–1905)*, edited by F. Botti (Rome: USMM, 1998).
16. Regarding Ferdinando Acton, see M. Gabriele, *Ferdinando Acton* (Rome: USMM, 2000).
17. G. Giorgerini and A. Nani, *Almanacco storico delle navi militari italiane, 1861–1995* (Rome: USMM, 1996), 186; and J. Roberts, "Warships of Steel, 1879–1889," in *Steam, Steel & Shellfire: The Steam Warship 1815–1905*, edited by A. Lambert (London: Conway Maritime Press, 1992), 101.
18. Roberts, "Warships of Steel, 1879–1889," 95.
19. J. Roberts, "The Pre-Dreadnought Age, 1890–1905," in Lambert, *Steam, Steel & Shellfire*, 119.
20. G. Giorgerini and A. Nani, *Almanacco storico delle navi militari italiane, 1861–1995*, 208–9.
21. G. G. Maldini, "La difesa marittima d'Italia," *Nuova Antologia* 15, ser. 3 (16 June 1888).
22. Commandant Z. and Montéchant, *Les guerres navales de demain*, 87; and V. U., "Die Strategische Bedeutung Maddalenas?" in *Marine Rundschau*, January–June 1901, 429–38. The main thinkers of the Jeune École were Admiral Aube's flag lieutenant, Matthieu Jean Henry Vignot (pseudonym Henry Montéchant), and his secretary, Commander Paul Jean Fontin (Commandant Z.). E. Ferrante, "The Impact of the Jeune École on the Way of Thinking of the Italian Navy," in *Marine et technique au XIXe siècle: Actes du colloque international Paris*. École militaire, 10, 11, 12 June 1987 (Paris: Services historique de la Marine, 1988), 519–24.
23. "Relazione sulla manovra coi quadri a partiti contrapposti dello ottobre 1883—battaglia di Fiumicino," Raccolta di Base (RdB), Busta 113, Folder 5, 1883, Archivio Ufficio Storico della Marina Militare (AUSMM), Rome.
24. O. T., "Appunti sulla capacità d'invasione marittima della Francia," in *Rivista Marittima* 17, no. 1 (January 1884): 5–25.
25. "Esercitazioni navali: Rapporti relativi," 1885, RdB, Busta 117, Folder 1, AUSMM.
26. Nautilus, "Le esercitazioni della Marina Italiana," in *Nuova Antologia* 11, ser. 3 (16 September 1887): 238–68.

27. "Esercitazioni navali e pratiche relative," RdB, Busta 124, Folder 1, AUSMM; and "Relazioni sulle manovre navali," 1887, RdB, Busta 125, Folder 2, AUSMM.
28. Micali Baratelli, *La Marina militare italiana*, 171; and M. Gabriele, Introduzione to R. Nassigh, *La Marina italiana e l'Adriatico, il potere marittimo in un teatro ristretto* (Rome: USMM, 1998), 10.
29. Nautilus, "Le esercitazioni della Marina italiana," 264–65.
30. "Esercitazioni navali e rapporti relativi," 1906, RdB, Busta 192, Folder 2, AUSMM.
31. F. Di Palma, "Le manovre navali del 1906 sul Mare Jonio," *Nuova Antologia* 126, ser. 2 (1 December 1906): 501–16.
32. "Studio in caso di conflitto tra l'Italia e Austria (formazione di base navale passeggera su territorio nemico)," 1909, RdB, Busta 199, Folder 5, AUSMM.
33. Mantegazza, *Il Mediterraneo e il suo equilibrio*, 200.
34. R. Nassigh, *La Marina italiana e l'Adriatico, il potere marittimo in un teatro ristretto* (Rome: USMM, 1998), 60–61.
35. Ferrante, "The Impact of the Jeune École," 519–24.
36. For the Regia Marina in World War I, see E. Ferrante, *La Marina in Adriatico* (Rome: USMM, 1987).

# PART III
# THE TWENTIETH-CENTURY GLOBAL WARS

CHAPTER 9

# THE HIGH SEAS FLEET DURING WORLD WAR I
## A Fleet in Being Contrary to Its Own Intentions (1914)

*Michael Epkenhans*

From 1897 until World War I, Germany expended enormous sums of money to implement a meticulously prepared plan to build a fleet to rival Britain's Royal Navy. The German High Seas Fleet's sheer size of 61 battleships and battle cruisers, 40 light cruisers, 144 torpedo boats, and 72 submarines on the opposite side of the North Sea could only be regarded as a hardly disguised dagger-at-the-throat-strategy, which in the end was supposed to force Britain—Germany's neighbor and, according to Grand Admiral Alfred von Tirpitz's reports to the emperor, its "most dangerous opponent"[1]—to make political and perhaps territorial concessions in Europe and overseas. Whatever the emperor or Tirpitz said in public, their secret documents left no doubt that their final aim was to replace Britain as the leading world and supreme naval power. The twentieth century was to become the German century just as much as the eighteenth and nineteenth centuries had belonged to Britain.[2]

Germany's naval buildup contributed to an unusual increase of political tensions across Europe. In response, Britain, France, and Russia signed political agreements starting in 1904 for differing complex reasons and aims that culminated in the Triple Entente. Soon, instead of a multipolar system, two political camps watched each other with increasing distrust, both accusing the other of wanting war. Tirpitz's plan began to go awry due to developments in shipbuilding and Britain's decision to outbuild the Kaiserliche Marine (Imperial German Navy) by increasing its building tempo. Rather than remain "a second-rate European continental power," Tirpitz believed Germany should persevere because "it seems more worthy for a great nation to fight for the supreme objective and maybe perish with honor rather than to relinquish its future ingloriously."[3] In the event of failure, he always warned the emperor as well as the chancellor of an "utter fiasco" that would shatter the foundations of the monarchy.[4] This thinking explains why Tirpitz and Germany's naval leadership clung to the idea of a major fleet-on-fleet engagement in the impending war. The Kaiserliche Marine had to prove its value with the battle fleet to justify its existence and the tradeoff of the vast sums invested in shipbuilding rather than in the buildup of more army corps and the purchase of more heavy artillery and machine guns.

In actuality, the battle fleet spent most of World War I in port, incapable of escaping German's constricted geography of narrow seas bordering its main enemies. German capital ships became an unplanned fleet in being that still had significant deterrent value: there were no Allied landings behind German lines on the German or Danish coasts. Britain had to devote considerable naval assets to blockade Germany. The fleet closed the Baltic to Russia so that desperately needed supplies could not reach it. The U-boat campaign nearly sunk an unsustainable percentage of British trade.

## THE WAR PLANS OF THE KAISERLICHE MARINE AGAINST ITS "MOST DANGEROUS OPPONENT"

Like all navies, the Kaiserliche Marine as a true disciple of Mahanian thinking had regarded a decisive battle against the Royal Navy as a means. Just before the war, the outlook remained bleak. In early 1914 even Tirpitz admitted that the Royal Navy under the leadership of the new First Lord of the Admiralty, Sir Winston S. Churchill, had won the naval race despite the enormous financial strain entailed, whereas Tirpitz could not finance building the vessels mandated by the navy law.[5] More importantly, whereas the army had its Schlieffen Plan, which determined the deployment and movements of troops according to a carefully devised and constantly updated timetable, the navy lacked such a plan.[6] Since the German navy had been built up only in order to help overcome Britain and its naval supremacy at almost any cost, one would have expected an operational plan to implement a strategy that promised success or at least instructed the commander in chief of the High Seas Fleet how to fight Britain.

What had happened? Since 1895 the Admiralty Staff, the command of the High Seas Fleet, the Imperial Navy Office, and the kaiser had discussed operational plans against Britain and, initially, even landings on Britain's East Coast. These plans contained two assumptions: First, at the outbreak of war, due to imperial commitments, only parts of the Royal Navy would be available in the North Sea, thus allowing the Kaiserliche Marine a favorable margin against its much superior enemy. Second, the Royal Navy would impose a close blockade against the German coast, and sooner or later a decisive battle would ensue under the guns of Heligoland, a small island only a few miles away from the navy's main base and a favorable position for an inferior naval power.

This scenario, however, seemed very unlikely on the eve of war. From 1904 to 1905 onward the Royal Navy redeployed the big ships to home waters and introduced a new strategy and battle tactics.[7] In 1912 German observations of British naval maneuvers indicated changes in the Admiralty's strategy against Germany. Battleships had become too vulnerable to submarines, torpedoes, and mines to risk in a battle that seemed unnecessary for one important reason: geography. As a result, Britain abandoned plans to establish a close blockade or even an observational blockade to force the German navy to break it by challenging the Grand Fleet. Instead, a distant blockade of cruisers between the Orkneys, Shetlands, and Faroes covered by the Grand Fleet from its new war base at Scapa Flow seemed sufficient to achieve the Royal Navy's main aim—namely, to cut off Germany's sea lines of communication. Many Royal Navy officers were uncomfortable with this change in naval strategy that renounced a decisive Trafalgar-like battle upon the outbreak of war and that accepted, as Churchill put it in September 1914, that the navy's main role would be to provide "the cover and shield" to allow Britain to create an army "strong enough to enable our country to play its full part in the decision of this terrible struggle."[8] German naval officers, for lack of hard knowledge about the operational implications of the new technologies at sea and more complex ideas of sea control and trade protection, also clung to traditional ideas of naval warfare that were no longer feasible.

The German naval leadership only very slowly realized the implications of Britain's new strategy for its own war plans—and was stunned by them. When asked in 1912 what the High Seas Fleet would do "if the Grand Fleet did not come [out to fight]," the chief of the Admiralty Staff, Admiral August von Heeringen, only answered: "Then, our submarines will have to make it [sortie]."[9] Two years later the Imperial Navy still had no idea how to solve this dilemma. In May 1914, during the last prewar maneuvers of the High Seas Fleet, its commander in chief, Admiral Friedrich von Ingenohl, only shrugged his shoulders when Tirpitz asked him the same question.

These reactions are in fact easy to explain: In 1912, in 1913, and once again in spring 1914, the navy had looked for alternatives in maneuvers and war games. The results were disappointing: the blue party representing the High Seas Fleet had always lost against the yellow party, the Royal Navy. Due to the disadvantages of geography, the German navy had no chance of breaking such a blockade or of forcing the Royal Navy to offer battle close to the German coast without risking total disaster. As a result, the High Seas Fleet would and could only be a fleet in being in a naval war with Britain, unless the Royal Navy offered a battle under favorable circumstances—a scenario difficult to plan for and very unlikely to happen.

### TAKEN BY SURPRISE: THE NAVAL WAR IN THE NORTH SEA

Many contemporaries who followed the speeches and writings of naval officers before 1914 and expected a great and decisive battle in the North Sea soon after the outbreak of war were soon deeply disappointed. Instead, the Grand Fleet as well as the High Seas Fleet restricted their actions to watching each other, awaiting the opportunity to strike under favorable circumstances. Due to an overwhelming superiority in modern as well as pre-dreadnought battleships and battle cruisers, the Grand Fleet with its new commander in chief, Admiral Sir John Jellicoe, could afford a wait-and-see attitude.

The High Seas Fleet was in a much more difficult position. Due to the change in British naval strategy, Operations Plan Number 1 ordered a defensive strategy at least for the time being. The goal was "to damage the English fleet through offensive advances against the observation and blockade forces of the German Bay, along with a bold mine offensive taken as far as the British coast, and, if possible, U-boat offensives." This strategy was intended to create the "balance of forces," necessary for a battle "under favorable conditions." Should "an earlier opportunity to attack" arise, then this was to be exploited.[10] Accordingly submarines and smaller vessels were to attack the Grand Fleet and infest the North Sea with mines.

Anything else would have been suicidal. Two weeks after the beginning of hostilities, Ingenohl justified this strategy in a speech to his commanding officers, who were disappointed that nothing had happened so far. Standing under the big guns of his flagship, the battleship *Friedrich der Grosse*, he told them: "This behavior of our enemies suggests that their intention is to remove themselves from all losses that they fear from us and to prompt us to come to their coast with our battleships to fall victim to their mines and U-boats. We must not do this favor for our enemy. They must and will come at last, and then accounts will be balanced. And for this settlement we must be in place with all of our battleships."[11] Ingenohl made clear the lack of any factual basis for his wishful thinking that Britain's Grand Fleet *must* stage an attack under conditions that were favorable to the High Seas Fleet and highly unfavorable to itself.

As a result, for the time being, the High Seas Fleet remained on the defensive in the North Sea, leaving the initiative to the Grand Fleet in the vague hope that a promising opportunity might arise. This "guerrilla war" or, as the Germans called it, *Kleinkriegs* strategy suffered a severe blow only a few weeks after the beginning of hostilities. On 18 August, just a fortnight after Ingenohl's speech, three German small cruisers and a torpedo boat sank after they had been surprised by superior British forces off Heligoland.[12] Due to bad preparations as well as the tides, the High Seas Fleet arrived on the scene too late.

The first encounter between the two fleets had far-reaching consequences: For years to come, the German naval and political leadership would discuss alternatives to the navy's operational plans, a problem that turned out to be closely related to the question of leadership.

When Ingenohl proposed in mid-September to deploy some battle cruisers further out, the emperor himself restricted his freedom of action: In early October Wilhelm II ordered "that the fleet hold back and avoid action that could lead to greater losses." "Favorable opportunities" should, of course, continue to be exploited. Nevertheless, it was expressly stated that "a use of the fleet outside of the German Bight, which the enemy is aiming for, for instance by his movements in the Jutland Strait, falls outside of the favorable opportunities mentioned in the operations order."[13]

Tirpitz believed these instructions would result in "the death of the fleet."[14] After a visit to the main navy base at Wilhelmshaven, he wrote to Ingenohl on 25 October 1914:

> After the war, the English will insist that we absolutely would never have come out of the harbors. If we had been sixty or eighty nautical miles north of Helgoland only once, . . . then we would be able to say that it was just the opposite. We would, in fact, have come out, but the English would not have. One assertion against the other. . . . It is, as I said, in my opinion, less of a question of battle than a question of prestige after the war. . . . The case would be all the more strengthened that the fleet had tried everything that was in its power.[15]

Such an approach was not a strategy but a desperate attempt to justify his life's work—namely, the buildup of a fleet that now seemed useless.

What alternatives did the German navy have? The number of options in the North Sea was indeed very limited. It simply amounted to a hit-and-run strategy against Britain's East Coast that aimed at enticing parts of the Grand Fleet to come out and offer battle under more favorable circumstances than in the open or even the northern parts of the North Sea, where the risks of meeting superior forces were simply too great. In September 1914 the first of these strikes was planned but canceled at the last minute due to German naval intelligence reports suggesting the location of the Grand Fleet made leaving port too dangerous.[16] In the following months German battle cruisers raided Britain's East Coast twice, shelling Whitby, Scarborough, and Hull and elsewhere without, however, achieving any strategic or even tactical successes. Although both fleets came close to each other and eventually exchanged fire, either poor visibility or Admiral Franz Ritter von Hipper's conclusion that running for home was preferable to falling into a trap prevented any bigger encounter. Moreover, the Battle of Dogger Bank in January 1915 clearly demonstrated the risks of this strategy. Unexpectedly, Hipper's battle cruisers, which had attempted to destroy British fishing vessels suspected of supporting the Grand Fleet with reconnaissance information, had run into the Grand Fleet's battle cruisers under Vice Admiral David Beatty. Although some of Beatty's vessels were severely mauled, they all reached their home ports in this first encounter between big ships. Hipper's squadron not only suffered severe damage to some ships but also lost the armored cruiser *Blücher*.

As a result, Commander in Chief of the High Seas Fleet Ingenohl, accused of not having sufficiently supported his battle cruisers, was sacked. Ingenohl was a scapegoat for a strategic dilemma for which he was by no means responsible. Even Vice Admiral Reinhard Scheer, commander in chief of the 3rd Battle Squadron and later Germany's only undisputed naval hero, concluded that Ingenohl had made no mistakes. "We have no motive to offer the English a battle under favorable conditions, they should instead come to us. If some of our own ships that are assigned to our fleet pursue an opposite tactic, then we can very probably count on a failure. . . . Have the political circumstances changed so much," he wrote to the new chief of the Admiralty Staff, Admiral Gustav Bachmann, "that we no longer sense the need for our fleet as a fleet in being? Or are other powers at work that, in order to lift the navy's prestige, would push the navy into a battle at any cost, that is, even at the cost of annihilation?"[17]

Despite the change in command and despite increasing criticism by younger officers of the new commander in chief, Admiral Hugo von Pohl, whom Wilhelm II had granted more freedom of action in late March 1915 than his predecessor, the High Seas Fleet remained on the defensive for over a year. It sortied no further than fifty miles out into the North Sea and carefully avoided coming close to any British ships. Not only Germans were dissatisfied with this development; in Britain, important voices time and again demanded a more active role for the Royal Navy in the North Sea, suggesting the occupation of one of the

Frisian Islands, Heligoland, or the Danish port of Esbjerg.[18] Jellicoe, however, was satisfied with his distant blockade strategy, for it achieved its main aim, interrupting German supply lines into the Atlantic Ocean and keeping the High Seas Fleet at arm's length without risking any losses.

Only in April 1916 did Admiral Reinhard Scheer, who became commander in chief of the High Seas Fleet in January 1916 after his predecessor's sudden death, again order more offensive missions into the North Sea. Scheer hoped to annihilate smaller parts of the Grand Fleet. For morale as well as political considerations—namely, the justification of the navy's existence—a more active role assumed great importance after two years of fighting in which the navy had not proven that it was worth the money spent on it. One of those missions accidentally led to the Battle of Jutland on 31 May 1916.[19]

Whatever German naval officers later said or wrote about this "Glorious 1st of June," as Kaiser Wilhelm II first wanted to call this battle, it was no German victory, although British losses of men and matériel were higher.[20] Losses for Britain and Germany in killed, wounded, or taken prisoner amounted to 6,945 and 3,058, respectively, and lost tonnage 115,025 and 61,180.[21] Strategically, the battle changed nothing. The High Seas Fleet had knocked at the door of its jail but had proven unable to open it, as a popular British caricature rightly soon suggested. Grudgingly, Admiral Scheer frankly admitted defeat in a memorandum to the kaiser in early July:

> Nevertheless there is no doubt that even the most favorable outcome of a naval battle in this war will not force England to peace: The disadvantages of our military geographical position with respect to the island empire, and the great materiel superiority of the enemy will not be able to be balanced out to the extent that we will become master over the blockade that is aimed at us, or over the island empire itself, even if the U-boats are completely available for military purposes. A victorious end to the war in the foreseeable time can only be achieved by wrestling down the English economic life—that is, by deploying the U-boats against English commerce.[22]

Despite acknowledging the inherent difficulties of German naval strategy, Scheer continued to regard a battle, although not against the whole Grand Fleet, as desirable. Subsequently, after the repair of his vessels, which had been severely mauled at Jutland, Scheer twice left Schillig Roads outside Wilhelmshaven, hoping to meet and annihilate parts of the enemy's superior forces. These hopes, however, were not fulfilled. When airships reported during his sortie on 16 August that not only parts but the whole Grand Feet were at sea, he returned to Wilhelmshaven immediately. The risk of running into another dangerous battle was too great. Like the much better-positioned Grand Fleet, the High Seas Fleet then stayed in harbor, only to leave again in April 1918 to make a raid into the northern North Sea against Allied convoys. It paid rather dearly when a British submarine torpedoed one its most modern battle cruisers, *Moltke*; no parts of the Grand Fleet came into sight. Subsequently, the German navy again restricted its role to that of a fleet in being, which protected Germany's coast from invasion and supported the increasingly difficult task of sweeping mines in the German Bight to allow submarines to exit into the North Sea for operations against Britain's merchant fleet.

When the German Empire verged on collapse in October 1918, the newly established naval command under Admiral Scheer, the Seekriegsleitung, again planned an offensive strike against the Grand Fleet. Fully aware that such a strike was a strategically useless and politically unnecessary provocation of the Allies, the Seekriegsleitung nevertheless hoped that a final great battle would demonstrate a willingness to sacrifice lives and ships to preserve the honor of the naval officer corps and thus pave the way for a postwar naval buildup. This was, of course, pure nonsense. Hardly astonishing, in the last days of October, the sailors mutinied on the vessels that were doomed to sink if they left port. Angry about the way they had been treated by their officers during the war, they saw no purpose in sacrificing their lives for a system that had denied them equal rights in politics, let alone the disastrous situation regarding the provision of food and other goods. Starting at Germany's main naval bases at Wilhelmshaven and Kiel, mutinying sailors, who quickly united with soldiers from the army and workers, brought down the existing political and social order.

The other possible theaters of war were at best sideshows, which might have offered even more opportunities had not German naval planners concentrated all their attention on one event: the battle against Great Britain, which, if successful, seemed to offer enormous political, economic, and military gains.

## THE NAVAL WAR IN THE BALTIC

Regarding Russia, due to the overall importance of the North Sea theater of war as well as Russian numerical and material superiority, the German navy also had no option but to stay on the defensive. The Kiel Canal, Germany's internal waterway allowing its fleet to move safely between the Baltic Sea and the German Bight in the North Sea, became operational only after many years of reconstruction made necessary by the increasing size of the newest capital ships. On 30 July 1914 it enabled Germany to reinforce its forces in the Baltic either to meet Russian challenges or to launch offensive strikes. This scenario had prompted the Russian navy to stay on the defensive. Although Russia had begun to rebuild its fleet in 1912, its forces remained too weak for an offensive role even against a smaller German fleet. More importantly, the traumatic experiences of the Russo-Japanese War (1904–5) made the Russian Baltic Fleet leadership cautious about losing the new fleet in a sudden encounter with numerically far superior German units. A German strike against Russia's long coastline and behind its armies, let alone a direct attack of its capital, St. Petersburg, could have had a disastrous impact upon Russia.

Geography, special hydrographic conditions, and climate deeply affected naval operations in the Baltic. Unlike the North Sea, the Baltic was nothing but a large lake with only one narrow entrance in the west. Whereas hydrographic conditions were favorable for the deployment of submarines and the use of mines, long nights and ice made operations very difficult, especially in the eastern parts of the Baltic between October and March. Since no modern means of reconnaissance were available at that time, enemy forces could advance and strike without early detection, if ice allowed any operations at all.

In contrast to the North Sea, where German forces were in an inferior position, the situation in the Baltic was largely the reverse. Although the number of vessels stationed at Kiel and other forward positions like Danzig or Pillau on the southern Baltic coast (eight mostly old light cruisers, eight torpedo boats, and three submarines) was smaller than the Russian Baltic Fleet (four older pre-dreadnoughts, five armored cruisers, four light cruisers, sixty-three torpedo boats, and twelve submarines as well as four modern capital ships that would become operational within less than a year), the German navy could always rely upon the High Seas Fleet for support for either defensive or offensive operations.[23]

This situation caused the German Baltic Fleet to start an offensive upon the outbreak of war. First, to prevent the Grand Fleet from entering the Baltic, Commander in Chief of the German Baltic Fleet Prince Henry, the emperor's younger brother, ordered the mining of its entrance. This measure, however, was only at first glance advantageous for the German navy. It prevented its direct enemy, the Russian Baltic Fleet, as well as, indirectly, the Grand Fleet, from forcing the Danish Straits. But the German naval leadership, by limiting the possibility of a raid of the High Seas Fleet out of the now mined Kattegat into the North Sea, also carelessly renounced a strategic option that would have kept the Grand Fleet in suspense and complicated its defense measures. Second, to discourage the Russian Baltic Fleet from offensive strikes against Germany's long coast, German cruisers and torpedo boats were dispatched into the eastern parts of the Baltic as a show of force. Unfortunately, this deployment turned out to be a disaster with far-reaching consequences. The small cruiser *Magdeburg* ran aground in the Gulf of Finland and had to be given up while the rest of the squadron made a narrow escape. The disaster was not the loss of the cruiser but rather the Russian discovery in the wreckage of the German navy's top-secret signal book, which the Russians soon handed over to the British. This signal book enabled the Grand Fleet to detect the movements of the German fleet at a very early stage and thus to remain "master of the situation" in the North Sea until the end of the war by taking precautionary measures.[24]

Although the Russians refrained from openly attacking their enemy, they were nevertheless quite successful. In autumn 1914 Russian minefields either severely damaged or sank several German warships. For the German Baltic Fleet, the situation became more complicated when, after the end of the winter, it successfully moved east with the victorious German armies. The scouting forces of the Baltic Fleet, established in April 1915 and based on the Russian port of Libau, Latvia, conquered in May, were now better positioned to try to secure the lines of communication in the Baltic, especially the important sea routes to Sweden. This task, however, soon proved more difficult than expected. Russian minelaying supported by British submarines allowed Russia and Britain to launch a successful campaign, sinking alarming numbers of German merchant vessels and warships. The failure of German attempts to force the entrance into Riga Bay in 1915 and the sinking of seven torpedo boats, which ran into Russian minefields entering the Bay of Finland in December 1916, illustrate the Russian mastery of minelaying. Fortunately for Germany, the collapse of the Russian Baltic Fleet after the outbreak of the first Russian revolution in 1917 paved the way for a joint amphibious operation of both the German army and navy to conquer the Baltic islands in October 1917, only weeks before the outbreak of the ensuing Bolshevik Revolution. Although successful, the loss of two modern capital ships to mines was an unnecessarily high price for an operation, which, as some commanding officers rightly assumed, had only been ordered, first, to prove to the army that the navy was capable and willing to strike successfully and, second, to divert attention from the first mutinies, which had seriously affected morale in the summer of 1917. The German naval expedition to Finland saw no combat action. The new government of this former part of the Russian Empire had requested German assistance to support Finnish forces to prevent Bolshevists from invading. The damage to the battleship *Rheinland*, which rammed a rock, was another severe and unnecessary loss in a situation that was already difficult enough for the navy.

## THE KAISERLICHE MARINE IN THE MEDITERRANEAN, ADRIATIC, AND FAR EAST

In the Mediterranean, an important lifeline between Britain and its empire, the situation was more complicated. In 1913 the navies of the Triple Alliance had signed a naval convention aiming at securing "the naval control of the Mediterranean through the swiftest possible defeat of the enemy fleets."[25] Using Messina, Sicily, as base, German forces were to operate against French troop transports after the outbreak of war before uniting with the fleets of their Italian and Austrian allies to fight the Royal Navy. This scenario, however, assumed that Italy would join Germany and Austria-Hungary, which it did not. Rather, Italy remained neutral, thus forcing the German Mediterranean Squadron, consisting of one battle cruiser and one light cruiser, *Goeben* and *Breslau*, respectively, either to reach an Austrian port in the Adriatic or, as they eventually did, hand themselves over to a new ally, the Ottoman Empire. After shelling French positions in Algeria, both ships successfully escaped their British pursuers and found refuge in the Dardanelles.[26] By supporting the Turkish navy after the signing of a German-Turkish alliance treaty in early August 1914, these vessels—as a small fleet in being—contributed enormously to the defense of both the Dardanelles and the Bosphorus against Allied attempts to open a new front to attack the Central Powers in their weak rear, although they played no active role in the fighting in the crucial months for the survival of the Ottoman Empire in 1915. Thus, in the Mediterranean, German submarines were the only platform to menace Allied traffic, a task they fulfilled with great success until the end of the war.

In naval history, cruiser or commerce warfare has always been a strategy implemented by numerically weaker navies to inflict losses upon an overwhelmingly superior enemy. Fast cruisers could pressure a powerful opponent to sue for peace by destroying enemy merchant vessels, thus causing serious problems for trade, industry, and the provision of food or for enemy military operations through the destruction of vessels transporting troops and war matériel from distant parts of the British and French Empires to the main theater in Europe. Cruiser warfare would have not only seriously threatened Britain's and even France's lifelines but also forced the Royal Navy to disperse its ships, possibly reducing the number of British vessels available in 1914 for a decisive battle in the North Sea.

Incredibly, due to the great impact of Mahanian ideas on naval warfare, cruiser warfare played an important role neither in preparing for the war at sea nor in fighting it. The lack of bases and coaling stations had been one reason why Tirpitz had always emphasized the need to build a battle fleet and not a fleet of cruisers waging commerce warfare on the oceans. It is true, on the eve of war Tirpitz apparently toyed with the idea of forming two "flying squadrons" consisting of battle cruisers to wage cruiser warfare in the Atlantic, but he never implemented such a strategy. In his eyes, oceanic warfare, as it was later called by one of his disciples, Grand Admiral Erich Raeder, would have undermined his battle-fleet concept.[27]

Against this background Germany's cruisers, scattered over distant parts of the world, were doomed to be sunk sooner or later. Although the German Admiralty Staff had issued orders in the spring of 1914 to the German East Asiatic Squadron based in Germany's colony in Qingdao recommending an attack on the British forces in East Asia immediately after the war "if circumstances for the Cruiser Squadron [. . .] are particularly favourable,"[28] Admiral Count Maximilian von Spee, the commander of Germany's most powerful squadron overseas, consisting of two armored and four small cruisers, decided to try to reach his home base. En route he defeated an inferior British squadron under Admiral Sir Christopher Cradock off the Chilean coast in November 1914. The British had allowed the German ships to escape Qingdao but struck back by dispatching superior forces to hunt them down.[29] Only a month after the Battle of Coronel off Chile, Spee's squadron was sunk off the Falkland Islands when preparing for an attack on Port Stanley. The remaining German small cruisers like the famous *Emden* (sunk in November 1914), *Dresden*, or *Königsberg* waging commerce warfare in the Indian and Pacific Oceans and off the coast of East Africa were all hunted down by the spring 1915.

Whereas the Royal Navy had no apprehensions of the impact of Germany's cruisers upon Britain's overseas lifelines, the prospect of fast German passenger and merchant vessels converted into auxiliary cruisers had increasingly worried the Admiralty. Due to their great speed and number, these vessels posed a much more serious menace to British trade routes than any German warship. Even these fears proved largely unjustified. Although most of Germany's auxiliary warships were sunk in the first months of the war, they could claim some successes. For example, one of Britain's newest dreadnoughts, *Audacious*, fell victim to a mine laid by the German auxiliary cruiser *Berlin* in the Irish channel in October 1914. After an interlude of almost two years, the lack of success in the main theater of war eventually caused the German naval leadership to resume the war against Britain's trade routes with auxiliary cruisers. Hoping to force the Admiralty to weaken its forces in the North Sea, the German navy again dispatched several converted merchant vessels like the old steamships *Möwe* and *Wolf* or *Seeadler*, a slow sailing ship. Whereas *Seeadler* was soon hunted down and sunk, *Möwe* and *Wolf* successfully waged commerce warfare in the Atlantic, Indian, and Pacific Oceans for almost two years before returning to Kiel in early 1917 and 1918, respectively.[30]

## ATTEMPTS TO BREAK THE DEADLOCK BY SUBMARINE WARFARE AND THE AFTERMATH

The only serious threat to British superiority in the Mediterranean, the North Sea, and the Atlantic was submarines. In late 1914, realizing that a Mahanian blue-water strategy would bring no success, the German naval command at least partly reverted to a completely different strategy: submarine warfare. The submarine had been invented in the mid-nineteenth century. Since the turn of the century, in a slow process of trial and error entailing many accidents and setbacks, all navies had developed this new type of vessel, with Britain having the largest submarine fleet, seventy-two vessels on the eve of war, whereas the German navy had only twenty-eight.

Despite their proven seaworthiness and capabilities in naval warfare before the war, submarines were still not regarded as an important weapon in future wars at sea. Although submarine warfare remained a question of trial and error for all navies throughout the war due to manifold technical problems either of the boat itself or of its armament, the success of the German submarine *U9* was something of a turning point despite many reservations by the adherents of battleships. Under very favorable circumstances, *U9* had sunk three old British armored cruisers within one hour off Dover in September 1914. In 1915 and 1916, however, attempts to introduce submarine warfare on a larger scale and more effectively by sinking Allied ships without warning faced severe opposition from Germany's political leadership. Until 1917 the danger of U.S. entry into the war on the side of the Allies, with all its repercussions on the Allied war effort, outweighed all Admiralty Staff promises of quick and decisive success against Allied shipping. Only in February 1917, when victory on land was still not in sight and when hunger as well as the lack of raw materials threatened political and social stability, did Germany's leadership unanimously decide to stake all on one last card to force Britain onto its knees—and it lost everything. Although German submarines inflicted heavy losses upon Allied shipping in the first months of 1917, the introduction of the convoy system soon mitigated the situation. Moreover, new forms of antisubmarine warfare and a large-scale mining offensive effectively blockading their exit routes proved successful in fighting German submarines, which soon suffered increasing losses totaling 4,474 men and 178 out of 335 vessels in service.

On 21 November 1918, the Day (*Der Tag*) that many British naval officers had longed for and that many German naval officers had hoped to avoid by winning a decisive battle arrived, although in a different form than expected when the war had begun. In a humiliating procedure from the German point of view, the Grand Fleet and Allied vessels, totaling more than 370 ships, met the disarmed High Seas Fleet in the North Sea to escort it into custody at Scapa Flow. Allied success on all fronts in the west, south, and southeast as well as the outbreak of revolutions in Austria-Hungary and Germany had brought the Central Powers and their navies down onto their knees. During this great struggle, both navies had played their part, although differently than anticipated. No Trafalgar-like battle had taken place; instead, different kinds of warfare like the blockade (distant, not close), the commerce war conducted by difficult-to-detect submarines, and the war from the air had become increasingly important. The era of powerful battleships fighting for naval supremacy seemed over.

So what had gone wrong from the German perspective?

A simple answer is impossible. Admiral Ingenohl, commander in chief of the High Seas Fleet until he was sacked after the Battle of Dogger Bank, offered one answer. In January 1918, long after his dismissal, he admitted,

> The entire prewar training of the fleet up to then—our tactics, our maneuvers, and of course our shipbuilding policy all the way

down to the details of ship construction—was based on the idea of a decisive battle within or directly near the German Bight, under the assumption that the English fleet, with its superior strength, would set up a rather narrow blockade of the German Bight of the North Sea in order to block off the access from the sea and at the same time force our fleet into the narrowest defensive position and cause it to engage in battle.[31]

This battle, however, never occurred. Contrary to what was happening in the North Sea and although Tirpitz, Scheer, and Ingenohl himself partly realized the risks of offensive sorties in the North Sea, they never fully grasped that Britain's Grand Fleet did not need to offer another battle at any time during the war. Despite great disappointment about the outcome of the Battle of Jutland, which had been no Trafalgar, the Grand Fleet saw no point in offering battle, which even if it had produced a great victory would not change anything strategically. Neither its commander in chief, Admiral John Jellicoe, nor his successor, Admiral David Beatty, were willing to risk too much for nothing.

But does this mean that the Kaiserliche Marine had achieved nothing during the war? No, it does not. As Werner Rahn rightly argued,

> The High Seas Fleet remained what it had been since the outbreak of war—"a fleet in being"—which had a strategic effect just because of its very existence. Its strong presence tied up the British Grand Fleet and, along with it, the light warships that were needed in the Atlantic for security escort tasks. The fleet provided security for its own coastal area, blockaded the Baltic Sea from relief shipments to Russia, and offered the U-boat war a certain amount of support in the securing of entrance and exit routes. Thus, contrary to popular opinion of historians, who deny that it had any strategic significance, the fleet did have its military value for the German conduct of the war. Still, a sober cost-effectiveness analysis inevitably leads to the conclusion that ultimately it did not accomplish what was expected of it or could have been expected.[32]

## NOTES

1. Memorandum by the State Secretary of the Imperial Navy Office, Rear Admiral Tirpitz, June 1897 [completed July 1897], cited in Matthew Seligman, Frank Nägler, and Michael Epkenhans, eds., *The Naval Route to the Abyss: The Anglo-German Naval Race 1895–1914*, Publications of the Navy Record Society, vol. 161 (London: Ashgate, 2015), no. 4.
2. Rear Admiral Tirpitz, Notes on his Report to the Sovereign on the Amendment to the Navy Law [Novelle], to be given on 28 September 1899, cited in Seligman et al., no. 7.
3. Imperial Navy Office meeting minutes of remarks by Tirpitz, 9 October 1913, cited in Seligman et al., no. 127.
4. Notes for a Report to the Sovereign, concerning the naval relation to England by Admiral von Tirpitz on 24 October 1910, cited in Seligman et al., no. 98.
5. Undated memo by Tirpitz, probably May 1914, cited in Michael Epkenhans, *Die wilhelminische Flottenrüstung 1908–1914: Weltmachtstreben, industrieller Fortschritt, soziale Integration* (München: Oldenbourg, 1991), 391. The best account of Churchill's naval policy is Christopher M. Bell, *Churchill & Seapower* (Oxford: University Press 2013), 15–48.
6. Ivo N. Lambi, *The Navy and German Power Politics, 1862–1914* (London: Allen & Unwin, 1984), 390–415.
7. Christopher M. Buckey, *Genesis of the Grand Fleet: The Admiralty, Germany, and the Home Fleet, 1886–1914* (Annapolis, MD: Naval Institute Press, 2021).
8. Bell, *Churchill & Seapower*, 53; see also 42–48.
9. Kurt Assmann, *Deutsche Seestrategie in zwei Weltkriegen* (Heidelberg: Kurt Vowinckel, 1957), 30.
10. Cited in Gerhard Granier, ed., *Die deutsche Seekriegsleitung im Ersten Weltkrieg*, vol. 1 (Koblenz: Bundesarchiv, 1999–2004), no. 8.
11. Ingenohl's Order of 14 August 1914, quoted in Reinhard Scheer, *Deutschlands Hochseeflotte im Weltkrieg* (Berlin: Ullstein, 1920), 56.
12. Eric W. Osborne, *The Battle of Heligoland Bight* (Bloomington: Indiana University Press 2006), esp. 27–46, 100–120.
13. Pohl to Ingenohl, 6 October 1914, in Granier, *Die deutsche Seekriegsleitung*, vol. 2, no. 164.
14. Hopman to Trotha, 10 October 1914, quoted in Albert Hopman, *Das ereignisreiche Leben eines Wilhelminers: Tagebücher, Aufzeichnung und Briefe 1901–1920* (Munich: Oldenbourg 2004), 459.
15. Tirpitz to Ingenohl, 25 November 1914, cited in Michael Epkenhans, "The Imperial Navy, 1914–1915," in *Jutland: World War I's Greatest Naval Battle*, edited by Michael Epkenhans, Jörg Hillmann, Frank Nägler (Lexington: University Press of Kentucky 2015), 130. Significantly, this letter is missing from Tirpitz's edited document collection.

16. Paul G. Halpern, *A Naval History of World War I* (London: Allen & Unwin 1994), 21–50.
17. Scheer to Bachmann, 24 February 1915, cited in Epkenhans, "The Imperial Navy, 1914–1915," 124–25.
18. Andrew Lambert, "The German North Sea Islands, the Kiel Canal and the Danish Narrows in Royal Navy Thinking and Planning, 1905–1918," in *The Danish Straits and German Naval Power 1905–1918*, edited by Michael Epkenhans and Gerhard P. Gross, 35–62 (Potsdam: Militärgeschichtliches Forschungsamt, 2010).
19. Werner Rahn, "The Battle of Jutland from the German Perspective," in Epkenhans et al., *Jutland*, 143–282; and Andrew Gordon, *The Rules of the Game: Jutland and British Naval Command* (Annapolis, MD: Naval Institute Press, 1997).
20. Emperor's speech in Wilhelmshaven on 5 June 1916, cited in Granier, *Die deutsche Seekriegsleitung*, 2:97–99.
21. Rahn, "The Battle of Jutland," 184.
22. Scheer's report to the emperor, 4 July 1916, cited in Rahn, 206–7.
23. Halpern, *Naval History*, 183–222; and Werner Rahn, "The Naval War in the Baltic, 1914–1918: A German Perspective" in Epkenhans and Gross, *The Danish Straits and German Naval Power*, 75–77.
24. Quotation from a secret service memorandum of the German Navy (1934), in Seligman et al. *Naval Route to the Abyss*, 81.
25. Lambi, *The Navy and German Power Politics*, 408.
26. James Goldrick, "The Battleship Fleet: The Test of War" in *The Oxford Illustrated History of the Royal Navy*, edited by J. R. Hill (Oxford: Oxford University Press, 1995), 299–300.
27. Memo by Admiral Capelle with Tirpitz's remarks, 17 May 1914, cited in Epkenhans, *Die wilhelminische Flottenrüstung*, 399.
28. Lambi, *The Navy and German Power Politics*, 410.
29. Halpern, *Naval History*, 88–100.
30. Richard Guilatt and Peter Hohnen, *The Wolf: How One German Raider Terrorized the Southern Seas during the First World War* (London: Bantam, 2009).
31. Undated, January 1918, memo by Admiral Ingenohl, cited in Epkenhans, "The Imperial Navy, 1914–1915," 121.
32. Rahn, "The Battle of Jutland," 191–92.

CHAPTER 10

# THE ITALIAN FLEET *"IN EFFICIENZA"* (1919-43)

Fabio De Ninno

The Regia Marina (Italian Royal Navy) developed a fleet-in-being approach to naval warfare during the nineteenth century to counter French naval superiority.[1] During the interwar era, this evolved into a doctrine defined as the defensive-offensive or fleet *in efficienza* (efficiency). The first section of this chapter discusses the evolution of this fleet in efficiency in relation to the role of Fascist foreign policy in influencing Italian naval development, strategic decision-making mechanisms, receptivity to technological changes, and the evolution of the Regia Marina's naval doctrine and strategy. The second section analyzes the conflict at sea of 1940–43, demonstrating the failure of the Regia Marina as a fleet in efficiency both in securing its operational objectives and in supporting Benito Mussolini's war aims in the Mediterranean.

**DEVELOPMENT OF THE FLEET-IN-EFFICIENCY CONCEPT (1919-40)**

During a series of conflicts from 1935 to 1943, the development of national naval power was central to the Mussolini regime's goal to control the Suez Canal and Gibraltar, which in turn would secure access to oceanic communications at the expense of the declining French and British empires.[2] However, Mussolini failed to coordinate domestic and foreign policy with military planning. Interservice rivalries undermined military coordination. The armed forces focused not on developing the long-term force structure necessary to secure the Fascist foreign policy goals but on the intermediate operational threat: France (1922–34), Britain (1935–36), France and Britain (1936–40), and Britain (1940–43). Therefore, during the second half of the 1930s, strategic goals and operational planning diverged, with navy planners fully absorbed in the latter.

Before 1935, Italian military preparations focused on a French–Yugoslav coalition.[3] France was the Regia Marina's traditional enemy. After World War I the Marine Nationale (the French Navy) wanted to build a fleet superior to those of Germany and Italy combined. Instead, the Washington Naval Conference (1922) imposed naval parity in capital ships with Italy.[4] Dreadnoughts were the backbone of the Italian and French navies (six versus five in 1922), but the efficiency of these aging warships was limited. Both powers could not build new battleships due to financial restrictions and the Washington "naval holiday." Therefore, France built a large submarine force (ninety-six units in 1934) that could attack Italy's vulnerable Mediterranean Sea communications. Both powers competed primarily in their light forces, which proved pivotal during World War I in the Mediterranean. Indeed, wartime light-force construction made the Regia Marina numerically superior to the French navy in this component of the fleet. Therefore, the French perceived Italy's numerical superiority in cruisers, destroyers, and torpedo boats as a threat despite their average smaller dimensions. This, combined with the peninsula's geographic position, threatened French maritime communications. So the French navy opposed the extension of naval parity to noncapital warships at the conferences of Geneva (1927) and London (1930) and in 1924 passed a Statut Naval to outbuild the Regia Marina in light units, with limited success.[5]

For the Regia Marina, World War I changed the confrontation. Italy had lost about 57 percent of its merchant fleet, suffered substantial food and raw material shortages from German submarine warfare, and believed the numerically superior French fleet threatened national survival.[6] Postwar, Italian admirals intended to profit from the disappearance of the Austro-Hungarian navy by concentrating ships in the central and eastern Mediterranean to secure communications with Suez and the Dardanelles, considering the western Mediterranean inaccessible in wartime.[7]

Overall Italian naval inferiority to France remained an insurmountable problem for these plans until the Washington Naval Treaty and the rise of Mussolini (1922).[8] Capital ship construction was blocked, allowing a focus on light forces, and Mussolini made naval parity with France

**TABLE 10.1.** ITALIAN ARMED FORCES EXPENDITURES, 1925–34

|  | 1925–26 £ (m) | 1926–27 £ (m) | 1927–28 £ (m) | 1928–29 £ (m) | 1929–30 £ (m) | 1930–31 £ (m) | 1931–32 £ (m) | 1932–33 £ (m) | 1933–34 £ (m) |
|---|---|---|---|---|---|---|---|---|---|
| Army | 2,795 | 3,112 | 2,705 | 2,856 | 2,943 | 3,230 | 3,067 | 3,068 | 2,700 |
| Navy | 1,080 | 1,320 | 1,210 | 1,262 | 1,298 | 1,582 | 1,626 | 1,614 | 1,440 |
| Air Force | 558 | 754 | 663 | 737 | 744 | 787 | 775 | 770 | 720 |
| Total | 4,433 | 5,186 | 4,578 | 4,855 | 4,985 | 5,599 | 5,468 | 5,452 | 4,860 |
| Total state expenditures | 23,000 | 24,600 | 29,650 | 20,480 | 20,860 | 25,580 | 25,230 | 22,850 | 28,140 |

Source: Lucio Ceva, *Storia delle forze armate in Italia* (Turin: Utet, 1999), 223.

**TABLE 10.2.** COMPOSITION OF THE FRENCH AND ITALIAN FLEETS, 1934

|  | France | | Italy | |
|---|---|---|---|---|
|  | Number | Tonnage | Number | Tonnage |
| Battleships | 9* | 185,925 | 4 | 87,917 |
| Carriers and aircraft tenders | 1 | 22,146 | 1 | 4,690 |
| Cruisers | 18 | 157,737 | 24 | 158,823 |
| Destroyers and torpedo boats | 70 | 106,723 | 99 | 91,477 |
| Submarines | 96 | 82,511 | 69 | 46,457 |
| Total | 194 | 555,042 | 197 | 389,364 |

\* 4 semi-dreadnoughts

Source: League of Nations, *Armaments Yearbook, 1935* (Geneva: League of Nations, 1935), 387, 540.

a cornerstone of his foreign policy.[9] Naval expenditures grew, and the fleet expanded over the next decade, despite their perennial inferiority to army expenditures, the creation of the Regia Aeronautica (Italian Air Force, 1923), and the consequent increased budgetary competition and interservice rivalry (see table 10.1).[10] By 1934 budget expansion and French difficulties allowed Italy to maintain a relative numerical superiority in light surface forces and reduce its tonnage disadvantage (see table 10.2).

Operational planning focused on defending Mediterranean sea lanes due to the influence of Romeo Bernotti, Italy's leading naval thinker and vice-chief of Naval Staff from 1927 to 1929.[11] His thinking focused on the defense of national seaborne communications and set the framework of the 1929 naval plans, which remained influential until 1934. Italian naval strategy assumed that geography and the superiority of the Franco-Yugoslav coalition would put the Regia Marina on the defensive, precluding significant offensive operations.[12] So the fleet must guarantee Italy's western maritime frontiers from incursion and landings while protecting trade via the Suez Canal and the Dardanelles. (The situation resembled the fleet-in-being strategy of the 1881–1914 period, described in chapter 8.) France could have sought major naval battles, given its superiority, while Italy had to avoid them: French neutralization of Italy's fleet would have opened the road to invade Sicily. A combination of secondary operations in the western Mediterranean harassing enemy communications and attacks on enemy traffic in the Indian Ocean would have diverted enemy forces from the main theater.[13] Interservice frictions influenced these plans, inhibiting attacks against the enemy traffic and bases west of Sardinia.[14]

Italy's defensive approach started changing in the 1930s, when battleships returned to the core of naval policy, due to both the end of the Washington naval holiday and a Fascist foreign policy that, at the turn of 1932–1934, moved to a more proactive stance. Indeed, increasing international disorder and especially the rise of Nazism in Germany allowed Mussolini to prepare for a total war against Ethiopia.[15] During this period France built the battleship *Dunkerque* (1932) in response to the German *Deutschland*-class pocket battleships. Italy followed with the reconstruction of the two *Conte di Cavour*–class battleships (1933) and financed the first two *Littorio*-class battleships (1934), Italy's largest capital ships, to regain offensive capacities at the operational level.[16]

The comeback of battleships reflected changes in Italy's naval doctrine related to the foreign policy turn. Giuseppe Fioravanzo, the most influential naval thinker of the 1930s, argued that a numerically superior enemy, contrary to the defensive-minded Royal Navy of 1914–18, would always search for an offensive and war-winning battle. To achieve success in face of a possible enemy naval offensive, the Italian fleet should revise the operational methods of Germany's fleet-in-being strategy in the North Sea after the Battle of Jutland[17]—specifically, the submarine barrages, mines, and early naval airpower used to harass the Grand Fleet and the cruisers and destroyer groups supported by fast battleships.[18] Fioravanzo blamed the German fleet for its excessive defensiveness but also recognized its pioneering attrition methods that could help the weaker fleet level the field for a victorious encounter, particularly in narrow seas like the Mediterranean and North Seas. Success required a defensive-offensive attitude. The weaker fleet had to harass the more potent enemy force entering a narrow maritime space with naval air power, torpedo units, submarines, and mines before a devastating strike by the main battleship force. Raids against enemy communications and bases could also distract enemy forces from the main theater of war. This more aggressive approach, according to Fioravanzo, allowed a shift from the fleet in being to a fleet that could remain "in efficiency": a fleet always ready to transition from its defensive posture to an offensive-counteroffensive one.[19] The fleet in efficiency or defensive-offensive became the cornerstone of Italian operational doctrine in World War II.[20]

The new doctrine required offensive capacities that the Regia Marina lacked, as exposed by the crisis of 1935–36 over Mussolini's invasion of Ethiopia and the League of Nations' retaliatory sanctions. The Italian and British navies mobilized in the Mediterranean. Britain's Mediterranean Fleet abandoned Malta due to the threat of Italian air attacks.[21] The naval balance in capital ships overwhelmingly favored the Royal Navy (see table 10.3). In May 1935, Plan B, a worst-case

**TABLE 10.3.** RELATIVE STRENGTH OF THE REGIA MARINA AND ROYAL NAVY, SEPTEMBER 1935

|  | Mediterranean | | Red Sea | |
| --- | --- | --- | --- | --- |
|  | Royal Navy | Regia Marina | Royal Navy | Regia Marina |
| Battleships | 5 | 2 |  |  |
| Battle cruisers | 2 | 0 |  |  |
| Carriers | 2 | 0 |  |  |
| 8-inch Cruisers | 5 | 7 | 1 | 0 |
| 6-inch Light cruisers | 10 | 10 | 2 | 2 |
| Flotilla leaders | 0 | 18 | 0 | 2 |
| Destroyers and torpedo boats | 54 | 65 | 5 | 3 |
| Submarines | 11 | 62 | 0 | 4 |
| Sloops | 0 | 0 | 5 | 2 |

*Source*: Arthur Marder, "The Royal Navy and the Ethiopian Crisis of 1935–36," *American Historical Review* 75, no. 5 (1970): 1338. Reproduced with permission of the American Historical Association.

contingency forcing a return to a fleet-in-being posture, would have waged "guerrilla warfare" at sea by harassing the superior enemy navy with submarines and air power but with no chance of a major victory.[22]

Because of the crisis, Admiral Domenico Cavagnari, undersecretary of the Navy since 1933 and chief of Naval Staff since 1934, scrambled for funds to expand the fleet.[23] By January 1936 the Naval Staff prepared a study for a six-year naval program (1936–42) to build an "escape fleet" to break out of the Mediterranean prison in case of war against France or Britain or to secure predominance between Gibraltar and Suez in case of a conflict with both. The plan envisaged a "maximum" fleet of nine battleships and three aircraft carriers or a minimum of six and one.[24] Critical voices like Bernotti and Admiral Gino Ducci, commander in chief of the main fleet, also asked for greater offensive and projection capabilities. Mussolini and Cavagnari, however, scrapped the proposal to build aircraft carriers in favor of battleships and submarines.[25] Assuming that Germany would reduce pressure in the Mediterranean, the Regia Marina secured resources for new battleships, improved naval bases, and planned to control the central Mediterranean.[26] By November 1936 a new main war plan (Alfa Uno) envisaged Anglo-French bases encircling Italy, the cut-off of all Italian oceanic trade, and possible limited Italian oceanic action from its Red Sea bases. Consequently, the Regia Marina would conduct defensive operations in the central Mediterranean with "active aggressivity," engaging the enemy's main forces if "there is some probability of success." The war aim was seizing the Suez, but the plan assumed a land invasion from Libya while maintaining a defensive posture in the western Mediterranean and a counteroffensive in the central Mediterranean to secure communications with Libya and the Dodecanese.[27] As one historian recorded, trying to seize a pivotal maritime choke point via a land invasion was an "unusual" strategic design for an admiral.[28] The navy leadership's defensive-offensive approach abdicated grand strategic designs to focus on a fleet in efficiency as an operational approach.

Operational planning for the fleet in efficiency depended on naval attrition and closing the Sicilian Strait, demonstrating the centrality of narrow seas for this strategy. A study completed by June 1938 examined the use of fixed minefields and long-range artillery from the Sicilian Strait island of Pantelleria and such mobile elements as submarine barrages, airpower, and torpedo-boat squadrons during night hours to block enemy passage between the two extremes of the Mediterranean and avoid the merging of British and French battle squadrons or at least to maximize damage before intercepting the enemy.[29] Italy's fleet in efficiency aimed to control the area between Cape Spartivento (Sardinia) and Cape Matapan (Greece), in a narrow maritime space likely to be contested.

These plans depended on a network of bases mainly covering the central Mediterranean's northern shore. The primary base was Taranto, with facilities expanded beginning in 1937. The other first-class base was the Ligurian port of La Spezia, modernized during 1930–34 when planning focused on France but far from the main theater of operations. A network of secondary bases included Naples, La Maddalena, Venice, Brindisi, Pola (Italian Dalmatia), Leros (Aegean Sea), Tobruk (Libya), and Massawa (Eritrea). Third-class bases, capable of accommodating light forces with limited repair facilities and no dry docks, included Cagliari (Sardinia) and, in Sicily, Messina, Augusta, and Trapani. Civilian shipyards concentrated around Genoa, Trieste, and Naples could also make major repairs.[30] The Italian fleet could quickly move within the "internal lines" along the Italian coasts and redeploy for contingent operations or project into the Sicilian Strait under the cover of land-based airpower.

Cavagnari established a centralized naval high command in Rome (later called the Supermarina) to coordinate all available forces.[31] Naval squadron commanders lost the authority to study operations autonomously. Naval operations fell under the strict supervision of the naval high command. Local commanders could respond autonomously to enemy actions only with minor units. Such rigid command and control deprived commanders at sea of the initiative to search for tactical success.[32]

Between 1936 and 1940 fleet expansion changed to a fleet-in-efficiency approach, but the navy remained third place in the interservice budget distribution (see table 10.4). However, it should be considered that much of the army and air force budgets were devoted to fighting the Fascist wars in Ethiopia (23.45 billion lire, with 2.52 for the navy) and Spain (8.5 billion, with just 150 million for the navy).[33] Inflation, scarcity of raw materials, and the worldwide arms race had a more significant impact on Italian naval programs.[34] Yet the fleet expanded steadily between 1935 and 1940. The tonnage ratio between the French and Italian fleets diminished from 1.62:1 in 1931 to 1.16:1 in 1940. By 1937 the navy began modernizing two *Duilio* and constructing two more

TABLE 10.4. ITALIAN MILITARY EXPENDITURES, 1934-40

| | | 1934 £ (m)* | 1935 £ (m) | 1936 £ (m) | 1937 £ (m) | 1938 £ (m) | 1939 £ (m) | 1940 £ (m) |
|---|---|---|---|---|---|---|---|---|
| Army | Ordinary | 2,355 | 2,539 | 2,368 | 2,513 | 2,995 | 3,769 | 3,954 |
| | Extraordinary | 564 | 801 | 4,852 | 4,711 | 3,315 | 3,614 | 11,597 |
| | Total | 2,919 | 3,340 | 7,220 | 7,224 | 6,310 | 7,383 | 15,551 |
| Navy | Ordinary | 1,088 | 1,241 | 1,554 | 1,705 | 2,037 | 2,131 | 2,207 |
| | Extraordinary | 288 | 256 | 1,298 | 1,566 | 793 | 894 | 1,248 |
| | Total | 1,376 | 1,497 | 2,852 | 3,271 | 2,830 | 3,025 | 3,455 |
| Air Force | Ordinary | 669 | 619 | 937 | 952 | 1,146 | 1,546 | 2,171 |
| | Extraordinary | 84 | 122 | 1,525 | 2,058 | 2,514 | 2,081 | 2,974 |
| | Total | 753 | 741 | 2,462 | 3,010 | 3,660 | 3,627 | 5,145 |
| Colonies | Total | 448 | 859 | 4,141 | 5,944 | 6,327 | 4,284 | 5,650 |
| Grand total | | 5,496 | 6,437 | 16,675 | 19,449 | 19,127 | 18,319 | 29,801 |

* All figures at current and constant 1938 prices.

*Source*: Adapted from Vera Zamagni, "Italy: How to Lose the War and Win the Peace," in *The Economics of World War II*, edited by Mark Harrison (Cambridge: Cambridge University Press, 1998), 201–2. Reproduced with permission of the licensor through PLSclear.

TABLE 10.5. ITALIAN FLEET IN THE MEDITERRANEAN, JUNE 1940

| | Italy | France | United Kingdom |
|---|---|---|---|
| Carriers | 0 | 0 | 1 |
| Battleships and battle cruisers | 4 (+2)* | 5 | 5 |
| Cruisers | 22 | 14 | 9 |
| Destroyers | 52 | 38 | 31 |
| Torpedo boats | 69 | 6 | 0 |
| Submarines | 105 | 40 | 12 |
| Escorts | 1 | 21 | 5 |
| Total | 253 | 124 | 63 |

* Two battleships were under reconstruction and ready between the summer and autumn of 1940.

*Sources*: Supermarina, ufficio statistica operativa, situazione naviglio dello stato, Maristat-Statistiche generali, busta 3, AUSMM; Duncan Redford, *A History of the Royal Navy: World War II* (London: I. B. Tauris, 2014), 136; and Philippe Masson, *La marine française et la guerre: 1939–1945* (Paris: Tallandier, 1991), 429–37.

*Littorio* battleships. The submarine arm rapidly expanded (the 1936–38 programs alone financed thirty-eight new boats), bringing the number of active units to over one hundred by 1939. Industrial problems delayed major warship construction and costs skyrocketed.[35] Nevertheless, the fleet in 1940 looked impressive compared to the French and British naval forces in the Mediterranean (see table 10.5).

In reality, Mussolini and Cavagnari's renunciation of aircraft carriers precluded operations outside the range of land-based airpower. Attrition in the central Mediterranean depended on air power, but interservice cooperation with the Regia Aeronautica, which controlled all air units, was poor. In 1940 no torpedo bombers were available, and planes for strategic reconnaissance were insufficient.[36] Like the fleet, the submarine arm, also critical for attrition, faced shortages of officers and qualified personnel. Defects in its tactics became manifest during the illegal commerce raiding campaign during the Spanish Civil War.[37] Italian naval technology was falling behind due to inadequate research and development, especially in electronics (radar) and electroacoustics (sonar), and a naval leadership unenthusiastic about cutting-edge but uncertain technologies.[38] Cooperation with the German ally finally improved little during 1936–40, with both navies jealous of their operational autonomy.[39]

## FROM A FLEET IN EFFICIENCY BACK TO A FLEET IN BEING: THE NAVAL WAR OF 1940–43

In March 1940, as war with France and Britain approached, Mussolini ordered a strictly defensive posture for the army and air force and a general offensive for the navy. In April Cavagnari reassessed Mussolini's directives. If the Anglo-French fleets stayed in the western and eastern basins of the Mediterranean, even with submarines, possible offensive actions were limited. If they launched an offensive, a major naval battle could ensue, with heavy losses on both sides that the enemy could more quickly replace.[40]

Consequently, the naval directives issued for war on 29 May 1940 called for a strictly defensive approach, ordering the fleet to maintain a defensive posture in the western and eastern Mediterranean while assuming an offensive-counteroffensive in the center, where it should blockade the Sicilian Strait to impede the merger of French and British forces; attack enemy sea lanes with submarines, special forces, and other light forces; avoid superior forces while attacking inferior ones; and defend the sea lanes to Libya and Albania.[41] With the fall of France and the consequent Italo-French armistice (24 June 1940) and in expectation of Britain's collapse, Italy planned an offensive into Egypt from Libya.[42]

The armistice with France left Italy facing a much more favorable force ratio against Britain's Mediterranean Fleet based at Alexandria, with an estimated force of four battleships and one carrier, and Force H based at Gibraltar, with two battleships and one carrier. The first significant but indecisive naval encounter occurred in the Battle of Calabria on 9 July 1940 under conditions regarded before the war as ideal for a major victory.[43] Both parties were escorting convoys, the British to Malta and the Italians to Benghazi, and engaged just thirty miles from the Italian coasts in striking range of Italian land-based air power. Italian submarines' interception of the Mediterranean Fleet near Crete before the battle proved ineffective. The morning of the battle Italian reconnaissance suffered a near blackout. Italians perceived their position to be inferior, having only two battleships against the enemy's three plus one carrier. Admiral Inigo Campioni, the Italian commander, broke contact after one of his two battleships was hit. The Regia Aeronautica did not significantly damage the Mediterranean Fleet but instead inadvertently attacked Campioni's forces. The German naval high command, privy to information provided by Italy, saw a missed opportunity to achieve a major success with torpedo units during the nights before and after the battle, and the liaison officer in Rome, Admiral Eberhard Weichold, spoke of a missed crucial hour for the Regia Marina.[44]

Due to faulty intelligence, the Supermarina concluded that an enemy warship and cruiser were hit, and at least seven destroyers were damaged.[45] Therefore, it proclaimed the operation successful, and Mussolini issued a new series of strategic directives for a fleet-on-fleet battle, given the imminent availability of two more *Littorio*s and the Regia Aeronautica's numerical superiority in the Mediterranean. On 14 July 1940 Cavagnari ordered engagement with the enemy battleships "as soon as possible" in the proximity of Italy's bases.[46] The supposed success at Punta Stilo apparently validated the Supermarina's prudent use of the fleet-in-efficiency doctrine.

In reality, the Regia Marina's attrition arms (air power and submarines) were ineffective, as noticed during the action off Calabria by Admiral Andrew Cunningham.[47] In the subsequent months, British antisubmarine technology and offensive escort groups, conducting aggressive patrols in advance of battleships, forced Italian boats to leave their position, forfeiting attack opportunities. Already by early July 1940 this, in combination with the lack of enemy merchant traffic, deprived Italian submariners of targets.[48] Italian air power fared no better, forcing the Supermarina to admit that "it will be dangerous to think that our offensive actions could impede the enemy from passing through the [Sicilian] channel with heavy losses." To secure traffic with Libya required intensified air attacks against Malta and Alexandria and German deployment of at least eighty Ju-87 dive bombers between Sardinia and Cyrenaica (Libya) to compensate for the Regia Aeronautica's ineffective high-altitude bombing attacks.[49]

Ensuing Italian attempts to intercept enemy forces crossing the central Mediterranean were ineffective, as proven during Operation Hats (30 August–5 September), targeting the first significant convoy to resupply Malta and reinforce the Mediterranean Fleet, which received the carrier *Illustrious* that later raided Taranto. Despite Admiral Campioni's five battleships, including the brand-new *Littorio* and *Vittorio Veneto*, poor reconnaissance, bad weather, and the Supermarina orders not to operate too far from Italian bases prevented engagement in favorable conditions.[50] His failure to engage before the arrival of British reinforcements from Gibraltar meant the Mediterranean Fleet now had five battleships to hinder Italy's advance on Suez.[51]

In July and August, the Supermarina refused to project its battle fleet north of the Egyptian coast to support Italy's invasion of Egypt (begun on 9 September). In late September it reiterated the impossibility of engaging the enemy outside the central Mediterranean and redefined the fleet's main task as securing communications between Italy and Libya.[52] The commander of the 2nd Naval Squadron, Admiral Angelo Iachino, protested to Cavagnari about the lack of offensive operations. According to Iachino, the forces at Alexandria always conducted movements with a maximum of four battleships. Although its six battleships and the availability of the two *Littorios* made the Italian battle fleet superior in number and firepower, the search for ideal conditions precluded possible successes and depressed morale.[53]

Cavagnari rebuffed Iachino's accusations; the Naval Staff considered Italian attritional instruments inadequate to weaken the enemy before any major battle. For example, after the first S.79 torpedo bomber squadron's activation in August, by mid-October the air force had exhausted its torpedo supply and was fighting with the navy for detonators to activate more weapons. Meanwhile, available aircraft for strategic maritime surveillance dropped from an average of fourteen in July to seven in September. Finally, to reduce losses, the Air Staff ordered SM.79 bombers not to attack enemy naval formations in the presence of fighters.[54] The submarine arm also continued to prove inadequate. According to the Supermarina's analysis, between 21 September and 28 October 1940, three units were lost in the eastern Mediterranean without "tangible advantages."[55] Cunningham correctly deduced that prewar planning had exaggerated the Italian air and submarine threats.[56]

Operational rigidity could not achieve strategic results. The fleet's ability to influence operations in the ill-fated invasion of Greece (28 October 1940) proved secondary, especially after the renunciation of an amphibious assault on Corfu. Nor could the Italian fleet's predominance in the central Mediterranean stop the reinforcement of Malta or Operation Compass, targeting Italian forces in North Africa.[57] Finally, Italy's proven difficulty in interdicting enemy movements in the central Mediterranean allowed the carrier-borne strike against the naval base of Taranto. Indeed, the Regia Marina intercepted only three of the Mediterranean Fleet's sixteen sweeps in the central Mediterranean, revealing the feasibility of safely approaching within striking distance of Taranto.[58]

Operation Judgement (11–12 November 1940), Britain's attack against Taranto, was a turning point for the Italian operational approach to the naval war in the Mediterranean. The attack severely damaged half of Italy's battleships: the *Cavour* remained under repair until the Italian armistice, the *Littorio* returned in service in four months, and the

*Duilio* after seven. The ensuing Battle of Cape Teulada, Sardinia (27–28 November 1940), ending in a draw against Britain's Force H, showed that the Italian fleet had not lost combativeness.[59] Nevertheless, Taranto profoundly affected Italy's fleet-in-efficiency concept. The Supermarina's strategic evaluation in December 1940 admitted that "the English have gained, without difficulty, the prevalence of forces in both basins of the Mediterranean. . . . [The] enemy has the most unchallenged freedom of movement" but, should both the new German air unit in Sicily and the Italian fleet erode the enemy force, "the possibility to engage [the enemy] in favorable conditions could emerge."[60]

Taranto resulted from the Supermarina's defensive application of Italy's fleet-in-efficiency doctrine without effective attritional weapons. Because the fleet in efficiency was falling apart, in December 1940 Cavagnari was sacked and replaced by Admiral Arturo Riccardi. This failure occurred within the wider collapse of Italy's parallel war between November 1940 and January 1941, which forced Mussolini to enter a subordinate strategic partnership marked by the arrival of German air and land forces (immediately) and submarines (from September 1941) in the Mediterranean.[61] Italy's entire operational scheme and, consequently, its naval strategy became dependent on German assistance.

The battle fleet was reorganized around a single squadron under the command of Iachino, whose memoirs harshly criticized the Supermarina's defensive-minded approach.[62] In March 1941, with the looming Axis invasion of Yugoslavia and the German intervention in Greece, the Kriegsmarine (the German navy) asked the Regia Marina to prepare an operation targeting British traffic in the Aegean Sea. The area was outside the range of previous Italian large-scale operations but promised a much-needed offensive against enemy naval forces. The Regia Marina could count on German air support, proven effective during Operation Excess (10–11 January 1941) by heavily damaging the carrier *Illustrious*. Instead the operation in Greek waters led to the catastrophic defeat of Gaudo-Matapan (26–29 March 1941). Italy lost three heavy cruisers and two destroyers, and the battleship *Vittorio Veneto* was torpedoed. Superior British intelligence, the use of radar, and Iachino's hazardous conduct caused the defeat. Afterward the Italian fleet retrenched in the central Mediterranean with a stricter fleet-in-being strategy.[63]

Thereafter until the fall of Tunisia (May 1943), the central Mediterranean naval war concerned attrition around the sea lanes to resupply Libya. The Supermarina assumed a defensive strategic outlook: It considered Britain to be on the offensive to disrupt the Axis communications; it refused to conduct large-scale operations in the eastern Mediterranean; and it used the battle fleet as an indirect instrument for traffic protection. During the summer of 1941 the Kriegsmarine pressed for an offensive with light forces in the eastern Mediterranean. The Supermarina refused because of commitments in the central Mediterranean and the looming fuel shortage.[64]

The strictly defensive posture left the initiative to Britain. The outcome revolved around the use of light forces, naval air power, and submarine and antisubmarine warfare. During 1941–42 Malta's aeronaval forces caused 63.7 percent of all Axis shipping losses in the central Mediterranean. Meanwhile, 42.1 percent of all tonnage lost by the Axis on the routes to North Africa was related to intelligence provided by Ultra, granting Britain an essential advantage by late 1941.[65]

The Axis shipping losses to Libya jumped from 30 percent in October to 80 percent in November 1941. According to Riccardi, Britain had acquired aeronaval superiority in the central Mediterranean without deploying a single battleship or aircraft carrier there. The only major surface force was the small Force K (two cruises and two destroyers).[66] Between December 1941 and March 1942, the Alexandria raid and the Second Battle of Sirte gave the Italian fleet surface control of the central Mediterranean until the arrival of Anglo-American forces in November 1942.[67] However, strategically, the key factor for the naval war was not the Regia Marina's surface control but Axis air power's suppression of Malta.[68] During the spring and summer of 1942, the aeronaval war in the Mediterranean focused on the resupply and possible invasion of Malta. The convoy battles of Operation Harpoon (June 1942) and Operation Pedestal (August 1942) showed again that the keys to naval warfare in such narrow seas were land-based aircraft, submarines, small surface combatants, mines, and an advantageous geographic position.[69]

Despite five available battleships, as soon as the Luftwaffe (the German air force) shifted its focus from Malta to supporting General Erwin Rommel's advance on El Alamein (in the spring and summer of 1942), the Axis surface forces could not suppress the air and submarine threat to their convoys. By October 1942 shipping shortages were already crippling Italian logistics.[70]

The strictly defensive fleet-in-being strategy launched after March 1941 proved that the numerical superiority in large surface units could not prevent the attrition and defeat of the Regia Marina while defending the communications with North Africa. An excessively defensive mindset and fuel shortages limited battle fleet operations. During Operation Pedestal, despite highly favorable conditions and massive Allied losses, Italian surface forces could not secure a major operational success by finishing off the crippled British convoy resupplying Malta.[71]

After the landings in Sicily unopposed by Italian main forces (July 1943), Allied naval leaders' perception of the Regia Marina as a threat disappeared.[72] By the summer of 1943, despite the willingness of the Italian admirals to launch the fleet in a last suicidal incursion in the southern Tyrrhenian Sea, the strategic value of the Regia Marina had changed from its potential actions to its potential as a bargaining chip in the ongoing Italian armistice negotiations.[73] Its relatively orderly surrender on 9 September 1943 ended its role as a fleet in being.

In conclusion, between 1919 and 1943, at the tactical and operational levels, the evolution of the Italian fleet in being shows that compensating for numerical inferiority required effective weapons for naval attrition. The centrality of resource-absorbing battleships in the Italian naval thinking in the late 1930s, interservice rivalry, and the limited Italian technological-industrial base precluded the acquisition of these weapons. The Regia Marina prioritized winning a major battle against a superior enemy, which distorted its force structure by focusing on battleships' strategic role and protection. Instead of imposing attrition, Italy suffered attrition in the face of more flexible enemies. In 1940 expensive Italian battleships had to be protected at all costs, transforming them into strategic assets with limited operational and tactical utility. This rigid force structure impeded adapting to the convoy war. While Italian communications were never completely cut, British sea denial in the central Mediterranean influenced the war in North Africa at key moments, such as early in the Battle of El Alamein.[74]

**TABLE 10.6. ALLIED LOSSES OF WARSHIPS AND MERCHANT SHIPS UP TO 8 SEPTEMBER 1943**

|  | Regia Marina | | Regia Aeronautica | | Kriegsmarine | | Luftwaffe | |
| --- | --- | --- | --- | --- | --- | --- | --- | --- |
|  | No. | Tons | No. | Tons | No. | Tons | No. | Tons |
| Warships | 58 | 99,606 | 29 | 30,692 | 70 | 160,027 | 133 | 182,641 |
| Merchant ships | 41 | 167,816 | 27 | 116,465 | 98 | 342,456 | 196 | 775,705 |

*Source*: Alberto Santoni and Francesco Mattesini, *La partecipazione tedesca alla guerra aeronavale nel Mediterraneo (1940–1945)* (Rome: Bizzarri, 1980), table A, B.

The Italian operational scheme could have worked, as shown by the massive casualties inflicted on the British convoys and their escorts during the spring–summer of 1942, but this depended on German submarines and air units, which overwhelmingly caused Allied naval losses in the Mediterranean (see table 10.6). However, even if the Italian operational theory had worked without German help, it did not serve the foreign policy needs of the Fascist regime to expand and defend its Mediterranean empire.

The characteristics of a fleet in being and the proper balance between a counteroffensive attitude and mere survival are subject to debate. However, scholars agree that it remains a defensive strategy.[75] In the Italian case, geography lessened the defensive utility of the fleet in being. As Milan Vego explains, a central position in narrow seas, like the Italian peninsula in 1940–43, offers potentially great defensive strength, but the occupation by the enemy of an opposing shore creates a flanking position, allowing it to launch offensive operations despite its defensive posture (as Britain did in 1940–42).[76] Italy's uncoordinated civil-military strategy-making process and the military's focus on operational matters produced armed forces incapable of breaking out from the central Mediterranean toward Suez or Gibraltar. Consequently, the Regia Marina's operational approach could not effectively serve the foreign policy objective of securing access to the oceans. This mismatch between strategic goals and operational possibilities arose not only from Mussolini's ignorance of military strategy and force structure building but also from the naval leadership's refusal to confront his views, demonstrating the impact of the dictatorship on selecting military leaders. In contrast, the preceding generation of Italian admirals, particularly the chief of Naval Staff and later minister of the navy, Grand Admiral Paolo Thaon di Revel, had pressed the government in 1913 to change its foreign policy or match its naval policy with its foreign policy that was on a collision course with Britain. His pressure proved pivotal in Italy's decision to remain neutral in 1914.[77]

From 1919 to 1940 Italy moved from a deterrent fleet-in-being strategy to an attrition fleet-in-efficiency strategy, which proved incapable of inflicting the necessary attrition for Italy to dominate its surrounding seas. Defeat at Taranto in 1940 then forced a return to a fleet in being. The history of Italy's fleet in efficiency demonstrates that an aggressive maritime foreign policy requires a fleet capable of projecting its power toward its targets and destroying the enemy with offensive actions there. However, the necessary fleet was neither a fleet in being nor a fleet in efficiency but the superior fleet that Fascist Italy was unable to build.

## NOTES

1. Brian R. Sullivan, "A Fleet in Being," *International History Review* 10, no. 1 (1988): 106–24.
2. G. Bruce Strang, *On the Fiery March: Mussolini Prepares for War* (Westport CT: Praeger, 2003), 9, 20, 32, 84; and Robert Mallet, *Mussolini and the Origins of Second World War, 1933–1940* (London: Palgrave Macmillan, 2003), 5, 9, 14.
3. Fortunato Minniti, *Strategie e conflitto nella politica di potenza di Mussolini: 1923–1940* (Naples: Esi, 2000), 39–81.
4. Joel Blatt, "The Parity That Meant Superiority," *French Historical Studies* 12, no. 2 (1981): 223–48.
5. Philippe Masson, "La belle marine de 1939," in *Historie militaire de la France*, vol. 4 (Paris: Presses Universitaires de France, 1992), 445–54.
6. Based on the data of Ludovica De Courten, *La marina mercantile italiana nella politica di espansione, 1860–1914: Industria, finanza e trasporti marittimi* (Rome: Bulzoni, 1989), 275.
7. Promemoria circa l'assetto militare marittimo dell'Italia, June 1921, Raccolta di base (RDB), box 1574, Archivio dell'Ufficio storico della Marina militare (AUSMM), Rome.
8. Studio di programma navale, December 1921, RDB, busta 1574, AUSMM.
9. Brian Sullivan, "Italian Naval Power at the Washington Conference," in *The Washington Conference 1921–1922*, edited by Eric J. Goldstein and John H. Maurer, 220–248 (London: Frank Cass, 2003).

THE ITALIAN FLEET *"IN EFFICIENZA"* 205

10. John Gooch, *Mussolini and His Generals: The Armed Forces and Fascist Foreign Policy, 1922–1940* (Cambridge: Cambridge University Press, 2017), 21–23, 32–37, 43, 47–49, 55, 81–88, 115, 118.
11. Pierpaolo Ramoino, *Romeo Bernotti* (Rome: Ufficio storico della marina militare [USMM], 2006), 61–70.
12. Libro di guerra, documento n. 1, Apprezzamento della situazione iniziale nella ipotesi di conflitto est-ovest, Situazione geografico-strategica in relazione alla guerra marittima, 1934, pp. 4, 6, Direttive Generali (DG), box 1-B,C, D, Pacco 12, busta 2, D3, AUSMM.
13. Libro di guerra, documento n. 1, 15–16.
14. Seduta del 7 novembre 1931, in Antonello Biagini and Alessandro Gionfrida, *Lo Stato Maggiore Generale tra le due guerre (Verbali delle riunioni presiedute da Badoglio dal 1925 al 1937)* (Rome: Ufficio storico stato maggiore dell'esercito [USSME], 1997), 280–81.
15. Robert Mallett, *Mussolini in Ethiopia, 1919–1935: The Origins of Fascist Italy's African War* (Cambridge: Cambridge University Press, 2015), 52, 55.
16. Erminio Bagnasco and Augusto De Toro, *The Littorio Class: Italy's Last and Largest Battleships, 1937–1948* (Annapolis, MD: Naval Institute Press, 2008); and Gooch, *Mussolini and His Generals*, 222.
17. Fabio De Ninno, "Continental Naval Doctrines between the Wars: The Impact of German Naval Experience on the Italian Navy (1919–1943)," *War in History* 29, no. 3 (2021): 1–20, https://doi.org/10.1177/09683445211043405.
18. James Goldrick, *After Jutland: The Naval War in Northern European Waters, June 1916–November 1918* (London: Seaforth, 2018), 283–84.
19. Giuseppe Fioravanzo, *La guerra sul mare e la guerra integrale*, vol. 1 (Turin: Schioppo, 1930), 446–63.
20. Luigi Donolo, *Storia della dottrina navale italiana* (Rome: USMM, 1996), 306.
21. Richard Hammond, "An Enduring Influence on Imperial Defence and Grand Strategy," *International History Review* 39, no. 5 (2018): 815–17; and Andrew Field, *Royal Navy Strategy in the Far East, 1919–1939: Preparing for War against Japan* (London: Frank Cass, 2004), 101–2.
22. Robert Mallett, *The Italian Navy and the Fascist Expansionism, 1935–1940* (London: Frank Cass, 1998), 8–37.
23. Considerazioni circa la necessità di aumentare la flotta, 24 October 1935, RDB, busta 2684, AUSMM.
24. Studio di programma navale sessennale 1936–1942, 13 January 1936, Ministero della Marina, Gabinetto 1934–50, box 295, Archivio Centrale dello Stato (ACS), Rome.
25. Fabio De Ninno, *Fascisti sul mare: La Marina e gli ammiragli di Mussolini* (Rome-Bari: Laterza, 2017), 212–14.
26. Mallett, *The Italian Navy*, 80.

27. Ufficio del capo di stato maggiore della R. Marina, Ufficio Piani di operazioni, Documento zero, studio sulla preparazione, November 1936, 33, 35, DG, DG, 1-D, E, pacco 14, fascicolo 1, AUSMM.
28. Minniti, *Strategie e conflitto*, 145.
29. Il canale di Sicilia, Studio indicativo per la realizzazione e l'esercizio del dispositivo di sbarramento, June 1938, DG, DG-10, busta 1, fascicolo, 3, AUSMM.
30. Maurizio Brescia, *Mussolini's Navy: A Reference Guide to the Regia Marina 1930–1945* (Annapolis MD: Naval Institute Press, 2013), 22–29.
31. Promemoria Funzionamento dell'Alto comando della marina in pace e in guerra, 18 March 1939, DG, DG, 0-B, pacco 2, busta 2, AUSMM.
32. Memorandum comandi in capo delle squadre e comando superiore in mare, 28 September 1938, 361–62, DG, DG-2, AUSMM; and Donolo, *Storia della dottrina*.
33. Giorgio Rochat, *Le guerre italiane 1935–1943: dall'Impero d'Etiopia alla disfatta* (Turin: Einaudi, 2005), 139; and Renzo De Felice, *Mussolini l'alleato: 1940–1945*, vol. 1 (Turin: Einaudi, 1990), 63.
34. Joseph Maiolo, *How the Arms Race Drove the World to War 1931–1941* (New York: Basic Books, 2010), 16–17, 19, 35, 149, 201, 233, 265.
35. Fortunato Minniti, "Il problema degli armamenti nella preparazione militare italiana dal 1935 al 1943," *Storia contemporanea* 11, no. 1 (1978): 41–50; and Fortunato Minniti, "Le materie prime nella preparazione bellica dell'Italia (1935–1943)," *Storia contemporanea* 17, no. 1 and 2 (1986): 5–40, 245–76.
36. Giorgio Giorgerini, *La guerra italiana sul mare: La marina tra vittoria e sconfitta, 1940–1943* (Milan: Mondadori 2002), 124–63.
37. Jack Greene and Alessandro Massignani, *The Naval War in the Mediterranean, 1940–1943* (Annapolis, MD: Naval Institute Press, 2002), 312–14; Fabio De Ninno, *I sommergibili del fascismo* (Milan: Unicopli, 2014), 246–70; and Franco Bargoni, *L'impegno navale italiano durante la guerra civile spagnola (1936–1939)* (Rome: USMM, 1992), 130–38, 202–10, 316–17.
38. Erminio Bagnasco, *Le armi delle navi italiane nella seconda guerra mondiale* (Parma: Albertelli, 2003); and Fabio De Ninno, "A Technological Fiasco," *Journal of Military History* 84, no. 3 (2020): 798–824.
39. Giorgio Giorgerini, *Da Matapan al Golfo persico: La marina militare italiana dal fascismo alla Repubblica* (Milan: Mondadori, 1989), 406–15; Mallett, *The Italian Navy*, 131–41; and Gerhard Schreiber, *Revisionismus und Weltmachtstreben: Marineführung u. dt.-ital. Beziehungen 1919–1944* (Stuttgart: DVA, 1979), 163–81.
40. Mussolini memo for the King, 30 March 1940, in Renzo De Felice, *Mussolini il Duce*, vol. 2 (Turin: Einaudi, 1981), 774; and Promemoria consegnato al Capo del Governo dal CSM della Marina, 14 April 1940, in USMM, *L'organizzazione della marina nel conflitto*, vol. 1 (Rome: USMM, 1972), 351–52.

41. Concetti generali di azione in Mediterraneo nella ipotesi di conflitto Alfa Uno, 29 May 1940, 4–5, DG, Di.Na-0 e 1, Di.Na 0, AUSMM.
42. "Gibilterra e Malta," in *Verbali delle riunioni tenute dal capo di SM Generale* (VCSG) (Rome: USSME, 1983), 1:63.
43. Vincent O'Hara, *"The Action off Calabria and the Myth of Moral Ascendancy,"* in *Warships 2008*, edited by John Jordan, 26–39 (Annapolis, MD: Naval Institute Press, 2008); and Francesco Mattesini, *Punta Stilo: 9 luglio 1940: 80 anniversario della prima battaglia aeronavale della storia* (Rieti: Ri-Stampa, 2020).
44. Werner Rahn and Gerhard Schreiber, eds., *Kriegstagebuch der Seekriegsleitung 1939–1945* (KDS), Band 11, July 1940 (Herford-Bonn: Mittle & Sohn, 1989), 13 July 1940, 148–49.
45. Relazione sulle operazioni navali dei giorni 6, 7, 8 e 9 luglio 1940, Azione di Punta Stilo, 44–45, Scontri navali e operazioni di guerra, busta 3, AUSMM.
46. Francesco Mattesini, comp., *Corrispondenza e direttive tecnico-operative di supermarina* (CDOS), tomo I, *Maggio 1939–luglio 1940* (Rome: USMM, 2000), 1:478–79, 483–84.
47. M. J. Pearce, *Confronting Italy: Mediterranean Surface Actions in 1940; Exploding the Myth of Mussolini's "Mare Nostrum"* (Plymouth, UK: University of Plymouth Press, 2019), 81–84.
48. Supermarina, Guerra con i sommergibili, 3° periodo, 28 June-12 July 1940, 2–3, 6, Marisegrege, busta 7, AUSMM.
49. CDOS, vol. 1, T. I, 531–32.
50. USMM, *Le operazioni navali nel Mediterraneo*, vol. 1 (Rome: USMM 1959), 191–92.
51. KDS, Mittelmeerkriegführung, Band 13, September 1940, 6 September 1940, 76–77.
52. Comando supremo capo di stato maggiore della Marina to Eccellenza il Capo di stato maggiore generale, 1 August 1940, Supermarina, Comando supremo, Box C, AUSMM; and Considerazioni sulla situazione strategica in relazione alle operazioni in Egitto, 22 September 1940, Supermarina, Comando supremo, Box C, AUSMM.
53. CDOS, vol. 1, T. II, 759–61.
54. Comando supremo, 1940, Riunione tenutasi presso il comando supremo, 14 October 1940, Supermarina, AUSMM.
55. Supermarina, Guerra con i sommergibili, IX e XI periodo, 21 September–28 October 1940, p. 6, Marisegrege, busta 7, AUSMM.
56. Hammond, "Enduring Influence," 823–24.
57. I. S. O. Playfair, *The Mediterranean and the Middle East*, vol. 1 (Uckfield: Naval & Military Press), 259–60.
58. David Hobbs, *Taranto and the Naval Air Warfare in the Mediterranean* (Barnsley, UK: Seaforth, 2020), 55, EPUB.

59. Francesco Mattesini, *La battaglia di Capo Teulada (27–28 novembre 1940)* (Rome: USMM, 2000).
60. Apprezzamento della situazione, 30 December 1940, pp. 2, 6, Supermarina, ODN, busta 7, AUSMM.
61. John Gooch, "Mussolini's Strategy 1939–1943," in *The Cambridge History of the Second World War*, vol. 1, *Fighting the War*, edited by John Ferris and Evan Mawdsley, 147–48 (Cambridge: Cambridge University Press, 2017).
62. Angelo Iachino, *Tramonto di una grande Marina* (Milan: Mondadori, 1959), 214–17, 239–40.
63. Vincent P. O'Hara, *Struggle for the Middle Sea: The Great Navies at War in the Mediterranean Theater, 1940–1945* (Annapolis, MD: Naval Institute Press, 2008), 98; and Green and Massignani, *The Naval War in the Mediterranean*, 157–60.
64. Situazione strategica e possibilità operative nel Mediterraneo, 19 July 1941, Supermarina, ODN, AUSMM.
65. Douglas Austin, *Malta and British Strategic Policy, 1925–1943* (London: Routledge, 2003), 99–170; and Alberto Santoni, *Il vero traditore: il ruolo documentato di ULTRA nella guerra del Mediterraneo* (Milan: Mursia, 2005), 271.
66. Verbale della riunione del 4 dicembre 1941, VCSG, 2:119.
67. A detailed description of the operations is in Vincent P. O'Hara, *Six Victories: North Africa, Malta, and the Traffic War, November 1941–March 1942* (Annapolis, MD: Naval Institute Press, 2019), however its conclusions are questionable because it attributes the shift in the naval war in the Mediterranean to surface actions by the Italian fleet, while the key question was the presence of German airpower and submarines. See Fabio De Ninno and Vincent P. O'Hara, "Six Victories: North Africa, Malta, and the Mediterranean Convoy War, November 1941–March 1942," *Naval War College Review* 74, no. 2, art. 12 (2021), https://digital-commons.usnwc.edu/nwc-review/vol74/iss2/12.
68. VCSG, 3:261, 274–75, 286, 292, 299, 304, 321, 324, 329, 334, 348–49.
69. Milan Vego, "Major Convoy Operation to Malta," *Naval War College Review* 63, no. 1 (2010): 147–48.
70. The shortage was 167,000 tons. Verbale della riunione tenuta il giorno 1° ottobre 1942 a Palazzo Venezia presso il Duce sull'argomento: potenziamento delle FF.AA, pp. 18–19, Spd, Carte della Valigia, ACS. On antishipping operations in August and September, see Richard Hammond, *Strangling the Axis: The Fight for Control of the Mediterranean during the Second World War* (Cambridge: Cambridge University Press, 2020), 135–39.
71. Giorgerini, *La guerra italiana sul mare*, 386.
72. Hammond, "Enduring Influence," 828.
73. Elena Aga-Rossi, *Una nazione allo sbando l'armistizio italiano del settembre 1943 e le sue seguenze* (Bologna: il Mulino, 2003), 108–9.

74. Mario Montanari, *The Three Battles of El-Alamein, June–November 1942* (Rome: USSME, 2003), 336.
75. John B. Hattendorf, "The Idea of a 'Fleet in Being' in Historical Perspective," *Naval War College Review* 67, no. 1 (2014): 3–5.
76. Milan Vego, *Naval Strategy and Operations in Narrow Seas* (London: Frank Cass 2004), 57.
77. Mariano Gabriele and Giuliano Friz, *La politica navale italiana dal 1885 al 1915* (Rome: USMM, 1982), 244; and Thaon di Revel to Salandra, Promemoria del capo di stato maggiore della marina in occasione della Proclamazione della neutralità italiana, 1 August 1914, Carte Salandra, busta 2, fascicolo, 16, ACS.

CHAPTER 11

# JAPAN AND THE INTERWAR NAVAL ORDER (1921-41)
Did the Imperial Navy Forgo a Fleet in Being to Contest Naval Dominance?

*Alessio Patalano*

Interwar Japan seems an ideal case to examine the value of a fleet in being as a strategy. First, at the structural level of international relations, a concept relevant for weaker naval powers to apply to stronger opponents fits Japan's situation. Japan was recognized as one of the top three naval powers. However, treaty arrangements relegated it to a position of relative inferiority compared to the other two, Britain and the United States. Second, the main naval literature on Japan has long assumed that the political frustrations of the Imperial Japanese Navy (IJN) with the arms control treaties reflected debates on force posture, capabilities, and doctrine that were predicated on a fleet designed for deterrence. Thus, as the naval order broke down and extreme military factions took control of the navy, they abandoned the fleet-in-being strategy and, with it, the strategy of deterrence that informed it.

The idea that Japan's behavior in the late 1930s unfolded from a rejection of a fleet-in-being strategy needs reexamination because of one unproven assumption arising from insufficient clarity about the fleet in being as a conceptual framework. Indeed, the assumption that Japan designed its fleet for deterrence reflects the naval literature's inadequate distinction between a fleet in being as an organizing principle for a peacetime fleet posture design from a fleet in being as a wartime operational preference—and, crucially, the relationship between the two.

This distinction is key because the literature assumes the fleet in being to be a peacetime strategy of deterrence, one aimed at war avoidance. Thus, it interprets Japan's eventual decision for a preemptive surprise attack against the United States and other Western powers in December 1941 as an abandonment of a fleet-in-being strategy.

Such an assumption is incorrect. In fact, the IJN never adopted a fleet-in-being strategy to avoid war. Rather, the navy pursued a fleet structure and capabilities that would operationally enable it to achieve victory from a position of relative inferiority without considering whether the buildup would invite the very war it was trying to avoid. The conviction among Japanese planners that it would be hard, if not impossible, to reverse Japan's condition as a weaker force in a fight against the U.S. Navy led them to develop the necessary capabilities to win with an active fleet-in-being operational strategy in wartime. The IJN did not consider a fleet in being as exclusively a peacetime strategy. Japanese naval planners never pursued a fleet that could deter through presence.

Throughout the first half of the twentieth century, as naval professionals and national elites of major powers came to understand the role of navies as tools of statecraft, an international naval order emerged.[1] This chapter first reviews the naval literature on the fleet-in-being concept to highlight its limitations. Simultaneously, it develops a clearer framework to review peacetime fleet-in-being strategies. It then uses the framework to assess the external structural circumstances that affected interwar Japanese naval thinking as well as the domestic dynamics that helped cement naval decision-making. The conclusion examines the extents to which Japan adopted a fleet-in-being strategy and to which the strategy's method of adoption led to the decision for war.

This approach, rather than assuming that the strategy's abandonment led to war, draws upon a variety of secondary and primary sources to make two distinct contributions to the wider naval literature. It offers the first systematic examination of a fleet in being as a peacetime deterrent strategy as well as a wartime operational approach. And it provides a different interpretation of Japanese naval behavior in the decision for war, one of historical and contemporary relevance as it emphasizes understanding the type of fleet-in-being approach in order to appreciate whether its purpose is to avoid war.

## UNDERSTANDING THE FLEET IN BEING AS A FRAMEWORK: THE STRATEGY OF THE WEAKER PARTY?

In the strategic studies literature focusing on maritime affairs, a fleet in being is a wartime operational approach available to navies unable to match enemy ship numbers in the expected theater of operation.[2] In a direct clash with the enemy's main force, such an inferior navy cannot gain command of the sea for sufficient duration or meaningfully contest it. A fleet-in-being strategy puts a premium on the value of a latent threat, one centered on a weaker force presenting a dilemma to a stronger opponent.[3] It attempts to overcome weaknesses by pursuing one or more of the following three main objectives: to preserve the main force; to deny a superior force from fully enjoying its operational advantage; or to secure war objectives short of defeating the adversary.[4]

Admiral Philip Colomb was the first author to systematically articulate the operational value of a fleet in being as pioneered by Admiral Arthur Herbert, First Earl of Torrington, who commanded a combined Anglo-Dutch fleet in the English Channel during the summer of 1690. Torrington realized that he faced a superior French force, one that put any possibility of a battle "besides the hopes of success," and decided to avoid engaging the enemy fleet.[5] Crucially, he was not convinced he needed to fight. He preferred to play for time by deploying his fleet in being within reach of the French navy to make an invasion of England by the latter too risky.[6] Torrington's superiors misunderstood his approach and pressured him to engage the French, a demand that led to the defeat of Beachy Head on 30 June 1690.[7]

For Colomb, Torrington's main option was to avoid an immediate clash and monitor French movements. This would have enabled him to select more favorable conditions to increase the odds of success. Torrington made clear, according to Colomb, he was not opting for a passive choice aiming to avoid fighting. He was trying to put the burden of the next move onto the French so that he would be in a more advantageous position to attack, should they decide to invade.[8] French Admiral Raoul Castex quoted Alfred Mahan to join the American writer in disagreeing with Colomb's analysis. They cast serious doubts on the operational value of excessive emphasis on the preservation of the fleet.[9] Other leading authors, including Julian Corbett, Cyprian Bridge, Herbert Richmond, Bernard Brodie, and Herbert Rosinski, retained positive views of what Torrington tried to achieve.[10]

Milan Vego, building upon Mahan's work, sought to resolve the tension inherent to these two primary interpretations of a fleet in being. He suggested that different authors have highlighted three methods to implement a fleet-in-being strategy: active, passive, and semiactive.[11] All three assume that a fleet in being is a defensive wartime strategy for a force that considers itself weaker than its opponent. The three methods of implementation reflect different tactical and operational choices. In the active and semiactive variants, a fleet seeks actively to deny the enemy command of the sea by avoiding a regular battle but seizing opportunities to counterstrike at every desirable opportunity. The purpose is to divert enemy forces from other theaters, to preserve some measure of control of a theater, to play for time to reconstitute to prevent the destruction of one's forces, or to ensure the most favorable bargaining position in the aftermath of a conflict.[12]

In the passive fleet-in-being method, the weaker force maintains a defensive posture both strategically and operationally. Force preservation through risk avoidance is the main objective. But it is not risk-free since it leaves the initiative to the enemy, with the inherent challenges unfolding from that choice. The weaker force aims to maximize the potential value of the fleet by remaining close to its bases, if not avoiding going out at sea altogether. Vego observed, based on Russia's experience in the nineteenth and early twentieth centuries, that the passive approach was far from successful. He found no discernible advantages in adopting a passive fleet-in-being strategy.[13]

In retrospect, the disagreement in the literature stems from understanding a fleet in being as a passive or an active military operation. For example, J. C. Wylie's seminal *Military Strategy* did not present a fleet in being as a wartime option. Instead it defined wartime activities as either sequential or cumulative strategies. He defined the latter as the "accumulation of little items piling one on top of the other until at some unknown point the mass of accumulated actions may be large enough to be critical."[14] For Wylie, war at sea is always about contesting control—however little of it, and for however limited a period of time.[15] Thus, an active or semiactive fleet-in-being strategy is a form of cumulative strategy in which available capabilities and the capacity to replace them constrain the pursuit of control.

An important question remains unaddressed. Is there a peacetime version of a fleet-in-being approach and, if so, what does it entail? Geoffrey Till briefly reviews a peacetime fleet-in-being strategy.[16] He draws on prior scholarship exploring Admiral Alfred von Tirpitz's adoption of the German Naval Law of 1900. Tirpitz designed a modern and powerful fleet to constrain the actions of the leading navy of the day, Britain's Royal Navy, through a dagger-at-the-heart strategy.[17] This approach, also known as risk theory, assumed that a sufficiently powerful fleet would prevent policies inimical to German interests since the resources demanded to deal with any direct conflict would have left the British Empire exposed overseas.[18] However, as the fleet expanded, Tirpitz regularly deployed the new navy in China, Morocco, and Bosnia to elevate Germany's international status and to sustain domestic momentum for the naval buildup.[19] This in turn consolidated views in Britain for the need to meet the German challenge with its own naval buildup, the opposite of the intended result.[20]

Tirpitz's naval strategy proved to be unsuccessful, thus raising questions about the relevance of a fleet-in-being approach as a peacetime organizing principle for a naval strategy. A closer examination of the literature reveals two tensions inherent to the fleet-in-being concept. The peacetime preparations for a fleet in being, designed to be active at the operational level of war, entail doctrinal and capability choices favoring military action. Do these preparations then make war more likely? Does a navy, intent on preparing for a war on advantageous terms, assume war will, at some point, occur? This leads to a second issue. Navies do not operate in a vacuum. In peacetime, navies are tools of national statecraft. Do perceptions at home and abroad of a fleet in being as a peacetime strategy depend on perceptions of the country's foreign and security policies as a whole? Specifically, how do forceful peacetime foreign activities affect the expectations and attitudes concerning war avoidance of both external observers and a country's own military leadership?

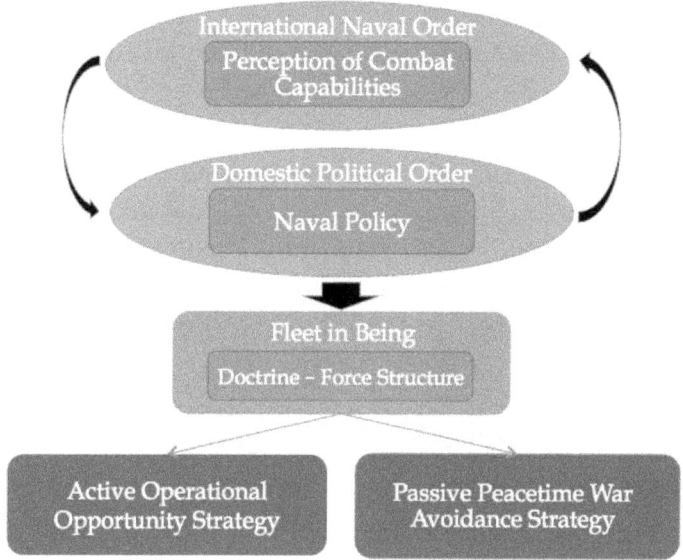

**FIGURE 1:** A FLEET IN BEING AS A STRATEGIC POSTURE AND AN OPERATIONAL APPROACH

This chapter presents a conceptual framework to answer these questions. Conceptually, a navy's choice for a fleet in being as a peacetime strategic posture or a wartime operational endeavor unfolds from a dynamic interaction of the international order with a country's specific domestic circumstances. At the structural level, interactions within international naval order create a perception of material and operational inferiority that determine the extent to which a fleet in being is designed to serve a strategy to deter war or as a doctrine to ensure victory under conditions of material inferiority. Crucially, the structural circumstances that inform naval elites' convictions of the absence of opportunities to redress their navy's condition may predispose a focus on the operational aspect of a fleet in being. In other words, naval planners are more likely to focus on doctrines that will facilitate operational solutions to inferior combat capabilities if they feel their greatest agency lies in this area.

Within this international context, domestic conditions reinforce such perceptions affecting choices in naval policies. These in turn inform doctrines and force structures aimed at overcoming or mitigating, strategically or operationally, issues of material inferiority. This dynamic interaction in turn determines the extent to which a fleet in being retains an active operational posture, whether to support national statecraft in peacetime or to seize opportunities in wartime. Operationally, an active fleet in being is an opportunistic strategy: it seeks to maximize opportunities as a way to mitigate risks and deficiencies. A fleet in being as a strategic posture is, by contrast, predominantly a passive posture as it emphasizes risk avoidance and force preservation. These observations are visually presented in Figure 1.

The sections below test this framework against the development of Japan's interwar naval strategy before drawing wider theoretical conclusions on the utility of the fleet-in-being concept.

## JAPAN AND THE INTERWAR INTERNATIONAL NAVAL ORDER: A FEELING OF ENTRAPMENT?

Historians, whether emphasizing cultural or economic explanations for interwar policy choices, agree on a pervasive sense of anxiety and uncertainty informing Japanese behavior.[21] Historians regard the transformation of Japanese anxieties about their role in the world into confrontational endeavors in the 1930s as a direct result from the simultaneous deterioration of regional stability after the Chinese warlord Zhang Zuolin's assassination in 1928 by the Kwantung Army (Japan's army in Manchuria) along with the global economic crisis of 1929.[22]

This context matters because no navy exists outside the society that produces its personnel and oversees the procurement of its capabilities. By the end of World War I, Japan stood as one of the world's leading naval powers. This gave imperial elites confidence in the military as a tool of statecraft to shape future regional affairs.[23] In 1919 British diplomat and minister plenipotentiary in Tokyo Sir Beilby Alston aptly captured this spirit after the conclusion of the Versailles peace treaty and the establishment of the League of Nations. He noted that this confidence had "lain most conspicuously along the lines of naval and military development."[24] More importantly, he added: "Now that she has diplomatically, financially, economically, and as a fighting Power attained so superior a position in international affairs, there seems no reason why she should any longer adhere to her antiquated diplomatic procedure of waiting on the other Powers for a lead whenever a difficult question arises."[25]

Like many others, Sir Alston recognized that Japan's rapid deployment of forces to take control of German possessions in East Asia had significantly advanced its strategic posture, not least vis-à-vis China.[26] By the time postwar negotiations had concluded, the confirmation of Japan's control over the islands of Micronesia (the Marianas, the Carolines, and the Marshalls) represented the crown jewel of a Pacific empire, which placed the IJN in a position of regional prominence.[27] Very early in the war, observers had foreseen that their retention would constitute a primary war gain for the IJN.[28] Throughout the 1920s and 1930s, these new possessions became a core component of Japanese war planning against the United States, designated in official documents from 1923 onward as Japan's main adversary.[29] The Mandates in the Pacific presented naval planners with a significant strategic asset but only with an adequate fleet.[30] As a result, throughout the interwar period, addressing the fleet's posture and numbers remained the IJN's priority.

Japan's weakened diplomatic ties, however, hampered this pursuit. The policies informing Japan's conduct throughout World War I had undermined Britain's trust in its naval ally. This was not for lack of naval support, since the IJN had proven to be a professional and proficient partner. In the words of the *Washington Post*, Japan's naval support to the British Empire relieved "English anxiety" over the safeguard of sea lanes from the South Seas to the Indian Ocean, including South Africa.[31] Moreover, in 1917 Japan stepped up its escort duties and deployed a squadron to the Mediterranean Sea. One Japanese admiral noted with pride at the time that "no one who has travelled lately in the Mediterranean could fail to see, from time to time, Japanese ships."[32] These contributions had been meaningful, but by the end of the war international observers perceived them as driven by pragmatic self-interest. Besides the acquisition of German possessions and greater political encroachment in China, Japanese business had also made striking commercial advances across the Pacific, with exports to Australia alone reportedly growing from £800,000 in 1913 to £2,800,000 in 1917.[33] The Japanese had acted throughout the war, it was perceived, in a way that first and foremost benefited them.

Such a change in perception informed dramatic developments in Anglo-Japanese relations when Britain terminated their alliance. As the postwar age of naval arms regulations dawned, Britain decided that the alliance did not align with its East Asian interests. In the final report of the Anglo-Japanese Alliance Committee, Japan's expansionist ambitions as much as its means to pursue them produced a unanimous recommendation to terminate the two-decade-long arrangement.[34] Instead the pursuit of a tripartite agreement with the United States and Japan could serve as a potential alternative to constrain the risk of Japan's further opportunistic "expansionism."[35] At the negotiations overseeing the international naval order of the 1920s and 1930s, Japan found in Britain a more ambivalent and less understanding interlocutor.

Indeed, the naval conferences in Washington (1921–22) and in London (1930 and 1935–36) did much to define the interwar naval order through arms control. They provided naval elites of the major powers a common forum to wrestle with the link between capabilities and future naval warfare.[36] These negotiations are important for examining the fleet-in-being concept as a peacetime naval posture for two reasons. First, the negotiations propelled Japan's naval community to challenge its own perception of material inferiority.[37] Second, the negotiations became the lightning rod in the early 1930s that assertive naval elites used to push designs like the *Mogami* class of cruisers to the limits of concentrated firepower while criticizing the failure of the arms agreements to improve the country's overall circumstances.[38] Limitations on the armament and tonnage for capital ships, especially cruisers, together with Japan's inferior ratios relative to the United States and Britain, set the stage for profound and enduring frustration.[39] By 1936 Tokyo's naval elites concluded that naval planning and procurement could not be geared toward a fleet in being with a passive operational doctrine; rather, an active operational doctrine was a much safer bet to mitigate inferior numbers. To that end, they tailored capabilities such as submarines and naval aviation (largely overlooked in the previous decade's regulations) to the needs of a fleet seeking an early clash on advantageous terms to prevent material inferiority from impeding victory.[40]

In part, Japanese naval elites' inability to negotiate themselves out of a situation of inferiority propelled this shift. Given their assumption that mathematical formulas could calculate the power balance, there were two primary ways to improve their material circumstances. In negotiating the first agreements in Washington, Japan's lead negotiator, Admiral Kato Tomosaburo, accepted an inferior ratio (60 percent instead of 70 percent of the British and U.S. strength in capital ships) in return for limits on U.S. strengthening of fortifications in Guam and the Philippines.[41] Because Japan's industrial base and national finances could not compete in naval capabilities with its main competitors, limiting others, although suboptimal, would work in Japan's favor.[42]

Other senior naval officers, initially led by Vice Admiral Kato Kanji, the chief naval representative in Washington, disagreed. They rejected that limiting competitors was sufficient. As negotiations for the failed Geneva conference and the subsequent meetings in London progressed, Japan's position regarding the 70 percent ratio for its fleet became a matter of dogma and prestige. Indeed, key followers of Admiral Kato Kanji—notably, admirals Suetsugu Nobumasa and Takahashi Sankichi—came to lead the IJN's Command Faction, which opposed the Treaty Faction, which included those who supported the treaties.[43] Remarkably, neither group's senior leaders actually proposed any alternative to a passive fleet in being that would overcome Japan's material inferiority. Implicitly, they always assessed the different diplomatic approaches based on the assumption of war. This led to a second assumption that both sides implicitly accepted. They shared a gloomy view of their country's naval might: by the mid-1930s, the interwar naval order had done little to mitigate Japan's inferior position to the United States.

In 1933 and 1934 irreconcilable policy disagreements within Japan's main factions resulted in the Osumi purge, named for Navy minister Osumi Mineo, who complied with demands for the early retirement of inconvenient naval officers that Takahashi conveyed on behalf of Prince Fushimi Hiroyasu, a member of the imperial family sympathetic to the Command Faction. The purge silenced the Treaty Faction's more moderate voice.[44] The reactionary leadership dominating the navy remained superficially committed to arms control regimes until their expiration in 1936. In practice, the IJN had already accelerated its design and procurement processes to create a fleet able to defeat a superior U.S. force in a decisive battle in the western Pacific. In 1935 plans for a superbattleship program—the gargantuan *Yamato* class—started in haste. All signs pointed to an operational approach that would be active, if not assertive, in pursuing an early solution to a war of Japan's choosing.[45]

## THE DOMESTIC POLITICS OF EMPIRE: WHAT ARE WE FIGHTING FOR?

Domestic politics provided the context for the navy's decisions on force structure and, by the time of the Osumi purge, on a doctrinal path that assumed a confrontation with the United States. This is not to suggest that war—as it came to be in 1941—was inevitable. Rather, although military organizations try not to become prisoners of deterministic escalation, dynamics at home, when coupled with the above international circumstances, informed the IJN's choice of war. Leading military scholars and observers have argued that Japan's army and naval education systems in the 1930s were also a contributing factor. These institutions reflected a military culture that imbued values and principles about the military profession that perceived war as a legitimate, if not desirable, tool to solve international disputes and reinforced organizational beliefs in its use.[46]

Budgets are particularly important for navies, given their technology-intensive requirements. Funding became fractious for the interwar IJN in two respects. First, technological innovation—with the correlated need for study to understand the potential implications and uses—and the expansion of submarine warfare and aviation as full-fledged components of naval warfare put exceptional pressure on fleet posture and capabilities procurement.[47] For the IJN the question did not merely concern numbers of surface combatants but also the necessary combination of the three dimensions of war at sea to ensure the fleet's victory. Second, the naval transformation coincided with army actions that made expansion in northern China the primary foreign policy objective.[48]

Meanwhile, economic changes, especially the downturn experienced in rural areas after the global crisis of 1929, brought both structural reforms and social discontent. When the Great Depression reached Japan, the Kanto region, including the capital area, was still recovering from the destructive 1923 earthquake that had also severely damaged the naval docks in Yokosuka and the hull of the battle cruiser *Amagi*. Between 1929 and 1931, the wholesale price index fell about 30 percent, and silk prices on the Yokohama exchange were down by about half. Rice prices, too, fell in 1930, with rural incomes particularly affected.[49] Home Ministry data indicated a simultaneous spike in unemployment. Between 1929 and 1932, the number of unemployed increased from 195,000 to 489,000, although these figures covered only main urban areas. Nationwide, the problem was probably much deeper.[50]

The economic crisis of the early 1930s prompted Japanese governments to enact major reforms creating industrial cartels to rationalize and regulate the economy. These initiatives in turn favored the development of industry—notably, iron, steel, and chemicals.[51] They also reinforced collusion among business, political, and military stakeholders in places like Manchuria—for example, Mantetsu, the South Manchuria Railway Company, which worked closely with the Kwantung Army to advance Japan's expansion in China. Indeed, the manufactured crises in Manchuria in 1931–32 and the establishment of the puppet state of Manchukuo reflected military designs of imperial expansion that army elites in China concocted and ambitious industrialists sustained.[52] These moves, presented as a way to render the empire more autonomous and self-sufficient, produced the opposite effects. From 1936 to 1937, the value of U.S. exports to Japan almost doubled, from $163,815,000 to $253,710,000, with war related matériel like gasoline, lubricating oil, iron and steel scrap reportedly representing key items in the increase.[53] Furthermore, in retaliation for Japan's China policy, by 1936 U.S. tariffs on products like textiles further strained trade.[54] If the domestic narrative for the expansion in China concerned autonomy, the opposite occurred in reality.

Naval plans faced an austere economic climate that restricted budget requests. Domestically, the government had not prioritized military expenditures since the mid-1910s. In 1920 the Diet finally agreed to fund the navy's proposed "eight-eight" fleet (a strike force composed of eight battleships and eight battle cruisers), only for the naval treaties to undermine this ambition once again.[55] Given that the international and domestic circumstances of the 1920s did not bode well for naval procurement, planners developed an interception-attrition strategy based on the IJN's existing preference for an interception strategy.[56] The naval treaties contributed to the IJN's greater focus on improving capabilities not covered in the agreements and useful for the attrition of the enemy before the main battle fleet engagement. The results were some of the world's most advanced and heavily armed cruisers, starting with the *Furutaka* class, armed with six 8-inch guns and twelve torpedo tubes, completed in 1926, and followed by the *Myoko* (1928), *Takao* (1932), and *Mogami* (1935) classes of heavy cruisers.[57]

By 1938, however, the raging war in China undercut the IJN's claims for a larger share of the budget, precluding full integration of new technology in sophisticated designs. As a result, the navy had to invest carefully in those capabilities necessary for the best possible version of the interception-attrition plan. For example, weapons like the long-lance torpedo Type-93 were developed to extend the reach and firepower of the ships delivering the attrition element of the navy's strategy.[58] Similarly, Japan developed submarines able to cruise long distances to meet a U.S. fleet crossing the Pacific and to make preliminary attacks against Guam and the Philippines.[59] In 1937 the navy's logic of attrition extended to a surprise strike in the war's opening stages by embarked air power from a multi-carrier strike force.[60] The IJN tasked the Institute of Navy Aeronautics to develop and deliver the required air assets.[61] This focus on one core plan and acquisitions tailored to it alone reduced these acquisitions' utility for unexpected contingencies.

Capabilities design, force structure, and doctrine all worked together to mitigate material inferiority by means of preemptive action. In the 1930s the competition with the army over budget allocations and support for wider operational activity in China contributed to the IJN's assumption of the inevitability of war and ensuing search for it. Following the clash of Chinese Nationalist and Japanese regular forces in the Marco Polo Bridge Incident on 7 July 1937, army operations assumed an unprecedented scale. During the previous four years the Imperial Japanese Army had sought to detach north China from Nationalist control through violence, agitation of anti-Nationalist unrest, and subversion.[62] As one U.S. report reflecting on the causes of the Sino-Japanese War observed, the army had deep-rooted links and interests in China: "With regard to the professional Japanese army, we know that it has a vested interest in continued military occupation of China and that it is in business and "rackets" in China on an all-out scale, and that the money is rolling into its pockets. We know that the army is enjoying power, wealth, authority and good living undreamed of before, and therefore we may be certain that the army is not going to give up China lightly."[63]

The 26 February 1936 Incident in Tokyo had eliminated the government's last powerful critics of unbridled expansion in China, allowing a consolidation of militarist leadership within the army. By the spring of 1937 this, combined with a renewed Soviet challenge in the north, brought about a major shift in military operations.[64] To the army, China was not merely a crucial source of power and influence, it was also a place to halt a Soviet advance against the Japanese empire. The ensuing campaigns aimed at bringing China more firmly under Japanese control as a preliminary step to meet any Soviet threat. By the end of 1937 large-scale operations to take control of Shanghai and, subsequently, central China and Hong Kong committed the equivalent of the army's peacetime force strength, some 600,000 personnel, to the mainland.[65] Numbers steadily grew in subsequent years. The army now set the tone of Japanese military statecraft. The navy was ancillary to these plans: its trademark contributions to statecraft down to 1940 were a sequence of bombardment campaigns against Chinese cities, support for amphibious landings, the invasion of Hainan, and the blockade of Hong Kong.[66]

The expanding scale of operations in China and, by late 1940, the lack of a clear way out from major army commitments had two primary effects on the IJN. On the one hand, it added strategic-level anxiety since the navy had consistently argued for guaranteeing Japan's resources by expanding into the resource-rich areas of Southeast Asia rather than attempting to control China.[67] By September 1940 the fall of France had offered the opportunity to overtake northern French Indochina, both to expand southward and to defeat the Nationalists by cutting their supply chains from southern China.[68] Further southward expansion looked increasingly undesirable, given the army's commitments in China. On the other hand, air operations against Chinese targets enabled the navy air corps to perfect its strike potential. By the spring of 1941 the navy's First Air Fleet comprised 7 carriers and 464 aircraft: 137 fighters, 144 diver bombers, and 183 torpedo planes.[69] This mighty force was designed to deliver attrition before the long guns of *Yamato* and *Musashi*, the warships leading the fleet, intercepted the enemy. Missing was a perfect opportunity to secure the IJN's desired outcome.

Resource constraints—notably, the steel and oil vital to the fleet—arose from the double pressure of escalating U.S. sanctions that culminated with an oil embargo and army operational demands. The constraints left the navy with ever-fewer options. Yet the longer the wait, the greater the risk of failure.[70] War became a question of now or never. An October 1941 agreement with the army, redistributing steel allocations for the following year in the navy's favor, determined the window for the war that the IJN now saw as the only way out of a nearly two-decade-long state of material inferiority.[71] The army had agreed to temporarily change the focus of its operations to enable the navy to eliminate its main adversaries. This was an incredible gamble, given the weak economic foundations of Japan's military machine. Such an approach when coupled with the navy's very limited interest in, and attention to, wartime convoy escort requirements suggests that the IJN did not envision fighting with a fleet-in-being strategy aimed at preserving forces. The fleet was going to be very active at the outbreak of hostilities to settle matters quickly.[72]

Earlier in March the U.S. secretary of state had observed to his ambassador in Japan that European events seemingly reinforced the navy's confidence in its ability to secure victory: "Officers of the Japanese Navy are reported to have expressed in conversation the opinion that in the anticipated German spring offensive British defeat is a foregone conclusion; that British sea power will probably be diminished to such an extent that control of the Atlantic will be lost to the British; and that as a result thereof a part of the American fleet will be withdrawn from the Pacific Ocean, enabling the Japanese to carry out their plans for expansion in southeast Asia without substantial opposition."[73]

Thus, the IJN never really implemented a fleet-in-being strategy that focused on conventional deterrence as a strategic posture. It never had such a strategy guiding naval development. Instead, throughout the 1920s and 1930s, naval planners developed an opportunistic strategy to win a war from a position of material inferiority by tailoring the IJN's capabilities, posture, and doctrine.

## DID JAPAN FORGO A FLEET-IN-BEING STRATEGY?

Distinguishing the use of the fleet-in-being concept as a peacetime posture from a wartime operational strategy offers three important insights. First, an examination of interwar Japan suggests that naval planners designed a fleet suitable for wartime fleet-in-being operations because this maximized the navy's agency in making the wider case for the service within Japan's straitened domestic and international circumstances. The IJN's main concern remained the development of a force strong enough to meet its potential enemies, not whether such a peacetime posture would make war more or less likely. The IJN's position of inferiority, made permanent by international negotiations combined with Japan's foreign policy focused on expansion in China, led the navy to concentrate on operational issues. Securing funds to meet them was the overarching concern.

This leads to a second conclusion. This case study indicates that those who fail to consider whether the adoption of a fleet-in-being strategy makes war more likely tend to take an active operational approach. From doctrinal, capabilities, and force structure perspectives, Japan's pursuit of a fleet in being is a story of early action to solve problems of material inferiority. Throughout the 1930s, decision-making in research and development, capabilities procurement, and doctrinal solutions aimed to enhance chances of success. The IJN processed even its experience in the supporting missions in China to improve doctrine and tactics for the next war. By the late 1930s the IJN considered war to be inevitable because it was tailoring its entire structure to fight that war. Accordingly, it was basing naval acquisitions on the assumption that success for the inferior force depended on early engagement. In this context the navy's focus on the fleet in being as an operational construct reinforced beliefs in the inevitability of war.

These two conclusions lead to a third one. The scholarly narrative of a navy that sought to constrain a warmongering army requires revision.[74] Japan's expansion in the second half of the 1930s does not support the idea that naval leaders placed peace with the United States above all considerations. Naval leaders were frustrated that operations in China drew resources away from them. They did not consider war with the United States to be a desirable strategy. Yet, since they had spent more than a decade preparing to fight the U.S. Navy, they were unwilling to consider alternatives that would preclude them from taking their chances. In so doing, the IJN became blind to issues that could undermine their plans, not least the eventuality of a U.S. strategy that eschewed battle or leveraged superior intelligence.

This final observation is relevant for today. In assessing any navy's force design and procurement plans, the key to a fleet-in-being strategy is not so much whether it helps deter war. Rather, it is how actively it fosters an active operational posture—regardless of the strategic consequences.

## NOTES

1. Alessio Patalano, "The Global Order at Sea," in *Power and the Maritime Domain*, edited by William S. Moreira and Greg Kennedy (Abingdon, UK: Routledge, 2023), 13–15.
2. Geoffrey Till, *Seapower: A Guide for the Twenty-First Century*, 2nd ed. (London: Routledge, 2009), 173; Ian Speller, "Naval Warfare," in *Understanding Modern Warfare*, edited by David Jordan, James D. Kiras, David J. Lonsdale, Ian Speller, Christopher Tuck, and C. Dale Walton (Cambridge: Cambridge University Press, 2008), 136; Hervé Coutau-Bégarie, *Traité de Stratégie*, 3rd ed. (Paris: Economica, 2002), 592–93; and Bernard Brodie, *A Layman's Guide to Naval Strategy* (Oxford: Oxford University Press, 1943), 62.
3. Milan Vego, *Maritime Strategy and Sea Denial: Theory and Practice* (London: Routledge, 2020), 130–32.
4. Till, *Seapower*, 173–74.
5. Philip Colomb, *Naval Warfare: Its Ruling Principles and Practice Historically Treated*, 2 vols. (London: W. H. Allen, 1891), 1:115.
6. Nicholas A. M. Rodger, *The Command of the Ocean: A Naval History of Britain, 1649–1815* (London: Penguin, 2006), 145.
7. Rodger, 145–46.
8. Colomb, *Naval Warfare*, 116.
9. Raoul Castex, *Strategic Theories* (Annapolis, MD: Naval Institute Press, 1993), 340.
10. Julian S. Corbett, *Some Principles of Maritime Strategy* (London: Longmans, Green, 1918), 195–201; Cyprian Bridge, *Sea-Power and Other Studies* (1910; repr., Cambridge: Cambridge University Press, 2013), 48; Brodie, *Layman's Guide*, 62; and John B. Hattendorf, "The Idea of a 'Fleet in Being' in Historical Perspective," *Naval War College Review* 67, no. 1 (2014): 46.

11. Vego, *Maritime Strategy and Sea Denial*, 132.
12. Vego, 132–48.
13. Vego, 148–52.
14. J. C. Wylie, *Military Strategy: A General Theory of Power Control* (Annapolis, MD: Naval Institute Press, 2014), 24.
15. Wylie, 124–25.
16. Till, *Seapower*, 175.
17. Michael Epkenhans, "How to Square the Circle?," in *Maritime Strategy and Naval Innovation: Technology, Bureaucracy, and the Problem of Change in the Age of Competition*, edited by Alessio Patalano and James A. Russell (Annapolis, MD: Naval Institute Press, 2021), 45–46.
18. Epkenhans, 46.
19. Epkenhans, 48–49; and Holger H. Herwig, *"Luxury" Fleet: The Imperial German Navy, 1888–1918* (London: Prometheus, 1987), 95–110.
20. Herwig, *"Luxury" Fleet*, 69–94.
21. Akira Iriye, *Power and Culture: The Japanese-American War, 1941–1945* (Cambridge, MA: Harvard University Press, 1981), 1–35; Michael A. Barnhart, *Japan Prepares for Total War: The Search for Economic Security, 1919–1941* (Ithaca, NY: Cornell University Press, 1987), 22–49; Joseph A. Maiolo, *Cry Havoc: How the Arms Race Drove the World to War, 1931–1941* (London: John Murray, 2010), 23–39; Frederick R. Dickinson, *World War I and the Triumph of a New Japan, 1919–1930* (Cambridge: Cambridge University Press, 2013), 1–12, 37–59; and Leonard A. Humphreys, *The Way of the Heavenly Sword: The Japanese Army in the 1920s* (Stanford, CA: Stanford University Press, 1995), 30–59, 147–170.
22. Takafusa Nakamura, *A History of Shōwa Japan, 1926–1989* (Tokyo: University of Tokyo Press, 1993), 48–49, 68–77; and S. C. M. Paine, *The Wars for Asia, 1911–1949* (Cambridge: Cambridge University Press, 2012), 19–23, 55–57.
23. Frederick R. Dickinson, "The Japanese Empire," in *Empires at War, 1911–1923*, edited by Robert Gerwarth and Erez Manela (Oxford: Oxford University Press, 2014), 208–212.
24. Mr. Alston, "No 432 to Earl Curzon, 18 July 1919," *Documents on British Foreign Policy 1919–1939*, Ser. 1, vol. 6, Ref: 118980/6579/23, Documents on British Policy Overseas, King's College London, hereafter DBPO, https://www.proquest.com/dbpo?accountid=11862.
25. Mr. Alston, "No 432 to Earl Curzon."
26. Sir J. Jordan, "No 416 to Earl Curzon, 28 June 1919," *Documents on British Foreign Policy 1919–1939*, Ser. 1, vol. 6, Ref: 118928/16000/10, DBPO; and Dickinson, "Japanese Empire," 201–7.
27. Dickinson, "Japanese Empire," 203.
28. "Japan and the War," *Times of India*, 10 December 1914, 4.

29. David C. Evans and Mark R. Peattie, *Kaigun: Strategy, Tactics, and Technology in the Imperial Japanese Navy, 1887–1941* (Annapolis, MD: Naval Institute Press, 1997), 191.
30. Chihaya Masataka, "Importance of Japanese Naval Bases Overseas," in *The Pacific War Papers: Japanese Documents of World War II*, edited by Donald M. Goldstein and Katherine V. Dillon (Washington, DC: Potomac Books, 2006), 64–66.
31. "Japan's Navy Is Busy," *Washington Post*, 23 August 1917, 2.
32. "Japan and the War," *South China Morning Post*, 26 September 1917, 4.
33. "Our Australian Letter," *Times of India*, 1 July 1919, 8.
34. "No 212 Report of the Anglo-Japanese Alliance Committee, 21 January 1921," *Documents on British Foreign Policy 1919–1939*, Ser. 1, vol. 14, Ref: F1169/63/23, DBPO.
35. "No 212 Report of the Anglo-Japanese Alliance Committee."
36. Joseph A. Maiolo, "Internationalism in East Asia," in *The International History of East Asia, 1900–1968*, edited by Anthony Best (Basingstoke, UK: Routledge, 2010), 69–70.
37. Sadao Asada, "From Washington to London," in *Culture Shock and Japanese–American Relations: Historical Essays*, edited by Sadao Asada (Columbia: University of Missouri Press, 2007), 117–19.
38. Evans and Peattie, *Kaigun*, 239; Sadao Asada, "The Japanese Navy's Road to Pearl Harbor, 1931–1941," in Asada, *Culture Shock and Japanese–American Relations*, 138–44; and Maiolo, "Internationalism in East Asia," 75, 77.
39. Maiolo, "Internationalism in East Asia," 73–74; and Asada, "From Washington to London," 127–35.
40. Evans and Peattie, *Kaigun*, 248–50; and Carl Boyd and Akihiko Yoshida, *The Japanese Submarine Force and World War II* (Annapolis, MD: Naval Institute Press, 1995), 4–7.
41. Asada, "From Washington to London," 112–13.
42. Asada, 113.
43. Asada, "The Japanese Navy's Road to Pearl Harbor," 138–39.
44. Asada, 139–40.
45. Evans and Peattie, *Kaigun*, 370.
46. Edward J. Drea, *In the Service of the Emperor: Essays on the Imperial Japanese Army* (Lincoln: University of Nebraska Press, 1998), 75–90; and Oi Atsushi, "The Japanese Navy in 1941," in Goldstein and Dillon, *The Pacific War Papers*, 5–7.
47. Evans and Peattie, *Kaigun*, esp. chap. 11.
48. W. G. Beasley, *Japanese Imperialism, 1894–1945* (Oxford: Oxford University Press, 1987), esp. chap. 12–13.
49. Nakamura, *A History of Shōwa Japan*, 71.
50. Nakamura, 73.

51. Nakamura, 75–76; and Yoshihisa Tak Matsusaka, *The Making of Japanese Manchuria, 1904–1932* (Cambridge, MA: Harvard University Press, 2003), 312–88.
52. Matsusaka, *The Making of Japanese Manchuria*, 381–408; and Nakamura, *A History of Shōwa Japan*, 77–97.
53. "Our Trade in the East Exceeds 1936 Total," *New York Times*, 19 December 1937, 39.
54. "Japan Is Saddened by Textile Tariffs," *Wall Street Journal*, 25 May 1936, 1.
55. Hirama Yoichi, "Japanese Naval Preparations for World War II," *Naval War College Review* 94, no. 2 (1991): 66.
56. Evans and Peattie, *Kaigun*, 201–5.
57. Hirama, "Japanese Naval Preparations for World War II," 67.
58. Evans and Peattie, *Kaigun*, 266–72.
59. Boyd and Yoshida, *Japanese Submarine Force*, 5–6.
60. Evans and Peattie, *Kaigun*; and Hirama, "Japanese Naval Preparations for World War II."
61. Nishiyama Takashi, *Engineering War and Peace in Modern Japan, 1868–1964* (Baltimore: Johns Hopkins University, 2014), 45–53.
62. Mark R. Peattie, "The Dragon's Seed," in *The Battle for China: Essays on the Military History of the Sino-Japanese War of 1937–1945*, edited by Mark R. Peattie, Edward J. Drea, and Hans J. van de Ven (Stanford, CA: Stanford University Press, 2011), 70.
63. William R. Langdon, "Observations of the Far Eastern Situation and on American Policy in Relation Thereto," Memorandum, 25 October 1941, *Foreign Relations of the United States Diplomatic Papers, 1941, The Far East*, vol. 4, https://history.state.gov/historicaldocuments.
64. Peattie, "Dragon's Seed," 75–80.
65. Edward J. Drea and Hans Van De Ven, "An Overview of Major Military Campaigns during the Sino-Japanese War, 1937–1945," in Peattie et al., *Battle for China*, 32.
66. Ken-ichi Arakawa, "The Japanese Naval Blockade of China in the Second Sino-Japanese War, 1937–41," in *Naval Blockades and Seapower: Strategies and Counter-Strategies, 1805–2005*, edited by Bruce A. Elleman and S. C. M. Paine (London: Routledge, 2006), 105–16; and Franco David Macri, *Clash of Empires in South China: The Allied Nations' Proxy War with Japan, 1935–1941* (Lawrence: University of Kansas Press, 2012).
67. Evans and Peattie, *Kaigun*, 453–56.
68. Macri, *Clash of Empires in South China*, 227–34.
69. Evans and Peattie, *Kaigun*, 349.
70. Barnhart, *Japan Prepares for Total War*, 144–45.
71. Barnhart, 255–57.

72. Toshiyuki Yokoi, "Thoughts on Japan's Naval Defeat," U.S. Naval Institute *Proceedings* 86, no. 10 (1960): 68–75.
73. "The Secretary of State to the Ambassador in Japan (Grew)," No. 2145, 15 March 1941, *Foreign Relations of the United States Diplomatic Papers, 1941, The Far East*, vol. 4, https://history.state.gov/historicaldocuments.
74. Sadao Asada, "From Washington to London: The Imperial Japanese Navy and the Politics of Naval Limitations, 1921–1930," *Diplomacy and Statecraft* 4, no. 3 (1993): 147–91; Sadao Asada, *From Mahan to Pearl Harbor: The Imperial Japanese Navy and the United States* (Annapolis, MD: Naval Institute Press, 2006); and Kiyoshi Aizawa, *Kaigun no Sentaku: Saikou Shinjuwankougeki no he Machi* [The navy's choice: Reconsidering the road to the attack on Pearl Harbor] (Tokyo: Chuokoron-shisha, 2002).

CHAPTER 12

# THE BRITISH AND U.S. REACTION TO THE JAPANESE NAVAL BUILDUP (1930-41)

John T. Kuehn

The United States and Britain responded differently to Japan's efforts to build a battle fleet to dominate the western Pacific and the waters of East Asia. The U.S. approach changed least with the Japanese challenge. In the aftermath of the 1930 London Naval Treaty, the U.S. Navy (USN) leadership focused on building a battle fleet that would prevail in a Mahanian-style clash with Japan.[1] This would facilitate an endgame strategy of blockade and economic strangulation to bring Japan into negotiations. Prior to the buildup, it retained a fleet in being in Hawaii.

Events in Europe, especially after German rearmament began in the mid-1930s, shaped Britain's response. Britain's use of economy of force in the Far East to protect imperial interests reflects what might be characterized as a "fortified fleet-in-being."[2] This approach, reflecting an "aggressive naval defense," was based on the fortress of Singapore.[3] Events in Europe only reinforced British imperial security policy that underwrote this approach, especially after the signing in 1935 of the Anglo-German Naval Agreement.

## FROM WASHINGTON TO LONDON

The eight years following the Washington Conference have been characterized as the "Period of Anglo-American Antagonism."[4] Although the 1902 Anglo-Japanese Alliance no longer remained in force, the Royal Navy (RN) continued to assist the Imperial Japanese Navy's (IJN) development of naval aviation.[5] However, the exclusion of Singapore from the Washington Naval Treaty's nonfortification clause clearly indicated Britain's concerns.[6] Admiral of the Fleet Earl Beatty forecast that if Britain did not build up Singapore, as the treaty allowed, Japan might seize Singapore and threaten "oil fuel storage and the ports of Colombo, Trincomali, Madras and Rangoon." Britain did not adopt the proposed "scheme" to make improvements to Singapore because it was "out of keeping with the spirit of [the] Washington agreement." Beatty and the senior member of the Board of the Admiralty were shocked.[7] A clear divergence existed in Britain's strategic polity between the government and the naval officer corps.

After the failure of the 1927 Geneva Naval Conference, Britain seemed to regard the United States as its primary enemy, with Japan a distant second. The United States and Japan each regarded the other as its primary naval opponent.[8] Japan used the 1920s to build every ton allowed by the Washington treaty, correctly surmising that Britain and the United States would economize and not build to the treaty limits.[9] The British–U.S. relationship vis-à-vis Japan remained unresolved until the period 1929–30, when Prime Minister Ramsay MacDonald and President Herbert Hoover acted to bring their naval officer corps to see each other more as allies than as enemies.

## LONDON AND AFTER—THE JAPAN RESPONSE

Naval arms limitations seemed to have succeeded with the 1930 London Naval Treaty.[10] The system established at Washington in 1922 had saved the world's major maritime powers money as well as curtailed a financially draining postwar naval arms race.[11] Success in London shed a ray of light onto the Depression-weary publics of the signatories. The Japanese public enthusiastically greeted the returning delegation at the Tokyo train station with shouts of "Banzai!" This reaction shocked delegate Admiral Yamamoto Isoroku into rethinking his hawkish position on the London treaty and align with the more moderate Treaty Faction inside Japan's Navy Ministry.[12]

The U.S. and British delegates congratulated themselves on getting Japan to maintain the capital ship–building holiday and other key features of the original Washington Naval Treaty. Japan had also agreed to extend the 5-5-3 tonnage ratio—for Britain, the United States, and Japan, respectively—for the cruiser class of warships (including heavy cruisers). When the United States agreed to delay building its final three heavy cruisers until the mid-1930s, this gave Japan a de facto 70 percent ratio for the treaty's duration from 1930 to 1936. Additionally, Japan received a 70 percent actual ratio in other auxiliaries (including destroyers) and parity in submarines.[13] The cruiser proviso was critical in convincing British and U.S. leaders of Japan's intent to maintain a defensive fleet in the Pacific rather than a fleet for offensive warfare against their interests in East Asia.

Britain and the United States succeeded at London in limiting Japan in the next most important class of ships—cruisers—where it had reached equivalency with the United States due to the latter's anemic ship construction. The United States had not commissioned a single cruiser of any class since Herbert Hoover had become president, and construction of cruisers prior to Hoover had also been anemic, despite the efforts of the USN to build as many 10,000-ton (later classified heavy) cruisers as possible.[14] Many Western officers disagreed with their diplomats' belief that the IJN remained a defensive rather than an offensive force. Such officers as Admiral Hilary Jones, USN, and Admiral Roger Keyes, RN, and retired officers such as Rear Admiral Bradley Fiske, USN, believed Japan had instead achieved a key goal: de facto if not de jure recognition of its right to naval equivalency with the two senior maritime powers.[15]

Japan's naval officer corps was more divided than their British and U.S. counterparts. London seemed to herald the triumph of the Treaty Faction of admirals who controlled naval policy from within the Navy Ministry, the heirs of Admiral Kato Tomosaburo. The so-called Fleet Faction, led by Baron Kato's archrival Admiral Kato Kanji (no relation), however, controlled a much broader group of rising young naval officers who favored an aggressive foreign policy and rejected the treaty system as an insult to Japan's national honor.[16] These Treaty Faction officers in 1930 looked at Britain and the United States as virtual allies, whose combined fleets dwarfed Japan's. The issue at stake at London in 1930 remained the same as at Washington in 1921–22: would Japan have a fleet in being relative to the "Anglo-American powers"?[17]

Japan's battle fleet (and, at London, the cruiser fleet) was limited to 60 percent of the size of the RN or USN (not 60 percent of their combined strength). But Japan had calculated that 70 percent was necessary to prevail in conflict with the United States on the assumption that refueling requirements and wear and tear meant fleets lost approximately 10 percent of their combat strength over every 1,000 nautical miles they steamed. Therefore, a U.S. fleet steaming from the Hawaii would lose 30 percent of its combat power en route to where the IJN estimated the battle would occur in western Pacific. However, if Japan's fleet were only 60 percent the size of the U.S. fleet, then the USN would retain a 10 percent superiority. In naval warfare the three-to-one offensive–defensive relationship did not apply. A 60 percent IJN would be a fleet in being, while a 70 percent IJN could match and fight the USN at near-equivalent combat power. To this end, the Japanese intended their margin of success to rely on superior training and tactics.[18] This is why they fought so hard at London for no less than a 70 percent ratio vis-à-vis the U.S. cruiser fleet. Kato Kanji's Fleet Faction allied with Japan's army factions to oppose the London treaty and defang its cruiser compromise.[19] The London treaty provided the occasion for the Fleet Faction to wrest control of naval building policy away from the Treaty Faction.[20]

Assassination and violence became increasingly frequent tools of political "speech" in Japan after the London conference. The Navy General Staff informed the emperor that it would not be bound by ratios at the next naval conference in 1936. On 30 November 1930 a young nationalist assassinated Prime Minister Hamaguchi Osachi because of the treaty, initiating a season of political violence that continued to a young officers' coup attempt in 1936. A purge by Navy Minister Osumi Mineo in 1933–34 culled the ranks of Treaty Faction admirals from key positions inside the Navy Ministry.[21]

Meanwhile, the IJN's offensive purpose became apparent when both the army and navy officers favoring a more aggressive and expansionist foreign policy initiated violence in China.[22] In 1931 Japan's army in Manchuria engineered an explosion on the South Manchurian Railway tracks near Mukden but blamed Chinese "bandits" as a justification for preplanned military operations that delivered Manchuria into Japan's control. The army quickly set up the puppet regime of Manchukuo under the last Qing emperor, Henry Pu Yi. Japan's government proved incapable of overruling the army's conquests.[23] The "Manchurian Incident" (as Japan called it) generated an international outcry against Japan's perceived violation of the Covenant of the League of Nations. The League condemned Japan, which formally withdrew from the League in 1933. The United States refused to recognize Manchukuo, and most other nations followed suit, including Great Britain.[24]

Japan's army fomented another incident in Shanghai that involved the IJN. After the Manchurian Incident, Nationalist China boycotted Japanese goods and nationwide demonstrations occurred, including in Shanghai, not far from the seat of the Chiang Kai-shek's Nationalist government in Nanjing. The army claimed in subsequent propaganda that innocent "Japanese Buddhist priests" were "outrageously attacked . . . by . . . Chinese workmen."[25] Actually, the "priests" were likely Japanese soldiers acting as provocateurs. Japan's local naval commander Admiral Shiozawa Koichi used this pretext to intervene with naval infantry. The Chinese 19th Route Army responded with veteran troops. Japan's naval troops fared poorly, and the IJN had to call on a corps-sized element of the army to prevent a defeat. The aircraft carriers *Kaga* and *Hosho* flew naval air missions in support of the troops ashore during the fighting, which lasted for months.[26] British and American observers needed no more striking example of the kind of fleet Japan was building and for what intent.

The "Shanghai Incident" further inflamed the international community, including the major powers, who regarded it as a violation of the Four-Power Pact and the Nine-Power Pact, both signed at Washington in 1921, that nominally guaranteed the peace in China. Japan's government brought the navy and army to heel and accepted a less-than-satisfactory ceasefire in Shanghai that only further aggravated the nationalists. Another round of assassinations occurred when eleven young naval officers assassinated Prime Minister Inukai Tsuyoshi on 5 May 1932 for negotiating with Chiang Kai-shek.[27]

## THE BRITISH RESPONSE

Britain and the United States faced difficult choices. For Britain, Japan's naval buildup threatened the empire, but this concern was secondary to the specter of the breakdown of the postwar peace in Europe. In the Pacific, Britain maintained a fleet-in-being defensive posture centered on the fortress of Singapore, which was a joint base with warships, military aircraft, and a large army garrison. The United States, on the other hand, focused on disputing any Japanese attempts to wrest command of the sea by building a fleet intended for fleet-on-fleet battle and sea control as reflected in War Plan Orange, the contingency plan for war with Japan.[28]

Japan's actions of the early 1930s came at a particularly bad time for the British government. It was still laboring under the "Ten Year Rule," a defense spending premise that limited expenditures on the assumption that no war with any major power would occur for ten years. Winston Churchill had initially implemented the rule when serving as chancellor of the Exchequer—the same Churchill who had scuttled expenditures on Singapore in the late 1920s, calling Japan a "fancied danger."[29] It was not one of Churchill's finer moments.

Japan's actions in China influenced the deliberations in Britain's Cabinet and the Committee of Imperial Defence (CID). In March 1932, as the Shanghai fighting worsened daily, the Cabinet took up the issue of Singapore again, under the leadership of Prime Minister MacDonald. At the top of the day's agenda was "Imperial Defense Policy: The Far East."[30] The Cabinet noted that the Ten Year Rule was moot in the following terms: "No dissent was expressed from the acceptance by the Committee of Imperial Defence of the recommendation of the Chiefs of Staff Sub-Committee in favour of the cancellation of the assumption on which the Estimates of the Defence Departments have been based in recent years."[31] A caveat soon followed emphasizing the "serious financial and economic situation." The CID asked specifically to reexamine the Ten Year Rule and forwarded a new proposal for the defense of Singapore. The Cabinet continued to hold out hope for "disarmament" but clearly recognized the inapplicability of the old rule. The chiefs of the services had seized the day to highlight the rule's obsolescence.[32] Subsequent attempts in 1932 to achieve further disarmament foundered.[33]

By February 1933 the First Lord of the Admiralty referenced Japan's naval actions at Shanghai the previous year in a "Most Secret" memorandum to the Cabinet recommending over £100,000 for "defensive equipment and reserves" for naval defense as well as expanding the operating budget for naval aviation. He again highlighted the need to abandon the "ten year rule."[34] As Adolf Hitler assumed power and Japan withdrew from the League of Nations, the Cabinet approved measures to "expedite" the improvement of Singapore's defense from 5 to 3.5 years, add a second military airfield, improve its basing for ships, deploy another aircraft squadron, and make "detailed plans" for the garrison's reinforcement. To defend Hong Kong, the Cabinet also approved the redeployment of one battalion of troops from Shanghai.[35]

German withdrawal from disarmament discussions in 1933 changed the Cabinet's mood concerning disarmament. Defense calculations entertained the possibility of war with either Germany or Japan. Accordingly, the Cabinet approved the "recommendations" of the CID with the Far East as the priority. There was concern about the formation of a "Fascist *bloc* outside the League of Nations."[36] From late 1933 rearmament became a probability, although "hope" remained for some new development in disarmament.[37] In Great Britain this "hope" became the basis for naval conferences in London, including preparatory talks from 1934 to 1936. These conferences shaped the course of rearmament, especially Britain's response to Japan's naval rearmament, clearly underway in 1934.[38] By March 1934 Britain's government was in a quandary. The Cabinet committed several meetings to addressing "our worst deficiencies in Imperial Defense." Of interest were "the Far East" and the Locarno Pact, which recognized the "inviolability" of French, Belgian, and German borders. Hitler's rearmament placed Germany's commitment in question, and the impact on the Far East meant Britain no longer had only Japan to worry about at sea.[39]

In a late July Cabinet discussion, First Lord of the Admiralty Sir Bolton Monsell criticized a "most secret" draft report by the Ministerial Committee on Disarmament for understating both the "deficiencies" in imperial defense vis-à-vis Japan while overstating the costs of rectifying them.[40] He told the Cabinet that the "prospects of the [ongoing] Naval Disarmament Conference did not appear favorable and the position as regards Japan was disturbing." He provided information that showed Japan's spending per annum as £2 million more than Britain's on their respective fleets and that the IJN outnumbered the RN by 10,000 personnel. He then stated: "The defence of our Empire necessitated as a minimum the maintenance of a One-Power Standard. Our annual building programmes were formulated and our existing deficiencies had been calculated with strict reference to that standard. If our building . . . could not be carried out, and equally if our deficiencies could not be made good, the One-Power standard could not be maintained . . . and we might as well have no Navy at all."[41] The "One-Power Standard" referred to the parity the Washington and London treaties granted to the U.S. fleet. This time, however, Monsell was alluding to Britain's falling behind Japan, not the United States. The Cabinet agreed with all his points and the restoration of the one-power standard (although without specifying Japan).[42]

RN officers' attitudes about the disarmament treaties, Singapore, and naval building had come up in a luncheon earlier in March attended by Admiral Sir Roger Keyes and Franny Colby, a known confidant of President Franklin Roosevelt. Keyes expected Colby to inform Roosevelt of the chat. When Colby pressed Keyes about naval construction in the light of the upcoming 1934 London talks, Keyes relayed his understanding that U.S. Navy officers were "pleased [about] construction of the British base at Singapore." He added that "I think we should approve of your building what you like so long as we may do the same." He also indicated he did not think much of light cruisers, indicating indirectly support for a U.S. heavy cruiser construction program. Keyes noted the criticality of the Mediterranean and specifically mentioned Italy as a problem.[43]

By November 1934 it was clear Japan would leave the treaty system if not allowed to build to parity with Britain and the United States. However, of greater concern to the Cabinet was the need for a naval agreement with Germany should it abandon the strictures of the Treaty of Versailles and the guarantees of the Locarno Pact. The Cabinet first tried a multilateral approach to avoid, as the minutes put it, "a purely Anglo-German" accommodation and to keep any agreement on a "European plane."[44] The Cabinet met again in November, after the failure of the 1934 naval talks. Rearmament had clearly become the dominant policy, shaped by Germany's rearmament and repudiation of the

Versailles and, soon, Locarno agreements. The Air Ministry reported plans for the early completion of twenty-two aircraft squadrons "for air defense" (i.e., fighters) for the Royal Air Force and another three squadrons for the RN's Fleet Air Arm. Germany more than Japan motivated the additional air power. The meeting ended with the laconic notation that the German military liaison officer had announced he was now also the "Air Attaché," thus affirming Germany's intent to build an air force in violation of Versailles.[45]

The following year Italy complicated Britain's naval policy and construction. By 1935, in addition to concerns about Germany and Japan, the Cabinet and the Admiralty had to include Italy as a naval threat. Italy's capable navy threatened Britain's sea lines of communications with the East—especially India. Because Italy's actions in Ethiopia elicited financial sanctions and arms embargoes, Britain now had to account for another fleet in its calculations.[46]

Britain reversed course regarding a bilateral agreement with Germany and in June of 1935 signed the Anglo-German Naval Agreement, which limited Germany's fleet to 35 percent of the size of the RN, except in submarines, which was 45 percent, and assumed these submarines would follow international rules governing "cruiser warfare." The Germans were still under these numbers in all categories, but their construction increased greatly.[47] The rapidity of this settlement in part reflected the Naval Staff's fears that if the negotiators dawdled, the German "demand should be increased." Home Secretary Sir John Simon passed this information on to the Cabinet on 5 June.[48] The choice of 35 percent gave the Germans the same ratio the Italians and French had received at Washington in 1922. Britain would need 35 percent of its fleet to deal with the Germans, leaving the other 65 percent available for imperial defense.

As rearmament proceeded, another naval entente with France would have helped a thinly stretched RN against Italy, leaving the bulk of the remaining fleet available for any crisis in the Far East, including a Japanese move on Singapore. Although the initial French reaction to the Anglo-German agreement was "troubled," Italy's barbaric conquest of Ethiopia, the outbreak of the Spanish Civil War, and the ensuing naval cooperation in response to covert Italian submarine operations drove

Britain and France together. The aftermath of the Munich Crisis saw the formalization of Anglo-French naval staff coordination that continued until the outbreak of war in 1939.[49]

In London a larger conference to bring Japan back into the system convened on 9 December 1935. For the next two months the talks revolved around Japan's demand for naval parity. Japan's only "concession" was to limit the three major powers to a much lower tonnage of overall ships without limiting any of the secondary powers—including Italy. Japan's chief delegate was Admiral Nagano Osami, who later became chief of Japan's Imperial Naval General Staff. He was an heir of the anti-American Admiral Kato Kanji. He demanded parity or Japan would not rejoin the treaty system. On the 15 January 1936 Japan's delegation formally withdrew from the conference.[50] A second London treaty was signed in March, but without Italian or Japanese accession. Its main result on paper was the limitation of battleship calibers to 14 inches, however, a key "escalator clause" allowed the construction of 16-inch-gun battleships if one of the signatories of the Washington Conference (i.e., Japan) exceeded the limitation. More importantly, it intensified the British-U.S. cooperation that had bloomed at Washington in 1929 and increased after London in 1930. Japan left the system, but it had guaranteed a British-U.S. partnership if war came to the Far East.[51]

## THE U.S. RESPONSE

As in Britain, "disarmament" and economy shaped the congressional and White House response to Japan's naval construction programs. U.S. officers, however, planned for a war with Japan as if these constraints did not exist.[52] This divergence ended in 1932 with the election of Roosevelt, who, unlike British leaders, aligned with his officer corps and began to ameliorate the deficiencies in the U.S. Fleet.[53] He used naval construction as a federal jobs program under the National Industrial Recovery Act and used the passage of the Vinson–Trammel bills to increase naval construction to the "treaty limits." Throughout all of this, the General Board of the USN emphasized the importance of maintaining the 5:3 ratio of superiority over the IJN in the most important ships, despite lagging in both cruisers and aircraft carriers by 1932.[54]

The General Board shaped fleet construction based on its *1922 Naval Policy*. The 1922 Washington Naval Treaty affirmed the General Board's position of a "navy second to none."[55] The United States had adopted Britain's "one-power standard," using the RN as the standard and the Washington treaty as the justification to build a fleet to that standard—that is, two-thirds bigger than Japan's fleet. By 1929 the General Board made it clear to President Hoover's secretary of the Navy, Charles F. Adams, that "we have not such a fleet [built to treaty limits] at the present time. Each postponement of the undertaking of . . . essential new construction increases the already pronounced inadequacy of the fleet . . . and extends the period of that inadequacy still further into the future."[56] The board went on to recommend the construction of "replacement shipping" over the next four years: five aircraft carriers; a larger acquisition of aircraft for these carriers; thirty-five submarines; thirty destroyers of various types; one large, deployable floating dry dock for carriers and battleships; twenty-five 10,000-ton cruisers; and five new 16-inch gun battleships, beginning in 1931 with the expiration of the Washington treaty.[57]

The report compared both Britain's and Japan's annual construction rates to U.S. rates. The General Board emphasized that the construction was needed mostly to replace older ships—especially cruisers, destroyers, and submarines. It also referenced gaming at the U.S. Naval War College and the plans of Chief of Naval Operations War Plans Division as supporting its recommendations. These two organizations' efforts for gaming and planning centered on War Plan Orange, a war plan against Japan, not Britain.[58]

Hoover's policies had focused on extending the treaty-system mandates at the London conference the following year. To that end, he had helped improve U.S.–British naval relations strained over the issue of heavy cruisers and enabled the success of the London conference in extending the Washington ratio to naval auxiliaries in the 1930 London Naval Treaty.[59] Hoover then had used the London Naval Treaty to prevent new naval construction. He had used the upcoming 1932 Geneva arms conference to cancel and "delay" further construction. By the time Hoover left office, his administration had not laid down a single warship and only built one small floating dry dock.[60]

The General Board and USN leadership were trying to build a fleet that could defend U.S. interests in the Far East against Japan, especially in the Philippines, to match War Plan Orange's projections. Instead the fleet was becoming inferior to Japan's in every respect except in battleship tonnage. However, if Japan left the treaty system and began building more modern battleships, the United States might fall behind in that category. The United States remained a party to the system that extended the "battleship building holiday" and prevented it from building or improving facilities to base the fleet in Guam and the Philippines.[61] The United States would have a fleet in being by default if nothing changed. One of the more important changes arising from the 1930 London treaty was the division of cruisers into two classes, light (generally armed with guns no larger than 6 inches) and heavy (armed with 8-inch main battery guns).

Lieutenant Commander Thomas C. Kinkaid analyzed the tonnage ratios for the General Board in October 1932. Kinkaid found that only in capital ships was the United States correctly aligned with Japan and Great Britain. In aircraft carriers, Japan lagged by only 15,000 tons, giving the United States a ratio of only 7.5 to 6, while Japan's submarines were both more numerous and more modern. The United States retained an almost 2 to 1 advantage in destroyers but was "shockingly deficient in modern destroyer tonnage." Most alarmingly, the USN was behind in both categories of cruisers: Japan had over 30,000 tons more of heavy cruisers and 23,000 tons more of light cruisers.[62] As for British–U.S. accord, it continued from 1930 to 1937 under the chiefs of naval operations William Pratt and William Standley, when these "staunch" friends of Great Britain led the USN. Pratt wrote that in "the final analysis the best hope of peace . . . is that the United States and United Kingdom must stand firmly side by side, shoulder to shoulder . . . in the case of a break [i.e., war] the mutual interest of Great Britain and ourselves in sea power will draw us inevitably closer."[63]

The General Board also played bureaucratic politics in holding its recommendation for arms limitations. The board delayed its response until after Hoover left office, ensuring that Roosevelt would see it. In it they cataloged the dearth of naval construction and closed by alluding to "national emergencies," a clear reference to the Far Eastern crises in

Manchuria and Shanghai. It warned: "Present preparedness must not be sacrificed to an illusory future readiness."[64] Roosevelt acted decisively by earmarking $238 million for naval construction. The first Vinson–Trammel Naval Bill, also passed in 1934, supported this expenditure. These two pieces of legislation set in motion a decade-long building program to "treaty limits."[65]

Japan reacted quickly. In the fall of 1934, the preliminary talks between the major naval powers were underway again in London. Japan's lead naval delegate was Assistant Naval Minister Rear Admiral Yamamoto Isoroku. Yamamoto had been instructed to demand naval "parity" with the United States and Great Britain because of Japanese intelligence that the U.S. battle fleet's improvements meant refueling mid-Pacific was no longer necessary. This capability undercut Japan's "attrition strategy" against the U.S. fleet.[66] Roosevelt's message to Britain of his intent to ask Congress for an additional $500 million of naval construction reflected U.S.-British unity. Roosevelt believed Japan's leaders "were pushing a very long distance program of imperial expansion in Asia."[67] Nonetheless, the U.S. secretary of state believed that if the United States and Britain made common cause at a new conference, Japan would have to rejoin the treaty system.[68]

When Yamamoto presented Japan's condition of parity at London in 1934, Britain and the United States refused, even though their delegations suspected Yamamoto's disagreement with his government's position. Although Japan remained a party to the Nine-Power Pact guaranteeing Chinese sovereignty, with the rejection of parity, its formal and public withdrawal from the treaty system began and the terms of the Washington and London treaties no longer constrained Japan. But the treaties required a two-year notification period of an intent to withdraw, meaning two years to convince Japan to reconsider. Civilian diplomats in Britain and the United States believed they could do so at the second London Naval Conference in 1935. Japan, however, began almost immediately to abrogate the treaty, seeing no reason to delay modifications or new construction.[69]

The advent of the treaty system had driven the longer range of the U.S. fleet that Japan had correctly identified. The plans for longer-range battleships, submarines, destroyers, cruisers, and aircraft carriers arose from the reaction of the officer corps, especially the General Board, to the status quo fortification clause of the original Washington Naval Treaty.[70] The same reasoning led to creation of a "fleet train" to support this longer-range fleet. Prior to Roosevelt's administration, the lack of construction created an urgency in the USN to make other operational innovations.

Pratt, one of the more progressive U.S. admirals of the period, outlined his views on naval warfare for the General Board in May 1930. After World War I the navy had reorganized itself into four parts: a battle fleet, a scouting fleet, a fleet base force (which contained the fleet train), and a control fleet (an advanced concept that accounted for command and control of the other three components).[71] Pratt conveyed lessons learned from his experience as commander in chief during the recent Fleet Problem X exercise. It was only the second exercise of its type conducted with the new, large carriers USS *Lexington* and USS *Saratoga* participating as integral components in both the battle fleet and the scouting fleet.[72] Pratt informed the board that once "sufficient carrier tonnage" was built, he would like to see the carrier operating with the new heavy cruisers for a "really effective scouting force" that would operate faster than the battleships and out in front of the force. When pressed on the issue of the numbers of cruisers by the former Asiatic Fleet commander, Admiral Mark Bristol, Pratt replied he would like to have "as many of the eight-inch cruisers as I have carrier tonnage to go with it." Pratt also recommended an entire "division of destroyer plane guards" with this force. Bristol clarified that this equated to one carrier, four heavy cruisers, and six destroyers. In the event of war, Pratt wanted at least three of these task forces. Thus, in May 1930 Pratt had detailed the composition of a carrier task force and the operational number of carriers in the Pacific in December 1941 (*Enterprise*, *Lexington*, and *Saratoga*).[73]

In 1937, when Japan failed to rejoin the treaty system and confirmed it was building battleships with 16-inch guns (they would in fact be the super battleships of the *Yamato* class, with 18-inch guns), the United States began to design and build battleships with 16-inch batteries.[74] The U.S. program, spurred on by a second Vinson bill, included two new battleships. By 1938 a new naval arms race was underway, with the

General Board intending to build three 45,000-ton battleships (which later became the four battleships of the *Missouri* class). Finally, later in 1938, the board recommended the construction in the next ten years of what became known as the "Two-Ocean Navy Act," which included fourteen battleships and five big fleet carriers (later the *Essex* class) in addition to another two hundred smaller warships.[75] With numbers like these, Japan was running out of time in the narrow window when it could reasonably assume it might win a naval contest in the Pacific.

Britain faced a much bigger problem that still seemed manageable given that the Kriegsmarine (the German navy) was small. If war did break out in Europe, the cooperation of the French fleet would help balance Italy in the Mediterranean. Sir Winston Churchill was back in his old job as First Lord of the Admiralty. He made it clear that he regarded the Mediterranean theater as secondary to the Far East and that Singapore would be held no matter what. New Zealand and Australia increased their naval construction and added significantly to the numbers of cruisers and destroyers that would join the RN operating from the impregnable base at Singapore. There were developing plans even to defend Singapore forward in Malaya rather than allow Japan an easy march down the peninsula, should it invade.[76] Although Britain would require time to send naval forces to the Far East, should the Japanese violate the peace, it had confidence that the U.S. Asiatic Fleet based in the Philippines and the Dutch naval forces would join forces to resist Japan. These assumptions were well founded. The Dutch had changed from plans to fight alone using submarines against Japanese troop transports to plans to coordinate with Britain. There would be significant naval forces already in the Far East, to say nothing of the powerful Pacific Fleet in Hawaii to underwrite Britain's fortified fleet-in-being approach.[77]

★ ★ ★

War in Europe in 1939 cemented the U.S. and British approaches: respectively, a forward-based fleet in Hawaii ready for immediate naval operations and a fortress-based, fleet-in-being strategy in Singapore but with no major fleet or air force deployments to the Far East until war actually began. After the fall of France and Japan's signing the Tripartite Pact in 1940, forming the Axis powers, the United States frantically prepared to build up and secure its Pacific bases, and its use of air power, especially via an air bridge to China.[78] Because of Britain's desperate struggle with Germany and Italy, the Far East remained an economy of force centered on Singapore. Only weeks before hostilities began did Britain deploy major naval forces to serve as the capital ship nucleus of the fleet in being under Admiral Tom Phillips, although their publicly proclaimed primary role was to deter Japan. Japan's leadership had decided for war before Phillips set sail.[79]

The British plan to defend the Far East against Japan assumed that the situation in Europe would not entail a measurable increase in Germany's naval strength, France would remain in the war for the long term, and Singapore would not fall. One by one these assumptions collapsed. The biggest setback was the fall of France in the summer of 1940. It not only took the French fleet out of the security calculations, it moved the Mediterranean theater up in priority for Britain because Italian belligerency came with a significant surface fleet. Unlike the situation in World War I, Germany had acquired a huge swath of Europe's West Coast—from the Bay of Biscay to the North Cape of Norway—from which to launch air and naval attacks against Great Britain proper as well as against its maritime commerce supplying and fueling its industrial base. With Germany's submarine attacks, Britain became desperately short of destroyers. Another unexpected result was Japan's entry into the Axis alliance, indicating that Japan might enter the war at any time against British, Dutch, and U.S. interests in the Far East.[80] The final fatal assumption about Singapore shattered with the outbreak of war in December 1941.

"The enemy gets a vote," and British and U.S. reactions to Japan's naval buildup fell victim to that aphorism. Japan's actions on 7–8 December 1941 throughout the Pacific almost overnight put the United States on the defensive, forcing it to adopt a fleet-in-being strategy, a strategy of defense until it could build up combat power to resume offensive operations against Japan's expanding defensive perimeter in the Pacific.[81] British assumptions about defending the Far East began to unravel shortly after Pearl Harbor. Admiral Phillips set sail with his task force (designated Force Z) organized around the battleship *Prince of Wales*, the battle cruiser *Repulse*, and four destroyers to interdict Japanese invasion shipping in the Gulf of Thailand on 10 December 1941.

Phillips accepted risk in this action, sallying forth with his ships before ensuring that he had land-based fighter cover. The same Japanese naval aviation that the British had helped foster famously dispatched this force, sinking both capital ships, with Admiral Phillips going down aboard *Prince of Wales*.[82]

Ashore, assumptions about Singapore's ability to hold out without supporting naval forces crumbled, and that fortress fell in perhaps the greatest Allied disaster of the war in Asia. Singapore fell to Japan's army on 15 February 1942.[83] In subsequent operations the IJN virtually annihilated the remnants of the Allied fleet in being in the Far East at the Battle of the Java Sea (27 February 1942), which paved the way for Japan to conquer the Dutch East Indies and threaten Australia itself.[84]

Britain tried to employ an economy-of-force, fleet-in-being strategy centered in Singapore to defend its Asian colonies, but Japan dispatched this fleet in being in the opening days of the war. In contrast, the Two-Ocean Navy Act would transform what had been at war's onset a fleet in being in Hawaii into part of a force capable of defeating the primary U.S. naval enemies in both the European and Asian theaters. During the naval buildup, the fleet in being—built mostly during the treaty period—inflicted important losses on the IJN.

## NOTES

1. Also called *guerre d'escadre* (lit., "war of squadrons"). Clark Reynolds, "The U.S. Fleet-in-Being Strategy of 1942," *Journal of Military History* 58, no. 1 (January 1994): 104–5n4.
2. Reynolds, 106–7.
3. John B. Hattendorf, "The Idea of a 'Fleet in Being' in Historical Perspective," *Naval War College Review* 67, no. 1 (2014): 46.
4. John T. Kuehn, *Agents of Innovation: The General Board and the Design of the Fleet That Defeated the Japanese Navy* (Annapolis, MD: Naval Institute Press, 2008), 58.
5. Mark R. Peattie, *Sunburst: The Rise of Japanese Naval Air Power, 1909–1941* (Annapolis, MD: Naval Institute Press, 2001), 17–19.
6. Stephen Roskill, *Naval Policy between the Wars*, vol. 1 (New York: Walker, 1968), 317, 318, 528–31.
7. Roskill, 1:420–21.

8. John T. Kuehn, "A Turning Point in Anglo-American Relations?," in *At the Crossroads between Peace and War*, edited by John H. Maurer and Christopher M. Bell (Annapolis, MD: Naval Institute Press, 2014), 7, 21–22.
9. Roskill, *Naval Policy*, 1:565–66.
10. Maurer and Bell, *At the Crossroads*, 1–2.
11. Kuehn, *Agents of Innovation*, 40–62.
12. Sadao Asada, "The London Conference and the Tragedy of the Imperial Japanese Navy," in Maurer and Bell, *At the Crossroads*, 117.
13. Asada, 106–7; and Kuehn, *Agents of Innovation*, 54–55.
14. Kuehn, "Turning Point," 19–21.
15. 17 May 1930 telegram, Bradley A. Fiske, to the General Board, RG 80, General Board (GB) Studies 438-1, National Archives and Records Administration (NARA), College Park, MD.
16. Asada, "London Conference," 89–92; and Sadao Asada, "The Revolt against the Washington Treaty," *Naval War College Review* 46, no. 3 (Summer 1993): 89–91.
17. Asada, "London Conference," 99–102.
18. Asada, "The Revolt," 83, 92–94; and Kuehn, *Agents of Innovation*, 26.
19. John T. Kuehn, *A Military History of Japan: From the Age of the Samurai to the 21st Century* (Santa Barbara, CA: Praeger, 2014), 176, 190–91.
20. Asada, "London Conference," 118–19.
21. Asada, 117–19.
22. Kuehn, *Military History of Japan*, 186.
23. Edward J. Drea, *Japan's Imperial Army: Its Rise and Fall, 1853–1945* (Lawrence: Kansas University Press, 2009), 168–69.
24. S. C. M. Paine, *The Japanese Empire: Grand Strategy from the Meiji Restoration to the Pacific War* (Cambridge: Cambridge University Press, 2017), 115–18.
25. "The Shanghai Incident and the Japanese Imperial Navy" (Tokyo: Navy Department, 1932), 4. Held in the Trinity College Moore Collection, Trinity College, Hartford, Connecticut.
26. Kuehn, *Military History of Japan*, 187–88.
27. Kuehn 188–89.
28. Edward S. Miller, *War Plan Orange: The U.S. Strategy to Defeat Japan, 1897–1945* (Annapolis, MD: Naval Institute Press, 1991).
29. Roskill, *Naval Policy*, 1:464; and Christopher M. Bell, "Winston Churchill and the Ten Year Rule," *Journal of Military History* 74, no. 4 (October 2010): 523–56.
30. Meeting, 23 March 1932 at 10 Downing Street, Cabinet (hereafter, CAB) 23/7019, CAB 19(32), National Archives, Kew, London (hereafter, NA, Kew).
31. Meeting, 23 March 1932, 391.
32. Meeting, 23 March 1932, 390–94.
33. Kuehn, *Agents of Innovation*, 56–57.

34. Minutes of meeting, 15 February 1933, CAB 9(33), 138–39, NA, Kew.
35. Minutes of meeting, 12 April 1933, CAB 27(33), 440–41, NA, Kew.
36. Minutes of meeting, 16 November 1933, CAB 62(33), 220–32 (emphasis original), NA, Kew.
37. Stephen Roskill, *Naval Policy between the Wars*, vol. 2 (South Yorkshire: Seaforth, 2016), 164.
38. Asada, "London Conference," 119.
39. Minutes of meeting, 7 March 1934, CAB 8(34), NA, Kew; and Roskill, *Naval Policy*, 1:438–439.
40. Minutes of meeting, 31 July 1934, CAB 31(34), 353–54, NA, Kew.
41. 31 July 1934, 355.
42. 31 July 1934, 356–58.
43. "Naval Disarmament," letter from Franny Colby to Franklin D. Roosevelt, 25 March 1934, RG80, GB 438-1 files, NARA.
44. Minutes of meeting, 26 November 1934, CAB 42(34), NA, Kew.
45. 26 November 1934.
46. Minutes of meeting, 9 October 1935, CAB 45(35), 243–44, NA, Kew.
47. Friedrich Ruge, *Der Seekrieg: The German Navy's Story, 1939–1945*, trans. M. G. Saunders (Annapolis, MD: Naval Institute Press, 1957), 28–32; and Roskill, *Naval Policy*, 2:303, 306.
48. Roskill, 2:303–304; and Minutes of meeting, 5 June 1935, CAB 32(35), NA, Kew.
49. Roskill, *Naval Policy*, 2:306–8, 436–49.
50. Sadao Asada, *From Mahan to Pearl Harbor* (Annapolis, MD: Naval Institute Press, 2006), 203–4; and Roskill, *Naval Policy*, 2:313–16.
51. Roskill, *Naval Policy*, 2:319–21; and Kuehn, *Agents of Innovation*, 59.
52. Miller, *War Plan Orange*.
53. Kuehn, *Agents of Innovation*, 58.
54. Kuehn, 60–61.
55. Subject: "Naval Building Program Fiscal year 1931," 4 April 1929 (serial 1415), RG80, GB 420-2, p. 1, NARA.
56. Subject: "Naval Building Program"; and John T. Kuehn, *America's First General Staff* (Annapolis, MD: Naval Institute Press, 2017), 227.
57. Subject: "Naval Building Program," 2–3.
58. Subject: "Naval Building Program" 4–8.
59. Kuehn, "Turning Point," 23–27, 34–36.
60. Kuehn, *Agents of Innovation*, 56–58, 139.
61. Kuehn, 25, 26, 55, and app. 1, 183–84.
62. Thomas C. Kinkaid, "A Study of the Relative Naval Strength of the United States vis-à-vis Great Britain and Japan," 14 October 1932, RG80, 438-1, NARA.

63. Roskill, *Naval Policy*, 2:161–63.
64. "Limitation and Reduction of Armaments," 18 January 1933, RG80, GB 438-1 (1521aa/1584), NARA; and Kuehn, *Agents of Innovation*, 58.
65. Kuehn, *Agents of Innovation*, 58.
66. Asada, *From Mahan to Pearl Harbor*, 198–200.
67. Asada, 201.
68. Asada, 201.
69. Asada, 202–3; and Kuehn, *America's First General Staff*, 178.
70. Kuehn, *Agents of Innovation*, chap. 3, 5, 6, 7, and 9, passim.
71. Proceedings and Hearings of the General Board (PHGB), "Testimony of Commander-In-Chief, in Regard to Needs of the Fleet," 27 May 1930, RG80, NARA. Pratt commanded the U.S. Fleet.
72. Scot MacDonald, "Last of the Fleet Problems," *Naval Aviation News* (September 1962): 34–38.
73. PHGB, "Testimony of Commander-In-Chief," 27 May 1930.
74. Kuehn, *Agents of Innovation*, 59.
75. Roskill, *Naval Policy*, 2:470; "Priorities in 2-Ocean Navy Building Program," 30 July 1941, RG80, GB 420-2, NARA.
76. Roskill, *Naval Policy*, 2:435–37.
77. Rene W. A. van den Berg, "Patterns of Innovation: A Historical Case Study of Military Innovation in the Netherlands East Indies Navy from 1900–1942" (master's thesis, Fort Leavenworth, KS: U.S. Army Command and General Staff College, 2013), 108–37.
78. Glen M. Williford, *Racing the Sunrise: Reinforcing America's Pacific Outposts, 1941–1942* (Annapolis, MD: Naval Institute Press, 2010).
79. Evan Mawdsley, *The War for the Seas: A Maritime History of World War II* (New Haven, CT: Yale University Press, 2019), 186; and Asada, *From Mahan to Pearl Harbor*, 271–75.
80. Asada, 221–29.
81. Reynolds, "U.S. Fleet-in-Being Strategy of 1942," 109–12.
82. Mawdsley, *The War for the Seas*, 187–90; and Craig L. Symonds, *World War II at Sea: A Global History* (New York: Oxford University Press, 2018), 188.
83. Richard B. Frank, *Tower of Skulls: A History of the Asia-Pacific War, July 1937–May 1942* (New York: Norton, 2020), 369–78.
84. Frank, 404–10.

CHAPTER 13

# GERMAN NAVAL STRATEGY BETWEEN 1928 AND 1945

*Jörg Hillmann*

From 1928 to 1938 the German navy developed a succession of force structure plans aimed at neutralizing an expanding list of enemies in ever more distant seas. The 1928 Plan A focused on fighting Poland in the Baltic. The 1932 Conversion Plan added fighting France in the North Sea, tiptoeing past some of the Versailles Treaty shipbuilding limits to do so. The 1938 Z-Plan then focused on a globally capable navy after a European war, then defeating Great Britain and ending its naval dominance. However, Germany lacked the funds to follow either Plan A or the Conversion Plan and lacked the time to complete Z-Plan, so it went to war ill-prepared. In the interwar period, what began as a fleet in being intended to deter Germany's immediate neighbors grew to dreams of a dominant and offensive fleet. These ambitions reflected the dreams of German naval officers, but their plans never matched the military or geographic realities facing Germany. The competing ideas of navy chiefs Erich Raeder and Karl Dönitz illustrate the tradeoffs between capital ships and submarines that Germany failed to make because the Naval Command (Marineleitung) failed to link feasible naval missions with national strategy.

## THE STRUGGLE TO ALIGN THE FLEET

On 1 October 1928 Raeder became the controversial successor to the Reichsmarine chief, Admiral Hans Zenker, who was cashiered for a secret rearmament program known as the Lohmann affair.[1] Raeder inherited a shipbuilding plan, Plan A, which reflected wishful thinking, not the state of technical development in 1928. It assumed a one- to two-year warning period, allowing preparations for war.[2]

| PLAN A 1927–28 |
| --- |
| 42 Destroyers (Type: large torpedo boat) |
| 42 Large destroyers |
| 36 Submarines, Type F, ~ 370 tons |
| 36 Submarines, Type G, ~ 650 tons |
| 36 Submarines, Type J, ~ 800 tons |
| 31 Minesweepers (diesel), ~ 625 tons |
| 98 Minesweepers (steam), ~ 525 tons |
| 98 Motorboats and fast patrol boats of different types |
| 120 Supply vessels (Type: trawler) of different sizes for North Sea tasks |
| 90 Seagoing tugs for Baltic Sea tasks |

Strategically, Plan A reflected the tasks necessary to defend the German coasts, to keep the Baltic Sea routes open, and to protect transports in the North Sea against enemy naval forces. It was also designed as an emergency shipbuilding plan. Despite the experience of World War I but like the Royal Navy, Germany's naval administration favored submarines for support duties, not for naval warfare.

Meanwhile, the existing shipbuilding program continued to expand and modernize the Reichsmarine (navy of the Weimar Republic) in accordance with the Versailles peace treaty as amplified by the Washington Naval Treaty.[3] If the torpedo boats and blockade vessels built up to 1928 reflected the Reichsmarine's naval strategic orientation, the post-1921 construction of the new 6,000-ton cruiser and the 10,000-ton A-class heavy cruiser, the "pocket battleship," continued the Alfred von Tirpitz era's unrestricted construction of capital ships. The justification for these new ships was initially not so much strategic as legalistic, the right under the Versailles Treaty to replace the outdated *Schlesien*-class ships. Upon establishing the right to modernize the Reichsmarine, the next justification for new construction concerned ships to be used primarily in the Baltic, although their real operating range was much wider. The Naval Command justified to the skeptical political leadership the construction of larger warships as necessary for the "forward defense" at sea against France, which could act in alliance with Poland in the Baltic. The construction of new cruisers and the A-class heavy cruiser reflected not official Weimar

Republic policy but the naval leadership's intent to reestablish larger ships in continuity with their predecessors in the Imperial Navy in order to become at least marginal players among other sea-power states.[4] As the revision to the Versailles Treaty approached, the Naval Command's justifications for expansion aimed for the North Sea, but politics restricted the navy to the Baltic Sea and its armaments remained unchanged.

Raeder's 1929 memorandum to Defense Minister Wilhelm Groener—"Does Germany need large warships?"[5]—emphasized that only large warships against Poland and France would guarantee German sea lines of communication and, thus, the transit of essential national supplies in the North and Baltic Seas.[6] Yet he stressed that "every armed conflict [must] be avoided, in which England is one of our opponents. It would be condemned to hopelessness from the outset." "The wishful thinking of reestablishing an outstanding naval power" should not be allowed to gain ground in Germany. Thus, he followed his predecessors and supported the defense minister, who had already agreed to construct heavy cruisers but remained critical of capital ship construction in the tradition of Tirpitz.[7]

Raeder followed his predecessors' strategic reasoning by emphasizing Reichsmarine tasks in the North and Baltic Seas but expanded their context by referencing the concepts of equality and equivalence regarding probable opponents among the second-tier naval powers, such as France. In this way he legitimized the role of the new larger ships, given their speed, fighting power, and their radius of action, and he confirmed the important supporting role of submarines and aircraft in a joint network.[8] He asserted, however, the larger the fleet, the better. The Reichsmarine command, like its international rivals, regarded capital ships as the backbone of the fleet, not solely a military necessity but also a key source of prestige. The latter reflected Raeder's deeply internalized self-image of his service, not the actual military situation.[9]

Groener's 1930 insistence that the Reichswehr (Defense Forces) required the capability to counteract in the shortest period possible any Polish encroachment onto German territory did not cause the Naval Command to concentrate solely on Baltic tasks. Rather, Raeder stuck to his postponed new construction program for the B- and C-class heavy cruisers and tried to orient them toward the upper limits of the

Versailles Treaty.[10] Groener's post-1928 policy seemed moderate externally but difficult and inconsistent for the military leadership internally since the approved public armaments measures and the ongoing secret armaments did not comport with official statements. Despite a clear, justified mission, the fleet under development after 1928 only partially corresponded to it and was thus diverging from the politically desired tasks of national defense.

A disastrous focus on naval construction in the pursuit of political prestige rather than military necessity and professionalism ensued.[11] Just as the political leadership could not moderate the navy's maritime course, the naval leadership was unable and unwilling to act as a trustworthy adviser to the politicians but instead prioritized institutional prestige over national interests in naval construction plans.

In June 1932 the conservative nationalist politician Franz von Papen took over government affairs after the Heinrich Brüning cabinet had resigned. Under Defense Minister Kurt von Schleicher, the see-sawing in military policy became more marked and the treaty revision process under Brüning continued.[12] The demand for equal rights in the armaments sector and the associated tacit repudiation of the Versailles provisions became an openly articulated goal of German foreign policy, with apparent implicit approval in signals from Geneva and London.[13] Everything indicated that revising the Versailles Treaty was now within reach, but this further strained the tense relationship with Poland.

By the summer of 1932 Raeder preferred to build a 22,000-ton battle cruiser, well below the upper limit of 35,000 tons under the Washington Naval Treaty. In August Raeder set the construction date for the C-class ship as 1 October and allowed it to slightly exceed the displacement specified in the Versailles regulations. All shipbuilding plans already concentrated on larger tonnage figures, thus prioritizing a military, mission-oriented armament over an armament aimed at equality and equal rights with other naval powers.[14]

Based on a concept endorsed on 15 November 1932, Schleicher drew up a conversion plan for the Reichswehr for 1933 that initiated the revision of the Versailles Treaty. Schleicher prioritized the formation of a naval air wing and a submarine force. For naval surface forces, the Conversion Plan took the Versailles Treaty figures and added sixteen submarines and an aircraft carrier.[15] This way Schleicher met Raeder's demands, formulated in 1928, for a combined fighting fleet, calling it an "organic fleet."[16]

### THE CONVERSION PLAN (15 NOVEMBER 1932)

- 6 Old pre-dreadnoughts (kept in service, to be replaced)
- 1 Aircraft carrier
- 6 Cruisers / heavy cruisers
- 6 Torpedo boat–destroyer flotillas
- 3 Mine sweeper flotillas
- 3 Fast patrol boat flotillas
- 3 Submarine flotillas (16 boats)
- 1 Sailing training ship
- 1 Minelaying flotilla

Although the Conversion Plan restrained armaments in new capital ships, it anticipated expanding the Reichsmarine based on Raeder's 1928 naval strategic orientation. This continuity in naval strategic thinking still failed to justify the military necessity of capital ships in the North and Baltic Seas. Rather, it reflected the traditional desire, articulated by the naval leadership since 1919, to build capital ships because Germany could under the Versailles Treaty. Moreover, it implied the long-term expansion of the area of operations from the North Sea to the Atlantic, but this was not publicly discussed.

## FROM THE REICHSMARINE TO THE KRIEGSMARINE: THE DEMAND FOR EVER-LARGER SHIPS

After the National Socialist coup (*Machtergreifung*) on 30 January 1933, the Reichswehr expanded to become an instrument of Adolf Hitler's power politics. Like other conservative former and new elites, Raeder sympathized with such National Socialist goals as preserving values, strengthening the national community, and revising policy.[17] However, Raeder reacted suspiciously to Hitler's statements on the Reichsmarine's future. In the newspaper *Völkischer Beobachter* on 21 October 1932, Hitler had disparaged the Reichsmarine's armament policy as too costly and slow for tasks outside the Baltic and warned that capital ship armament could "confuse foreign policy perspectives" by disturbing relations with France and Britain.[18] In a private letter to friend and Nazi Party member Rear Admiral Magnus von Levetzow, Raeder described Hitler's statement as "the most foolish" thing he had done so far; it disrupted "foreign policy in a criminal manner" and demoted the navy to a coastal navy, even though tasks in the North Sea remained paramount.[19]

In his first briefing before Hitler on 16 March 1933, Raeder pushed the Conversion Plan by highlighting the need for equality with France at sea. His handwritten notes indicate great continuity in maritime and naval strategic thinking since 1928; Raeder worried that Hitler's fixation on the army would curtail planned naval rearmament.[20] Raeder's inconsistent thinking in advocating more capital ships but, due to a lack of resources, with inadequate armaments for their likely missions reflected the Reichsmarine's survival struggle against the political leadership, the Reichswehr, and international interests seeking to delay further German naval rearmament. In 1928 Raeder had warned against causing tensions with Britain by rearmament measures. In 1933, when the political leadership raised these arguments, he no longer saw them as dangerous and insisted on rearmament aimed at France in accordance with the existing plans.[21] The numerous foreign and military policy negotiations between Germany and Britain largely bypassed the naval leadership, which became increasingly active only after Germany left the League of Nations on 14 October 1933.

A new shipbuilding plan replaced and reduced the 1932 Conversion Plan, specifying the completion of the D-class battleship, four destroyers, eight minesweepers, and four fast patrol boats in 1934; the keel laying of the fifth battleship in 1935; and the commissioning of a sixth small cruiser and completion of four destroyers and four minesweeping boats in 1936.[22] Strikingly, the Naval Command's strategic orientation did not change from 1928 to the end of 1933. Instead it avoided its actual and primary task in the Baltic by continually looking toward the North Sea. Raeder's statement in the autumn of 1933 that his fleet could "sweep the Polish fleet from the sea and eliminate its only naval base" documented his personal self-confidence.[23] Raising questions linking ship construction with actual naval missions would have been politically disadvantageous for the Reichsmarine.

Raeder's proposal on 19 November 1933 to offer a larger German fleet to the British as an allied fleet strengthened the rationale for German naval rearmament. Both Hitler and Raeder seemed convinced of the need for an Anglo-German alliance.[24] Raeder might have made a tactical calculation that initial loyalty to the naval alliance would mask the intended revenge for World War I. He supported the alliance in the event of war against the United States.[25] The alliance was a new development in German naval strategic thinking that did not gain traction until the beginning of 1934. The conclusion of the German-Polish nonaggression pact on 26 January 1934 significantly relieved pressure on the Baltic Front at sea and on the Eastern Front, permitting Germany to concentrate on the North Sea. The Naval Command intended to use the upcoming naval conference in 1935 to justify building as much new tonnage as possible to make Germany an equal partner with Britain and gain a favorable negotiating position.

Prior to the conference Germany based its equal "partner at sea" status at parity with France, meaning 35 percent of British tonnage as accorded to France under the 1922 Washington Naval Treaty.[26] Germany's Naval Command highlighted quantitative equality without consideration of qualitative equivalence or required French naval missions concerning their colonies. Although the Naval Command portrayed its naval missions as founded strategically in the narrow Baltic and North Seas, it envisioned an Atlantic-oriented mission to interrupt sea lines of communication.[27]

The aim of parity with France implied a decisive Franco-German fleet-on-fleet confrontation in distant waters as envisioned by Alfred T. Mahan. Raeder rejected such thinking. During his time at the Navy Archives (1920–22), Raeder had studied cruiser warfare intensively and highlighted its crucial advantages over Tirpitz's battle fleet principle.[28] Raeder's theory that an "organic fleet" could provide both national defense and a diversionary effect rested on his deeply rooted convictions about World War I's ignominious end. Long-range heavy cruisers and battleships in distant waters could tie up enemy naval warfare resources for the long term, providing quantitative relief for the home front at sea, thus preserving naval supremacy in areas necessary for national defense. The Reichsmarine's parallel interruption of enemy sea lines of communication would relieve pressure on the home front on land by starving the enemy of personnel and matériel. Cruiser wars overseas and the use of the home fleet were therefore not mutually exclusive. This thinking was probably the most drastic break between the Kriegsmarine and the Imperial Navy.[29] The new naval strategy aimed at extreme offensive power that actively influenced the course of the war and that seized the initiative from the outset to fragment the enemy's naval forces. The desire for parity thus became the desire for supremacy.

The 1934 construction plan envisioning eight battleships, three aircraft carriers, eighteen cruisers, forty-eight destroyers, and twenty-four large and twenty-four small submarines fit this thinking. It clearly exceeded the previous tonnage restrictions and broke with the Versailles Treaty, but it did not represent a consensus within the Naval Command. The files of the Naval Command do not reveal any alignment with France against Britain.[30] However, the naval officer corps shared a resentment against British maritime superiority expressed in the private letters of the "old" admiralty and in the speeches during the annual Jutland Day celebrations.[31] The twin desires for revenge and a return to the ranks of the sea-power states were deeply embedded throughout all ranks of the officer corps.

Study IV reflected the findings of Raeder's headquarters' wargame conducted at the end of April 1934 "to represent aggressive naval warfare against France." It demonstrated that the relief of the Baltic Front at sea, due to "the ingenious initiative of the Führer," offered the opportunity to concentrate on warfare in the Atlantic if Germany developed the battleships, aircraft carriers, and submarines for long-range operations.[32] Current bases could not guarantee logistical support for Atlantic operations without future afloat logistics and improvements in the stability and endurance of capital ships. Although A-, B-, and C-class pocket battleships were therefore unsuitable for Atlantic operations, in April 1934 their construction went ahead.

D- and F-class ships would have the tonnage and armaments necessary for an "Atlantic capability."[33] The future F-, G-, and H-class warships would be 35,000-ton ships. Total tonnage was anticipated to be 280,000 tons, just over 50 percent of the British total.[34] Taking account of the waiver on building replacements of equivalent tonnage based on the 35 percent rule, only ships of 21,000 tons could have been built, but they would have been inadequate for warfare in the Atlantic.

Hitler rejected these plans. He intended to win over Britain as a negotiating partner and thus legitimize his land and air force armaments. Only on 27 June 1934 did Raeder persuade Hitler to consider increasing warship tonnage to 35,000 tons for the long term, but not with the recommended large guns.[35] Hitler supported the naval strategic orientation to fight France in the Atlantic offensively. First, however, he wanted to stick to the 35 percent rule vis-à-vis the British fleet to underpin the political alliance with the planned German–British naval agreement. This would form the political basis for naval armaments negotiations. Raeder, however, remained fixated at the operational level of warfare and rearmament.

The assassination of the last Weimar chancellor, Kurt von Schleicher, on 30 June 1934 weakened Germany's international reputation and led to a reassessment of its naval and air rearmament measures. Hitler had no interest in confronting Britain at sea. He focused primarily on the Baltic at least until November 1934, thus paving the way for the Anglo-German Naval Agreement based on a 35 percent rule. The naval leadership complied since Raeder anticipated implementing his second shipbuilding replacement plan by 1938 with political support and British consent to prepare for war against France. Only after 1938 would these plans have exceeded the 35 percent margin. Furthermore, Raeder might have hoped Hitler regarded such limitations as temporary since, over the winter of 1934–35, Raeder was emphasizing that the "skillful use of type displacement" would allow Germany to match British warship construction.[36]

As a result, the June 1935 Anglo-German Naval Agreement degenerated into a tactically calculated farce. In late 1934 or early 1935, Hitler and Raeder accepted possible antagonism with Britain by 1938–39, or at least a political "deterioration of the climate" over Germany's post-1938 naval rearmament.[37] If Britain refused to ally with Germany, Raeder would urge augmenting the naval rearmament already completed under the camouflage of the naval agreement.[38]

After the agreement, the pace of new construction increased while naval strategy stagnated: the Baltic and North Seas remained the areas of operations, while Atlantic naval warfare aspirations remained secret, despite their reflection in the design and construction of large ships. Lacking was both a guiding strategy linking the force structure to national objectives and coordination between the surface and submarine fleets. The first 250-ton submarine was commissioned revealing years of secret development under Commander Karl Dönitz. As the "submarine leader," promoted to full captain, he relentlessly pursued submarine technical development and tactics but failed to influence the strategic thinking of Raeder, who in the meantime had attained the rank of Generaladmiral in command of the Kriegsmarine. (In another step toward Hitler's dictatorship, the Reichsmarine had been renamed as Kriegsmarine on 1 June 1935 after Hitler's declaration of military sovereignty and reintroduction of conscription.)

Raeder remained convinced of the synergy between battleships / heavy cruisers and the home fleet, which—in combination but in different geographical areas depending on the situation—could create mutually supporting conditions to protect German sea lines of communication while disrupting those of the enemy. The 1937 Anglo-German Agreement, limiting naval armaments and exchanging information on naval construction, linked Germany quantitatively to the 1936 British-French-U.S. armaments treaty.[39] In 1937 a Naval War Staff study first addressed the likelihood of "active English intervention sooner or later" in a two-front war against France in the North Sea and the Atlantic, and against Russia and Poland in the Baltic. Yet the study emphasized that Germany's lack of resources ruled out a war against Britain. Significantly, the analysis did not include the German-Polish nonaggression agreement.[40]

This assessment contrasted with Hitler's objective articulated to the heads of the Wehrmacht (German military) on 5 November 1937, to use force to "gain more living space." Yet Raeder announced on 12 April 1938 at the end of a war game that, henceforth, Britain alongside France was a possible opponent—an old idea under discussion in the Admiralty since 1937.[41] After the March 1938 annexation of Austria and the increasing international pressure on Germany over the Sudeten crisis, in May 1938 Hitler ordered that Britain should be included alongside France and Russia in future war preparations. He also ordered immediate rearmament in submarine capability and warship production, exceeding the displacement of those already under construction.

In the summer of 1938 a Kriegsmarine Operations Department's planning study concluded that joint air and naval operations would be necessary to pressure Britain to negotiate a peace deal. This more realistic study and assessment by the Naval War Staff analyzed hostile naval action *against* German naval supremacy although it simultaneously anticipated a fight *for* supremacy at sea. This attitude, underpinned by National Socialism, reflected the unbridled desire for world status as well as the continuing desire for revenge against Britain. Yet the two approaches required different strategies and force structures.[42]

Raeder reacted quickly to the changed threat situation. In late 1938 he formulated alternative naval armaments to optimize shipyard utilization. Although Raeder and Hitler considered the construction of (already proven) heavy cruisers urgent, further parallel development of battleship and aircraft carrier construction continued.[43] They favored "forced rearmament without foreign policy safeguards" despite the naval agreement with Britain.[44] The Z-Plan submitted in late 1938 represented a consensus among the Naval War Staff, Raeder, Hitler, and the Kriegsmarine for construction to be completed by 1946.

### Z-PLAN (INCLUSIVE OF EXISTING UNITS)

| | |
|---|---|
| 10 | Battleships (including 6 H-class, 52,600-ton heavy battleships with 8 40.6-cm [16-inch] guns) |
| 10 | Cruisers |
| 3 | Pocket battleships (cruisers) |
| 4 | Aircraft carriers |
| 5 | Heavy cruisers |
| 12 | Light cruisers |
| 20 | Scout cruisers |
| 58 | Destroyers |
| 78 | Torpedo boats |
| 249 | Submarines |
| 75 | Fast patrol boats |
| 112 | Minehunters |
| 50 | Minesweepers |
| 12 | Submarine hunters |

In January 1939 the completion date was brought forward to 1944, and three more P-class, 30,500-ton heavy cruisers with six 38-cm (15-inch) guns were scheduled for 1945.

The strategic orientation of the navy was strikingly separate from the overall military orientation of the "Third Reich."[45] Naval strategy's incorporation into Hitler's overall strategy was rudimentary.[46] Due to a lack of internal dialogue, the naval leadership did not transparently convey its strategic considerations to its own service, so the "inner unity" invoked by Raeder and his predecessors was less based on a common understanding than on a traditional straitjacket of values.[47]

Until war broke out on 1 September 1939, Raeder, as the commander in chief of the navy, based the implementation of his concepts on the establishment of an "organic fleet" that would develop complementary and supporting capabilities in the overseas cruiser war and in the home-seas naval war. This orientation was offensive, regarding France as the enemy. British belligerency left the Naval War Staff with an offensive naval warfare strategy aimed at the immediate paralysis of the Royal Navy to neutralize its material superiority. This required capabilities different from those in the navy's new construction plans that targeted France and Russia until the end of 1938. Despite the changing threats, the Naval War Staff and Raeder stuck to their existing shipbuilding plans that Hitler seemed to support. Raeder, however, lacked the time to build the ships.

## THE BEGINNING OF WORLD WAR II: FIRST SUCCESSES, FIRST LOSSES

Raeder assumed he had several more years of naval expansion and so was not prepared when war came.[48] For the Atlantic campaign, on 1 September 1939 Germany had two battleships, three pocket battleships, one heavy cruiser, six light cruisers, the U-boat Salzwedel Flotilla (two Type I-A and ten Type VII-A submarines), the Wegener Flotilla (eight Type VII-B submarines), and the Hundius Flotilla (seven Type IX-A submarines). On 3 September, *U30* torpedoed the British passenger steamer *Athenia*, which soon sank. Germany sank a British steamer on 5 October and a Norwegian freighter on 14 October. *Admiral Graf Spee* operated successfully in the South Atlantic and received regular supplies of fuel, ammunition, and food far from shipping routes from the 12,000-ton supply ship *Altmark*, which also embarked the captured crews of the sunk ships. *Admiral Graf Spee* sank nine British merchant ships with a total tonnage of over 50,000 gross register tonnage (GRT) between 30 September and 7 December.[49]

Raeder had ordered the two battleships *Gneisenau* and *Scharnhorst* to the North Atlantic to relieve *Admiral Graf Spee* operating in the South Atlantic. They targeted the so-called Northern Patrol from 21 to 27 November 1939. *Scharnhorst* sank the British auxiliary cruiser *Rawalpindi* between Iceland and the Faroe Islands on 23 November. The British unsuccessfully deployed a strong contingent in pursuit, but the German battleships retreated into the far north of the North Sea. They then broke out undetected on 26 November in heavy weather and returned to Kiel. On the German side, however, the four submarines stationed east and west of the Shetland and Orkney Islands could do nothing against the British Home Fleet. The British located and so badly damaged *Admiral Graf Spee* that its commander scuttled his ship on 17 December in the Rio de la Plata estuary before committing suicide. The loss triggered heated discussions in Berlin.

At the end of 1939, despite the small number of warships, the results satisfied the naval leadership. The sinking of enemy merchant ship tonnage fell short of expectations, but the navy had already contributed to the war, despite its anticipated subordinate role. Above all, the submarines of Types II, VII, and IX had made an important contribution. The latter two submarine classes operated primarily in the North Atlantic and gravely threatened the enemy's sea lines of communication. In the first four months of the war, *U48* sank twelve ships totaling 77,000 GRT on three patrols. These early successes confirmed calls for more U-boats from the leader of the submarines, Rear Admiral Dönitz, calls that Raeder relayed to Hitler as early as September and October 1939.[50] Germany's insufficient resources repeatedly delayed the promised rapid growth of the submarine force. Torpedo failures, which thwarted some sinkings, were also of particular concern. The mines planned for Britain's eastern coastal waters fell behind schedule; in addition, the British captured the firing mechanism of the mines.

Although Britain diverted considerable resources and energy to counter German units operating alone, geography operated against Germany. To protect German sea lines of communication and impose diversionary effects on Britain, units had first to get into the Atlantic and, much more difficult, return past Britain to reach their bases on the North and Baltic Sea coasts. Thus, every deployment was dangerous and potentially quickly spotted by the enemy.

During World War I a distant British blockade had cut off Germany, and the Imperial Navy's ships had remained in Wilhelmshaven and Kiel as a fleet in being for more than two years. The Reichsmarine considered how to improve the geostrategic situation. Denmark, Norway, the Faroe Islands, and Iceland could play an important role in the absence of Atlantic coast basing. Ports such as Brest in France and El Ferrol in Spain became the focus of attention. Raeder made clear the urgent need for better naval bases. He also had information that Britain planned to land in Norway, which would cut off Germany from Swedish iron ore shipped via northern Norway. Raeder saw Norway as a springboard into the Atlantic, which was achieved through Operation Weserübung (the German invasion of Denmark and Norway), but with important naval losses.[51] The 1940 lightning victory in France opened better possibilities. The massive Atlantic port expansion began, including large submarine bases welcomed by Dönitz.[52]

The Naval War Staff intended Operation Rheinübung to tie up the Royal Navy for a diversionary effect from other areas where Germany would continue sinking enemy merchantmen. But only two of the planned five capital ships were available (*Bismarck* and *Prinz Eugen*). *Bismarck*'s sinking then severely damaged the prestige of the navy, the Reich, and Hitler. Raeder nevertheless stuck to the use of capital ships and demanded more Luftwaffe support. Hitler agreed, but Supreme Commander of the Luftwaffe Reichs-Marshal Hermann Göring did not cooperate. Yet the Atlantic ports used to expand capital ships' operational radius required Luftwaffe protection. As the war on the Eastern Front increasingly preoccupied Hitler, he lost interest in the navy.

While Raeder and the Naval War Staff focused on surface forces, Dönitz fought his own war from the submarine pens of Lorient (in occupied France) and Trondheim (in occupied Norway). He fought the Battle of the Atlantic with U-boats. Capital ships remained in Brest attracting repeated heavy bombing raids. In February 1942, to secure the Norwegian coast from British invasion, Hitler relocated the battleships *Scharnhorst, Gneisenau,* and *Prinz Eugen,* based in Brest, to the North Sea (Operation Cerberus).[53] Thereafter, U-boats fought the Battle of the Atlantic against enemy convoys alone.[54]

As part of Operation Paukenschlag, U-boats also operated off the East Coast of North America, which surprised the Allies, as had the improved Enigma M4 cipher machine introduced in February 1942. They also feared Admiral Dönitz's wolf-pack tactics, which stipulated that submarines maintain contact with any convoy encountered and radio its position to Dönitz's headquarters to enable more submarines to attack the convoy.[55] The British, however, intercepted this radio traffic so that destroyer escorts could sink the converging submarines.[56] Specialists in the Bletchley Park decryption center near London decoded German radio messages in an operation codenamed Ultra.

Although Dönitz steadily increased the number of U-boats targeting the North Atlantic convoy routes, sinkings still fell short of expectations. The Allies expended great effort but only partly succeeded in diverting the convoys, which were vital for Britain's survival, away from the submarine operating areas.[57] Even more concerning was the loss in early July 1942 of almost the entire Allied convoy PQ17 (twenty-four ships) in the northern North and Norwegian Seas, en route from Reykjavik to Murmansk with war matériel for the Soviet Union.

In November 1942 alone, the Allies lost 126 ships totaling more than 800,000 GRT worldwide, including 29 that U-boats sank in the North Atlantic. The British Admiralty stated that the U-boat threat had never been more serious. By the end of 1942, over 200 U-boats were operating in the Atlantic. The Allies upgraded convoys with destroyer escorts and carrier escorts (support groups), long-range reconnaissance aircraft, searchlights and radar for nighttime attack on surfaced submarines, and ASDIC and, later, sonar to detect submerged submarines. The hunters now became the hunted when the submarine became the Wehrmacht's last offensive weapon.

## 1943: THE TURNING POINT

The first half of 1943 was a turning point in German naval warfare. At the end of January 1943 Raeder resigned amid rising tension with Hitler and the unsuccessful attack on British convoy JW51B by a task group consisting of the Kriegsmarine's remaining valuable units that Hitler believed should have been used to protect Norway instead. Hitler laid up the surface fleet to free up armaments elsewhere, thus ending decades of navy aspirations for a dominant surface fleet. Dönitz replaced Raeder as commander in chief of the navy and chief of the Naval War Staff.

Dönitz immediately implemented Hitler's stipulations, but with a sense of proportion and suggested a compromise solution.[58] In February 1943 he stopped repair work on *Gneisenau* and the construction of the aircraft carrier *Graf Zeppelin*. He also presented a plan for the decommissioning of the capital ships or their further use. The battleships *Scharnhorst* and *Tirpitz* as well as the heavy cruisers *Prinz Eugen*, *Admiral Scheer*, and *Lützow* initially remained in service in their current state, while the navy concentrated all available capacity on the expansion and use of submarines.

FLEET CONSTRUCTION PROGRAM 1943
(PRODUCTION PER YEAR UNTIL 1948)

| | |
|---|---|
| 480 | Submarines |
| 8 | Destroyers |
| 12 | Torpedo boats |
| 108 | Fast patrol boats |
| 100 | Minehunters |
| 96 | Minesweepers |
| 35 | Barrier breakers |
| 400 | Multipurpose boats |
| 900 | Ferryboats |
| 96 | Light gunboats |
| 15 | Support boats for the torpedo flotillas |

In March 1943 the Allies once again could not read the radio traffic due to a key change in German encryption. This resulted in the loss of 20 percent of the escorted ships for the targeted convoys. However, within ten days, the British cryptanalysts resumed decryptions and improved destroyer escort direction-finder equipment. Because of heavy losses, Dönitz ended the Atlantic convoy attacks on 24 May and either recalled or sent the U-boats to find targets in remote sea areas.[59] Dönitz explained to Hitler on 31 May that enemy air superiority and "tracking devices" made German losses too high, with no prospect of replacements. Dönitz demanded improvements in technical performance, new weapons systems, new classes of electric submarines, new decoy countermeasures, and a naval air wing. Hitler agreed and increased the number of planned new submarines from thirty to forty per month.[60]

From then on, German submarines fought in distant waters, further southward along the East Coast of North America and in the Mediterranean and the Norwegian Seas. However, they remained vulnerable to enemy air superiority. Nevertheless, Dönitz kept U-boats in the fight and endeavored with technical innovations such as the snorkel to increase their survival rate. The promised new electric submarines, which had been praised as a "miracle weapon," were ineffective and only partially ready for service by war's end. After the capitulation, the surviving units turned themselves in to the Allies, were interned in neutral ports, or were sunk. Hitler's successor, Grand Admiral Dönitz, led a provisional Reich government until his arrest on 23 May 1945.[61]

## FINAL REMARKS: GERMAN NAVAL STRATEGY IN WORLD WAR II?

Until removed in January 1943, Raeder stuck to his concept of naval warfare with large surface units, although the rationale disappeared with *Bismarck*'s sinking, or at the latest when the capital ships were relocated back to the North Sea. Hitler preferred working with Dönitz, whom he later called his "best man."

Neither Raeder nor Dönitz could expand on any successes during the naval war. They discarded a concentration of forces in favor of forces scattered where Hitler demanded their presence. The supreme commanders were less advisers than recipients of orders. The German naval intelligence service grossly underestimated enemy decryption capabilities. This produced high U-boat losses, which could not be replaced due to the scarcity of resources and the slow development of more modern U-boats. As a result, Dönitz sent his crews into action with outdated equipment while trying to serve all theaters of war equally.

Raeder's prewar demands for an "organic fleet" would have been effective if the navy had had its own functioning air wing. Due to interservice rivalry, the Luftwaffe did not provide adequate protection either at sea or along the Atlantic coast. Ultimately, enemy air superiority and technical innovations brought the German naval war to a halt independently of the German losses ashore.

The navy lacked a clear strategic orientation as the war progressed. It was consistently involved in commerce raiding, which was initially to be waged with capital ships. When this concept failed, it relied solely on submarines. Given the experience of commerce raiding in World War I, this essential U-boat mission was foreseeable in the interwar period. But Dönitz successfully pushed for more submarines only in 1943, which was too late.

Both Raeder and Dönitz agreed that their ships and boats had to be used visibly in the war to guarantee a postwar navy. In this they resembled their predecessors in the Imperial Navy and Reichsmarine, who also followed the principle of "die and become" and preferred to "die gloriously" rather than to give up—reminiscent of their scuttling of the Imperial Navy in Scapa Flow in 1919.

Both the Reichsmarine and Kriegsmarine shared a common conceptual inability to fit into the overarching political and military strategies. Raeder's misjudgment that the war would be fought solely on the European continent and that the navy would have only a supporting role was just as fatal as the underestimation of the enemy's naval combat capability. Perhaps there is some truth in the assessment of the naval adjutant, Captain Karl-Jesko von Puttkamer, who said that Hitler did not understand the sea and was afraid of it. This is reminiscent of the end of World War I when Grand Admiral Tirpitz told the Germans they did not understand the sea.

Germany's naval access via narrow seas along the coast of its primary naval enemy required a force structure different from that of Britain with its unfettered access to the high seas. Germany was inherently susceptible to blockade, which meant its surface fleet lacked reliable oceanic access in wartime. This left it with commerce raiding as the main viable naval operation against Britain. Commerce raiding required U-boats, not capital ships. German naval officers' infatuation with a prestige fleet matching Britain's meant inadequate numbers of U-boats at war's start. Had Germany built U-boats instead of capital ships, it might have starved Britain before the United States joined the war. The German navy never planned to use a fleet-in-being strategy of deterrence but always wanted to match British warships and cut their sea lines of communication by using large battleships. That should have forced the enemy to use the full strength of its fleet against Germany. But finally in 1943–44 *Tirpitz* and *Scharnhorst* acted as a fleet in being in northern Norway.

## NOTES

1. RM/6–15, National Archives, Military Archives, Freiburg i. Br. (hereafter, BA-MA); and RM/6–16, BA-MA.
2. Werner Rahn, *Reichsmarine und Landesverteidigung 1919–1928* (Munich: Bernard & Graefe, 1976), 229.
3. Jost Dülffer, *Weimar, Hitler und die Marine: Reichspolitik und Flottenbau 1920–1938* (Düsseldorf: Droste, 1973), 87ff, 563.
4. Dülffer, 110ff.
5. Rahn, *Reichsmarine*, 281–86.
6. Dülffer, *Weimar*, 192f.
7. Tirpitz papers, vol. 20, 23–24, N 253/261, BA-MA.
8. Werner Rahn, "Vom Revisionskurs zur Konfrontation: Deutsche Marinepolitik und Seestrategie von 1928–1939," in *"Der Fall Weiß": Der Weg in das Jahr 1939*, edited by Jörg Hillmann (Bochum: Winkler, 2001), 81f.
9. Dülffer, *Weimar*, 564.
10. Rahn, "Revisionskurs," 83.
11. Dülffer, *Weimar*, 120ff., 182f.
12. Michael Salewski, "England, Hitler und die See," in *Die Deutschen und die See*, edited by Jürgen Elvert and Stefan Lippert, vol. 1 (Stuttgart: Steiner, 1998), 218.
13. Dülffer, *Weimar*, 167–82, 229.

14. Rahn, "Revisionskurs," 82f.
15. Dülffer, *Weimar*, 565f.
16. BA-MA, RM/46–147, Groener, Marineetat 1929.
17. Michael Salewski, "Marineleitung und politische Führung 1931–1935," in *Die Deutschen und die See*, edited by Jürgen Elvert and Stefan Lippert, vol. 2 (Stuttgart: Steiner, 2002), 128–74.
18. Rahn, "Revisionskurs," 84.
19. Salewski, "England," 219.
20. Salewski, "Marineleitung,"138ff.
21. Dülffer, *Weimar*, 243.
22. Salewski, "Marineleitung," 144.
23. Quote from Michael Salewski, *Die deutsche Seekriegsleitung 1935–1945* (Frankfurt am Main: Bernard & Graefe, 1975), 1:2. See also Michael Salewski, "Die Verteidigung der Ostsee 1918–1939," in *Die Deutschen und die See*, 1:199–214.
24. Michael Salewski, "Die deutsche Kriegsmarine zwischen Landesverteidigung und Seemachtambitionen," in *Die Deutschen und die See*, 1:191–98.
25. Erich Raeder, *Mein Leben* (Tübingen: Schlichtenmayer, 1956), 1:284.
26. Salewski, "Marineleitung," 145f; and Michael Salewski, "Die Washingtoner Abrüstungskonferenz von 1922: Ein Beispiel für geglückte Abrüstung?" in *Die Deutschen und die See*, 2:79–92.
27. Raeder, *Mein Leben*, 1:256f.
28. Erich Raeder, *Der Kreuzerkrieg in den ausländischen Gewässern*, vol. 1, Band 1 (Berlin: Mittler, 1922); and Erich Raeder, *Der Kreuzerkrieg in ausländischen Gewässern*, vol. 2 (Berlin: Mittler, 1923).
29. Jörg Hillmann, "Seestrategische Überlegungen und Planungen in der Reichsmarine und in der Kriegsmarine bis zum Kriegsausbruch 1939," *Seestrategische Konzepte vom kaiserlichen Weltmachtstreben zu Out-of-Area-Einsätzen der Deutschen Marine*, edited by Eckardt Opitz (Bremen: Temmen, 2004), 25–91.
30. Salewski, "Marineleitung," 147f.
31. Dieter Hartwig, "Das Marine-Ehrenmal in Laboe: Kontinuität und Wandel einer nationalen Gedenkstätte," in *Nordlichter: Geschichtsbewußtsein und Geschichtsmythen nördlich der Elbe*, edited by Bea Lundt, 413–438 (Köln/Weimar/Wien: Böhlau, 2004).
32. Lecture 66: "Gedanken über Kriegführung zur See zwischen Frankreich und Deutschland" (Rear Admiral Otto Groos, May 1934), Archivs 14098, Wehrgeschichtliches Ausbildungszentrum, Marineschule Mürwik.
33. Salewski, "Marineleitung," 149.
34. Dülffer, *Weimar*, 284f.
35. Letter Vice Admiral Hoffmann to Admiral Foerste (20 February 1957), N 328/33, BA-MA.

36. Salewski, "Marineleitung," 155ff.
37. Speech Raeder 1938, p. 36ff, N/391–2, BA-MA; and Robert Ingrim, *Hitlers glücklichster Tag. London, 18. Juni 1935* (Stuttgart: Seewald, 1962).
38. Salewski, *Seekriegsleitung*, 1:3.
39. Speech Raeder 1938, 37, N/391–2, BA-MA.
40. Werner Rahn, "Strategische Wechselwirkung zwischen Nord- und Ostseekriegführung im 19. und 20. Jahrhundert," in *Kiel, die Deutschen und die See*, edited by Jürgen Elvert and Michael Salewski, 89–103 (Stuttgart: Steiner, 1992).
41. Dülffer, *Weimar*, 442, 462ff.
42. Rahn, "Revisionskurs," 91f.
43. Salewski, *Seekriegsleitung*, 1:57f.
44. Michael Salewski, "Die Deutsche Seestrategie des Zweiten Weltkrieges," in *Die Deutschen und die See*, 1:246–60.
45. Knut Stang, *Das zerbrechende Schiff. Seekriegsstrategien und Rüstungsplanung der deutschen Reichs- und Kriegsmarine 1918–1939* (Frankfurt am Main: Lang, 1995), 389–94.
46. Jörg Hillmann, "Maritimes Denken in der Geopolitik Karl Haushofers," in *Deutsche Marinen im Wandel*, edited by Werner Rahn (München: Oldenbourg, 2005), 265ff.
47. Dülffer, *Weimar*, 345–48.
48. Rahn, "Revisionskurs," 98.
49. Hans-Jürgen Kaack, *Kapitän zur See Hans Langsdorff* (Paderborn: Schöningh, 2020).
50. Gerhard Wagner, ed., *Lagevorträge des Oberbefehlshabers der Kriegsmarine vor Hitler 1939–1945* (Munich: Lehmanns, 1972), 134ff.
51. Geoffrey P. Megargee, *Inside Hitler's High Command* (Lawrence: University of Kansas Press, 2000), 77ff; and Jörg Hillmann, "Die Kriegsmarine und ihre Großadmirale im kollektiven Gedächtnis," *Historische Mitteilungen* 20 (2007): 5–73.
52. Lars Hellwinkel, *Hitlers Tor zum Atlantik. Die deutschen Marinestützpunkte in Frankreich 1940–1945* (Berlin: Links, 2012).
53. Rüdiger Schiel, "'Cerberus,' 'Mandarine,' 'Donnerkeil'—Aspekte eines Wendepunktes," in *Die Kriegsmarine*, edited by Stephan Huck, 81–103 (Bochum: Winkler, 2016).
54. Jörg Hillmann, "The Case of Germany in the First Part of World War II, 1939–1942," in *The Sea in History*, vol. 4: *The Modern World*, edited by N. A. M. Rodger and Christian Buchet, 462–70 (Bognor Regis: Boydell, 2017).
55. Karl Dönitz, *Die U-Bootswaffe* (Berlin: Mittler, 1942).
56. Clay Blair, *Hitler's U-Boat War: The Hunters 1939–1942* (New York: Random House, 1996); and Clay Blair, *Hitler's U-Boat War: The Hunted 1942–1945*

(New York: Random House, 1998).
57. Werner Rahn, "Der Einfluss der Funkaufklärung auf die deutsche Seekriegführung im Ersten und Zweiten Weltkrieg," in *Führung und Führungsmittel*, edited by Winfried Heinemann (Potsdam: MGFA, 2011), 15–56.
58. Karl Dönitz, *10 Jahre und 20 Tage* (Munich: Bernard & Graefe, 1977), 303ff.
59. Hajo Neumann, "Der U-Boot-Krieg im Atlantik 1942/43—Höhepunkt und Zusammenbruch," in *Die Kriegsmarine*, edited by Stephan Huck, 105–113 (Bochum: Winkler, 2016).
60. Wagner, *Lagevorträge*, 507ff.
61. Herbert Kraus, "Das Kriegsende in Flensburg," in *Die Kriegsmarine*, edited by Stephan Huck (Bochum: Winkler, 2016), 205–11; and Klaus Hesse, *Das "Dritte Reich" nach Hitler* (Berlin: Hentrich & Hentrich, 2016).

# PART IV
# THE COLD WARS

CHAPTER 14

# THE SOVIET SQUADRON-IN-BEING AND SUBMARINE-IN-BEING STRATEGIES

*S. C. M. Paine*

Soviet naval strategists faced both geographical and technological constraints. To overcome the former, they pursued a far seas squadron-in-being strategy, requiring overseas basing and overflight rights, to acquire a veto-player role in the Middle East and Africa. To overcome the latter, they pursued a near seas submarine fleet-in-being strategy to ensure a second-strike nuclear capability as a guarantee for homeland security. The squadron-in-being strategy did constrain U.S. and Israeli strategy in the Middle East, and the submarine fleet in being proved very costly for the U.S. Navy to counter. Nevertheless, by the 1980s, the combined expenditures for both helped to bankrupt the Soviet Union.

## THE GEOGRAPHIC PROBLEM

Soviet geography provided landward defense but hindered both global access and a unified fleet. For land warfare, sheer size offered endless possibilities for strategic retreat to overextend enemy forces before counterattacking a beleaguered foe. For naval warfare, its only high-seas coastline was largely unpopulated because, except for Murmansk, it faced frozen Arctic waters. Its recessed seas suffered isolation by land and sea so that ports on different seas were not mutually supporting. The narrow Baltic and Black Seas were nearly landlocked.[1] This "recessed position" created "fragmented fleets":[2] the Baltic Fleet based at Baltiysk in Kaliningrad Oblast, the Black Sea Fleet based at Sevastopol in Crimea, the Northern Fleet based at Severomorsk on the Barents Sea within the Arctic Circle, and the Pacific Fleet based at even more remote Petropavlovsk-Kamchatsky on the Kamchatka Peninsula.

Russia had little ability to protect the long sea lines of communication separating the four fleet headquarters. From Vladivostok, the main Far Eastern commercial port, to Leningrad (St. Petersburg), the main Baltic port, entailed a 19,000-mile journey via the Cape of Good Hope or 15,800 miles via the Suez Canal.[3] Between its ports, Russia lacked access rights to any naval base with major repair facilities through the early 1970s.[4] Internal land lines remained underdeveloped. A single 5,778-mile rail line, potentially vulnerable to air strikes, linked Moscow with Vladivostok: 450 miles of this Trans-Siberian Railway ran within 30 miles of China, a hostile country from the 1960 Sino-Soviet split until the end of the Cold War. From 1974 to 1984, Russia built the parallel Baikal–Amur Mainline further north that serviced a negligible population.[5]

Soviet trade, the crucial source of hard currency, flowed mainly through the Baltic and Black Seas, narrow seas likely to be closed by mines, shore artillery, and hostile navies in wartime. They in turn empty into other narrow seas, the North and Mediterranean Seas, respectively, before reaching the high seas that tend to be safer for wartime traffic. All these seas border on NATO members. Severomorsk and Petropavlovsk-Kamchatsky—the two naval bases most inhospitable and distant from population and industrial centers—had relatively unfettered ocean access. By geography, Russia could close the Black and Baltic Seas to NATO, but NATO could close the Mediterranean and North Seas to Russia—cutting off Soviet commercial access to noncontiguous parts of the globe. Thus, its recessed geographic position yielded four far-flung fragmented fleets reliant on the vulnerable Suez Canal as a key connector.

## THE FOUR PLUGS: THE BALTIC, DARDANELLES, ADRIATIC, AND SUEZ

Four chokepoints restricted access to the high seas: the Baltic, the Dardanelles, the Adriatic, and the Suez plugs. To exit the Baltic Sea required transiting first one of the three Danish Straits of Lillebaelt (Little Belt), Storebaelt (Great Belt), and Øresund (the Sound) and then a succession of two Swedish straits, first Kattegat and then Skagerrak, just to enter the North Sea, another narrow, shallow sea. To reach the high seas entailed skirting other NATO-member coastlines either via the Strait of Dover or by Britain's naval base at Scapa Flow.

The equally fraught egress from the Black Sea requires transit through the Turkish straits comprising the Bosphorus, the Sea of Marmora, and the Dardanelles before transiting the Aegean to reach the Mediterranean—hence the importance of Turkish and Greek NATO membership and the 1936 Montreux Convention governing the Turkish straits. The convention precludes the transit of submarines except for repairs or purchase and allows warships reliable access only in peacetime and then only in daytime, but only with eight days' notice and with restrictions on the numbers and types of ships that can transit simultaneously.[6] In June 1945 Stalin unsuccessfully demanded basing in Turkey's Dardanelles and Greece's Dodecanese islands, Turkish cession of the Kars and Ardahan Provinces, and amendment of the Montreux Convention to put him in charge of the straits.[7] This helped elicit the 1947 Truman Doctrine, promising to support democracies against communist encroachment as well as Turkish and Greek entry into NATO in 1952, leaving the Montreux Convention and the Dardanelles plug intact. Because Russia could not reliably deploy its Black Sea Fleet beyond that sea, naval reinforcements had to come from within, including via the Volga-Don Canal linking the Caspian Sea, or from the outside for external contingencies. The vast distances separating the Northern and Pacific fleets made this logistically challenging. For Mediterranean contingencies, warships required ports outside the Black Sea, necessitating overseas basing, which the distances made difficult to support.[8]

A less obvious plug was the Adriatic. From a continental perspective, security concerns radiate from a continental center toward the seas. By the end of World War II, Soviet armies occupied central Europe, and Tito had established a Communist government in Yugoslavia. If Tito had been as cooperative in the 1950s as Mao Zedong was, the Communist Bloc would have extended from the shores of the Pacific to the Adriatic that flowed into the Mediterranean. This would have offered promising basing possibilities, but Tito did not cooperate. Instead, Stalin's territorial demands propelled Yugoslavia and NATO members Greece and Turkey to sign the 1953 Balkan Pact. Thus, upon the formation of the Warsaw Pact in 1955, the 1,068-mile Yugoslav land border became a dividing line separating Russia from the sea, closed Yugoslavia's 2,885-mile-long coast to Soviet access, and interposed thirty Yugoslav divisions between the Soviet army and the Adriatic.[9] Nonaligned Yugoslavia and soon-to-be-nonaligned Albania controlled the entire eastern Adriatic coast. Yet the shortest route from central Europe to the Mediterranean crossed Yugoslavia via the Ljubljana Gap into the Gulf of Trieste in the Adriatic's far north and past the Strait of Otranto, controlled by Albania in the far south. Likewise, the shortest air route from the Warsaw Pact to the Middle East and Africa overflew Yugoslavia.[10] Although the 1954–55 Cyprus crisis undermined the Balkan Pact by setting Greece and Turkey at odds, enduring Yugoslav and Albanian nonalignment plugged the Adriatic.

The most important plug was the Suez Canal, which saved Russia 33 days at 10 knots and 7,900 nautical miles (nm) to transit from Odessa on the Black Sea to the Persian Gulf (4,100 vs. 12,000 nm). Likewise, it saved 29 days at 10 knots and 6,900 nm from Odessa to Singapore (6,200 vs. 13,100 nm). Given that the main Soviet commercial port, Ilychevsk (now Chornomorsk, Ukraine), was located on the Black Sea, the canal's long closure, from 1967 to 1975 due to the 1967 Arab–Israeli War, had serious commercial and military implications: Pacific Fleet ships had to deploy for operations in the West.[11] The closure coincided with the Vietnam War, doubling the Soviet supply route to Vietnam and forcing refueling at sea. During the late Cold War, Bruce W. Watson, a U.S. Navy commander–turned–top Soviet navy analyst, argued that "the Suez Canal was perhaps the most strategically important waterway to the USSR in the post-war period" as its denial would undermine Soviet operations in Africa and Asia, while Soviet dominance would have limited Western military responses and trade—most notably, oil.[12]

Thus, Soviet egress to the high seas from the Black Sea faced the double airlock of the Dardanelles plug and the Suez Canal plug. To unplug the plugs required the command of a succession of narrow seas: the Black Sea, the Aegean, the eastern Mediterranean, the Suez Canal, and the Red Sea for commerce or warships to reach the Middle East and Africa, let alone the high seas.

The operational effectiveness of overseas deployments depends on a strategic package of capabilities. Although Russia had a variety of anchorages, ships need repairs and supplies, which necessitated bases. Naval bases in turn require permanent ship deployments. Unindustrialized countries—the locations of most Soviet overseas bases—depended on parts and other supplies delivered mostly by air, necessitating overflight rights—also problematic when Yugoslavia, a key location to break out of Eurasia, did not always cooperate. Given the difficulty of assembling these many capabilities, Russia sought reliable basing, which proved difficult in the unstable parts of the world that often issued invitations to leave after a few years of expensive investments. Everything about Soviet bases was tenuous: the double-airlocks to reach them, the fragmented fleets to support them, the unreliable overflight permissions, and the ambient political instability.

## A SOLUTION: FAR SEAS SQUADRONS IN BEING

Given these limitations and propelled by pivotal events, the Soviet navy gradually settled on a strategy of far seas squadrons in being whose existence constrained U.S. freedom of action. The 1956 Suez Crisis, the 1958 Lebanon Crisis, and the Arab–Israeli June 1967 Six-Day War were three such pivotal events. In 1956 the United States intervened against its NATO allies Britain and France to prevent them, along with Israel, from taking over the Suez Canal after Egypt's new president, Gamal Abdel Nasser, had nationalized it.[13] Marshal Georgy Zhukov allegedly waved a map at the Kremlin leadership to explain his inability to intervene.[14] The following year the Eisenhower Doctrine aspired to prevent the spread of communism in the Middle East. In the 1958 Lebanon Crisis, the United States deployed Marines to ensure the victory of the Christian president, Camille Chamoun, when a civil war broke out on the eve of elections. As in the Suez Crisis, Russia did little, not for lack of interest but for an inadequate naval presence to sustain intervention.[15]

In the year of the Suez Crisis, Russia increased its Mediterranean naval presence. In 1957 it had negotiated basing rights in Albania and in 1958, right after the Lebanon crisis, began staging submarine operations from Valona. The naval base remained under construction in 1961 when Albania supported China in the Sino-Soviet split and ejected

Russia. The divorce entailed the shooting deaths of Soviet sailors and Albanian confiscation of their submarines, suspending Soviet submarine operations in the Mediterranean for three years.[16] Rather than reliable basing in Albania, Russia ended up with an incomplete arc of neutrality, a de facto buffer zone separating Warsaw Pact and NATO members that extended from neutral Finland and Sweden in the north, through neutral Austria and Switzerland in central Europe, to nonaligned Yugoslavia and Albania in the south.

As relations with Albania deteriorated, Russia sought ports in Egypt in 1960 from an unenthusiastic Nasser, who feared for his independence if he hosted foreign troops.[17] Another pivotal event changed his mind: in the 1967 Six-Day War, Israel launched a preemptive attack to take the Golan Heights from Syria, the West Bank from Jordan, and Sinai from Egypt.[18] For the first time since World War II, the U.S. Sixth Fleet faced naval opposition when Soviet naval forces harassed its ships.[19] Yugoslavia opened its airspace and airfields to Soviet resupply of Arab armies. For several weeks one Soviet transport plane landed every quarter hour in Egypt.[20] Throughout the hostilities, Russia maintained a large Mediterranean naval presence plus thousands of military advisers in Egypt and Syria.[21] To deter a U.S. attack on either, Soviet ships deployed to Alexandria, Port Said, and Latakia to serve as a visible trip line, risking global war if tripped. Since Russia could not provide military aid efficiently without basing, disassembled MiGs arrived on transport planes, two per plane.[22]

Due to the war, Egypt allowed Soviet basing.[23] Permanent basing of spy planes for Mediterranean intelligence gathering began in the fall of 1967. A spring 1968 five-year agreement established permanent naval bases at Alexandria and Port Said with fuel and supply depots, early-warning systems, intelligence systems to monitor the Sixth Fleet, and rights to logistical services and weekly flights to Russia.[24] During the war, Russia assembled a large naval presence comprising elements of the Black Sea and Northern Fleets.[25] The latter provided submarines that had to transit 2,000 nm to reach Gibraltar because the Montreux Convention barred passage of Black Sea Fleet submarines.[26] On 14 June 1967, right after hostilities ended, Russia formally created the Fifth Eskadra or Mediterranean Squadron, subordinate to naval headquarters.[27]

The 1967 war realigned the great powers in the Middle East. Upon Israel's founding, Russia and the United States had attempted to befriend both Israel and its neighbors (also its primary enemies), only to discover that trying to befriend primary adversaries alienated both rather than befriending either. In 1955 Russia had abandoned neutrality to provide military aid to Egypt via Czechoslovakia.[28] A dozen years later in the 1967 war, the United States, not yet dependent on Arab oil, supported Israel.[29] This did not resolve the dilemma: such support radicalized Arab countries, which facilitated the expansion of the Soviet influence at U.S. expense.[30]

In 1957 Deputy Premier Anastas Mikoyan observed, "Earlier we had no access to Arab countries. . . . But then then we sold arms to Egypt, we bared our teeth to our enemies, and . . . now they cannot any longer resolve the issues of the Near East without us."[31] Andrei Gromyko, the long-serving foreign minister from 1957 to 1985, understood that a political solution to Middle Eastern animosities would expand U.S. influence. So the Soviet goal became to keep tensions simmering—a veto-player role, denying peace to the region.[32] Gromyko noted, "As long as the region remains tense, the Soviet Union is assured a role there."[33] In 1971 Ambassador to the United States Anatoly Dobrynin concurred: "We can always prevent a settlement."[34] Political instability in the Middle East and Horn of Africa have compounded ever since. An expanding list of intervening powers, each vetoing the plans of the others, has produced an endless stalemate, whose costs in deaths and depressed living standards the local population bears. Particularly hard hit have been the countries that granted Soviet bases: Egypt, Syria, Ethiopia, Somalia, and Yemen.

After the 1967 war, the Mediterranean Squadron, combined with the airlift over Yugoslavia, enabled Russia to support noncontiguous partners in the Middle East and Africa while restraining U.S. naval intervention. Efficacy depended on three prerequisites: Soviet naval presence in the conflict zone, a quick-reaction capacity with amphibious capabilities, and airlift. Basing underwrote it all.[35]

In the ensuing Israeli–Egyptian War of Attrition, lasting until 1970, Russia reprised its 1967 war airlift over Yugoslavia.[36] Nasser unsuccessfully tried to regain Sinai. The Suez Canal became the battlefront. The Israeli air force pounded Egypt throughout 1969 until early 1970, when—for the first and only time—the USSR risked its troops for a Middle Eastern country in Operation Kavkaz (Caucasus). In the spring, it deployed a 10,000-man air-defense division, including two fighter aircraft regiments. Israel started losing planes both to Soviet surface-to-air missiles and to Soviet pilots in dogfights. A cease-fire ensued—the war had become too costly for both sides.[37] Soviet intervention curtailed Israeli ambitions without realizing Egypt's.

During the 1970 Jordanian Civil War, when the Palestinian Liberation Organization attempted to overthrow King Hussein, Russia deployed naval ships among Sixth Fleet task forces, precluding naval attacks on land by either side for fear of vulnerabilities at sea. Thus, Soviet and U.S. naval presence canceled each other out, precluding a military solution to the crisis.[38] Amid the Jordanian Crisis in September 1970, Nasser died of a heart attack immediately after brokering a cease-fire for the War of Attrition.[39]

In 1973 Egypt and Syria tried to recover their lost territories in the Yom Kippur War (6–25 October) with a surprise attack, underwritten by Soviet aid, on Israeli-occupied territories. The preceding April and July, Russia had sealifted several thousand Moroccan troops and sixty tanks to Syria and over the summer sealifted troops to South Yemen. Once war broke out, the Soviet navy resupplied Egypt and Syria with over a million tons of military supplies, convoyed merchantmen that Israel had been sinking, and established a defensive blockade line between Cyprus and Lebanon. For the first time since World War II, Russia deployed its navy into a naval war zone, assembling its largest squadron ever of ninety-five ships. In a reprise of the 1967 war and the War of Attrition, it conducted its largest airlift to date, again via Yugoslav airspace.[40] On 17 October the Organization of Arab Petroleum Exporting States retaliated against Israel's supporters with an oil embargo that surged oil prices fourfold. This all imposed costs on Israel, which realized the days of lopsided victories against neighboring states were over. Nevertheless, Israel initially retained most of the disputed territory.

Nasser's successor, Anwar Sadat, reassessed after Russia refused to resupply Egypt's military or reschedule its debt.[41] As long as Egypt hosted Soviet troops, the United States refused to pressure Israel for concessions.[42] In 1976 Egypt abrogated its friendship treaty with Russia—no more basing or advisers—removing the veto player from the equation, and in 1978 signed the Camp David Accords with Israel, establishing diplomatic relations and regaining Sinai.

As tensions mounted with Egypt, Russia turned to Syria, which proved a reliable partner but with inferior ports.[43] In the fall of 1972 Russia reportedly signed a basing agreement to use Latakia and Tartus, which were small, overcrowded, and lacked Egypt's maintenance facilities.[44] So Russia sought additional ports in Somalia.[45] Even prior to the Cuban Missile Crisis, Russia and Somalia had signed a protocol on 27 March 1962 that would lead to the development at Berbera of, initially, a naval communications center and, eventually, a base, which was completed in 1969, the year the Marxist general Mohamed Siad Barre replaced the assassinated pro-Western president Abdirashid Ali Shermarke.[46]

Upon the closure of the Suez Canal in the 1967 war, Russia needed a base to the south. During the Yemeni Civil War—what Britain called the Aden Emergency for the 1963 to 1967 phase—Britain's side lost. Britain's reassessment led to its decision, initially announced in 1966 and followed by a 1971 deadline finalized in November 1967, to withdraw from its naval base at Aden, strategically located near the exit of the Red Sea.[47] Russia seized the opportunity so that by the early 1970s Aden became an important logistical center and base for its naval aircraft.[48] In 1972 military aid increased and Aden sustained subsequent Soviet interventions in the Horn of Africa.[49]

This facilitated the expansion of the small Soviet naval presence in the Indian Ocean established in 1968 from elements of the Pacific Fleet. It became known as the Indian Ocean Squadron.[50] From 1969 to 1976, Somalia hosted the largest Soviet military mission in Africa with 1,500–2,000 personnel.[51] By 1973 Russia had installed a powerful telecommunications station so that until 1977 Berbera became the command-and-control center for the Indian Ocean Squadron that conducted naval operations in the Red Sea, the Persian Gulf, and the Indian Ocean.[52] Berbera became Russia's closest equivalent to a base in Africa. It did not last.[53]

Aden became essential after the overthrow of Ethiopia's Emperor Haile Selassie in 1974.[54] Despite Marxist governments in both Ethiopia and Somalia, the impossibility of befriending primary adversaries forced a choice. Russia chose Ethiopia when Somalia invaded Ogaden, Ethiopia, triggering the Ogaden War (1977–78). Somalia retaliated on 13 November 1977, giving Russian personnel a week to leave, costing Russia access to all facilities there, including Berbera.[55] In the Ogaden War, Russia supported Ethiopia militarily from Aden, delivering supplies to Assab and Massawa. Its ships transported 16,000–17,000 Cuban troops from Cuba and Angola to Ethiopia, while its planes flew in supplies in one of its largest military resupply operations. Aden became the staging base for the Indian Ocean Squadron, and the island of Socotra off Yemen served as an anchorage.[56] With the loss of Berbera, Russia soon created an alternate but much more limited base on the island of Nokra in the Dahlak Archipelago off Massawa, Eritrea, then in the midst of its own war of independence from Ethiopia (1962–91). It became the Indian Ocean Squadron's main logistical base.[57]

Domestic instability in Somalia, Ethiopia, Eritrea, and Yemen made secure basing on the Red Sea or Gulf of Aden problematic, with the host country too often subject to regional and civil wars. The poverty of these areas hindered modern basing since they lacked basic infrastructure and industry to support a fleet. Nevertheless, the mere presence of a Soviet squadron in being complicated U.S. strategy. It denied the United States complete freedom of maneuver, lost after the Suez and Lebanon crises of the 1950s. Henceforth, when calculating the risks of intervening in any unfolding crisis in the Mediterranean or Suez Canal, it had to consider Russian naval presence and the possible escalation of a regional, medium-value conflict into a global existential one. Even Israel, which considered these regional wars existential, ultimately had to scale back its attacks on its neighbors because of Soviet military aid to them. U.S. and Soviet naval intervention, actual or threatened, precluded either side from winning and guaranteed roles for each as the regional antagonists sought foreign aid to prevent defeat. This yielded frozen conflicts not conducive to economic growth.

## THE TECHNOLOGICAL PROBLEM: NUCLEAR-POWERED AND -ARMED SUBMARINES

Russia faced not only geographical limitations but also technological problems. The advent of nuclear weapons meant that the Strategic

Rocket Forces, no longer the ground forces, guaranteed Soviet security.[58] Nuclear weapons required a broad array of technology to ensure adequate range, precision, lethality, and reliability. By the 1970s Russia's computer chip industry was woefully behind, which meant that U.S. ballistic missiles had superior ranges and accuracy.[59]

The first U.S. nuclear-powered submarine (SSBN) with submarine-launched ballistic missiles (SLBMs) armed with nuclear warheads went to sea in 1960. These Polaris A-1 missiles were first-generation SLBMs with a range of 1,200 nm and armed with a single warhead. U.S. SLBM ranges rapidly increased to 1,500 nm in 1961 (Polaris A-2), then to 2,500 nm with multiple warheads in 1964 (Polaris A-3), and then the same range but armed with multiple independently targetable warheads in 1971 (Poseidon), and attained a range of over 4,000 nm in 1982 (Trident I).[60] Russia was well aware of these developments, with Fleet Admiral Sergey G. Gorshkov providing a largely accurate table highlighting this information in his widely read book *The Sea Power of the State*, originally published in Russian in 1976.[61]

Russia had no counter for Polaris, which undermined its reliance on anticarrier capabilities because submarines, not aircraft carriers, would now deliver strategic nuclear weapons.[62] Immediately after Polaris A-1 deployments, Russia delivered medium-range ballistic missiles to Cuba in the fall of 1962, precipitating the Cuban Missile Crisis that resulted in Nikita Khrushchev's removal of the missiles and, later, his own removal from office for this and other setbacks.[63] Russia lacked the naval support capacity to defend Cuba at such distance from itself and such proximity to the United States.

To help counter Polaris submarines, Russia built its Yankee and Delta class SSBNs, but they could not locate U.S. SSBNs in open oceans and struggled to tail them as they left port.[64] In the 1960s, Russia also developed new ship classes, such as the missile-armed helicopter carriers *Moskva* and *Leningrad*, which were not very effective at antisubmarine warfare.[65] With trailing impossible, Russia focused on detecting SSBNs using seafloor acoustic sensors, land-based air, and surface combatants. Initially, an area-watch strategy was possible because the SSBNs armed with Polaris A-1 missiles had to approach close to Soviet shores to put Moscow within range.[66]

The longer-ranged A-2 and A-3 missiles forced Russia to extend its zonal defense outward. Soviet military doctrine of the mid-1950s had emphasized three concentric rings for maritime defense. A "Near Zone" barring enemy amphibious landings extended from the shore out about 100 miles, the maximum range of the Russian navy's land-based fighter planes for continuous air cover. A "Far Zone" of 300–400 miles in depth extended out to the maximum range for hostile carrier-based air attack on land targets. The Far Zone exceeded land-based Soviet air cover and its navy's ability to command these seas, but it could keep their command in dispute. Finally, an "Open Ocean Zone" comprised everything further out—areas where the U.S. Navy overmatched the Soviet navy.[67]

With the advent of Polaris submarines, the outer defense zone extended 1,500 nm from Moscow to include the eastern Mediterranean and Norwegian Seas. With the extension of U.S. SLBM ranges, in 1967–68, this arc of operations expanded to 2,500 nm to encompass the eastern half of the North Atlantic and the northern half of the Arabian Sea. The increased range of U.S. SLBMs beyond the Arctic Ocean and Barents Sea undermined Soviet progress in antisubmarine warfare because its submarines could not cover this vast area at such a distance.[68] While most Soviet forces could not reach the continental United States, Trident missiles could target strategic nuclear weapons on Russia from virtually any ocean.[69]

In 1970 Secretary of Defense Melvin R. Laird stated, "We believe that our Polaris and Poseidon submarines at sea can be considered virtually invulnerable today."[70] Meanwhile, U.S. submarines were trailing Russian SSBNs immediately after they left port for the high seas, undermining Russia's second-strike capability. Polaris gave the United States nuclear superiority that endured with subsequent generations of SLBMs until the end of the Soviet Union.

## A SOLUTION: NEAR SEAS SUBMARINE FLEETS IN BEING

With new U.S. submarine types—one fast, the other quiet—coming online in the early 1970s, Russia countered with a bastion strategy protecting a submarine fleet in being.[71] In fortifications, bastions are the parts projecting outward at an angle from the line of the wall to permit defensive fire from multiple directions. Russia would deploy its submarines in near sea–protected bastions to guarantee a reliable second-strike capability in the event of a nuclear war. To do so required missiles of sufficient range and quieter submarines. Espionage contributed to Russia's success. The spies responsible and their years of activity include retired Chief Warrant Officer John Walker (1967–84), FBI agent Robert Hanssen (1979–2001), and CIA officer Aldrich Ames (1985–94).[72]

In 1977 Admiral Stansfield Turner, Supreme Allied Commander NATO Southern Europe, observed that the postwar Soviet navy had transitioned from a coastal defense force to one aspiring to "(1) strategic deterrence; (2) naval presence; and (3) sea denial." In his estimation, this indicated that the "Soviet strategists had read Mahan."[73] Alfred T. Mahan, however, wrote for countries with a maritime geography of open, populated shores, not those with coastlines constricted by plugged narrow seas, teaming with hostile neighbors. Gorshkov oversaw a massive fleet buildup for a country lacking the geographic prerequisites enumerated by Mahan. Many of his new ships did not come online until the 1980s.[74]

Prior to the mid-1960s, the Soviet navy's primary mission had been near seas maritime defense; thereafter it became strategic strike with sea-based nuclear weapons aimed at distant targets on land.[75] In 1960, at about the time the first Polaris submarines deployed, Gorshkov wrote, "Leading military thought correctly considers that the fleet which most fully answers the demands of modern warfare must be based on submarines. It is precisely in this direction that the Navy of the Soviet Union is now developing."[76] His fascination with submarines went back to World War II. He calculated that each Nazi U-boat had tied up twenty-five Allied warships and a hundred aircraft, while each German submariner at sea had preoccupied a hundred Allied antisubmariners. He concluded that "one can hardly find a similar ratio of forces between attacking and defending forces among all of the other branches of the armed forces."[77] Gorshkov made SSBNs the priority force of Soviet navy.[78] In 1971 the 24th Party Congress greatly increased naval funding, adding new classes of warships to be delivered in early 1980s.[79]

In 1972 and 1973 Gorshkov published eleven articles in *The Soviet Naval Journal* (Морской сборник) that the Center for Naval Analyses interpreted in 1973 as a new Soviet naval doctrine, an "apparent adoption of a strategic 'fleet in being' concept for at least a portion of their SSBN force," intended as a strategic reserve to gain leverage during war termination. It believed SSBNs would operate within "bastions" protected by naval forces.[80] Very long-range SLBMs allowed SSBNs to remain in local waters, "security sanctuaries" primarily in the Barents Sea but also in the Sea of Okhotsk.[81] In both editions of *The Sea Power of the State*, published in 1976 and 1979, Gorshkov wrote: "History provides examples in which fleets by their presence alone, or even just by their existence, have exercised a certain, sometimes even very substantial, influence on the course of an armed struggle in ground theaters—if only by appearing in the capacity of a potential threat of further prolongation of the war."[82]

By the early 1970s SLBMs could target the United States from Soviet coastal waters, where Soviet submarines preferred to remain, as they were noisier than U.S. submarines and therefore vulnerable to detection, and where familiarity with the terrain, combined with air and surface support, offered protection.[83] To protect against SLBMs, the Soviet navy also needed the capability to destroy U.S. missile submarines and make nuclear strikes against the United States. This required antisubmarine warfare forces to protect Soviet SSBM sanctuaries.[84] Russia built light carriers for helicopters and others for vertical-takeoff-and-landing aircraft. In 1982 it laid down the first of multiple attack carriers.[85]

In 1980–81, U.S. naval intelligence confirmed the new Soviet doctrine reliant on SSBN bastions in northern waters with the bulk of general purpose forces deployed to defend them.[86] By the 1980s, after fifteen years of debate, this became the consensus view of the U.S. intelligence community.[87] The Soviet navy tested the doctrine in wargames and exercises.[88] In 1991, at the end of the Cold War, glasnost publications confirmed these assessments: by the late 1970s Soviet SSBNs were conducting combat patrols from home water bastions and mainly stuck to coastal waters.[89]

This bastion strategy caused a major reallocation of capital ships and submarines among Russia's four fleets. From the mid-1970s onward, submarines and large surface combatants were reallocated from Baltic and Black Sea Fleets to the Northern and especially the

Pacific Fleets.⁹⁰ Because the bastion strategy deferred cutting Western sea lines of communication, the United States—for the first time in fifty years—no longer prioritized protecting them, freeing up assets to target the bastions.⁹¹

During the Reagan administration (1981–89), chiefs of naval operations (CNOs) Thomas B. Hayward (1978–82) and James D. Watkins (1982–86) responded to the Soviet submarine fleet-in-being bastion strategy by changing from a defensive to an offensive strategy.⁹² From 1977 to 1978 numerous classified discussions analyzed Hayward's Sea Strike war plan. It entailed drawing Soviet assets away from Europe to the Far East and enlisting Japan's help. This became one of the bases for the 1980s Maritime Strategy.⁹³ In January 1979 the "CNO Strategic Concepts" highlighted the denial of sanctuaries to force Soviet naval operations back to home waters, which would preclude their attacking U.S. sea lines of communications.⁹⁴

Secretary of the Navy John Lehman (1981–87) and admirals Hayward and Watkins were the most prominent authors of the fully developed U.S. maritime strategy of the 1980s. President Ronald Reagan's 1987 unclassified version of the *National Security Strategy of the United States* promised that U.S. maritime superiority would permit "the United States to tie down Soviet naval forces in a defensive posture protecting Soviet ballistic missile submarines and the seaward approaches to the Soviet homeland, and thereby to minimize the wartime threat to the reinforcement and resupply of Europe by sea."⁹⁵

The strategy succeeded in a serendipitous way—by helping bankrupt Russia. When Watkins' successor, CNO Admiral Carlisle A. H. Trost, hosted Marshal Sergei F. Akhromeyev in 1987, the marshal complained, "We are surrounded. That is why we are concerned. We are concerned about our defense and our survival. . . . We know you know where our submarines are but we don't know where yours are. That's destabilizing." He revealed that, by tracking U.S. P-3 aircraft, "I know they're flying over my submarines. That's why I know where my submarines are at any given time. All I have to do is look and see where your airplanes are flying. . . . You . . . you the United States Navy, are the problem"—to which Trost replied, "I am pleased to hear that we're being effective . . . that our strategy is in fact working."⁹⁶

## BANKRUPTCY AND FROZEN CONFLICTS

In 1956 Gorshkov had inherited a coastal defense fleet aspiring to command seas limited to the immediate theater of operations or to the duration of hit-and-run raids. The fleet had no attack aircraft carriers. After Russian naval weakness in the 1956 Suez Crisis, 1958 Lebanon Crisis, 1962 Cuban Missile Crisis, June 1967 War, and the 1970 War of Attrition made clear the utility of a forward-deployable fleet, Russia bought the platforms necessary for a far seas, squadron-in-being denial strategy.[97] Russia simultaneously bought the whole suite of platforms for a deterrent submarine fleet-in-being strategy. Together this transformed Russia into the world's second sea power for the first time in history.[98] But navies require extraordinary maintenance to keep steel afloat in salt water; without funding, ships rapidly rust out—the fate of Gorshkov's prestige fleet. Gorshkov's ship deliveries coincided with the collapse of the USSR. The costs of his sustained naval buildup—in combination with the proliferation of Soviet third-world interventions, the militarization of Sino-Soviet border, maintaining the Warsaw Pact, and Russia's own underperforming economy—bankrupted the USSR. Among Mikhail Gorbachev's first reforms was replacing Admiral Gorshkov in 1985 with Admiral Vladimir Chernavin, who subordinated the navy to the army to support land operations.[99] In 1994 Russia sold to South Korea as scrap two aircraft carriers for $8 million, and thirty ships, submarines, and supply vessels for another $3 million.[100] Other ships rusted out in home waters, so within fifteen years of the end of the Cold War, "fully three-quarters to five-sixths of the Soviet-era inventory was written off."[101] It is unclear what the nuclear submarine fleet-in-being bastion strategy accomplished since spy Clyde Lee Conrad revealed to the USSR that NATO had no plans to attack, and, in the war that never happened, no one knows how the equipment would have performed.[102] In any case, the costs were unsustainable. In contrast, the more economical squadron-in-being strategy proved capable of denying peace to others to maintain the Soviet ability in the Middle East and Africa—if not to further its own aims, then to balk those of others.

## NOTES

1. Charles C. Petersen, "Trends in Soviet Naval Operations," in *Soviet Naval Diplomacy*, edited by Bradford Dismukes and James M. McConnell (New York: Pergamon, 1979), 38.
2. Kenneth Wayne Malbon, "Admiral Gorshkov and Russia's Naval Heritage" (Ph.D. diss., Fletcher School of Law and Diplomacy, Tufts University, 1993), 88–89.
3. George W. Baer, *One Hundred Years of Sea Power* (Stanford, CA: Stanford University Press, 1993), 425.
4. Malbon, "Admiral Gorshkov," 34.
5. Baer, *One Hundred Years*, 425.
6. League of Nations, "Convention Regarding the Régime of the Straits," *Treaty Series*, vol. 173, *1936–1937*, no. 4015, 221–27.
7. John Broderick Chomeau, "Seapower as a Political Instrument" (Ph.D. diss., University of Notre Dame, 1974), 20–21; and Ivan Laković and Dmitar Tasić, *The Tito-Stalin Split and Yugoslavia's Military Opening toward the West, 1950–1954: In NATO's Backyard* (Lanham, MD: Lexington, 2016), 53.
8. Bruce Wallace Watson, "The Mission and Operations of the Soviet Navy, 1956–1977" (Ph.D. diss., Georgetown University, 1979), 266.
9. Milan Vego, "Communist Navies in the Adriatic," in *The Soviet and Other Communist Navies: The View from the Mid-1980s*, edited by James L. George (Annapolis, MD: Naval Institute Press, 1986), 369; and Laković and Tasić, *Tito-Stalin Split*, vii.
10. Vego, "Communist Navies," 355.
11. Christopher S. Wren, "Soviet Building Port in Far East," *New York Times*, 11 November 1975, 47.
12. Watson, "Mission and Operations," 186–87, 259–60; see also Malbon, "Admiral Gorshkov," 34.
13. Jovan Čavoški, "Constructing Nasser's Neutralism," in *The Regional Cold Wars in Europe, East Asia, and the Middle East: Crucial Periods and Turning Points*, edited by Lorenz M. Lüthi (Stanford, CA: Stanford University Press, 2015), 88–107, 99–102.
14. Galia Golan, *Soviet Policies in the Middle East: From World War Two to Gorbachev* (Cambridge: Cambridge University Press, 1990), 49.
15. Salim Yaqub, *Containing Arab Nationalism: The Eisenhower Doctrine and the Middle East* (Chapel Hill: University of North Carolina Press, 2004), 210, 219, 223, 228, 230; Chomeau, "Seapower as a Political Instrument," 113; and Watson, "Mission and Operations," 212, 214, 320.
16. Watson, "Mission and Operations," 50–51, 320; Mikhail Monakov, "The Soviet Naval Presence in the Mediterranean at the Time of the Six Day War," in *The Soviet Union and the June 1967 Six Day War*, edited by Yaacov Ro'i and

Boris Morozov (Stanford, CA: Stanford University Press, 2008), 145; and Bruce W. Watson, "Submarine Operations," in *The Soviet Naval Threat to Europe: Military and Political Dimensions*, edited by Bruce W. Watson and Susan M. Watson (Boulder, CO: Westview, 1989), 105.
17. Watson, "Mission and Operations," 223; Monakov, "Soviet Naval Presence," 146–47; and Dima P. Adamsky, "The 'Seventh Day' of the Six Day War," in Ro'i and Morozov, *Soviet Union and the June 1967 Six Day War*, 223.
18. Peter L. Hahn, "The Cold War and the Six Day War," in *The Cold War in the Middle East: Regional Conflict and the Superpowers, 1967–73*, edited by Nigel G. Ashton (London: Routledge, 2007), 16; and Galia Golan, "The Cold War and the Soviet Attitude towards the Arab-Israeli Conflicts," in Ashton, *Cold War in the Middle East*, 95.
19. Bryan Ranft and Geoffrey Till, *The Sea in Soviet Strategy*, 2nd ed. (Annapolis, MD: Naval Institute Press, 1989), 226; and Watson, "Mission and Operations," 58.
20. Milan Vego, *Yugoslavia and the Soviet Policy of Force in the Mediterranean since 1961*, Center for Naval Analyses, Professional Paper 318 (August 1981), 25.
21. Chomeau, "Seapower as a Political Instrument," 115.
22. Isabella Ginor and Gideon Remez, *The Soviet–Israeli War 1967–1973: The USSR's Intervention in the Egyptian–Israeli Conflict* (Oxford: Oxford University Press, 2017), 6.
23. Monakov, "Soviet Naval Presence," 170.
24. Adamsky, "The 'Seventh Day'," 224, 226–27; and Yuri M. Zhukov, "Time Line," in *The Evolution of the U.S. Navy's Maritime Strategy, 1977–1986*, by John B. Hattendorf, Naval War College *Newport Papers* 19 (2004): 282.
25. Zhukov, "Time Line," 282; and Monakov, "Soviet Naval Presence," 167.
26. Wayne A. Wright, "Soviet Operations in the Mediterranean," in George, *Soviet and Other Communist Navies*, 223.
27. Ginor and Remez, *Soviet–Israeli War*, 28.
28. Golan, "Cold War," 60.
29. Jeremi Suri, "American Perceptions of the Soviet Threat before and during the Six Day War," in Ro'i and Morozov, *Soviet Union and the June 1967 Six Day War*, 105, 120–21.
30. Salim Yaqub, "The Politics of Stalemate," in Ashton, *Cold War in the Middle East*, 37; and Yaqub, *Containing Arab Nationalism*, 240.
31. Yaqub, *Containing Arab Nationalism*, 40.
32. Golan, *Soviet Policies in the Middle East*, 22, 358.
33. Adamsky, "The 'Seventh Day'," 234.
34. Ginor and Remez, *Soviet–Israeli War*, 232.
35. Vego, *Yugoslavia and the Soviet Policy of Force*, i.
36. Vego, 62.

37. Adamsky, "The 'Seventh Day'," 113, 198–99.
38. Chomeau, "Seapower as a Political Instrument," 120–21.
39. Ginor and Remez, *Soviet–Israeli War*, 207.
40. Ranft and Till, *Sea in Soviet Strategy*, 218, 225–26; and Vego, *Yugoslavia and the Soviet Policy of Force*, 86.
41. "Egypt Seeks to Improve Bad Relations with Soviet," *New York Times*, 9 May 1976, p. 3.
42. Yaqub, "Politics of Stalemate," 49.
43. Richard B. Remnek, "Appendix D: The Politics of Soviet Access to Naval Support Facilities in the Mediterranean," in Dismukes and McConnell, *Soviet Naval Diplomacy*, 379.
44. Chomeau, "Seapower as a Political Instrument," 103.
45. Radoslav A. Yordanov, *The Soviet Union and the Horn of Africa during the Cold War* (Lanham, MD: Lexington, 2016), 85.
46. E. M. Zaitsev, "Soviet-Somalian Agreements," *Great Soviet Encyclopedia*, 3rd ed. (1970–1979), The Gale Group, 2010, accessed 5 September 2023, https://encyclopedia2.thefreedictionary.com/Soviet-Somalian+Agreements; Yordanov, *Soviet Union and the Horn of Africa*, 103; and Watson, "Mission and Operations," 400–401, 403.
47. William James, "There and Back Again: The Fall and Rise of Britain's 'East of Suez' Basing Strategy," *War on the Rocks*, 18 February 2021, https://warontherocks.com/2021/02/there-and-back-again-the-fall-and-rise-of-britains-east-of-suez-basing-strategy/; Spencer Mawby, "The 'Big Lie' and the 'Great Betrayal'," in Ashton, *Cold War in the Middle East*, 164, 184; and Yordanov, *Soviet Union and the Horn of Africa*, 86.
48. Mark A. Carolla, "The Indian Ocean Squadron," in Watson and Watson, *The Soviet Naval Threat to Europe*, 241–46.
49. Golan, *Soviet Policies in the Middle East*, 229, 232.
50. Fred Joseph Zuniga, "Soviet Naval Diplomacy" (Ph.D. diss. George Washington University, 1979), 39; Watson, "Mission and Operations," 382–85; Carolla, "Indian Ocean Squadron," 241; and Bruce W. Watson, "The Soviet Navy in the Third World," in George, *Soviet and Other Communist Navies*, 258–60.
51. William H. Mott IV, *Soviet Military Assistance: An Empirical Perspective* (Westport, CT: Greenwood, 2001), 195.
52. Yordanov, *Soviet Union and the Horn of Africa*, 106; and Watson, "Mission and Operations," 385, 392–93, 401–9.
53. Mott, *Soviet Military Assistance*, 195.
54. Carolla, "Indian Ocean Squadron," 243; and Watson, "Mission and Operations," 410–11.
55. Watson, "Mission and Operations," 412–13; and Yordanov, *Soviet Union and the Horn of Africa*, 182–83, 188, 208.

56. Yordanov, *Soviet Union and the Horn of Africa*, 190–91; and Carolla, "Indian Ocean Squadron," 243.
57. Yordanov, *Soviet Union and the Horn of Africa*, 208; and Watson, "Soviet Navy in the Third World," 260.
58. Ranft and Till, *Sea in Soviet Strategy*, 65.
59. Chris Miller, *Chip War: The Fight for the World's Most Critical Technology* (New York: Scribner, 2022), 98–99, 117, 141–44.
60. U.S. Navy, Strategic Systems Programs, "Facts: Polaris-Poseidon-Trident," https://web.archive.org/web/20171201033311/https://www.ssp.navy.mil/about/history_facts_2.html.
61. S. G. Gorshkov, *The Sea Power of the State* (Oxford: Pergamon, 1979), 193; and С. Г. Горшков, *Морская мощь государства* (Moscow: Воениздат, 1976).
62. Robert Waring Herrick, *Soviet Naval Doctrine and Policy, 1956–1986* (Lewiston, NY: Edward Mellen Press, 2003), 1:132, 268; 2:523, 525, 553.
63. Norman Polmar, *Admiral Gorshkov*, Report prepared for director, Defense Research and Engineering, Department of Defense (Washington, DC: U.S. Department of Defense, April 1974), 107, 102.
64. Herrick, *Soviet Naval Doctrine*, 2:553; 1:136.
65. Stansfield Turner, "The Naval Balance Not Just a Numbers Game," *Foreign Affairs*, January 1977, 341.
66. Polmar, *Admiral Gorshkov*, 113–14.
67. Herrick, *Soviet Naval Doctrine*, 1:62–65, 91.
68. Malbon, "Admiral Gorshkov," 13, 15.
69. Alexei Arbatov, "The Soviet Union, Naval Arms Control and the Norwegian Sea," in *Europe and Naval Arms Control in the Gorbachev Era*, edited by Andreas Fürst, Volker Heise, and Steven Miller (Oxford: Oxford University Press, 1992), 47. For a Moscow-centered map, see U.S. Central Intelligence Agency, "Azimuthal equidistant projection centered on Moscow," https://www.loc.gov/item/86692614/. Herrick, *Soviet Naval Doctrine*, 2: 534.
70. Polmar, *Admiral Gorshkov*, 106, 114.
71. Malbon, "Admiral Gorshkov," 17.
72. John F. Lehman, *Oceans Ventured: Winning the Cold War at Sea* (New York: Norton, 2018), 58, 125–30.
73. Turner, "Naval Balance," 342.
74. Lehman, *Oceans Ventured*, 143–44.
75. Ranft and Till, *Sea in Soviet Strategy*, 187–88; and Herrick, *Soviet Naval Doctrine*, 2:547.
76. Watson, "Mission and Operations," 96.
77. Polmar, *Admiral Gorshkov*, 115.
78. Herrick, *Soviet Naval Doctrine*, 3:1106.
79. Malbon, "Admiral Gorshkov," 9.

SOVIET SQUADRON-IN-BEING STRATEGIES 295

80. Cited in John B. Hattendorf, *The Evolution of the U.S. Navy's Maritime Strategy, 1977–1986*, Naval War College Newport Papers 19 (2004), 25; and Christopher A. Ford and David A. Rosenberg, "The Naval Intelligence Underpinnings of Reagan's Maritime Strategy," *Journal of Strategic Studies* 28 no. 2 (April 2005): 384.
81. Ranft and Till, *Sea in Soviet Strategy*, 193; Malbon, "Admiral Gorshkov," 16; and Arbatov, "Soviet Union," 51.
82. Cited in Herrick, *Soviet Naval Doctrine*, 2:551–52.
83. Jan S. Breemer, "Estimating the Soviet Strategic Submarine Missile Threat" (Ph.D. diss. University of Southern California, 1987), 358–59.
84. Milan Vego, *Soviet Naval Tactics* (Annapolis, MD: Naval Institute Press, 1992), 87.
85. Herrick, *Soviet Naval Doctrine*, 3:1380.
86. Hattendorf, *Evolution of the U.S. Navy's Maritime Strategy*, 32.
87. Ford and Rosenberg, "Naval Intelligence Underpinnings," 385; and Breemer, "Estimating the Soviet Strategic Submarine Missile Threat," 2.
88. Hattendorf, *Evolution of the U.S. Navy's Maritime Strategy*, 32.
89. Herrick, *Soviet Naval Doctrine*, 2:627.
90. John Kristen Skogan, "The Evolution of the Four Soviet Fleets, 1968–87," in *Soviet Seapower in Northern Waters: Facts, Motivation, Impact, and Responses*, edited by John Kristen Skogan and Arne Olav Brundtland (New York: St. Martin's Press, 1990), 20–31.
91. Ford and Rosenberg, "Naval Intelligence Underpinnings," 386; and Breemer, "Estimating the Soviet Strategic Submarine Missile Threat," 6.
92. Edgar F. Puryear Jr., "Readiness: Carlisle Albert Herman Trost (1930– )," in *Nineteen-Gun Salute: Case Studies of Operational, Strategic, and Diplomatic Naval Leadership during the 20th and Early 21st Centuries*, edited by John B. Hattendorf and Bruce A. Elleman (Newport, RI: Naval War College Press, 2010), 208; and CIA, Directorate of Intelligence, "Soviet Perceptions of U.S. Naval Strategy," SOV 86-10009D, July 1986.
93. Lehman, *Oceans Ventured*, 56.
94. Hattendorf, *Evolution of the U.S. Navy's Maritime Strategy*, 38–39.
95. Hattendorf, 36, 89–90.
96. Quoted by Puryear, "Readiness," 203.
97. Malbon, "Admiral Gorshkov," 9, 25; and "Draft Guidance Telegram to Post on Soviet Naval and Military Expansion in the Mediterranean and Indian Ocean Areas," enclosed in A. B. Urwick, Defence Dept., 7 December 1970, FCO 46/652, item 69, paragraph 8, British National Archives.
98. Gunnar Åselius, *The Rise and Fall of the Soviet Navy in the Baltic, 1921–1941* (London: Frank Cass, 2005), 234.
99. Malbon, "Admiral Gorshkov," v.

100. М. П. Комаров and В. В. Матвеев, *Системная хроника развал СССР и становление новой России (1983–2014 гг.)* (St. Petersburg: «Стратегия будущего», 2017), 163.
101. Office of Naval Intelligence, *The Russian Navy: A Historic Transition* (December 2015), vi, https://nuke.fas.org/guide/russia/historic.pdf.
102. Memcon Bush and Jozsef Antall, 18 October 1990, Robert L. Hutchings, chronological files, National Security Council, George H. W. Bush Presidential Library.

CHAPTER 15

# A FLEET IN BEING IN THE PARACEL ISLANDS
## Chinese Sea Denial (1974–79)

*Bruce A. Elleman*

The South China Sea and its associated island chains, like the Paracel Islands, are a contested space. Because the Paracels have some of the few freshwater sources and provide a dependable shelter for ships from hurricanes, they have served many times as temporary locations for fleets in being, which can then be deployed to enforce sea-denial strategies. During the early 1970s, the Soviet navy regularly used them for this purpose, positioning its ships just southeast of the Paracels. Following China's expeditionary campaign in January 1974, which resulted in its taking control of these islands away from South Vietnam (Republic of Vietnam), China also established a fleet in being there. The Paracel Islands–based sea-denial strategy relying on a permanent naval base then became especially useful during the 1979 Sino-Vietnamese War.

One of the most interesting questions about China's 1974 expeditionary campaign is why the U.S. Navy failed to intervene. After all, South Vietnam was a firm ally. Possible reasons are numerous. First, after President Richard Nixon's visit to Beijing in February 1972, the U.S. government agreed to respect the People's Republic of China's (PRC) twelve-mile sovereignty claims around the Paracel Islands. Second, as part of its January 1973 negotiations with North Vietnam, the United States agreed not to send U.S. Navy aircraft carriers within three hundred nautical miles of North Vietnam; the Paracel Islands were well within this exclusion zone. A third possibility concerns U.S. suspicions that North Vietnam might soon defeat the South and take the Paracel Islands. Given Hanoi's close relations with the Union of Soviet Socialist

Republics (USSR), a unified Vietnam might have allowed the Soviet navy to use the Paracel Islands as a naval base.

This chapter explores a fourth possible reason: a Chinese fleet in being in the Paracels worked to the U.S. government's advantage to preclude a future Soviet military intervention in support of Vietnam. During the 1979 Sino-Vietnamese War, the Paracels became a safe haven for a Chinese fleet in being that prevented the USSR from honoring its military alliance with Vietnam.

## CONFLICTING CLAIMS TO THE PARACEL ISLANDS AND THE SOUTH CHINA SEA

China took advantage of the unclear legal claims to sovereignty over the Paracels and its own long history of record keeping. Chinese records going back to the second century BCE predate any other historical claims over the South China Sea. This does not mean that Vietnamese or Filipino fishermen never explored or used the various island chains but that the Chinese have better documentation proving they were there, which "may reflect mainly the greater industry of traditional Chinese authors in keeping geographical and historical records."[1]

China, Japan, and France all tried to dominate the South China Sea in the 1880s. France made Annam (Vietnam) first a protectorate and then a colony by means of the Sino-French War of 1884–85. Japan annexed Taiwan as a result of the first Sino-Japanese War of 1894–95. In 1907 Qing admiral Sa Zhenbing led a naval force to halt illegal Japanese phosphorus and guano mining operations on several Pratas and Spratly islands. During 1909–10, China formally annexed the Paracel and Pratas islands to Guangdong Province. Thereafter, it sent a naval ship to keep in touch with its citizens living on these islands.[2]

Following the Qing Dynasty's collapse in 1911, China remained in turmoil for many decades. In 1932 French Indochina occupied the Paracel Islands. On 4 July 1938 France claimed them as part of Annam, which resulted in a Japanese protest on 8 July 1938 that France was violating Chinese sovereignty. The Nationalist government-in-exile in Chongqing also protested on its own behalf. France next claimed the Paracels as part of the French Union in 1939, but on 31 March 1939 Japan claimed them on behalf of the governor general of Taiwan as part of the Japanese empire. But when Japan occupied the Paracels in 1940, it did so as Japanese territory based on a 1917 claim. From 1939 to 1945, the Japanese also occupied Itu Aba Island in the Spratlys and built a fuel depot, submarine base, and a radio station. Near the end of the war the Japanese had to withdraw.[3]

Soon after World War II ended, the Republic of China (ROC) built a garrison on Itu Aba (Taiping Island). Two destroyers defended it.[4] Since Nationalist troops were the first to occupy one of the Spratlys after the Japanese withdrawal in 1945, Taipei says its claim to the Spratlys is stronger than other local countries. Surprisingly, Beijing agrees and supports an ROC eleven-dash-line map issued in 1947, often referred to as the "cow tongue" map. The PRC argues that when the Chinese Communist Party took power in 1949, it inherited all ROC territory. Accordingly, it has created its own nine-dash-line map and has used it to assert its territorial claims from the early 1950s onward.

The PRC Foreign Ministry stated on 29 May 1956 that Itu Aba and Spratly Island in the South China Sea, "together with the small islands in their vicinity," were called the Nansha Islands. Beijing then insisted: "These islands have always been a part of Chinese territory. The People's Republic of China has indisputable, legitimate sovereignty over these islands."[5] The U.S. ambassador to Taipei reassured the ROC foreign minister on 2 June 1956 that the United States did not intend to become involved in South China Sea matters. Only after receiving this assurance from Washington that it would not intervene did the Taiwanese government also officially reclaim Itu Aba as part of the ROC.

Taiwan's action prompted the South Vietnamese minister Cao Bai to state on 5 June 1956 that the Spratly and Paracel Islands had been under the jurisdiction of the French colonial government and that Vietnam subsequently had jurisdiction by virtue of a grant of sovereignty by France; soon afterward South Vietnam landed naval units in the Spratlys. In response, Beijing insisted that the 1887 Sino-French Tonkin Treaty ceded to China the Paracel and Spratly groups. But other scholars argued that, despite the historical claims of the Chinese and Vietnamese, "only those events that took place since the 1930s are relevant to the analysis of the present dispute," which would make the 1887 treaty largely moot.[6]

The ownership disputes over the Paracels and the Spratlys soon became even more complicated. For example, Beijing issued its own Declaration on Territorial Waters on 4 September 1958. This new PRC claim stated that the Paracel (Xisha) and Spratly (Nansha) Islands were Chinese territory.[7] This Chinese declaration put the Communist government of North Vietnam on the spot. On the one hand, Hanoi needed military and economic aid from Communist China, but on the other hand, it also claimed these same islands. In a note to Chinese premier Zhou Enlai dated 14 September 1958, North Vietnamese premier Pham Van Dong expressed his government's support for China's declaration, stating "the Government of the Democratic Republic of Viet Nam recognizes and supports the Declaration of the Government of the People's Republic of China on China's territorial sea made on September 4, 1958."[8] This Vietnamese statement appeared to accept Chinese sovereignty over the Paracel and Spratly islands. The PRC later cited this statement by the North Vietnamese government as recognition of China's sovereignty over the islands.[9] Later Vietnamese government officials clarified that Hanoi had accepted China's claim to sovereign waters to a distance of twelve miles but not to the islands.

Both China and Taiwan agree that the Paracel Islands are Chinese. In January 1974 the People's Liberation Army Navy (PLAN) forcibly took them from South Vietnam. Following Vietnam's military reunification during 1975, Hanoi disputed China's possession, even though Hanoi had apparently recognized the PRC claim in 1958. On 1 July 1976 Vietnam restated its position that the Paracel Islands were Vietnamese territory. When the PRC pointed to Premier Dong's September 1958 recognition of China's maritime borders, the Vietnamese government issued a statement during August 1979 clarifying that "the spirit and letter of the note were strictly confined to recognition of China's 12-mile territorial waters."[10]

## SOVIET USE OF THE PARACELS FOR A FLEET-IN-BEING BASE

The geographic position of the Paracel Islands made them a perfect location to base a fleet in being to block access to Vietnam's central and northern coastline, including its main port of Haiphong. As part of President Nixon's visit to Beijing in early 1972, the U.S. government promised to respect the PRC's territorial sovereignty there. Later, during peace negotiations with North Vietnam, Washington agreed not to send ships—including, in particular, aircraft carriers—within three hundred miles of Vietnam's shore. Both actions gave China the opportunity to reclaim control over the Paracel Islands since the agreements guaranteed the U.S. Navy would not intervene.

Following Nixon's visit to Beijing, Huang Hua, the PRC ambassador to the United Nations, met on 24 March 1972 with Alexander Haig, deputy assistant to the president for national security affairs. Huang protested that the U.S. warship USS *George K. MacKenzie*, along with a U.S. aircraft, had intruded into or over Chinese waters near Dong Island, just off the Paracel Islands. Haig reassured the Chinese ambassador that "it is against our policy to do that" and, after promising an investigation, said: "I can assure you that penetrations of your territorial waters and air space are not authorized."[11]

About ten days later the U.S. government confirmed that a U.S. warship and airplane had indeed intruded within "twelve nautical miles of the Paracel Islands but at no time moved closer to the islands than three nautical miles." As part of an agreement with the PRC, this note then stated: "In the interest of U.S.-Chinese relations the U.S. side has issued instructions that henceforth a distance of at least twelve nautical miles should be maintained from the Paracel Islands. This is without prejudice to the U.S. positions either on the territorial sea question or the various claims to the Paracel Islands."[12]

The U.S. Navy was prohibited from coming within twelve miles of the Paracels. But the Soviet navy was clearly using waters off the Paracel Islands to support its own fleet-in-being strategies. From time to time Soviet naval forces would congregate just to the south of the island chain. According to a June 1972 U.S. government report: "Early last month, the Soviet ships deployed to the South China Sea, apparently to establish a token force there."[13] According to a 13 May 1972 report, "Soviet naval activity probably related to the increased U.S. operations in the Gulf of Tonkin includes a naval force anchored southeast of the Paracel Islands. The force is currently made up of a *Kashin*-class guided-missile frigate, a guided-missile destroyer, a destroyer, a J-class cruise-missile submarine, and a naval oiler." In addition, a *Mayak*-class intelligence collector,

*Kursograf*, was patrolling the Gulf of Tonkin. Additional Soviet ships were on the way, passing through the Tsushima Strait on 12 May 1972. These included a *Sverolov*-class light cruiser, a *Kotlin*-class destroyer, and an *E-11*-class cruise-missile submarine.[14] In late June a second report stated: "Soviet surface combatants and submarines are returning to Pacific Fleet home waters from the South China Sea, ending [their] naval reaction to increased US operations against North Vietnam."[15]

It was in the PRC's interest to control the Paracel Islands if for no other reason than to exclude the Soviet navy from these waters.[16] During U.S.-North Vietnamese peace negotiations, Le Duc Tho had insisted that the U.S. government agree to keep its ships three hundred miles offshore: "Our territorial waters is 300 miles." In response, U.S. National Security Adviser Henry Kissinger stated: "We cannot accept any legal inhibitions on the deployment of our aircraft carriers because that is inconsistent with our position with respect to the international law of the sea. But we will repeat our assurance of yesterday that we will keep our aircraft carriers a distance away from the coast."[17]

According to the final U.S.-Vietnamese peace treaty, signed in January 1973, the exact wording was "The U.S. Government will move its aircraft-carriers to three hundred nautical miles off the coasts of Viet Nam." This agreement further stipulated that "the removal of the aircraft carriers will be accompanied by that of other U.S. warships."[18]

Interestingly, the Paracel Islands were well within this 300-nautical-mile exclusion zone, at just around 250 miles from central Vietnam, which meant U.S. Navy ships were no longer supposed to approach within 50 miles of the Paracel Islands after the treaty went into effect. These two U.S. diplomatic agreements—one with Beijing and the other with Hanoi—gave the PRC implicit guarantees that the U.S. Navy would not intervene should the PLAN mount an expeditionary campaign to take the Paracel Islands away from South Vietnam.

## CHINA'S 1974 NAVAL EXPEDITION

China's 1974 naval expedition to claim the Paracel Islands was arguably the first time that the PRC conducted an overseas naval operation—called expeditionary warfare—against a foreign country. Beijing called this naval expedition Xisha Ziwei Fanjizhan (西沙自衛反擊戰), or

Counterattack in Self-Defense in the Paracel Islands.[19] It argued that the fishing grounds in the South China Sea were traditionally China's and that Vietnam was trying to oust Chinese fishermen illegally from the Paracel Islands. Another interpretation is that the operation was all part of a Chinese effort to keep Vietnam from reuniting, which included a whole series of border conflicts to turn Hanoi's "military attention away from South Vietnam."[20]

Rather than allow the Soviet navy to use these waters with impunity or cede them to a unified Vietnam, China arguably sought to deploy its own fleet in being in the South China Sea. This required naval basing. Control over the Paracel Islands would position China to block North Vietnam's main port of Haiphong. After Nixon's trip to China, Mao Zedong endorsed a major military modernization program that called for developing an oceangoing navy as well as the continued expansion of coastal defense. Perhaps concerned that a unified Vietnam might use the Soviet Union to counterbalance China, Beijing decided to take the islands immediately prior to the North's reunification with South Vietnam.

The Chinese navy invaded the Paracel Islands on 19 January 1974. Beijing's version was that during November 1973 a number of Chinese fishermen had been illegally arrested by South Vietnam. On 11 January 1974 the PRC foreign ministry even accused South Vietnam of invading Chinese territory. Although the main Sino-Vietnamese conflict on 19 January lasted less than an hour, when four Chinese ships fought with four South Vietnamese ships, one Vietnamese ship was sunk outright and the three others were damaged. Reportedly, China's ships were also damaged but none sank.[21]

This naval expeditionary operation was commanded by Deng Xiaoping, the chief of the People's Liberation Army (PLA) general staff.[22] The 19 January battle—on the twenty-fourth anniversary of the PRC's recognition of the North Vietnamese government—was not a coincidence. The lengthy time it took to deploy the PLAN ships to the area and the long distance involved prove this date was intended to send a political signal to Hanoi, showing Beijing's displeasure with Hanoi's close relations with Moscow.[23] On 20 January 1974 the PRC officially annexed the islands and made them an integral part of Guangdong

Province. China did so despite Soviet protests on behalf of their North Vietnamese ally: supporting Hanoi's claim to these islands, Moscow immediately denounced China's actions in the 1 February 1974 edition of the magazine *Novoe Vremya*.[24]

This diplomatic incident was almost unique during the Cold War since Washington declined to support its ally, South Vietnam, in favor of China, while Moscow appeared to support diplomatically its archenemy, the South Vietnamese government, in opposition to its supposed socialist ally, China.

The Chinese attack on the Paracel Islands was also an unusual example of an expeditionary naval attack by a land power. As one expert concluded, China felt it had no choice: "By 1974, China's leaders must have concluded that if they did not act, they would be increasingly vulnerable in the South China Sea, especially if the Soviet Union assumed control over the Paracels as a forward base for operations against China."[25] Rather than potentially facing a major sea power like the Soviet Union, the PLAN took the islands away from the much weaker South Vietnamese navy, which was in the final full year of its existence.

The PLAN consolidated control over the Paracel Islands by the end of January 1974. After Vietnam reunified during 1975, there was a break between Beijing and the Communist government in Hanoi. The Vietnamese government stated on 1 July 1976 that the Paracel Islands were Vietnamese territory. To punish Hanoi, Beijing recalled its advisers from Vietnam and "delayed work on a number of projects being built with Chinese aid."[26] Sino-Vietnamese tensions have existed ever since. One Vietnamese scholar explained that the Paracels are "strategically important" to Vietnam since they are "located on one of the world's most important sea-lanes."[27]

## THE MILITARY UNIFICATION OF VIETNAM AND ELIMINATION OF VIETNAM'S NAVY

Not only did Vietnam lose the islands but it also lost the naval assets it expected to inherit from the defeated South Vietnamese government. In April 1975, as North Vietnam invaded South Vietnam, Richard Armitage, an emissary working for the secretary of defense, led a secret U.S. Navy mission to save or destroy as much sensitive U.S. material and technology as possible so it would not fall into the hands of the invading North Vietnamese army. Although most of the South Vietnamese Army had already surrendered, senior South Vietnamese navy officers refused to give up their ships. With time running short, Armitage offered U.S. Navy assistance to rescue what remained of their navy. As a result, USS *Kirk* safely escorted thirty-two ships and approximately 30,000 South Vietnamese refugees across the South China Sea to Subic Bay in the Philippines.

When *Kirk* approached Con Son Island on 30 April 1975, the crew saw scores of Vietnamese ships packed with refugees. Commander Paul Jacobs recalled the sight: "As we approached we could see their fleet there . . . and swift boats just milling around dead in the water. Some of them were anchored, some were not. They were adrift. You could look over and see the ships just loaded with people all the way up to the bridge. I would estimate 2,000 or 3,000 people on one of these Coast Guard WHECs [high endurance cutters]. I said, 'Oh, my God!' . . . no water, no food—and this is going to be an insurmountable problem. How are we going to pull this off?'" Another crewman recalled: "But above deck, there were just thousands of people, as many as you could get on board. And they were sitting, standing. They were just overloaded to the max."[28]

*Kirk* escorted 30,000 people safely across nearly one thousand miles of the South China Sea to the Philippines. The significance of this operation went virtually unnoticed for many years. As a bribe to Philippine president Ferdinand Marcos, the U.S. ambassador to the Philippines, William H. Sullivan, agreed to give the ships to the Philippines navy. The mission achieved its primary strategic and operational objectives by denying the thirty-two surviving ships of the South Vietnam navy to North Vietnam. This meant that unified Vietnam's naval forces in the upcoming Sino-Vietnamese War played little or no role in the fighting. The lack of a North Vietnamese navy facilitated China's goal of using a fleet-in-being strategy to prevent the Soviet navy from intervening to support Vietnam in a war against China.

## THE 1979 SINO-VIETNAMESE WAR

China's decision to take the Paracels from South Vietnam in 1974 led to a break between China and unified Vietnam, and to a warming of

Soviet-Vietnamese relations. For example, the Vietnamese government joined the Soviet-led economic group Comecon in 1978. Some four thousand Soviet military and technical advisers were working in Vietnam by August 1978. The USSR increased arms shipments, both by sea and air, in September 1978, including shipments of missiles, tanks, aircraft, and ammunition.[29] Meanwhile, Sino-Soviet relations remained tense.

On 2 November 1978 improving Soviet-Vietnamese relations culminated in the Treaty of Friendship and Cooperation between the Socialist Republic of Viet Nam and the USSR. This treaty was aimed at China, as best shown by the sixth clause, which states that Moscow and Hanoi would consult each other if either were "attacked or threatened with attack . . . with a view to eliminating that threat."[30] Reportedly, a secret protocol also granted the USSR military access to Vietnam's "airfields and ports."[31] Beijing was clearly worried about the Soviet-Vietnamese treaty. One Chinese newspaper, *Renmin Ribao*, even warned that Moscow was using Vietnam against Beijing as it had earlier tried—and failed—to use Cuba against Washington, and that Moscow's objective was to dominate all Indochina. In fact, the Soviet-Vietnamese defense treaty did give the USSR a number of military bases in Vietnam to outflank China from the South.[32]

Meanwhile the United States and China announced their intention to normalize relations on 15 December 1978. Vietnam attacked Cambodia soon afterward, with the Soviet Union's support. The Vietnamese forces had secured Phnom Penh by 7 January 1979. The PRC response was to invade Vietnam in February 1979. Beijing's goal was to prove that the Soviet government would not uphold its promise to assist Vietnam militarily.[33]

On 1 January 1979 Washington and Beijing officially normalized diplomatic relations. President Jimmy Carter's national security adviser, Zbigniew Brzezinski, reportedly backed Beijing's use of military force to undermine the Soviet-Vietnamese treaty. President Carter even gave Deng Xiaoping "American 'moral support' for the forthcoming Chinese punitive war against Vietnam."[34] The war tested the Soviet-Vietnamese strategic alliance. Would the USSR stand by its treaty with Vietnam, or would it back down and refuse to intervene? During a January 1979 meeting with Carter, Deng said that a Sino-Vietnamese conflict would "disrupt Soviet strategic calculations."[35]

Deng declared that China would conduct a limited attack on Vietnam beginning on 15 February 1979, the twenty-ninth anniversary of the Mao-Stalin agreement on Outer Mongolia that had made Mongolia a Soviet protectorate.[36] To halt a possible Soviet intervention, Beijing organized a new military command in Xinjiang, all Chinese troops along the Sino-Soviet border were put on an emergency war alert, and an estimated 300,000 civilians were evacuated from the frontier. Deng stationed a total of 1.5 million troops along China's borders with the USSR, which was the bulk of China's active forces. Deng was clearly warning Moscow that China was prepared for a full-scale war.[37]

On 17 February 1979 China's invasion of Vietnam began when 30,000 PLA troops crossed the 480-mile-long Sino-Vietnamese border at fourteen different points. To prove China's resolve, they were commanded by the former deputy commander of Chinese forces in the Korean War. By 25 February the troop strength had risen to 75,000 Chinese troops out of a total of 180,000 troops deployed along the Sino-Vietnamese border. By early March 1979, 120,000 Chinese troops were fighting an equal number of Vietnamese.[38]

China employed an effective sea-denial strategy. The PLAN's South Sea Fleet deployed two missile destroyers, four missile escort destroyers, twenty-seven patrol boats, and twenty submarines. Some three hundred PLAN ships were located in the South Sea Fleet.[39] In addition to stationing patrol boats around the Paracel Islands, a thousand-man garrison manned antiaircraft guns on the islands. The Paracels served both as a buffer area between the PRC and Vietnam and potentially as a strategic "area to stage punitive naval strikes against the Vietnamese."[40] Chinese land and naval forces in the Paracels also provided an important forward outpost to observe the Soviet navy and to deny it anchorage off the islands.

After three weeks of intense fighting, China could claim that it captured three of Vietnam's six provincial capitals—Cao Bang, Lang Son, and Lao Cai—that bordered on China. Meanwhile, the USSR did little to honor its treaty with Vietnam. During the height of the war, four Soviet warships attempted to intervene on Vietnam's behalf.[41] But the

Chinese naval forces based in the Paracel Islands successfully countered this threat.

It is important to emphasize that neither the Vietnamese navy nor the Soviet navy played a major role in this war. Arguably, this was due to China's fleet in being in the Paracels that blocked Soviet maritime access. If China had not taken these islands in 1974 and fortified them by basing ships and troops there, Soviet military aid might have cost China even more severe military losses than it suffered. The U.S. government clearly did not fear China's occupation of the islands since it did nothing to stop the PLAN from taking them.

## THE PARACEL ISLANDS AND CHINA'S FLEET-IN-BEING STRATEGY

China's fleet in being on the Paracel Islands hurt Vietnam in both the short and the long run. Soviet supplies to Vietnam could neither pass by land through the PRC nor be delivered by sea. China's fleet in being not only blocked the Soviet navy's entry into the war, but also ensured that naval forces were never widely used on either side. Xiaoming Zhang, for example, has commented how the 1979 war was "two-dimensional" since "air and naval forces did not participate."[42] The decision not to use airpower followed a pattern set during the 1969 Sino-Soviet border conflicts, when the two sides apparently agreed that an air war might too easily escalate into a nuclear confrontation. Chinese ships based at the Paracel Islands successfully deterred the Soviet navy from accessing Haiphong. The Vietnamese navy was also much smaller than it would have been had it inherited the South Vietnamese navy that fled to the Philippines.

There were also long-term consequences from China's taking the Paracel Islands. The rebuilding of a Chinese marine force separate from the PLA and PLAN coincided with the invasion of the islands.[43] The structure and training of these Chinese marines closely paralleled the U.S. Marine Corps. China's presence there checkmated "Hanoi's hopes for a foreign exchange bonanza based on being able to lease clear titles for offshore drilling in the South China Sea."[44] Finally, if there had been no Chinese fleet in being, the war might have played out very differently, with Soviet naval forces openly assisting Vietnam. In fact, the USSR looked feckless as a result of its forces being checkmated by China, with one scholar commenting: "Hanoi's reliance on the Soviet

Union for security was clearly a disappointing and even disillusioning experience."[45]

Thus, the Chinese fleet in being worked as intended by keeping the Soviet navy from intervening in the conflict on Vietnam's behalf. In the end, the Soviet government did not honor its mutual defense treaty with Vietnam and declined to ship weapons to Haiphong, in part because China could block the sea lanes.[46] Sending a potent anti-Soviet message to Moscow, Beijing then announced a troop withdrawal on 5 March 1979, the twenty-sixth anniversary of Stalin's death. Claims that China suffered a military loss overlook that China was not allocating even a fraction of its resources to the conflict in Vietnam but was directing its main forces against the USSR.[47]

On 3 April 1979 Beijing announced its intention to terminate the 1950 Sino-Soviet Treaty of Friendship, Alliance, and Mutual Assistance. Subsequently, Beijing condemned Soviet foreign intervention on 31 December 1979 and warned on 19 January 1980 that a Soviet invasion of Afghanistan threatened "world peace" and "Chinese security." To Beijing, the USSR's invasion of Afghanistan appeared to be an attempt to outflank China's ally Pakistan. To punish Moscow, Beijing announced on 20 January 1980 that it would stop all Sino-Soviet negotiations on a new Sino-Soviet treaty.[48] The Sino-Soviet monolith was dead. A new Sino-American political, economic, and military coalition opposing the USSR had coalesced.

## USING THE PARACEL ISLANDS TO ADOPT A SEA-DENIAL STRATEGY

Soon after China's 5 March troop withdrawal from Vietnam, Sino-Vietnamese peace talks opened in April 1979. As a first step, China immediately demanded that Vietnam recognize PRC claims concerning the South China Sea, especially concerning the Paracel Islands, but Hanoi refused. Tensions continued to simmer. During 1988 fighting broke out in the Spratly Islands when Chinese naval forces drove Vietnamese troops from Johnson Reef. China established a new island province, Hainan, and made the Paracels and the Spratlys part of this province on 13 April 1988.[49]

During the following decades, China shifted from a fleet-in-being strategy to a more active sea-denial strategy. PRC control of these strategic islands has given it a base of operations to claim even greater territory in the South China Sea. Beijing announced on 4 December 2007 that it had created a new "city" called Sansha. This new city in Hainan Province would thereafter administer the Spratlys, Macclesfield Bank, and the Paracels. According to news reports, "Shock waves were felt immediately throughout the region: both Vietnam and Indonesia formally protested China's unilateral and preemptive move."[50] One assessment of Sino-Vietnamese relations concluded that the "Paracels remain a standing bilateral issue that is unlikely to be resolved."[51]

In response, during February 2008 Taiwanese president Chen Shui-bian flew to Itu Aba for an official visit. Chen's trip not only proved that the recently lengthened runway could accommodate C-130 cargo planes but also publicized Taiwan's claim to these disputed territories.[52] The PRC and the ROC each argues it represents Chinese claims, and they agree that "historically, there is no question that the Paracels and Spratlys belong to China."[53] However, "Taiwan cannot deduce from this any claim to the whole archipelago (which is, after all, an arbitrary definition in regard to insular affiliation and dimension) just because it occupies one feature of the group."[54]

China's disputes over the Paracel, Pratas, and Spratly Islands show that sea-denial strategies do not necessarily have to sever all sea communications but can deny only certain types of traffic or can halt movement in one direction but not the other. This allows for fine-tuning maritime strategies. The control of key islands can potentially position a country to deny passage to others. Thus, the geography of the theater is perhaps the most important single factor in undertaking or withstanding sea denial through the use of fleets in being. Countries hemmed in by islands can fortify such islands to close their own waters to others. Conversely, an enemy sea power can take advantage of such restricted geography to deny its rival use of its merchant marine and navy. For example, regarding the ROC's Itu Aba (Taiping Island) naval base, Liang Kung-kai, head of Taiwan's Ministry of National Defense's Department of Strategic Planning, stated in 2006 that "if war broke out between Taiwan and China, Taiwan's submarines would definitely have the ability to make ambush attacks against China's oil tankers in the South China Sea."[55]

On 26 July 2012 Senior Colonel Cai Xihong took command of Sansha garrison on Woody Island to defend China's South China Sea claims to the disputed Paracel chain. China also sponsored massive island reclamation operations. Although dispersed over an enormous area, many islands in the Spratly group have now been turned into Chinese bases with significant airfields of their own. Johnson South Reef, Subi Reef, and Mischief Reef are the main bases. Beginning in 2016 China reclaimed an estimated 3,200 acres of land on these three different islands, plus on Johnson Reef, Gaven Reef, Calderon Reef, and Fiery Cross Reef. Reclamation allowed for new airfields to be built on Subi Reef and Mischief Reef.

While these reclamation projects will not necessarily give China any new territorial rights, they will "significantly enhance" China's position in the South China Sea by improving "China's ability to detect and challenge activities by rival claimants or third parties, widen the range of capabilities available to China, and reduce the time required to deploy them."[56] All of these developments will assist PLAN expeditionary operations in the Spratlys by providing additional air support. Daily civilian flights began from Hainan Island to Woody Island in December 2016. Chinese strategic bombers circled the contested Spratlys twice in a show of force in January 2017.

However, sea denial is not just one-sided. Other countries could just as easily retaliate by cutting off the PRC's commercial traffic through a combination of submarine attacks on merchant shipping and by actively blocking more distant choke points such as the Strait of Malacca. A recent RAND study has suggested that the United States and its allies incorporate a far-blockade strategy by encouraging the PRC's neighbors to position short-range (100–200 km), land-based antiship missiles (ASMs) at a variety of chokepoints throughout East Asia, such as the straits of Malacca, Sunda, and Lombok. According to RAND, this would "shut down China's naval movements," undermine its ability to project power, and vastly complicate its problems, should it initiate a conflict with its neighbors.[57]

Vietnam, the Philippines, Brunei, Malaysia, and Indonesia also have valid territorial claims that must be considered. On 12 July 2016 the Permanent Court of Arbitration ruled in favor of the Philippines and against China when it determined that "certain sea areas are within the exclusive economic zone of the Philippines, because those areas are not overlapped by any possible entitlement of China."[58] Even though China both signed and ratified the UN Convention on the Law of the Sea, Beijing's rejection of the 2016 Permanent Court of Arbitration decision "increased tensions in the South China Sea and delayed both co-operation and progress towards an agreed Code of Conduct."[59] During May 2017, China and the ten Association of Southeast Asian Nations countries reported that they had agreed on a rough outline to prevent clashes over the South China Sea islands. Although the text was secret, Chinese vice foreign minister Liu Zhenmin told *Xinhua News Agency* that it would create a "solid foundation" for resolving outstanding problems through negotiations.[60] To date, however, these lofty words have failed to produce a completed code of conduct.

★ ★ ★

The PRC has used its South China Sea islands, including the Paracel Islands, to base fleets in being to enforce sea-denial strategies. On 11 June 1975, Moscow's *Radio Peace and Progress* accused China of using its new Paracel bases as a "springboard to attack South-East Asia," and on 21 July 1975 *Moscow Radio* stated that China's action was "a pretty precise demonstration of the methods Peking intends to use to put its expansionist ambitions into practice."[61] Sure enough, this strategy worked well in the 1979 Sino-Vietnamese War, successfully keeping the Soviet navy at bay.

Given the PRC's dependence on trade to maintain its economic growth, however, adopting a maritime strategy of sea denial aimed at halting or limiting foreign shipping would hurt Beijing more than help it. Such strategies carry the additional risk of second-order effects such as skyrocketing insurance rates that might effectively halt not just targeted but all commercial traffic through contested waters. As Naval War College professor Peter Dutton has argued, "The impact of a disruption for even a period of three weeks would be substantial," and for those shipping companies attempting "to pass through the area during a conflict—whether to access the resources there, or to cut transit times—the insurance costs 'would be prohibitive.'"[62]

Rather than risk the probable backlash of adopting such a sea-denial strategy, therefore, China may be seeking to exert more limited sea control to apply pressure and incrementally dominate its smaller neighbors. For example, during May 2014, when China stationed an oil rig in disputed waters off the west coast of the Paracels, this sparked anti-China riots in Vietnam resulting in damage to many PRC and ROC-run factories and the deaths of four people. In retaliation, China recalled over seven thousand workers from Vietnam due to safety concerns but really to punish Hanoi. One Vietnamese woman belonging to a Buddhist movement even "immolated herself to protest the Chinese incursions into Vietnamese waters."[63] Vietnam has already responded to PRC pressure by rapidly expanding its air and naval forces. China's naval strategy, while successful at denying others access, may ultimately undercut its economic growth.

---

Parts of this chapter originally appeared in my monograph *The U.S. Navy and the South China Sea: American, Chinese, and Vietnamese Maritime Relations, 1945–2023* (New York: Routledge, 2025) and have been reproduced here with permission from the publisher.

## NOTES

1. John K. T. Chao, "South China Sea: Boundary Problems Relating to the Nansha and Hsisha Islands," *Chinese Yearbook of International Law and Affairs*, vol. 9: *1989–1990*, edited by Hungdah Chiu (Taipei: Chinese Society of International Law, 1991), 113.
2. Bruce Swanson, *Eighth Voyage of the Dragon: A History of China's Quest for Seapower* (Annapolis, MD: Naval Institute Press, 1982), 117–20.
3. Bruce Elleman, *China's Naval Operations in the South China Sea: Evaluating Legal, Strategic and Military Factors* (Folkestone, UK: Renaissance Books, 2018), 7–8, 41; some of this chapter originated from this book.
4. Elleman, 113.
5. Jianming Shen, "China's Sovereignty over the South China Sea Islands: A Historical Perspective," *Chinese Journal of International Law* 1, no. 1 (2002): 146.
6. Hungdah Chiu and Choon-Ho Park, "Legal Status of the Paracel and Spratly Islands," *Ocean Development and International Law*, no. 3 (1975): 19.

7. "Declaration on China's Territorial Sea," *Beijing Review*, no. 1 (9 September 1958): 21.
8. "Declaration," A photographic image of this letter, accessed 11 January 2012, http://en.wikipedia.org/wiki/File:1958_diplomatic_note_from_phamvandong_to_zhouenlai.jpg.
9. "China's Indisputable Sovereignty over the Xisha and Nansha Islands," *Beijing Review*, no. 23 (18 February 1980): 21.
10. "Vietnam–China: Background to the Conflict," *Keesing's Contemporary Archives* 25 (October 1979): 29870.
11. 24 March 1972, NSC-HAK, Box 97, Richard M. Nixon Presidential Library (RMNPL).
12. 3 April 1972, NSC-HAK, Box 97, RMNPL.
13. 26 June 1972, NSC-V, Box 133/3, RMNPL.
14. 13 May 1972, NSC-V, Box 133/2, RMNPL.
15. 26 June 1972, NSC-V, Box 133/3, RMNPL.
16. 10 January 1973, NSC, Vietnam Negotiations, Box 859/4, RMNPL.
17. 8 October 1972, NSC, Vietnam Negotiations, Box 856/3, RMNPL.
18. 17 October 1972, NSC, Vietnam Negotiations, Box 856/5, RMNPL.
19. 杨志本 [Yang Zhiben], ed., 中国海军百科全书 [China navy encyclopedia] (Beijing: 海潮出版社 [Sea Tide Press], 1998), 2:1747.
20. Hemen Ray, *China's Vietnam War* (New Delhi: Radiant, 1983), 58.
21. Yang, *China Navy Encyclopedia*, 2:1747.
22. David G. Muller, *China as a Maritime Power* (Boulder: Westview Press, 1984), 86–90.
23. Bruce A. Elleman, "Sino-Soviet Relations and the February 1979 Sino-Vietnamese Conflict" (20 April 1996), Vietnam Center & Sam Johnson Vietnam Archive, Texas Tech University, https://www.vietnam.ttu.edu/events/1996_Symposium/96papers/elleviet.php.
24. Kimie Hara, *Cold War Frontiers in the Asia-Pacific* (London: Routledge, 2007), 156.
25. M. Taylor Fravel, *Strong Borders Secure Nation* (Princeton, NJ: Princeton University Press, 2008), 287.
26. Stephen J. Morris, *Why Vietnam Invaded Cambodia* (Stanford, CA: Stanford University Press, 1999), 174.
27. Nguyen Van Canh, *Vietnam under Communism, 1975–1982* (Stanford, CA: Hoover Institution Press, 1983), 242.
28. Jan K. Herman, "After the Fall of South Vietnam: Humanitarian Assistance in the South China Sea," in *Navies and Soft Power: Historical Case Studies of Naval Power and the Nonuse of Military Force*, edited by Bruce A. Elleman and S. C. M. Paine (Newport, RI: U.S. Naval War College Press, 2010), 91–107.

29. Robert S. Ross, *The Indochina Tangle: China's Vietnam Policy, 1975–1979* (New York: Columbia University Press, 1988), 208.
30. Foreign Broadcast Information Service (FBIS) SU, 6 November 1978, 6–9.
31. Ramesh Thaku and Carlyle Thayer, *Soviet Relations with India and Vietnam* (New York: St. Martin's, 1992), 61.
32. William J. Duiker, *China and Vietnam: The Roots of Conflict* (Berkeley, CA: Institute of East Asian Studies, 1986), 80.
33. Elleman, "Sino-Soviet Relations."
34. Marilyn B. Young, *The Vietnam Wars, 1945–1990* (New York: Harper Collins, 1991), 309–10.
35. Ross, *Indochina Triangle*, 225.
36. Zhou Enlai told Nixon that the treaty was signed on 15 February but that Stalin had backdated it a day to 14 February to make it appear the PRC upheld the Yalta Agreement, so starting the war on 15 February had a clear anti-Soviet meaning.
37. Robert A. Scalapino, "Asia in a Global Context: Strategic Issues for the Soviet Union," in *The Soviet Far East Military Buildup: Nuclear Dilemmas and Asian Security*, edited by Richard H. Solomon and Masataka Kosaka (Dover, MA: Auburn House, 1986), 28.
38. Michael Clodfelter, *Vietnam in Military Statistics: A History of the Indochina Wars, 1772–1991* (London: McFarland, 1995), 287–88.
39. Spencer C. Tucker, *Vietnam* (Lexington: University Press of Kentucky, 1999), 199.
40. Steven J. Hood, *Dragons Entangled: Indochina and the China–Vietnam War* (Armonk, NY: M. E. Sharpe, 1992), 129.
41. Pao-min Chang, *The Sino-Vietnamese Territorial Dispute* (New York: Praeger, 1986), 86.
42. Xiaoming Zhang, *Deng Xiaoping's Long War: The Military Conflict between China and Vietnam, 1979–1991* (Chapel Hill: University of North Carolina Press, 2015), 114.
43. You Ji, *The Armed Forces of China* (New York: I. B. Tauris, 1999), 193.
44. Qiang Zhai, *China and the Vietnam Wars, 1950–1975* (Chapel Hill: University of North Carolina Press, 2000), 210.
45. Zhang, *Deng Xiaoping's Long War*, 121.
46. Bruce A. Elleman, "China's 1974 Expedition to the Paracel Islands," in *Naval Power and Expeditionary Warfare: Peripheral Campaigns and New Theatres of Naval Warfare*, edited by Bruce A. Elleman and S.C.M. Paine (London: Routledge, 2011), 149.
47. John Blodgett, "Vietnam: Soviet Pawn or Regional Power?" in *Emerging Powers: Defense and Security in the Third World*, edited by Rodney W. Jones and Steven A. Hildreth (New York: Praeger, 1986), 98.

48. Alfred D. Low, *The Sino-Soviet Confrontation since Mao Zedong* (New York: Columbia University Press, 1987), 52.
49. Sheldon W. Simon, "ASEAN Security in the 1990s," *Asian Survey* 29, no. 6 (June 1989): 595.
50. Vu Duc Vuong, "Between a Sea and a Hard Rock," *Asian Week*, 8 January 2008.
51. Brantly Womack, *China and Vietnam: The Politics of Asymmetry* (New York: Cambridge University Press, 2006), 253.
52. Brian McCartan, "Roiling the Waters in the Spratlys," *Asia Sentinel*, 4 February 2008.
53. Peter Kien-hong Yu, *The Four Archipelagoes in the South China Sea* (Taipei: Council for Advanced Policy Studies, 1991), 10–18.
54. R. Haller-Trost, *The Spratly Islands: A Study on the Limitations of International Law*, Occasional Paper No. 14 (Canterbury: University of Kent Centre of South-East Asian Studies, 1990), 61.
55. Edward Chung, "MND Says Spratly Airport Strategic," *Taipei Taiwan News* (Internet Version-WWW) in English, 6 January 2006, FBIS CPP20060106968041.
56. "China Has Reclaimed 3,200 Acres in the South China Sea, Says Pentagon," *Guardian*, 13 May 2016.
57. Wendell Minnick, "RAND Suggests Using Land-based ASMs against China," *Defense News*, 7 November 2013.
58. Matikas Santos, "Philippines Wins Arbitration Case v. China over South China Sea," *Inquirer*, 12 July 2016, http://globalnation.inquirer.net/140358/philippines-arbitration-decision-maritime-dispute-south-china-sea-arbitral-tribunal-unclos-itlos, citing *South China Sea Arbitration (Philippines v. China)*, Award of 12 July 2016.
59. Sam Bateman, "The Impact of the Arbitration Case on Regional Maritime Security," in *Arbitration Concerning the South China Sea: Philippines Versus China*, edited by Wu Shicun and Zou Keyuan (London: Routledge, 2016), 239.
60. "Progress Made on Draft of South China Sea Code of Conduct," *Associated Press*, 19 May 2017, http://www.foxnews.com/world/2017/05/18/china-reports-progress-on-south-china-sea-code-conduct.html.
61. "Vietnam and the Sino-Soviet Dispute," *Asian Analysis*, November 1975, FCO 95/2027, p. 3, National Archives, United Kingdom.
62. Everett Rosenfeld, "Chinese Naval Push Could Affect Global Trade," *CNBC*, 29 August 2014, http://www.cnbc.com/id/101952236.
63. T. T. Nhu, "Vietnam and China: Conflict over Islands Arouses Vietnamese Patriotism," *San Jose Mercury News*, 23 September 2014, http://www.mercurynews.com/opinion/ci_26591028/vietnam-and-china-conflict-over-islands-arouses-vietnamese.

CHAPTER 16

# THE IMPACT OF THE U.S. PACIFIC FLEET ON CHINESE STRATEGY

*Joel Wuthnow*

In late April 2022 the U.S. guided-missile destroyer *Sampson* conducted a "routine transit" through the Taiwan Strait, prompting a PLA spokesman to accuse the United States of carrying out "provocative acts" and sending "wrong signals to 'Taiwan Independence' forces."[1] The deployment of U.S. Navy ships in this location has long been a point of concern for Beijing: in June 1950, President Harry Truman ordered the Seventh Fleet into the strait to block a potential invasion of Taiwan by the People's Liberation Army (PLA); in March 1996 two U.S. aircraft carriers appeared near Taiwan at the height of an ongoing cross-strait missile crisis. In these cases, it was the use of U.S. naval assets in a specific location at a sensitive period that drew attention.

From Beijing's perspective, the U.S. naval threat lies not only in the employment of forces but also in the formidable capabilities that the United States has distributed across the Pacific—which can be mobilized to intervene in a future Taiwan conflict or to support Japan, the Philippines, or another regional actor in their own disputes with China. The U.S. Pacific Fleet, headquartered in Honolulu, consists of about 200 ships and submarines, 1,500 aircraft, and more than 150,000 active-duty and civilian personnel.[2] Major port facilities are in Japan (Sasebo and Yokosuka), Guam, Honolulu, San Diego, and Washington state. PLA analysts regularly assess the capabilities and disposition of the Pacific Fleet, and U.S. Navy forces globally to understand modern naval capabilities and assess the threat that could materialize in a crisis.[3]

China's attention to U.S. forces throughout the Pacific raises the question of whether a fleet-in-being strategy might be effective in influencing PLA strategy and Beijing's use of force calculations, especially in a Taiwan conflict (which the U.S. Department of Defense defines as the "pacing scenario" for U.S. planning).[4] In its classic version, the strategy would involve stationing some assets in distant ports to draw the adversary fleet away from the primary theater. This chapter argues that such an idea, on its face, conflicts with the reality of modern warfare in the Pacific, in which China holds U.S. ships at risk in their staging areas through long-range missiles launched from Chinese territory or bombers. Beijing also hopes to use military and political leverage to dissuade Japan and other nations from hosting U.S. forces and allowing them to conduct combat operations against China in the first place.

However, a modified fleet-in-being strategy could help deter or respond effectively to Chinese aggression against Taiwan in three ways. First, emphasizing the reliance of U.S. naval forces on Japanese ports would force Beijing to decide whether to attack Japan and risk bringing another major power into the conflict. Second, U.S. naval support for other allies in Asia requires the PLA Navy (PLAN) to disperse its capabilities along its maritime frontier and train for multiple contingencies, reducing its ability to focus on Taiwan. Third, the possibility of a U.S. distant blockade of Chinese imports in a crisis could require the PLAN to dispatch assets to Southeast Asia or the Indian Ocean region, reducing its capacity to support an invasion. Deterrence is strengthened in each of these ways by presenting Beijing with the risk of a conflict that expands in number of participants and geographic scope.

This chapter develops these arguments in four sections. The first sketches the recent modernization and expansion of the PLAN and explains how the U.S. Navy has been a factor both as a benchmark of modern naval capabilities and as an operational challenge that needs to be countered. The second critiques a classic fleet-in-being strategy in a Taiwan scenario based on China's counterintervention doctrine and capabilities and the political realities of U.S. basing in Asia. The third develops a counterargument that U.S. reliance on foreign basing and ability to maneuver far from the main theater could be useful in creating dilemmas for Beijing and reducing the PLAN's capacity to support cross-strait operations. The conclusion discusses implications for the United States and offers recommendations for how the U.S. Pacific Fleet can heighten China's concerns about a conflict that cannot be controlled.

## THE U.S. FACTOR IN CHINESE NAVAL STRATEGY

From its origins as a costal defense force, the PLAN has emerged as a modern navy able to project power at significant distances from mainland China.[5] China's 2015 defense white paper described a shift in PLAN strategy from defending Chinese interests within the "near seas"—referring to the South China Sea, East China Sea, and Yellow Sea—to a combination of "near seas defense" and "far seas protection."[6] The latter phrase alluded to increasing PLAN deployments far beyond the Asian littoral, most notably antipiracy patrols carried out in the Gulf of Aden since 2008.[7] The 2019 defense white paper added that the PLAN was "speeding up" its transformation into a navy able to meet its requirements in the "far seas" and sharpening its ability to conduct complex overseas missions, including "strategic deterrence and counterattack," "maritime maneuver operations," and "maritime joint operations."[8]

An expansion of PLAN capabilities has accompanied and enabled China's evolving naval strategy. By 2022, the PLAN was the world's largest navy, with 351 platforms (compared to 294 for the U.S. Navy).[9] Many of these assets are smaller ships such as corvettes, suitable for "near seas" missions, although additions that enable "far seas" missions include two aircraft carriers, with a third (the Type 003) soon to be commissioned, six ballistic missile submarines and another six nuclear-powered attack submarines, six 12,000-ton displacement Type-055 cruisers with several more in production, and three Type-075 landing helicopter docks capable of transporting thirty attack helicopters.[10] The U.S. Department of Defense assesses that the PLAN will grow to about 460 ships by 2030, although some analysts suggest that actual growth could be even higher given China's large shipbuilding capacity.[11] To sustain overseas operations, the PLAN relies on a base in Djibouti and more than ninety dual-use ports, many operated by Chinese firms.[12]

Several factors have contributed to the modernization and growth of the PLAN over the last two decades. The primary impetus has been the expansion of China's overseas interests. Beginning in the early 2000s, Chinese leaders emphasized the maritime economy, which required a stronger PLAN, as well as Coast Guard and maritime militia, to enforce China's claims in the resource-abundant South China Sea.[13] The East China Sea dispute escalated after the Japanese government purchased three of the Senkaku Islands from a private owner in 2012, putting pressure on the PLAN and its sister services to defend China's claims. Throughout the first two decades of the 2000s, economic interests and nationals abroad increased, which drew the Chinese leadership's attention to overseas security, resulting in new requirements for the navy to carry out such missions as noncombatant evacuations and antipiracy patrols. The 2011 Libya evacuation was also a key moment. The PLAN was not well-equipped to assist with the evacuation of more than 30,000 citizens that year and subsequently sharpened its focus on nontraditional security in the "far seas."[14] China's naval lobby took overseas missions as a cue to push for a larger and more capable PLAN.[15]

Amid other factors, the U.S. Navy has unintentionally spurred the PLAN's development in two ways. First, it has served as an inspiration for the types of capabilities a modern navy should possess. Chinese observers have frequently weighed PLAN capabilities through the benchmark set by the U.S. Navy. The Type 052 destroyer, for instance, has been portrayed as possessing an "Aegis-like" capability, albeit with different characteristics.[16] The Type 003 aircraft carrier has been compared to the U.S. *Gerald R. Ford*–class carriers, a key similarity being an electromagnetic launch system.[17] Chinese analysts have also studied the U.S. logistics model, looking with envy on a global network of support facilities the PLAN has only begun to emulate with its first base in Djibouti.[18] The PLAN has viewed engagements with the U.S. Navy as a useful opportunity to learn from an advanced navy, although those events focused on nontraditional security; exercises with Russia were more useful in sharpening combat skills. The PLAN arguably has gained more insight into naval combat from the Russian navy.

Second, the U.S. Navy has served as an operational challenge that needs to be countered. The most worrisome threat for the PLAN is the prospect of U.S. naval intervention in a Taiwan crisis, which is the key warfighting scenario for the PLA writ large. (Taiwan became the major planning scenario, or "main strategic direction," for the PLA in 1993.) The U.S. decision to deploy two aircraft carriers in the 1995–96 Taiwan Strait crisis underscored the likelihood of U.S. intervention and galvanized the PLA to reflect on how to secure maritime dominance in a conflict, which has both an antisurface and antisubmarine warfare dimension.[19] Even before that crisis, the specter of U.S. naval involvement in a regional conflict prompted former PLAN Commander Liu Huaqing to describe "command of the seas" as a major PLAN goal for the "near seas," leading to greater emphasis on building modern surface combatants as well as submarines and carriers able to push China's defensive perimeter past the first island chain.[20]

For Beijing, the U.S. Navy has also been a persistent challenge to enforcing China's maritime territorial claims. Chinese observers perceive U.S. post–Cold War strategy as designed to maintain a hegemonic position in Asia by strengthening military deployments and encouraging U.S. allies to be more confrontational in their disputes with China. Such critiques were common throughout China's defense white papers between 1998 and 2019.[21] These attitudes frame Chinese perceptions of U.S. naval activities in the region, including freedom of navigation patrols in the South China Sea, carrier operations in the Yellow Sea, and exercises such as Malabar (with Japan, India, and Australia), Balikatan (with the Philippines), and Talisman Saber (with Australia), which are often described as part of a containment plot.[22] U.S. Navy presence and activities have thus become a rationale for a more modern and capable PLAN, coast guard, and maritime militia, which frequently shadow and sometimes harass U.S. ships. To reduce the chance of unintentional escalation, the two sides approved a code of conduct for naval interactions in 2015. However, the success of that initiative has at best been mixed.

Beyond the Asian littoral, the U.S. Navy has also indirectly contributed to China's pursuit of a blue-water navy. The primary concern is that in a conflict, the United States would blockade China's seaborne trade crossing the Indian Ocean or in a chokepoint such as the Strait of Malacca where the PLA is at a relative disadvantage. This concern became a rallying call for China's "naval nationalists" to demand greater investments in aircraft carriers, nuclear-powered attack submarines, and other assets that might counter a blockade and protect critical sea lanes.[23] In short, the U.S. Navy has been not only a benchmark for PLAN modernization but also a challenge that needs to be addressed in each of the PLAN's major roles: the maritime component of a joint force preparing for a Taiwan conflict, a coercive tool for enforcing China's claims in the "near seas," and an expeditionary force that needs to operate beyond China's periphery.[24]

## UNSAFE HARBORS

How to deter and, if necessary, defeat China's navy has been the subject of much discussion. Most U.S. analyses focus on the application of military power to achieve these effects. The 2020 U.S. tri-service maritime strategy describes operations that will "mass the effects of joint, sea-based, and land-based kinetic and nonkinetic fires" on adversary targets.[25] Former undersecretary of defense for policy Michèle Flournoy writes that credibly threatening "to sink all of China's military vessels, submarines, and merchant ships in the South China Sea" within seventy-two hours of the start of a Taiwan conflict could lead Chinese leaders to consider "whether it is worth putting their entire fleet at risk."[26] Other analysts argue that U.S. nuclear attack submarines and long-range fires will play critical roles in targeting PLA forces inside the first island chain.[27] These concepts are in line with the Mahanian notion that direct action is necessary to command the seas in wartime.[28]

A classic fleet-in-being strategy, by contrast, might have less influence on Chinese naval capabilities in a conflict. In the traditional concept, the idea would be to keep U.S. Navy ships in protected harbors across the Pacific to compel Beijing to send fleets to conduct blockades or maritime strike missions against them.[29] This would diminish China's ability to attain maritime superiority in the main theater (assumed here to be the Taiwan Strait).

However, there are two basic flaws to this argument. First, advances in precision-guided munitions mean that the PLA can target U.S. ships in port without needing to deploy the navy.[30] The 2006 *Science of Campaigns*, a key PLA doctrinal teaching volume, describes missile bombardments by the Second Artillery Force, ground and air forces against "enemy bases and harbors" to "paralyze" assets "over a relatively long time."[31] Chinese analysts have paid special attention to U.S. naval facilities in Japan, given their proximity to regional flashpoints.[32] Table 16.1 documents PLA ballistic and cruise missiles that can target U.S. Pacific Fleet combatants based in Japan (an amphibious squadron at Sasebo and a carrier strike group and destroyer squadron at Yokosuka). Many of these systems could also target U.S. ships seeking shelter in other allied or partner ports, such as Busan (South Korea), Puerto Princesa (Philippines), or Cam Ranh Bay (Vietnam).

TABLE 16.1. PRC MISSILE THREATS TO U.S. PACIFIC FLEET BASES

| Chinese Designation | U.S. Designation | Type | Range | Payload | Launchers | U.S. Naval Bases in Range |
|---|---|---|---|---|---|---|
| DF-15 | CSS-6 Mod 3 | SRBM | 600–850+ km | 500–750 kg | 81 | Sasebo |
| DF-16 | CSS-11 Mod 2 | SRBM | 800–1,000 km | 500–1,000 kg | 36 | Sasebo |
| DF-21C | CSS-5 | MRBM | 1,500–1,750+ km | 600 kg | 30 | Yokosuka |
| CJ-10 | | GLCM | 1,500+ km | 400 kg | 72 | Sasebo |
| YJ-63 | | ALCM | 200 km | Unknown | Unknown | Sasebo, Yokosuka, Guam (from H-6s) |
| CJ-20 | | ALCM | 2,000 km | Unknown | Unknown | Guam (from H-6s) |
| DF-17 | CSS-22 | MRBM with HGV | 1,800–2,500 km | Unknown | 48 | Yokosuka |
| CJ-100 | CSS-13 | GLCM | 2,000 km | 400 kg | 54 | Yokosuka |
| DF-26 | CH-SS-18 | IRBM | 4,000 km | 1,200–1,800 kg (nuclear or conventional) | 250 | Guam |
| JL-2 | CSS-N-14 | SLBM | 8,000–9,000 km | 1,050–2,800 kg (nuclear) | 72 | Pearl Harbor (from SCS), San Diego, Bremerton (from Pacific) |

Sources: CSIS Missile Defense Project, https://missilethreat.csis.org/; *The Military Balance 2025* (London: International Institute for Strategic Studies, 2025), https://www.iiss.org/publications/the-military-balance/; and *China Military Power* (Washington, DC: Defense Intelligence Agency, 2019), 93.

Notes: ALCM = air-launched cruise missile; GLCM = ground-launched cruise missile; HGV = hypersonic glide vehicle; IRBM = intermediate-range ballistic missile; MRBM = medium-range ballistic missile; SCS = South China Sea; SLBM = submarine-launched ballistic missile; SRBM = short-range ballistic missile

The PLA has also been developing longer-range missiles to target U.S. bases farther into the Pacific. The DF-26 intermediate-range ballistic missile, fielded in 2016, can range U.S. naval and air force facilities on Guam. That island is also in range of cruise missiles launched at standoff distances from H-6K bombers in the western Pacific; to prepare for such contingencies, the PLA Air Force has increasingly flown those assets past the first island chain.[33] The PLA has fewer strike assets that can target Pearl Harbor or U.S. naval facilities on the West Coast: at present, only JL-2 submarine-launched ballistic missiles could range these ports. Nevertheless, these would likely be less important from a targeting perspective given transit times to the Western Pacific (seven days from Hawaii and ten from the West Coast).[34] In the coming years the PLA will also field new systems with extended ranges capable of threatening those targets.[35]

Second, China might be able to dissuade host nations from allowing U.S. naval forces to use ports to support combat missions in the first place. To the west of Guam, the U.S. Navy relies on facilities on foreign territory, including Japan, the Philippines, South Korea, Vietnam, Singapore, and Australia. In a Taiwan conflict, it is uncertain whether those ports would be available; countries might decide that the threat of Chinese military or economic retaliation is too great, and the likely benefits to their own interests too small, to permit usage. According to one U.S. analysis, among U.S. allies and partners, only Japan and Australia are poised to allow U.S. forces access to facilities to support intervention in a Taiwan conflict, and even then, these would involve politically "fraught" decisions in Tokyo and Canberra that cannot be taken for granted.[36]

In wartime U.S. Navy ships in port would be so vulnerable—both to Chinese missile strikes and to political decisions that limit access—that a tenet of U.S. doctrine is *not* to consolidate those assets in fixed locations. The tri-service maritime strategy holds that "distributing and maneuvering our forces across all domains allows us to exploit uncertainty and achieve surprise."[37] The Navy has pursued a "distributed lethality" concept in which surface forces are dispersed in "hunter-killer surface action groups" equipped with advanced missile and air defenses so that "adversary targeting is complicated and attack density is diluted."[38]

Analysts have also proposed similar solutions for U.S. Air Force units concentrated in vulnerable bases in Japan.[39] Such ideas are counter to a fleet-in-being strategy.

## CONTINUING RELEVANCE OF A FLEET-IN-BEING STRATEGY

A critique of the fleet-in-being strategy focuses on the vulnerabilities of U.S. naval facilities in the Pacific and the benefits of direct strikes, but there are three ways in which an indirect approach could be useful in promoting deterrence and strengthening U.S. warfighting advantages in a Taiwan conflict. First, concentrating U.S. capabilities in ports on allied territory could force China to make difficult choices to widen the conflict or allow U.S. forces to remain intact. Second, U.S. naval forces operating across China's vast periphery in peacetime require the PLAN to disperse its assets, reducing its ability to prepare for contingencies in a single theater. Third, a distant seas blockade could tie up the PLAN and distract Beijing during a conflict. This section explains each of these arguments.

## TOUGH DECISIONS

Reflecting a desire to manage the risks of war and succeed with its finite capabilities, PLA doctrine emphasizes limiting a conflict to the fewest possible opponents.[40] While China has the military capabilities to strike U.S. ships in Japan, it might refrain from using them because those strikes would also likely produce Japanese casualties, destroy Japanese infrastructure, and ultimately prompt Tokyo to abandon neutrality. However, Chinese self-deterrence would allow critical U.S. capabilities to survive the opening phase of the conflict and be used in subsequent phases if Tokyo eventually allows those facilities to be used for wartime purposes against China. Beijing would have fewer reservations about striking U.S. ships that have already left port since this would not draw in third parties.

Alternatively, China might conclude that it has no choice but to conduct preemptive strikes against U.S. assets in Japan.[41] One reason would be to eliminate the possibility that U.S. forces near the conflict could survive and be used later. Another would be the conclusion that Tokyo is likely to enter the conflict regardless of whether it is attacked first, which China might assume based on recent Japanese discussions about planning with the United States for a Taiwan contingency (driven in turn by Japanese fears that any PLA offensive on Taiwan would necessarily involve Chinese attacks on Japan's southwestern islands).[42] Although perhaps less likely, China might also target facilities in northern Australia, which has also been discussing involvement in Taiwan.[43] If China recognizes that it will have to prepare for a large conflict involving one or more U.S. allies, it might have to reserve key air, naval, and missile forces that otherwise would have been dedicated to Taiwan.

Since self-deterrence and preemptive strikes both carry risks, Beijing might decide that it should attempt to keep U.S. naval forces on allied territory out of the conflict through less escalatory means. One option would be cyber or electronic warfare strikes on U.S. fleet headquarters or ships in port, although this would not ensure that those assets could not be used later (and could tie up specialized PLA units that might be needed in the main theater). A more proactive option would be to send submarines and surface combatants into the East China Sea to confront U.S. ships leaving port. However, this would reduce PLAN capacity to operate elsewhere, meeting the requirements of a classic fleet-in-being strategy to disperse adversary forces.

## STRETCHING THE CHINESE FLEET

A revised fleet-in-being strategy would focus on the use of naval forces in secondary theaters to disperse adversary capabilities. Such an approach could be effective in the Chinese case because Beijing must worry not only about U.S. intervention in a Taiwan conflict but also about U.S. involvement in other disputes along China's extensive maritime periphery. The U.S. Navy maintains a regular presence in all of the "near seas," including transits and unilateral or combined exercises, and has pledged that its defense treaties with the Philippines and Japan cover the South China Sea and East China Sea, respectively.[44] The U.S. Navy also maintains a base in South Korea and could be mobilized to participate in a Korean Peninsula conflict near Chinese territory.

China's concerns about regular U.S. presence in different locations mean that PLAN needs to be prepared to confront the U.S. Navy (and other regional antagonists) outside the main theater. This concern is

IMPACT OF THE U.S. PACIFIC FLEET ON CHINA 327

TABLE 16.2. DISTRIBUTION OF PLA NAVY CAPABILITIES

| | Eastern Theater Command Navy | Southern Theater Command Navy | Northern Theater Command Navy |
|---|---|---|---|
| Aircraft carrier (CV) | 0 | 1 | 1 |
| Guided-missile cruiser (CGHM) | 0 | 4 | 4 |
| Guided-missile destroyers (DDGHM/DDGM) | 16 | 14 | 12 |
| Guided-missile frigates (FFGHM/FFG) | 20 | 14 | 11 |
| Guided-missile corvettes (FSGM) | 24 | 20 | 10 |
| Landing platform docks (LPD) | 3 | 5 | 0 |
| Landing ship tank (LST) | 16 | 20 | 2 |
| Landing helicopter dock (LHD) | 2 | 1 | 0 |
| Ballistic missile submarines (SSBN) | 0 | 6 | 0 |
| Diesel attack submarines (SSK) | 18 | 16 | 12 |
| Nuclear attack submarines (SSN) | 0 | 2 | 4 |

*Source: The Military Balance 2025* (London: International Institute for Strategic Studies, 2025), https://www.iiss.org/publications/the-military-balance/.

reflected in a roughly even distribution of naval capabilities among three fleets, as shown in table 16.2.[45] The Eastern Theater Command Navy (ETCN), responsible for Taiwan, has about the same number of large surface combatants and submarines as the Southern Theater Command (STCN) and Northern Theater Command (NTCN) navies. Even the ETCN cannot focus singularly on Taiwan since it also has responsibilities to handle U.S. and Japanese challenges around the Senkakus. Moreover, the large range of contingencies it faces means that the PLAN has incentives to develop fungible assets such as destroyers and avoid overinvesting in capabilities such as small landing craft that might be produced for one-time-use in a Taiwan campaign.[46]

In wartime, Beijing would likely augment the ETCN with forces from other theaters. Nevertheless, Chinese leaders would be hesitant to deplete too much capacity from the other two fleets because of threats elsewhere. They might assume, for instance, that the U.S. Navy will intervene through the South China Sea or strike PLA facilities in the Spratlys as a form of horizontal escalation. They would also be concerned about the likelihood that another regional rival, such as the Philippines, emboldened by the United States, could exploit the situation to press its own territorial agenda. Chinese writings refer to such gambits as "chain reaction warfare," and encourage a high state of readiness in all theaters during a conflict.⁴⁷ These factors could promote deterrence by reducing Beijing's confidence in its ability to prevail in an expanding conflict or make the conflict more manageable for the defense by dispersing the Chinese fleet.

### COUNTERBLOCKADE

A variation of a more proactive fleet-in-being strategy would use U.S. Navy assets to impose a distant blockade on Chinese imports. This would leverage China's reliance on seaborne trade, especially oil (most of which passes through maritime chokepoints such as the Strait of Hormuz and Strait of Malacca), and the PLA's relative disadvantage in projecting combat power into the Indian Ocean. U.S. analysts argue that a blockade could change China's decision calculus by increasing the economic costs of a protracted conflict while keeping escalation risks at a level that would be easier to manage than strikes on the mainland.⁴⁸

Beijing would have several options in responding to a blockade. Gabriel Collins suggests that the primary response would be economic: China would impose constraints on domestic oil consumption and maximize the use of overland pipelines; this would not eliminate economic costs but would allow the PLA and critical sectors to "ride out the storm."⁴⁹ Diplomatically, China would also organize a coalition of partners, such as Russia and Iran, to increase oil production or even actively engage in counterblockade operations against the United States.⁵⁰ China could also respond militarily in another domain, such as by conducting cyber strikes on U.S. interests or launching air or missile strikes on U.S. allies supporting the blockade.⁵¹

The most direct approach, however, would be to contest the blockade using Chinese naval and air forces. The 2020 *Science of Military Strategy*, published by China's National Defense University, describes a new class of "mobile maritime operations" that require seizing "control of important sea areas or control of important strait passages," signaling a view that the PLAN might need to operate far from home to safeguard maritime imports in wartime.⁵² Using its blue-water capabilities and access to naval facilities in friendly countries such as Myanmar or Cambodia, the PLAN would seek to prevent a foreign blockade by strengthening its presence in critical sea lanes, or would respond to threats. In combination with the need to preserve forces in the South China Sea and Yellow Sea, dispatching ships to contest a blockade in the Indian Ocean or beyond would reduce capabilities available in the Taiwan Strait.

## IMPLICATIONS AND RECOMMENDATIONS

The existence, and not just the employment, of the U.S. Navy is etched in the Chinese mindset and has shaped Chinese naval strategy. China's navy looks to its U.S. counterpart as a gold standard for the capabilities a modern navy should possess and interprets hostile U.S intent as a reason to worry about U.S. naval capabilities, even if they are not actively being used. The PLA has thus pursued a counterintervention doctrine and capabilities, such as long-range missiles, to hold U.S. Navy forces at risk at long distances from mainland China.

A classic fleet-in-being strategy would appear to be misguided. China has a range of capabilities to target U.S. forces in their staging areas without needing to reposition naval forces; even before hostilities commence, China hopes to leverage U.S. reliance on foreign bases in the Pacific by persuading host nations to deny access in wartime. Under these conditions, U.S. doctrine emphasizes mobility, concealment, and dispersion of forces. Counterintuitively, however, retaining some assets in forward ports creates a conundrum for Beijing: either conduct strikes that would likely bring U.S. allies into the conflict or allow those assets to survive and be used later—recreating Japan's critical failure to destroy U.S. aircraft carriers underway during the Pearl Harbor attack in 1941. A less escalatory option would involve more traditional means of holding U.S. ships at risk after they leave port, which would require some PLAN ships to operate far from the main theater.

A reinterpretation of the fleet-in-being strategy would focus on U.S. operations outside the Taiwan Strait that require the PLAN to disperse forces. Regular presence and alliance commitments mean that Beijing needs to plan for U.S. intervention in conflicts in secondary theaters. This not only requires capabilities to be distributed among the three fleets but also serves as a justification for the STCN and NTCN commanders to demand resources commensurate with their "important" missions.⁵³ The possibility of a distant blockade would create a challenge in the "far seas" that would also need to be addressed prior to or during a Taiwan conflict. These planning factors dilute the PLAN forces available for operations closer to the Taiwan Strait and divide PLA leadership attention in multiple directions.

These approaches would enhance deterrence by increasing the risk of a conflict that expands beyond China's ability to control. Beijing wishes that any war would be limited in terms of number of participants and geographic scope. In a Taiwan conflict, the need to defeat Japan or other U.S. allies as well as U.S. forces in secondary theaters would reduce China's confidence in a quick victory at an acceptable level of risk. Overconfidence in PLA capabilities, or an underestimation of the willingness of other countries to enter the conflict, might lead China to discount those risks. Even then, however, the PLA would be in a weaker position. PLAN assets would be dispersed, allowing Taiwan to use its limited capabilities more effectively and diminishing the PLAN's chances of achieving maritime supremacy in the Taiwan Strait—a key task in any landing campaign.⁵⁴ The conflict would still be won or lost in the primary theater, but operations elsewhere would influence the chances of victory.⁵⁵

The U.S. Navy can take several steps to heighten Chinese sensitivities about a conflict that cannot remain limited. While U.S. doctrine correctly emphasizes reducing reliance on vulnerable forward bases, U.S. strategic communications should highlight the continued reliance of U.S. forces on ports (and airfields, fuel storage, and maintenance facilities) in allied territory—Beijing would be on notice that it would have to risk drawing in other countries to ensure that U.S. forces could not successfully intervene. The logic would be strongest if China assumes that allies such as Japan and Australia prefer to remain neutral but would likely enter the fight if they are directly attacked.

Reiterating commitments to assist U.S. allies responding to Chinese aggression in the "near seas" would also reaffirm the PLAN's need to prepare for conflict beyond the Taiwan Strait. U.S. policy should be matched with sustained naval presence in these areas and combined exercises with allies and partners. The United States should also continue to increase the capacity of Southeast Asian navies to defend their own sovereignty through the sale or supply of ships, antiship missiles, air and missile defenses, and training assistance. Even without direct U.S. involvement in a South China Sea conflict, those states would pose greater risks to PLAN forces in that theater and reduce Beijing's ability to focus on Taiwan.[56] Moreover, regular naval exercises in the Strait of Malacca and along critical sea lanes in the Indian Ocean, such as the Malabar series conducted by the Quad countries (United States, Japan, Australia, and India), could influence Chinese assessments of the likelihood of a blockade.

A final element in U.S. strategy should be unpredictability. The logic is that, in the context of a Taiwan conflict, the PLA would be unable to anticipate from what direction, where, and in what form U.S. forces would intervene, and thus would fail to build adequate counters for those operations into their own plans. The 2018 National Defense Strategy referenced "dynamic force employment," referring to options to "flexibly use ready forces to shape proactively the strategic environment" as a key concept.[57] In the Pacific theater, the U.S. Navy might conduct unscheduled exercises, sometimes in concert with the other services and foreign allies and partners, to demonstrate an ability to present threats in difficult-to-anticipate locations with a mix of capabilities.[58] As with the other options, this approach would incentivize the PLAN to disperse its surveillance and strike assets while increasing the chance that Taiwan, supported by the United States, would be able to hold off Chinese forces.

## NOTES

1. Alex Wilson, "China Protests Another 'Routine' U.S. Navy Transit through Taiwan Strait," *Stars and Stripes*, April 27, 2022, https://www.stripes.com/theaters/asia_pacific/2022-04-27/us-navy-taiwan-strait-uss-sampson-destroyer-china-5814609.html.
2. "About Us," website of the U.S. Pacific Fleet, https://www.cpf.navy.mil/About-Us/.
3. See, e.g., Zhao Xiaozhuo, "The Transformation and Revelation of Current Great Powers' Military Strategy" [当前大国军事战略转型及启示], *Forum on Leadership Science* [领导科学论坛] 14 (2018): 74–96; and Zhao Yi, "The

Current U.S. Military Presence in Southeast Asia" [当前美国在东南亚的军事存在的探析], *Southeast Asian Studies* [东南亚研究], no. 5 (2014): 59–64.
4. Jim Garamone, "Defense Official Says Indo-Pacific Is the Priority Theater; China Is DOD's Pacing Challenge," *DOD News*, March 9, 2022, https://www.defense.gov/News/News-Stories/Article/Article/2961183/defense-official-says-indo-pacific-is-the-priority-theater-china-is-dods-pacing/.
5. Bernard D. Cole, *The Great Wall at Sea: China's Navy in the Twenty-first Century* (Annapolis, MD: Naval Institute Press, 2012); and Michael McDevitt, *China as a Twenty-First Century Naval Power: Theory, Practice, and Implications* (Annapolis, MD: Naval Institute Press, 2020).
6. "China's Military Strategy (full text)," *Xinhua*, May 27, 2015, http://english.www.gov.cn/archive/white_paper/2015/05/27/content_281475115610833.htm.
7. Christopher H. Sharman, *China Moves Out: Stepping Stones toward a New Maritime Strategy*, INSS China Strategic Perspectives 9, July 2015; and Andrew S. Erickson and Austin M. Strange, *Six Years at Sea . . . And Counting: Gulf of Aden Anti-Piracy and China's Maritime Commons Presence* (Washington, DC: Brookings Institution Press, 2016).
8. "Full Text: China's National Defense in the New Era," *Xinhua*, July 24, 2019, https://english.www.gov.cn/archive/whitepaper/201907/24/content_WS5d3941ddc6d08408f502283d.html.
9. *China Naval Modernization: Implications for U.S. Navy Capabilities—Background and Issues for Congress* (Washington, DC: Congressional Research Service, December 1, 2022), 8.
10. *Military and Security Developments Involving the People's Republic of China 2021* (Washington, DC: Office of the Secretary of Defense, 2021), 48–54.
11. James E. Fannell, "China's Global Navy—Today's Challenge for the United States and the U.S. Navy," *Naval War College Review* 73, no. 4 (2020): 24–25.
12. Isaac B. Kardon and Wendy Leutert, "Pier Competitor: China's Power Position in Global Ports," *International Security* 46, no. 4 (2022): 9–47.
13. Daniel M. Hartnett, "The 'New Historic Missions': Reflections on Hu Jintao's Military Legacy," in *Assessing the People's Liberation Army in the Hu Jintao Era*, edited by Roy Kamphausen, David Lai, and Travis Tanner (Carlisle, PA: U.S. Army War College, 2014), 49–52; Michael McDevitt, *Becoming a Great "Maritime Power": A Chinese Dream* (Arlington, VA: CNA, 2016); Ryan D. Martinson, *Echelon Defense: The Role of Sea Power in Chinese Maritime Dispute Strategy*, U.S. Naval War College China Maritime Studies Institute Red Book No. 15, 2018; and McDevitt, *China as a Twenty-First Century Naval Power*.
14. Zhou Hang, Mathieu Duchatel, and Oliver Brauner, *Protecting China's Overseas Interests: The Slow Shift Away from Non-interference* (Stockholm: SIPRI,

2014); and Andrea Ghiselli, *Protecting China's Interests Overseas* (New York: Oxford University Press, 2021).
15. Ghiselli, *Protecting China's Interests Overseas*, 56.
16. James R. Holmes, "Fleet Design with Chinese Characteristics," Testimony before the U.S.–China Economic and Security Review Commission, February 15, 2018, 3–4.
17. Matthew P. Funaiole, Joseph S. Bermudez Jr., and Brian Hart, "China's Third Aircraft Carrier Takes Shape," *CSIS Commentary*, June 15, 2021, https://www.csis.org/analysis/chinas-third-aircraft-carrier-takes-shape.
18. Isaac B. Kardon, "China's Overseas Base, Places, and Far Seas Logistics," in *The PLA beyond Borders: Chinese Military Operations in Regional and Global Context*, edited by Joel Wuthnow and the National Defense University Press (Washington, DC: National Defense University Press, 2021), 76–77; and Peter A. Dutton, Isaac B. Kardon, and Conor M. Kennedy, *Djibouti: China's First Overseas Strategic Strongpoint*, China Maritime Studies Institute China Maritime Report No. 6, April 2020.
19. Arthur S. Ding, "The Lessons of the 1995–1996 Military Taiwan Strait Crisis: Developing a New Strategy toward the United States and Taiwan," in *The Lessons of History: The Chinese People's Liberation Army at 75*, edited by Laurie Burkitt, Larry M. Wortzel, and Andrew Scobell, 379–402 (Carlisle, PA: U.S. Army War College Press, 2003).
20. Ryan D. Martinson, "Counter-Intervention in Chinese Naval Strategy," *Journal of Strategic Studies* 44, no. 2 (2021): 271–81.
21. Adam Liff, "China and the U.S. Alliance System," *China Quarterly* 233 (2018): 137–65.
22. As just one example, China's Defense Ministry spokesperson accused the United States of using the 2021 Malabar exercise to "instigate confrontation" by building "confrontational blocks" with its allies and partners. "Regular Press Conference of the Ministry of National Defense on August 26," PRC Ministry of National Defense, August 30, 2021, http://eng.chinamil.com.cn/view/2021-08/30/content_10082775.htm.
23. Robert S. Ross, "China's Naval Nationalism: Sources, Prospects, and the U.S. Response," *International Security* 34, no. 2 (2009): 70–71.
24. Ian Burns McCaslin and Andrew S. Erickson, "The Impact of Xi-Era Reforms on the Chinese Navy," in *Chairman Xi Remakes the PLA: Assessing Chinese Military Reforms*, edited by Phillip C. Saunders, Arthur S. Ding, Andrew Scobell, Andrew N. D. Yang, and Joel Wuthnow, 125–70 (Washington, DC: National Defense University Press, 2019).
25. U.S. Department of the Navy, *Advantage at Sea: Prevailing with Integrated All-Domain Naval Power* (Washington, DC: Department of the Navy, 2020), 13.

26. Michèle A. Flournoy, "How to Prevent a War in Asia," *Foreign Affairs*, June 18, 2020, https://www.foreignaffairs.com/articles/united-states/2020-06-18/how-prevent-war-asia.
27. Bryan Clark, Peter Haynes, Jesse Sloman, and Timothy A. Walton, *Restoring American Lethality: A New Fleet Architecture for the United States Navy* (Washington, DC: Center for Strategic and Budgetary Assessments, 2017), 60–64.
28. Kenneth Weisbrode, "The Fleet in Beijing: An Alternative U.S. Strategy," *Survival* 63 no. 3 (2021): 59.
29. John B. Hattendorf, "The Idea of a 'Fleet in Being' in Historical Perspective," *Naval War College Review* 67, no. 1 (2014): 42–60.
30. More generally, advances in adversary ballistic and cruise missile systems have created risks for many overseas U.S. facilities over the last few decades. See Joel Wuthnow, *The Impact of Missile Threats on the Reliability of U.S. Overseas Bases: A Framework for Analysis* (Carlisle, PA: U.S. Army War College, 2005).
31. Zhang Yuliang, *Science of Campaigns* [战役学] (Beijing: National Defense University Press, 2006), 316–30. See also Roger Cliff, Mark Burles, Michael S. Chase, Derek Eaton, and Kevin L. Pollpeter, *Entering the Dragon's Lair: Chinese Antiaccess Strategies and Their Implications for the United States* (Santa Monica, CA: RAND, 2007), 67–71.
32. Toshi Yoshihara, "Chinese Missile Strategy and the U.S. Naval Presence in Japan," *Naval War College Review* 63, no. 3 (2010): 39–62.
33. Daniel J. Kostecka, "China's Aerospace Power Trajectory in the Near Seas," *Naval War College Review* 65, no. 3 (2012): 114; and Derek Grossman, *China's Long-Range Bomber Flights: Drivers and Implications* (Santa Monica, CA: RAND, 2018), 13–17.
34. Jaganath Sankaran, "Missile Wars in the Asia Pacific: The Threat of Chinese Regional Missiles and U.S.-Allied Missile Defense Response," *Asian Security* 17, no. 1 (2021): 30.
35. These include the JL-3 submarine-launched ballistic missile and the H-20 bomber. In November 2022 U.S. Pacific Fleet commander Admiral Samuel Paparo stated that the JL-3 is already in service.
36. Zack Cooper and Sheena Greitens, "What to Expect from Japan and Korea in a Taiwan Contingency," in *New Frontiers for Security Cooperation with Seoul and Tokyo*, edited by Henry D. Sokolski (Arlington, VA: Nonproliferation Policy Education Center, 2021), 17–18.
37. U.S. Department of the Navy, *Advantage at Sea*, 13.
38. Thomas Rowden, Peter Gumataotao, and Peter Fanta, "Distributed Lethality," U.S. Naval Institute *Proceedings* 141, no. 1 (2015).
39. Stacie L. Pettyjohn, "Spiking the Problem: Developing a Resilient Posture in the Indo-Pacific with Passive Defenses," *War on the Rocks*, January 10, 2022,

https://warontherocks.com/2022/01/spiking-the-problem-developing-a-resilient-posture-in-the-indo-pacific-with-passive-defenses/.
40. Lonnie D. Henley, "War Control: Chinese Concepts of Escalation Management," in *Shaping China's Security Environment: The Role of the People's Liberation Army*, edited by Andrew Scobell and Larry M. Wortzel (Carlisle, PA: U.S. Army War College Press, 2006), 83.
41. A tension in PLA writings on war control is the advocacy of reducing the number of participants with a priority on preemptive strikes to seize an early victory. On the latter, see Alison A. Kaufman and Daniel M. Hartnett, *Managing Conflict: Examining Recent PLA Writings on Escalation Control* (Arlington, VA: CNA, 2016), 68–70.
42. "Japan and U.S. Draft Operation Plan for Taiwan Contingency," *Japan Times*, December 23, 2021, https://www.japantimes.co.jp/news/2021/12/23/national/taiwan-contingency/; and "U.S. Should Abandon Ambiguity on Taiwan Defense: Japan's Abe," *Nikkei Asia*, February 27, 2022, https://asia.nikkei.com Politics/U.S.-should-abandon-ambiguity-on-Taiwan-defense-Japan-s-Abe.
43. Andrew Greene, "Australia Discussing 'Contingency' Plans with United States over Possible Taiwan Conflict," *ABC News*, March 31, 2021, https://www.abc.net.au/news/2021-04-01/australia-discuss-contingency-plans-us-possible-conflict-taiwan/100043826; and Paul Dibb, "Australia and the Taiwan Contingency," *ASPI The Strategist*, February 6, 2019, https://www.aspistrategist.org.au/australia-and-the-taiwan-contingency/.
44. "Secretary Blinken's Call with Philippine Secretary of Foreign Affairs Locsin," U.S. State Department, April 8, 2021, https://www.state.gov/secretary-blinkens-call-with-philippine-secretary-of-foreign-affairs-locsin-2/; and "Japan Foreign Minister Says Blinken Gave U.S. Commitment to Defend Japan," Reuters, November 12, 2021, https://www.reuters.com/world/asia-pacific/japan-foreign-minister-says-blinken-gave-us-commitment-defend-japan-2021-11-13/.
45. Cole, *Great Wall at Sea*, 84–85, 134–35.
46. Acquisition tradeoffs could be one explanation for the shortfall in assets such as tank landing ships, although it is also possible that the PLA intends to deliver some forces by civilian means. *Military and Security Developments involving the People's Republic of China* (Washington, DC: Office of the Secretary of Defense, 2022) 127.
47. Joel Wuthnow, *System Overload: Can China's Military Be Distracted in a War over Taiwan?* INSS China Strategic Perspectives 15 (June 2020): 10–11; and M. Taylor Fravel, "Securing Borders: China's Doctrine and Force Structure for Frontier Defense," *Journal of Strategic Studies* 30, nos. 4–5 (2007): 716.
48. T. X. Hammes, "Offshore Control: A Proposed Strategy for an Unlikely Conflict," *INSS Strategic Forum 278*, June 2012; and Fiona S. Cunningham,

"The Maritime Rung on the Escalation Ladder: Naval Blockades in a U.S.-China Conflict," *Security Studies* 29 no. 4 (2020): 730–68.
49. Gabriel Collins, "A Maritime Oil Blockade against China," *Naval War College Review* 71, no. 2 (2018): 59.
50. Sean Mirski, "Stranglehold: The Context, Conduct and Consequences of an American Naval Blockade of China," *Journal of Strategic Studies* 36, no. 3 (2013): 392–96.
51. Hammes, "Offshore Control," 7–8.
52. Xiao Tianliang, *Science of Military Strategy* [战略学] (Beijing: National Defense University Press, 2020), 233–34.
53. Wuthnow, *System Overload*, 15–16.
54. For PLA concepts of phasing in a Taiwan campaign, see Michael Casey, "Firepower Strike, Blockade, Landing: PLA Campaigns for a Cross-Strait Conflict," in *Crossing the Strait: China's Military Prepares for War with Taiwan*, edited by Joel Wuthnow, Derek Grossman, Phillip C. Saunders, Andrew Scobell, and Andrew N. D. Yang (Washington, DC: National Defense University Press, 2022).
55. Elbridge A. Colby, "The Implications of China Developing a World-Class Military: First and Foremost a Regional Challenge," Testimony before the U.S.–China Economic and Security Review Commission, June 20, 2019, 6–8.
56. Michael Beckley argues that the United States should turn not only Taiwan but also other Asian states into "prickly porcupines." Michael Beckley, "The Emerging Military Balance in East Asia: How China's Neighbors Can Check Chinese Naval Expansionism," *International Security* 42, no. 2 (2017): 78–119.
57. *Summary of the 2018 National Defense Strategy of the United States of America* (Washington, DC: Department of Defense, 2022), 7. It is unclear if this concept is retained in the 2022 NDS.
58. For an example, see "Air Force, Navy Exercise Dynamic Force Employment in the Indo-Pacific," *Pacific Air Forces Public Affairs*, July 8, 2020, https://www.af.mil/News/Article-Display/Article/2266002/air-force-navy-exercise-dynamic-force-employment-in-indo-pacific/.

CHAPTER 17

# A FLEET-IN-BEING STRATEGY THROUGH CHINESE EYES

Toshi Yoshihara

The People's Liberation Army Navy (PLAN or PLA Navy) embraces an offensive version of a fleet-in-being strategy. In a war at sea, the PLAN will employ aggressive tactics and counterattacks to achieve its aims in home waters and distant theaters. The PLAN's strategy, if understood in terms of a fleet in being, could pose significant challenges to its main rival, the U.S. Navy.

The following draws extensively from Chinese-language sources, including official writings, to describe the PLAN's strategy and its interpretations of the fleet-in-being concept. The PLAN has its own theories, ideas, and lexicon—drawn from its historical experiences, military traditions, and interpretations of naval affairs—that reflect its unique strategic and operational outlook. It is therefore crucial to discern how the PLAN relates its strategy to the fleet-in-being concept on its own terms and in its own words. This chapter lets the PLAN speak for itself.

The chapter first examines the key guiding concepts of the PLA Navy's wartime and peacetime functions, including near seas defense and far seas protection, and Beijing's ambitious aim of building a world-class navy. It assesses the trajectory of the force structure and posture to discern whether the buildup will adequately support the PLAN's local and out-of-area missions. The chapter tests whether such concepts as near seas defense and far seas protection rhyme with the logic of a fleet in being.

## NEAR SEAS DEFENSE

Active defense (积极防御) is a foundational concept for understanding Chinese naval strategy and operations.[1] The idea dates to the 1930s when

Mao Zedong developed his theory of victory for the Red Army. Mao referred to active defense as "offensive defense" or "defense through decisive engagements."[2] Since then, it has remained a central tenet in China's defense policy.[3] At the operational level of war, active defense is the use of offensive operations and tactics in the service of strategically defensive goals. Active defense is thus the use of a campaign, or a series of campaigns, to achieve the Chinese Communist Party's aims.

Active defense seeks to uphold China's vital national or "core" interests. It is a military response to threats to all territories Beijing claims as its own, including Taiwan, the Senkaku Islands, and the Spratly Islands. The 2013 *Science of Military Strategy* by the PLA Academy of Military Science describes it as a "homeland defense-type strategy" encompassing a wide range of contingencies, from a geographically confined conflict against one of China's neighbors to a major regional war involving the United States and other third parties.[4]

Active defense is reactive in that it awaits the adversary to strike first—either politically or militarily—before delivering a riposte. It presumes China's relative inferiority to its opponent and seeks to use offensive campaigns to reduce the enemy's fighting power, thereby leveling the playing field. The concept's operative word is active. It envisions violent clashes of arms, including battles of annihilation, to shift the contest in China's favor.

Near seas defense or offshore waters defense (近海防御) transposes key elements of active defense to the maritime domain.[5] Near seas defense also covers a broad geographic space akin to a surrounding maritime buffer. As Admiral Liu Huaqing—the founding father of China's modern navy—notes in his memoir, "The 'near seas' refer to our nation's Yellow Sea, East China Sea, South China Sea, the Spratly archipelago, and the waters within and beyond the Taiwan-Okinawa island chain, as well as the northern sea area of the Pacific."[6] The official PLA dictionary on military terms states that the "near seas include the Bohai Sea, the Yellow Sea, the East China Sea, the South China Sea, and sections of water east of Taiwan Island."[7]

Thus, the near seas are not bounded strictly by the first island chain, the transnational archipelago that runs south from Japan through Taiwan to the Philippines. There is purposeful ambiguity about how far the near seas extend east beyond the first island chain. This geospatial vagueness confers strategic and operational flexibility. Sometimes Chinese naval power may need to exert control over adjacent waters to achieve war aims in the near seas.[8]

Like active defense, the operational area encompasses territories, such as Taiwan, the Senkakus, and the Spratlys, that Beijing considers inseparable from the homeland. It covers sea lanes that are vital to China's economic well-being. The near seas are the main and most direct avenues for hostile powers to reach mainland shores. Conversely, they are the enclosed waters that China's military and commercial ships must traverse to reach the open thoroughfares of the Pacific and Indian Oceans. In short, Chinese leaders attach extraordinary value to the near seas and will likely fight very hard to defend and control them.

Like active defense, near seas defense is a warfighting concept concerning offensive operations and tactics. According to the PLAN's official encyclopedia, near seas defense involves "the combined use of all kinds of methods to exercise the overall effects of maritime power to preserve oneself to the maximum extent while unceasingly exhausting and annihilating the attacking enemy." It "requires a sufficient grasp of mobile combat capabilities to search and destroy the enemy, gradually shift the power balance, change the strategic situation, and thereby appropriately time the transition to the strategic counteroffensive and attack."[9]

It follows that near seas defense would entail combined arms and joint operations involving every combat branch of the PLAN and the PLA's other services. Consonant with active defense, it would feature tactically decisive engagements. The PLA would initially fight from a position of relative inferiority that battles of attrition and annihilation would reverse. Near seas defense would degrade enemy strength sufficiently to command the maritime commons so that the PLA could assume the counteroffensive.

It would also involve irregular warfare at sea, or what the PLAN calls "sabotage warfare at sea," a concept originating in the 1950s.[10] Sabotage warfare at sea would employ hit-and-run tactics to harass and to ambush the enemy, supplementing main force unit operations. It would seek opportunities to inflict substantial damage against isolated or exposed adversary forces. Fast attack ships, for example, would exploit China's complex coastal terrain to screen their movements and launch salvos of antiship cruise missiles against approaching hostile warships.

The operational aim of near seas defense is to shift sea control from the adversary to the PLAN. As early as 1986, Admiral Liu anticipated that the PLAN required sea control for reliable wartime transit of the near seas.[11] The PLAN's official encyclopedia states that command of the sea "involves one side in war using maritime capabilities to control a certain maritime area within a predetermined period of time." The goals of command are "to eliminate possible threats to one's own side within the prescribed sea area, thereby achieving the freedom of movement at sea for oneself" and to "deprive the enemy's command of the sea, precluding it from using the sea and limiting the enemy's maritime movement."[12]

China's strategic community widely accepts the idea that the PLAN must dominate the near seas in wartime. Hu Bo, director of the Center for Maritime Strategy Studies at Peking University and close adviser to the PLAN, argues that China must develop significant maritime power to achieve "near seas control," which "refers to a type of power or latent strength to assert local sea control at a predetermined time and place in order to achieve other aims."[13] He then describes the "near seas combat cluster"—forming a reconnaissance-strike complex (or theater battle network)—necessary for near seas control (see table 17.1).[14]

**TABLE 17.1. COMBAT POWER COMPOSITION**

| Platforms by Domain | Sensors | Strike Systems |
|---|---|---|
| Land | Radars, short-wave direction-finding stations, satellite-receiving stations | Antiship cruise missiles (ASCM), antiship ballistic missiles (ASBM), combat aircraft, air-defense systems, unmanned aircraft, directed energy weapons (DEW) |
| Sea | Shipborne radars, sonars, undersea navigation systems, undersea surveillance systems | Unmanned undersea vehicles (UUV), surface combatants, shipborne strike weapons, shipborne helicopters, shipborne unmanned aerial vehicles (UAV) |
| Aerospace | Reconnaissance aircraft, early-warning aircraft, reconnaissance satellites | Aircraft, directed energy weapons (DEW), kinetic weapons, unmanned aircraft |

Hu Bo's conception of near seas control and the methods to obtain it are consistent with the PLA's understanding of near seas defense. His description of a "near seas combat cluster" shows that the PLA intends to employ all elements of its power to influence events at sea. PLA sensors and firepower—deployed on the mainland and offshore islands, in the air, on the sea surface, and beneath the waves—would blanket the battlespace across the near seas and beyond. Near seas defense would be a joint effort involving all the services and the combat arms of each service in a high-end naval war.

## FAR SEAS PROTECTION

As China's maritime interests have proliferated overseas, so have the PLAN's missions. Beyond the offshore tasks dictated by near seas defense, the PLAN must respond to threats far from the homeland. Since Beijing's late 1990s "go global" economic policy, China's overseas trade, investment, and nationals working abroad have multiplied. Integration into the global economy has deepened its dependence on seaborne commerce and on the sea lanes to and from mainland ports. Therefore, General Secretary Hu Jintao in 2004 charged the PLA to "defend China's expanding national interests" and to "safeguard world peace" in keeping with the military's "New Historic Missions." As a result, the protection of China's far-flung economic interests and potentially vulnerable sea lines of communications (SLOCs) has emerged as a major responsibility for the PLAN.

The concept of far seas protection (远海防卫) encompasses various naval missions reflecting China's growing global footprint. Although it became official strategy as early as 2007, the 2015 defense white paper was the first authoritative policy document to declare publicly that the PLAN would adopt a combined posture of "offshore waters defense" and "open seas protection."[15] It contended that China needed to build "a modern maritime military force structure" to "safeguard its national sovereignty and maritime rights and interests" and to "protect the security of strategic SLOCs and overseas interests."[16] The 2019 defense white paper confirmed that "the PLAN is speeding up the transition of its tasks from defense on the near seas to protection missions on the far seas." It called on the PLAN to construct "far seas forces," build "overseas logistical facilities," and fulfill "diversified military tasks," including "vessel protection operations," "the security of strategic SLOCs," and "overseas evacuation and maritime rights protection operations."[17]

Beginning in the late 2000s, the PLAN has progressively expanded its far seas–protection capabilities. In December 2008 Beijing dispatched its first flotilla to support counterpiracy operations in the Gulf of Aden and, since then, has maintained a continuous three-ship task-force presence on a rotational basis off the Horn of Africa. The PLAN conducted noncombatant evacuation operations to rescue Chinese nationals in Libya and Yemen in 2011 and 2015, respectively. In 2017 China established its first overseas military base in Djibouti and is reportedly seeking more locations for its out-of-area logistical and basing infrastructure.

The PLAN has regularly exercised, trained, sortied, visited foreign ports, and so forth across the world's oceans. As a U.S. congressional report notes, "Chinese navy ships are conducting increasing numbers of operations away from China's home waters, including the broader waters of the Western Pacific, the Indian Ocean, and the waters surrounding Europe, including the Mediterranean Sea and the Baltic Sea."[18] It cited then-commander of the Indo-Pacific Command, Admiral Philip Davidson, who in late 2019 observed that the PLAN had deployed globally more frequently in the last thirty months than the preceding thirty years.

While far seas protection appears to connote peacetime constabulary activities, the concept likely includes coercive and warfighting missions. As Rear Admiral Michael McDevitt, USN (Ret.), contends, China's political and security imperatives likely accompany its global economic interests, requiring "offshore shows of strength . . . or in extreme cases, the use of force."[19] Two analysts from the Office of Naval Intelligence concur that far seas operations might require the PLAN to use force to break distant blockades or to disrupt the adversary's ability to project power toward the mainland by striking its logistical nodes, staging areas, and expeditionary forces located far away.[20] Ryan Martinson similarly concludes that far seas protection seeks to deny the U.S. Navy sanctuary in the Philippine Sea and to defend distant sea lanes essential to China's economy.[21]

## A WORLD-CLASS NAVY

To near seas defense and far seas protection, General Secretary Xi Jinping has added an ambitious long-term goal: the construction of a "world-class navy (世界一流海军)." Xi unveiled his vision at the Nineteenth Party Congress in October 2017, pledging "to create a mighty force for realizing the Chinese Dream and the dream of building a powerful military."[22] Notably, he set a timetable: the PLA would "basically complete" its modernization by 2035 and be "fully transformed into a world-class military" by mid-century. During the Twentieth Party Congress in October 2022, Xi reaffirmed his commitment to raising the PLA to "world-class standards."[23] While the phrase "world-class military" remains undefined, it implies the capacity to influence events and to project power far beyond China's shores, entailing parity with—if not superiority, in various respects, over—the U.S. armed forces.

The PLAN is integral to these plans. On 12 April 2018 Xi gave a speech at a massive naval review in the South China Sea involving 48 ships, 76 aircraft, and about 10,000 personnel. He declared, "Building a powerful navy is an important symbol of building a world-class military, a strategic pivot for building the nation into a great maritime power, and an important component of realizing the great rejuvenation of the Chinese nation."[24] To Xi, naval modernization not only concerned fighting and winning future wars but also China's emergence as a world power.

The former commander of the PLAN, Vice Admiral Shen Jinlong, elaborated on Xi's exhortations. He called on the PLAN to construct "a powerful maritime armed force" comprising "strategic fists (战略拳头)," including carrier groups and amphibious assault forces commensurate with China's global status and able to "counterbalance and exchange blows with the strong enemy on the distant oceans and seas."[25] In PLA writings, the phrase "strong enemy" or "powerful adversary" means the United States.[26] In other words, a world-class navy is a great power navy that can compete with and fight against the U.S. Navy on an equal footing.

Given that a world-class navy is an aspirational goal requiring decades to reach, it is unclear how big the PLAN will become. Andrew Krepinevich and Robert Work argue that a global military posture—comprising forward-deployed forces, bases, logistics, a capacity to project power ashore, command-and-control networks, and foreign basing arrangements—would be essential to the kinds of global naval operations envisioned by Vice Admiral Shen.[27] Even a limited extraregional presence confined to the Indian Ocean would require China to possess all the elements of a global military posture, albeit at a modest scale.

As two researchers from China's Naval Research Institute acknowledge, "While the People's Navy has developed rapidly, modernized at scale, and possesses a level of deterrent and combat capabilities, it still must close a somewhat large gap when compared to other great power navies, the missions it must carry out, and the goal of a strong military."[28] Chinese strategists are clear-eyed about the time and resources necessary to construct a world-class navy. In the meantime, China has been methodically laying the foundation for such a posture and its key component: its oceangoing fleet.

## PLAN FLEET STRUCTURE AND POSTURE

To achieve Beijing's local and oceangoing ambitions, the PLAN has undergone a staggering expansion. According to a research team at the Center for Strategic and International Studies, "Between 2017 and 2019, China reportedly built more vessels than India, Japan, Australia, France, and the United Kingdom combined."[29] Martinson aptly describes China's scale and speed of the buildup as being on a "near wartime footing."[30] In testimony to the Senate Armed Services Committee, Admiral John Aquilino, the commander of the Indo-Pacific Command, described the PLAN's modernization as an element of "the most extensive military build-up since WWII [World War II]."[31]

The building spree over the past two decades not only transformed the PLAN but also upended the naval balance in Asia. The Pentagon's 2022 annual report on Chinese military power states: "The PLAN is numerically the largest navy in the world with an overall battle force of approximately 340 ships and submarines, including approximately 125 major surface combatants. As of 2021, the PLAN is largely composed of modern multi-mission ships and submarines."[32] Beyond fleet size, the PLAN has grown substantially by almost every measure of naval power, including the surface fleet's total tonnage, the average tonnage of a PLAN surface combatant, and the surface forces' missile launch capacity.[33]

All projections of the PLAN battle force ships point to a much larger force a decade hence. The Pentagon foresees the PLAN growing from 400 ships in 2025 to 440 ships by 2030.[34] The U.S. Office of Naval Intelligence estimates that the PLAN would expand from 400 battle force ships in 2025 to 425 battle force ships in 2030.[35] Among those ships, ballistic missile submarines, nuclear-powered attack submarines, diesel attack submarines, aircraft carriers, cruisers, destroyers, frigates, and corvettes would increase from 246 ships in 2025 to 276 ships in 2030. For the same ship types, a separate U.S. Navy study anticipates the fleet increasing from 238 ships in 2025, to 268 ships in 2030, and to 298 ships in 2040.[36] Beijing has been mum on how big it wants the PLAN to become, but U.S. forecasts hint at its ambitions.

In terms of force posture, as long as Taiwan and other offshore disputes remain unresolved, Beijing will concentrate most PLAN assets in the near seas for possible immediate action in home waters. In a cross-strait contingency, these forces would seek to destroy the Taiwanese navy, clear the seas and air around Taiwan, transport forces to the main island and offshore islands, and deter or defeat U.S. intervention. To be sure, the PLAN has already globalized, and a fleet component will likely operate permanently in the far seas. But Beijing will still fixate on the near seas if Taiwan is out of its hands. Reflecting this regional orientation, diesel attack submarines, frigates, and corvettes—combatants especially well-suited for near seas defense—are expected to constitute most of the fleet in the 2030s. Indeed, the buildup of frigates and corvettes has driven the surface force's growth over the past decade. Armed with antisubmarine warfare suites and ship-killing missiles, these smaller ships would be especially useful for sea lane defense, submarine hunting, and screening larger combatants in the East and South China seas. The PLA's air force and rocket force, employing shore-based aircraft and long-range missiles, respectively, would join the fray to clear the near seas. A war in offshore waters will not be an exclusively naval affair. China will draw on its land, sea, and air forces to impose its will.

## A FLEET IN BEING, CHINESE STYLE

As Geoffrey Till notes, the fleet-in-being approach comes in many varieties. It can range from a "moderated offensive" to a passive defense.

It can take place in blue water or littoral settings. It can last a long time or not. It can be employed via "a roundabout route avoiding a decision by battle" to obtain "a useful degree of command of the sea," or it can be used simply to survive. Fundamentally, it is an approach for a weaker or temporarily weaker navy that must make "best use of resources too limited to risk in a straightforward pursuit of battle with a superior adversary."[37]

The PLAN appears to favor the offensively minded version of a fleet-in-being strategy. As its official encyclopedia explains, a fleet in being (存在舰队) is an inferior but "highly capable (精干)" fleet that uses "appropriate deterrence (适当的威慑)" methods to "hold back (遏制)" a powerful enemy's navy. Such a fleet relies on "skill and flexibility (技巧和灵活)" to attack weaknesses, "tie up (牵制)" the adversary, or manipulate the opponent's attention. The goal is to preoccupy the enemy with potential threats so it cannot act effectively to achieve its aims. A fleet in being, the PLAN's encyclopedia observes, reflects "an offensive mentality (攻势意识)" and "confers a superior choice for implementing active defense."[38]

Conceptually, near seas defense, originating as it did from active defense, and an offensively oriented fleet-in-being strategy resemble each other. They are relevant to fleets that must fight from temporary or permanent positions of inferiority in quantity and quality. Near seas defense and the aggressive versions of a fleet-in-being strategy would employ offensive means—while eschewing battles of decision—to obtain some degree of sea control to achieve larger war aims. Liu Jin, a naval theorist, asserts, "A fleet in being is a kind of active defensive naval strategy. It refers to a weak or temporarily weak navy that uses every means to prevent a superior navy from exercising command of the sea. It is an active defense maritime strategy that exploits every possible situation and is ready to counterattack at any time."[39] This definition dovetails with the offensive spirit of near seas defense and echoes Mao Zedong's conception of active defense.

As Liu sees it, the PLAN's near seas forces are ideal for a fleet-in-being strategy. He contends that advances in sensor technologies, the mobility of naval forces, and the growing range and accuracy of firepower will "expand the scope and methods of an inferior navy that is pursuing a fleet-in-being strategy to exercise its influence." In other words, technology has opened new tactical vistas for the weaker side. As Liu explains, "Just as the Chinese navy has recently taken measures against U.S. naval warships in the South China Sea, when facing a superior navy, an inferior navy can actively demonstrate its political presence and perform missions to strive mightily for important gains."[40] To him, the mere presence and activity of the PLAN in the near seas could complicate the adversary's calculations in peace and in wartime.

McDevitt concurs that China's naval fleet, missiles and aircraft based on the mainland, and assets deployed on the manmade island bases in the Spratlys would make the South China Sea "an extremely dangerous place" for the U.S. military. He contends that U.S. forces would "struggle to gain sea and air control there" during hostilities. Given the expected difficulties, he speculates that Washington might decline to contest Chinese control of the South China Sea and instead might opt to inflict costs on the PLAN operating in the area. McDevitt further observes that U.S. reinforcements would have to flow across the Central Pacific to reach East Asian waters, implying that the U.S. Navy would write off the South China Sea as a viable avenue of approach.[41] Presumably, U.S. naval forces located in the Indian Ocean, Persian Gulf, the Mediterranean, and elsewhere would have to find alternative routes to transit around the South China Sea to reach the Philippine Sea and waters to the north.

In a war, the PLAN and the other services would make the approaches to and operations within the Philippine Sea hazardous for the U.S. Navy. The combined use of land-based antiship ballistic missiles, shore-based aircraft, surface combatants, and submarines, according to McDevitt, could "add up to a serious operational challenge for the U.S. Navy when it penetrates the second island chain into the Philippine Sea."[42] Indeed, aggressive tactics, skill, and sheer numbers could slow or preclude the flow of U.S. reinforcements into the Philippine Sea and surrounding areas to such an extent that China might be afforded the time and maneuver room to accomplish its operational objectives before the United States can meaningfully intervene on behalf of Taiwan or other Asian allies.

Hu Bo, too, sees much relevance in the fleet-in-being concept to Chinese naval strategy and applies the idea to the PLAN's far seas mission and its operational and force structure requirements. According to Hu, "A fleet in being usually refers to a weaker or a temporarily weaker navy using every means at its disposal to thwart (阻挠) the opponent's superior navy from obtaining absolute command of the sea." The weaker navy would "under all possible conditions" seek to counterattack the superior opponent through "integrated offensive and defensive operations."[43] His emphasis on going on the offense to preclude the enemy from making use of the seas is consistent with the definitions of fleet in being by the PLAN and Liu Jin cited above.

To Hu, a Chinese far seas fleet in being would operate beyond the first island chain in the open waters of the western Pacific and the northern Indian Ocean and would maintain an "effective presence (有效存在)" in those two areas. As Hu explains, "An effective presence refers to capabilities, which China must construct, that cannot be ignored and that cannot be easily defeated. These capabilities include a certain number of overseas support bases and a blue-water fleet formed by two to three carrier strike groups."[44] In other words, the fleet must be big enough and strong enough to draw the enemy's attention to it. In a crisis or war, the adversary must devote some portion of its forces to defend against or defeat this far seas fleet in being, thereby diverting scarce resources that it would otherwise use for other priority missions.

To Hu, an effective presence would require the PLAN to keep one carrier task force on station permanently in the western Pacific and the Indian Ocean, respectively. To maintain such a continuous presence on a rotational basis, Hu envisions a fleet of five to six medium and large carriers.[45] Beijing appears committed to developing such a force structure. The 2020 edition of Chinese National Defense University's *Science of Military Strategy* calls for a "new type of force structure" organized around aircraft carriers and nuclear-powered submarines.[46] The authoritative document identifies aircraft carriers, multirole destroyers, big-deck amphibious assault vessels, nuclear-powered submarines, oceangoing combat logistics ships, long-range carrier-borne aircraft, carrier-based unmanned aerial vehicles, and unmanned undersea vehicles as key constituents of this new naval force. Over the past decade, the PLAN has been constructing such blue-water capabilities at breakneck speed. China launched its third aircraft carrier—the first indigenous flattop designed and built from the keel up—in June 2022, with more likely to follow. The far seas fleet in being, as Hu understands it, is already in the making.

In a major conflict originating in the western Pacific, horizontal escalation is likely, if not certain. As McDevitt predicts, a war at sea over Taiwan "would likely spread globally very fast, after which whenever and wherever around the world the U.S. Navy and the PLA Navy encountered one another, combat would ensue."[47] The global element of Chinese naval power that Hu Bo depicts could engage in commerce raiding, harassment attacks against enemy bases, blockade and counterblockade operations, local sea denial and sea control, and limited power projection. Beijing could employ its forward-deployed units to open new fronts. Such peripheral operations or the threat to conduct them could compel China's opponents to draw possibly substantial resources and attention away from the main theater to cope with dangers in more distant areas. Indeed, with a fleet-in-being approach, Beijing could stimulate adversary responses disproportionate to the actual threat posed, especially if the PLAN were to hold the initiative in the far seas. The diversionary effects of the PLA's away team, even if modest in size and capabilities, could have an outsize impact on its adversary's strategy. Purposeful horizontal escalation to different maritime theaters could figure prominently in the PLAN's strategy in the coming years.

The effectiveness of a far seas fleet in being would depend on how China develops its power projection capabilities, including expeditionary logistics and basing arrangements, to sustain distant operations. A Chinese fleet in being in the Indian Ocean would have to fight far away from home ports and without the support of land-based air and missile cover. In a conflict with the United States and its allies and partners, including India and Australia, a far seas fleet would risk being cut off from reinforcements, resupply, and access to overseas bases.[48] The deployment of a well-balanced fleet, including a sizable at-sea replenishment flotilla as well as reliable access to foreign ports, facilities, and airbases would be crucial to sustain distant operations and to mitigate the vulnerabilities of a Chinese fleet in being. In recent years Beijing has worked hard to establish a network of dual-use commercial port facilities along major sea lanes to support the PLAN, although the wartime utility of these access points remains uncertain.[49]

In conclusion, the PLAN is rapidly aligning its doctrine, strategy, and means to achieve its local and extraregional maritime aims. Near seas defense will be central to the PLAN's strategy so long as disputes in the maritime direction remain unresolved and the prospect of third-party intervention over those disputes is probable, if not certain. The PLAN will assume ever more far seas responsibilities as Beijing's global interests and associated vulnerabilities proliferate. The naval buildup's trajectory suggests that the PLAN will be well positioned to meet the demands of near seas defense and far seas protection over the next decade. Although a global sea control force is still a distant goal, the contours of a world-class navy are already discernible in the force structure.

If China's near seas and far seas strategies are understood as an aggressive variety of a fleet in being, then significant operational challenges await the United States, should it choose to intervene against Chinese aggression. Given the PLAN's sheer size, it could "flood the zone" in the South China Sea to dissuade the U.S. Navy from contesting China's control of the sea and air there. The PLA's sea, air, and missile forces could make the Philippine Sea inhospitable enough to delay U.S. reinforcements that are essential to sustaining operations. China could deploy a far seas fleet in being to complicate U.S. and allied naval operations by posing threats in theaters outside of the western Pacific. The options collectively could pose severe dilemmas to U.S. commanders while buying critical time for Beijing to achieve its operational objective before U.S. forces can assemble enough power to stop China.

## NOTES

1. M. Taylor Fravel, *Active Defense: China's Military Strategy since 1949* (Princeton, NJ: Princeton University Press, 2019), 61–63.
2. Mao Zedong, "Problems of Strategy in China's Revolutionary War, December 1936," in *Selected Works of Mao Tse-Tung* (Peking: Foreign Languages Press, 1975), 1:207.
3. State Council Information Office of the People's Republic of China [hereafter, SCIO], *China's National Defense in the New Era* (Beijing: Foreign Languages

Press, July 2019), 7; SCIO, *China's Military Strategy* (Beijing: Foreign Languages Press, May 2015), 2; SCIO, *China's National Defense in 2010* (Beijing: Foreign Languages Press, March 2011), 10; and SCIO, *China's National Defense* (Beijing: Foreign Languages Press, July 1998), 7.
4. 寿晓松 [Shou Xiaosong], ed., 战略学 [Science of military strategy] (Beijing: Academy of Military Science, 2013), 104.
5. SCIO, *China's National Defense in the New Era*, 18; SCIO, *China's Military Strategy*, 12.
6. 刘华清 [Liu Huaqing], 刘华清回忆录 [Liu Huaqing memoir] (Beijing: Liberation Army Press, 2004), 434.
7. 中国人民解放军军事科学院 [PLA Academy of Military Science], 中国人民解放军军语 [Military terms of the PLA] (Beijing: Military Science Press, 1997), 440.
8. Toshi Yoshihara and James R. Holmes, *Red Star over the Pacific*, 2nd ed. (Annapolis, MD: Naval Institute Press, 2019), 125–28.
9. 中国海军百科全书编审委员会 [Editorial board of the Chinese navy encyclopedia (hereafter, EBCNE)], 中国海军百科 [Chinese navy encyclopedia] (Beijing: Haichao Press, 1999), 1154.
10. EBCNE, 731.
11. Liu Huaqing, *Memoir*, 438.
12. EBCNE, *Chinese Navy Encyclopedia*, 1928.
13. 胡波 [Hu Bo], 后马汉时代的中国海权 [Chinese sea power in the post-Mahanian era] (Beijing: Haiyang Press, 2018), 137.
14. Hu Bo, 171–72.
15. Ryan Martinson, "China's Oceanic Aspirations," *Orbis* 66 no. 2 (Spring 2022): 253–55.
16. SCIO, *China's Military Strategy*, 13–14.
17. SCIO, *China's National Defense in the New Era*, 14.
18. Ronald O'Rourke, *China Naval Modernization: Implications for U.S. Navy Capabilities—Background and Issues for Congress* (Washington, DC: Congressional Research Service, 2020), 27.
19. Michael A. McDevitt, *China as a Twenty-First Century Naval Power: Theory, Practice, and Implications* (Annapolis, MD: Naval Institute Press, 2020), 44.
20. Jennifer Rice and Erik Robb, "The Origins of 'Near Seas Defense and Far Seas Protection,'" *CMSI China Maritime Reports*, no. 13 (February 2021): 5–6.
21. Martinson, "China's Oceanic Aspirations," 267.
22. Xi Jinping, Secure a Decisive Victory in Building a Moderately Prosperous Society in All Respects and Strive for the Great Success of Socialism with Chinese Characteristics for a New Era, 19th National Congress of the Communist Party of China, 18 October 2017, 48.

23. Xi Jinping, Hold High the Great Banner of Socialism with Chinese Characteristics and Strive in Unity to Build a Modern Socialist Country in All Respects, Report to the 20th National Congress of the Communist Party of China, 16 October 2022, 47.
24. 海军党委 [PLAN Party Committee], "努力把人民海军全面建成世界一流海军 [Strive to build the People's navy into a world-class navy in an all-round way]," 求是 [*Qiushi*], no. 11, 31 May 2018.
25. 沈金龙 秦生祥 [Shen Jinlong and Qin Shengxiang], "人民海军 (People's Navy)," 求是 [*Qiushi*], no. 8, 16 April 2019.
26. Shou Xiaosong, *Science of Military Strategy*, 106.
27. Andrew Krepinevich and Robert O. Work, *A New Global Defense Posture for the Second Transoceanic Era* (Washington, DC: Center for Strategic and Budgetary Assessments, 2007), 4.
28. 杨晓丹 杨志荣 [Yang Xiaodan and Yang Zhirong], "人民海军所处的历史方位与战略要求 [The Historical Position and Strategic Requirements of the People's Navy]," 海军工程大学学报 [Journal of Naval University of Engineering] 16, no. 4 (December 2019): 49.
29. China Power Team, "How Is China Modernizing Its Navy?" *China Power*, April 20, 2022.
30. Ryan D. Martinson, "Deciphering China's 'World-class' Naval Ambitions," *Proceedings* no. 146 (August 2020), 8.
31. Statement of Admiral John C. Aquilino, Commander, U.S. Indo-Pacific Command, Before the Senate Armed Services Committee on U.S. Indo-Pacific Command Posture, 10 March 2022, 4–5, https://www.armed-services.senate.gov/imo/media/doc/INDOPACOM%20Statement%20(ADM%20Aquilino)%20_SASC2.PDF.
32. Office of the Secretary of Defense, *Annual Report to Congress: Military and Security Developments Involving the People's Republic of China 2022* (Arlington, VA: Department of Defense, 2022), 50.
33. Toshi Yoshihara, *Dragon against the Sun* (Washington, DC: Center for Strategic and Budgetary Assessments, 2020), 7–19.
34. Office of the Secretary of Defense, *Annual Report to Congress*, 52.
35. Ronald O'Rourke, *China Naval Modernization: Implications for U.S. Navy Capabilities—Background and Issues for Congress* (Washington, DC: Congressional Research Service, March 2021), 32.
36. O'Rourke, 33.
37. Geoffrey Till, *Seapower: A Guide for the Twenty-First Century*, 2nd ed. (London: Routledge, 2004), 173.
38. EBCNE, *Chinese Navy Encyclopedia*, 132.
39. 刘晋 (Liu Jin), "回到朱利安科贝特: 存在舰队再阐释 [A Return to Julian Corbett: A Reinterpretation of Fleet in Being]," 太平洋学报 [*Pacific Journal*] 25, no. 2 (2017): 52.

40. Liu Jin, 60.
41. McDevitt, *China as a Twenty-First Century Naval Power*, 147–48.
42. McDevitt, 115.
43. Hu Bo, *Chinese Sea Power*, 145.
44. Hu Bo, 144.
45. Hu Bo, 181.
46. 肖天亮 主编 [Xiao Tianliang], ed., 战略学 [Science of military strategy] (Beijing: National Defense University, 2020), 366.
47. McDevitt, *China as a Twenty-First Century Naval Power*, 89.
48. Toshi Yoshihara and Jack Bianchi, *Seizing on Weakness: Allied Strategy for Competing with China's Globalizing Military* (Washington, DC: CSBA, January 2021), 99–100.
49. Isaac B. Kardon and Wendy Leutert, "Pier Competition: China's Power Position in Global Ports," *International Security* 46, no. 4 (Spring 2022): 9–47.

CHAPTER 18

# COMBAT STABILITY AND THE RUSSIAN FLEET IN BEING

*Andrew Monaghan*

What is the purpose of today's Russian navy in peace and in war? To what extent has this purpose evolved, and what kind of strategies does it pursue? Does today's Russian navy, as some suggest, pursue a recognizable fleet-in-being strategy—and, if so, what does this concept look like in Russian thinking?[1] In sum, for what should the U.S. Navy prepare when facing the Russian navy?

To answer these questions, this chapter begins with some essential foundation points about the Russian navy, briefly sketching some background history that echoes through today's debate about war and strategy in Russia and highlighting some of the ways the Russian navy is distinct in its thinking and activity. This provides a platform to frame where and how Russian naval strategy fits in Moscow's approach to power at sea and purpose for the navy, looking at the key strategic documents and debates underway—and problems encountered.

### THE REEMERGENCE OF A RUSSIAN NAVAL CHALLENGE
During the 2010s Moscow began to make a substantial and sustained effort to reestablish Russia as a maritime power. Indeed, following Russia's annexation of Crimea in 2014 and the sanctions imposed by the Euro-Atlantic community, the sea became ever more important to Russia. Trade with the Middle East, North Africa, and the Asia-Pacific regions grew, and the development of the Northern Sea Route took on added significance as part of a persistent attempt to diversify both the economy and trading partners. If maritime infrastructure and the civilian fleet benefited from increased financial support from the

government during this time, the Russian navy became a priority in defense spending, given the largest share of the State Armaments Program to 2020. The Russian navy received between one-quarter and one-fifth of all military expenditure from 2015 to 2020, or some $35 billion a year in purchasing power parity terms—some of the highest spending on a navy in the world.[2]

This sustained investment yielded substantial results. By tonnage, Russia has one of the largest navies in the world, and Russian shipyards are currently operating at almost full capacity to modernize Soviet-era vessels and to build new ones. And the navy has begun to increase significantly its activity in numbers and types of missions both in waters close to home, for instance, in the Arctic, and further afield. In 2019 a Northern Fleet task force led by the frigate *Admiral Gorshkov* completed a circumnavigation, calling at Djibouti, Sri Lanka, China, Ecuador, Cuba, and Trinidad and Tobago, sailing through the Suez and Panama Canals.[3]

By the end of the 2010s and into the early 2020s, President Vladimir Putin made Russian ambitions explicit by emphasizing Russia's status as a great maritime and naval power. He repeatedly underlines, for instance, that the navy is an important "if not key component ensuring national defense and security in the 21st century" and that "we must also preserve and enhance our country's status as one of the world's leading seafaring nations." Moreover, he stated his intent that the navy be modernized to include high-precision, state-of-the-art weapons to create a fleet of "unique capabilities," a fleet of a "strong and sovereign nation."[4]

Such ambition might appear counterintuitive to a Euro-Atlantic audience. Russia is widely seen as a traditional continental power with a limited naval capacity largely dedicated to local, coastal defensive naval tasks and supporting the army. Russia's navy has a checkered history—while there have been some great naval victories, there have also been numerous calamitous defeats. And if under Admiral Sergey Gorshkov the Soviet navy achieved a powerful global naval presence in the 1970s and 1980s, this withered with the collapse of the USSR: in the 1990s the Russian navy halved in strength and suffered an acute socioeconomic crisis due to a lack of funding. The sinking in 2000 of the nuclear-powered *Kursk*, one of the largest submarines in the Russian inventory, with all hands lost, was just one of many tragedies that characterized a difficult period that lasted for nearly thirty years.

Nevertheless, by the mid-2010s senior Western naval officers began to recognize the growing capability of the Russian navy, asserting that its activity was reaching Cold War levels.[5] Since then they have argued that Russian naval activity poses a wide range of challenges, from threatening undersea infrastructure to persistent presence in the Mediterranean and sea denial, and even a "fourth battle of the Atlantic," akin to the challenges posed by the German navy in the two world wars. Moreover, there has been extended discussion about Russia's supposed anti-access-/-area denial (A2/AD) capabilities.[6]

Three incidents emphasized the sense that Russian power at sea posed a challenge. The first came in late 2015, when vessels in the newly modernized Caspian Flotilla launched missile strikes in support of Russian forces against targets in Syria. The second came in late 2018, when Russian boats fired on and then captured three Ukrainian vessels during the Kerch Strait confrontation, where the Sea of Azov and Black Sea meet. And the third came during 2022, when Moscow launched a full-scale invasion of Ukraine; although most of the fighting was carried out by Russian ground forces, the Russian navy played a significant role in blockading the Black Sea, providing logistical support to ground forces, and bombarding targets in Ukraine.

This reemergence of the Russian navy as a challenge led to the reestablishment of the U.S. Second Fleet and NATO's Joint Forces Command in Norfolk in 2018. Yet the strength of the Russian navy, the threat it poses, and even its purpose are all debated questions. Some analysts reject, for instance, the idea of a "fourth battle of the Atlantic," noting that this was never the purpose of the Russian navy, neither during the Cold War nor today: it is not equipped for or preparing to fight NATO on the sea lines of communication across the Atlantic.[7] Similarly, Russian modern weapons systems and A2/AD capabilities have been overemphasized. Indeed, the term "A2/AD" misdiagnoses the nature of the challenge: there is no such Russian doctrine or strategy.[8] Others question the strengths of the Russian navy and the nature of the modernization, as well as the ability of the Russian navy to conduct sustained activity further afield.[9] As we shall see, in so doing, they echo ongoing debates in Russia about the utility of naval power.

Before attempting to answer the questions initially posed, three important related caveats should be noted. First, this chapter focuses on the Russian navy, where it "fits" in Moscow's national and military strategy, its concepts, and its evolving tasks in wartime. At the outset, it should be acknowledged that Russian maritime power is multifaceted, with other entities explicitly working with the navy, such as the Ministry of Foreign Affairs, and other organizations such as the Federal Security Service Border Guards and the Ministry of Defense's Main Directorate of Deep Sea Research having roles in naval operations.

Second, the Russian navy's activity must be seen in the wider context of Moscow's view of international affairs and strategic activity. The Russian policy community often appears to have similar debates about international affairs as those underway in the Euro-Atlantic community: the emergence of a "new cold war," "hybrid warfare," and "great power competition." But care must be taken to not "mirror image" these debates and assume that Moscow sees the world in the same way as Western capitals do. In Moscow these are all understood very differently in terms of their causes, chronology, and consequences. The latter is particularly relevant: if the Euro-Atlantic community began to debate the emergence of a great power competition with Russia and China in the mid-2010s, framing it in strategic documentation in 2017 and 2018, Moscow had already concluded that such a competition was underway a decade earlier and that it was likely to last through the 2020s.[10] Other relevant documents, including the Maritime Doctrine, as discussed below, and the web of strategic plans for the Arctic all have a similar horizon of 2030–35.

Senior Russian officials, including Putin, Defense Minister Sergei Shoigu, and Chief of the General Staff Valery Gerasimov, have long pointed to the intensifying global competition over access to resources, transit routes, and markets that (in their view) increasingly characterize international affairs. This view of a global geoeconomic contest has been at the heart of Moscow's effort to generate grand strategy—formulating and sustaining a strategic agenda and effort to resource and implement it. Such activity has been (and remains) strategic, not merely "ad hoc," "opportunistic," or tactical. This has consequences for understanding Russian naval power: Moscow has a pronounced maritime agenda, including competition for the global commons and over maritime strategic choke points. The Russian navy should therefore be seen in this context: as a tool in a sustained effort by Moscow to link global regions, establish a global economic and military presence, and link economic and military activity to compete in an era of geoeconomics at sea.[11]

The third caveat regards Russia's full-scale invasion of Ukraine that began in 2022. At the time of writing, Russia is still conducting what it calls a "special military operation" against Ukraine. This represents Moscow's escalation of a conflict that simmered between Moscow and Kyiv since 2004 and then broke out in 2014 with the Russian annexation of Crimea and armed intervention in eastern Ukraine. It also relates to the long-standing policy and value dissonance between the Euro-Atlantic community and Russia, intensifying since the mid-2000s.

The war has accelerated a very sharp deterioration in relations between the Euro-Atlantic community and Russia, with Western states giving considerable political, economic, and military support to Ukraine and imposing harsh sanctions on Russia. While sanctions may slow Russian shipbuilding, Moscow's investment in the military, including its maritime power, is sustained. As Putin has stated, there are no funding restrictions, and this is likely to reap some rewards looking ahead into the 2020s. In the autumn of 2022 Putin put the Russian defense industry onto a war footing, and the military has outlined a plan for growth through 2026.[12] This will face numerous problems, but the intent and resources dedicated cannot simply be written off.

The war has become the primary focus of analysis of Russia over its military failings (including at sea) and even whether Russia faces strategic defeat. But much remains unclear, even through the short- to medium-term outlook. So, although this chapter notes episodes in the war in passing, it does not examine the war specifically, instead looking to the longer trajectory of Russian naval power in the post–Cold War era.

This is important because thinking about how Russia reconstitutes its military must remain flexible. A large part of the Russian navy—for instance, including its strategic capabilities—is not actively involved in the war. The possibility for the war to escalate, both specifically in Ukraine and (potentially) more widely in the region, emphasizes the importance of grasping how the Russian navy would act in war with the West. There is much discussion in the Euro-Atlantic community about having overestimated the Russian military prior to the war, which has now turned to a strong emphasis on examining the Russian military's failings. But this see-saw analysis has highlighted a black-and-white, either/or approach to the assessment of Russian military capabilities when there is instead a complex blend of both strength and weakness— and the task is to clarify more specifically the nature and balance of these strengths and weaknesses. This is important because the Russian military is a learning organization, and it is essential for Western armed forces to reflect on the lessons the Russians are learning from this war (the Russian navy is already attempting such work).[13] In sum, how Moscow launched and then pursued its "special military operation" is neither how it had trained nor how it would have gone to war against an adversary like NATO—which means that the U.S. Navy (and its allies) should adopt a sophisticated approach to interpreting the lessons to learn from it.

Finally, for Moscow the war is part of an intensified, multifaceted global contest that includes greater competition in the Arctic and the Asia-Pacific: Russian officials point to "provocations" by the United States over Taiwan and the establishment of AUKUS (the trilateral security pact among Australia, the United Kingdom, and the United States) as part of a destabilizing global agenda.[14] Whatever happens in the war, therefore, Moscow is increasingly dependent on the sea for international trade and essentially committed to a wider and longer contest that in many ways is increasingly maritime in nature.

## RUSSIAN NAVAL CONCEPTS—FAMILIAR, BUT DISTINCT

In the Russian policy and expert community, there are a number of debates underway about maritime power and the navy that will appear very familiar to Euro-Atlantic observers. Not only is a maritime turn in international affairs also recognized in Russia, but there is discussion about a possible paradigm shift in naval affairs due to new technology. There is extensive debate, for example, over the value or vulnerability of large vessels, especially aircraft carriers. Just as in the United States and Europe, there are those in Russia who argue that because of longer-range missiles and other capabilities, fleets have a very "ambiguous survival rate" and are now vulnerable even when moored in their home ports. If some Russian observers question the value of investing in the navy when it still results in local weakness compared to regional powers, others question the value of having a fleet at all.[15] Underway before Russia's full-scale invasion of Ukraine in 2022, these debates are only likely to intensify given Ukraine's sinking in April 2022 of the guided-missile cruiser *Moskva* and attacks on the Russian Black Sea Fleet in port at Sevastopol in occupied Crimea.

But different experiences shaped by geography and history have driven rather different Russian traditions and concepts in the use of naval power. This creates a multifaceted and complex picture in which strength and weakness, success and failure are intertwined, and in which the main characteristics of Russian power have evolved over time. Two points particularly stand out for our purposes.

The first is easily and quickly set out: geography puts the Russian navy immediately at a disadvantage. Russia's coastline is nearly 40,000 km long, and although it opens onto three oceans and numerous seas, the Russian navy has few viable outlets. It faces accessing isolated theaters via narrow exits and choke points that are often commanded by hostile states. The Russian navy is thus fragmented into four fleets, a flotilla, and a "permanent presence"—all separated by great distances: The Northern Fleet and Pacific Fleet are Russia's two strategic, oceangoing fleets, supplemented by the Baltic Sea and Black Sea Fleets, the Caspian Flotilla, and the "permanent presence" in the eastern Mediterranean. The Russian navy often rehearses linking these forces and regions in major exercises. This underlines not only funding challenges but also logistical questions. In short: while, in peacetime, the Russian navy plays a major role acting as a platform on which Moscow's diplomacy and trade is advanced, in wartime, today's Russian navy from the outset faces (often much) superior naval forces ranged against it.

The second point relates to how the Russian navy has attempted to cope with this situation in theory and practice. In fact, the character of Russian naval power has evolved substantially, and this evolving inheritance sheds light on Moscow's strategy today. Because Russia has traditionally been (and often still is) considered a continental power, and its navy has been secondary to ground forces, its naval power has constantly waxed and waned since the turn of the seventeenth to eighteenth centuries.

Initially Russia used its navy largely to assist the army's advance and in territorial defense. Thus, Russian naval power was as much to be found in the building of coastal defenses such as the Kronstadt Fortress and of floating batteries, as in fleets. Indeed, in wartime, Russian fleets were often either sacrificed in the defense of territorial interests or converted to land defense forces—for instance, during the so-called Crimean War (which in fact involved important naval operations elsewhere, including in the Baltic, high north, and Far East) and the Russo-Japanese War. Although fleet action occurred, it was largely avoided, especially against major navies.[16] The most notable cases occurred at the battles of the Yellow Sea and Tsushima in the Russo-Japanese War, when the tsar himself overruled Admiral Wilgelm Vitgeft, the commander of the 1st Pacific Squadron by ordering him to sortie from the safety of Port Arthur (Lüshun) to attack the Japanese fleet. Vitgeft died in the ensuing battle and the Russian fleet dispersed, with part of it returning to Port Arthur. Then, at Tsushima, one of the most lopsided naval battles in history, Japan sank or commandeered virtually the entire Imperial Russian Navy.

The navy's approach of providing support for ground force operations rather than concentrating on fleet-on-fleet operations evolved during the Soviet era, and especially during the Cold War under Admiral Gorshkov, when the Soviet navy began to grow again and play an active role well beyond Russia's shores in the world's oceans. Technological developments meant that the Soviet navy began to blend powerful offensive and defensive capabilities. Gorshkov advocated the adoption of a strategy that encompassed littoral protection as well as strategic deterrence and the building of a fleet that could not only protect the USSR's ballistic missile submarines in "bastions"—essentially protected operating areas—but also establish a forward presence mission. For Gorshkov, the navy should play a role in peacetime in advancing Russian national interests through soft power and should in wartime contribute to the wider national war effort. In this latter task, because the outcome of the war would be decided on land, the fleet's primary purpose should not be "fleet against fleet" (*flot protiv flota*) but "fleet against the shore" (*flot protiv berega*).[17]

As some of this suggests, the concept and features of a fleet in being appear to resonate with some aspects of Russian naval activity. If a fleet in being describes a strategy that reflects a naval force that adopts a defensive, "survival" approach, avoiding decisive battle or sheltering in port to remain in existence and prevent a superior enemy from exploiting command of the sea, then both Admirals Vitgeft and Gorshkov, in their different ways and different eras, offered something of a fleet-in-being approach (both are examined in detail in chapters 7 and 14 respectively). This history matters to the contemporary debate: not only does Putin repeatedly refer to these examples, but the contemporary military and naval debate in Russia also often draws on historical "lessons," including from the Russo-Japanese War, World War I, and World War II (in Russia called the Great Patriotic War), and some suggest that today's Russian naval strategy is "neo-Gorshkovian."[18]

But care is necessary here since Russian naval strategy is formulated on different concepts. Although "fleet in being" can be rendered in the Russian language literally as *sila flota v nalichii* (strength of the fleet available) or as *flot kak faktor v prisutstviya* (the fleet as a factor of presence) and is recognized as a Western naval concept or strategy, it is not a Russian naval concept or strategy. Like "command of the sea" (*gospodstvo na more*), it is considered to be a Western concept that does not satisfactorily describe the Russian navy's tasks and that does not reflect the Russian navy's priorities.[19]

Where Western navies might think of concepts such as "command of the sea," the Soviet and now the Russian navy thinks more in terms of "defending the country's maritime frontiers," "concentration of force," or "combat stability." This latter, combat stability, or *boevaya ustoichivost*, is a concept denoting the ability to give, take, and recover from damage, often in adverse conditions.[20] It reflects survivability and effective use of forces. Today the Russian Ministry of Defense defines combat stability as the "best use of forces and means in adverse conditions," and the "retention of the ability" to perform the "assigned combat mission with the required efficiency under the influence of the enemy and to ensure the fulfilment of the combat mission."[21]

Indeed, even the idea of a "naval strategy" does not accurately apply to Russian military (and naval) thought: as suggested above in the fleet-against-shore approach, the navy does not have a separate or independent "strategy" but instead contributes to a wider national warfighting effort. It is just one of several of the state's tools wrapped into the successful fulfillment of wider national tasks, political or military.

This means that while some features appear familiar, since some tasks do align with the concept of a fleet in being, they must be understood as having different roots and intent; if parts of the image look familiar, the overall picture is (sometimes subtly) different and must not be mirror imaged. Moreover, they must also be seen in the context of other aspects and characteristics of wider Russian military culture and art, such as how to seize the initiative in war and the constant tension between warfighting strategies of annihilation or attrition (and the common consequent hedge of adopting both simultaneously) while coping with an often flawed and disjointed chain of command and risk-averse commanders.[22]

This means that our understanding of the activity of the Russian navy has to be constructed first from an understanding of the key features of national, or grand, strategy, briefly sketched out above, then in the context of concepts of Russian military strategy, which concerns the operational level of war. Military strategy is the theory and practice of the state's military activity. It connects the political purpose of the grand strategy to military activity, defining priorities and directions and tasks. As defined by the Russian Ministry of Defense, "policy presents military strategy with tasks, and military strategy ensures their implementation." Military strategy assesses the "likely character of war and . . . the goals and tasks."[23]

In this respect, two characteristics stand out. The first is the long-running discussion in Russian military strategy about "sixth-generation warfare," emphasizing stand-off precision strike. (In Russian military thinking, the preceding five generations of warfare highlighted, respectively: the massed manpower of the ancients; gunpowder weapons; rifled, breach-loading weapons; automatic weapons; nuclear weapons.) The discussion flourished in the 1990s as military analysts such as

Major General Vladimir Slipchenko reflected on the Falklands War in 1982, Operation Desert Storm in 1991, and then NATO's bombing of Yugoslav forces in 1999. Slipchenko argued that technological changes, especially in information operations (network centric warfare) and (conventional) long-range precision-guided missiles amounted to a "new generation" in warfighting. Such weapons systems could be used as part of deterrence and to deliver simultaneous attacks on different axes of a theater of military activity, even beginning to link different theaters. Russian military theorists call this "noncontact" warfare: long-range strikes would obviate the need for large groupings of forces.[24]

This is the basis on which the Russian navy has sought to modernize its capabilities—including the so-called Kalibrisation of the navy, the use of the Kalibr "family" of long-range missiles for striking targets at sea and on land. But there have been problems with this.[25] Moscow has also emphasized the introduction of other weapons systems, including hypersonic missiles: in early January 2023 the frigate *Admiral Gorshkov* set out on a long-distance mission to the Atlantic, Mediterranean, and Indian Ocean equipped with Zircon hypersonic missiles, "capable of inflicting pinpoint and powerful strikes against an enemy at sea and on land."[26] As discussed below, this forms an important part of the evolution of tasking for the Russian navy, giving it added flexibility and thus new tasks and even a more central role in military strategy.

The second relates to the refresh of military strategy of the 2010s, developing this "sixth-generation warfare" (which in many ways echoed and built on the work of late Soviet military strategists such as Gorshkov and Nikolai Ogarkov).[27] Through the 2010s, Gerasimov drove the Russian debate about the changing character of war with a series of articles that were essentially write-ups of his yearly speeches to the Russian General Staff Academy. They examined Western strategy, the experience of (and lessons to be drawn from) the Great Patriotic War, and Russia's experience in its operations in Syria. Western attention focused, often misleadingly, on a 2013 article "The Value of Science in Foresight," but other articles in subsequent years were revealing, including one in 2017 titled "The World on the Brink of War." A number of common themes permeated these reflections, including what Gerasimov described as twenty-first century blitzkrieg, aerospace operations, and the planetary nature of warfare, and he emphasized the need to defend Russia and its immediate environment against those seeking to seize natural resources and deploy groups of forces to strategic parts of the world and the need to defend transit routes in a likely competition for the global commons.[28]

Writing in 2019 as part of a wider refresh of Russian military strategy, given the changing international context and changing character of war, Gerasimov reflected more specifically on military strategy, emphasizing three main contemporary themes. These were territorial defense, a "strategy of limited operations" (essentially expeditionary warfare), and active defense.[29] In all of these, the navy plays an important role, and in his writings Gerasimov has indicated the intent to shape more flexible military strategies, shifting away from the traditional reliance on ground forces toward basing a campaign on the most relevant service for the circumstances. In theory, this could mean that in a campaign, the navy could be the foundation service, with the other services in support of it. Indicating this shift in practice, the Northern Fleet Joint Strategic Command was established in 2014, and in 2021 the Northern Fleet became the only command with the status of Military District.[30]

Of particular interest here is "active defense" (*aktivnaya oborona*), which blurs the lines between the offensive and the defensive. The Russian Ministry of Defense defines *aktivnaya oborona* as a means not only of holding territory but of "mainly exhausting and bleeding large enemy forces" and using the counteroffensive. It includes the "intensive fire engagement" of the enemy during the preparation and conduct of this offensive, striking at troops and equipment, command and logistics.[31] Active defense involves the sustained disruption of and engagement with the adversary, and it includes preemption and preventive measures to deflect, disorganize, and neutralize threats before they strike as well as during an offensive. As we will see below, given the introduction of new weapons systems into service, this again increases the role of the Russian navy.

Rather than a Russian concept of fleet in being, therefore, we are better served by thinking first in terms of the state's broader intent, then in terms of military strategy, and then of "fleet against shore," "combat stability," and "active defense," which together represent "fleet survivability" and a more dynamic form of war fighting.[32] These concepts situate Russian thinking. With this in mind, we can now turn to Moscow's maritime priorities and tasks for the navy.

## RUSSIA'S MARITIME PRIORITIES AND THE PURPOSE OF THE RUSSIAN NAVY?

A web of strategic planning documents offer insight into the linking of Moscow's strategic agenda and use of naval power. These range from broader national strategies, such as the National Security Strategy and Foreign Policy Concept, down to more regional and thematic ones, for instance, for the development of the Arctic and shipbuilding. For our purposes here, though, the relevant documents are the Maritime Doctrine of 2015 and the updated version published in 2022, and the 2017 document The Foundations of State Policy of the Russian Federation in the Sphere of Naval Activity in the Period to 2030.[33] Such documents emphasize—and officially codify—the points made in speeches by senior officials about the establishment of Russia as a leading seafaring nation and the geoeconomic contest. In broad terms, both show Russia's shift toward greater attention to the sea, a more central role for the navy in military strategy, and the continuing evolution of naval power from a largely coastal defense force to one that, while it continues to have a defensive role, includes a more offensive capability. More specifically, they indicate strategic direction and priorities and tasks.[34]

If the Maritime Doctrine paints the broader, global horizon (the intent to show the Russian flag in the "world ocean" and maintain political stability) and frames regional prioritization, the 2017 Foundations of the State Policy is the key document setting out the navy's tasks. The Foundations underline Moscow's view both that Russia is a great maritime power and that competition between states for access to resources and transit routes is intensifying as part of a global rivalry between the world's centers of power. Describing a wide range of potential threats, the Foundations state that Moscow will seek to ensure that Russia retains its position as the second (after the United States) most-combat-capable navy in the world, and that naval power is an essential feature of maintaining strategic stability and strategic deterrence and of ensuring favorable conditions for Russia's socioeconomic development. Moreover, the Foundations set out naval strategic requirements, objectives, and priorities. These include the deterrence of the use of force and aggression against Russia and its allies, the capability to challenge a high-tech adversary's strike groups both at distance and near to Russia's shores, and the ability to promptly deploy and conduct extended autonomous operations in remote areas of the world ocean.

The Ministry of Defense builds on this, framing the navy's objectives, including in war. To deterrence, it adds the provision of protection through military methods of Russia's sovereignty in its internal sea waters, exclusive economic zone and continental shelf, and the security of Russia's maritime activity in the world ocean. In the transition to war, the navy would be involved in containing conflicts and protecting industrial activities and navigation. And in war, the priorities are set out as follows: destroy enemy land-based facilities at long range, ensure the sustainability of ballistic missile submarines, destroy enemy antisubmarine and other forces as well as coastal facilities, maintain a favorable operational environment, provide maritime support of contact troops during maritime defensive and offensive operations, and maintain seacoast defense.[35]

This list emphasizes traditional missions, such as coastal defense, the sustainment of ballistic missile submarines, and the support of ground forces. And many of these missions essentially reflect the importance of combat stability and the survival of fleet. Successful deterrence demands that the ballistic missile fleet is kept "in being." But it also reflects an important evolution in the modern Russian navy's missions, with the added adoption of the task to destroy enemy land-based facilities at long range. This reflects the combination of deterrence with sixth-generation warfare and active defense, offering a more offensive role to the navy, with a fleet-against-shore offensive mission.

There is, to be sure, much debate among specialists in both Russia and the Euro-Atlantic community about the strengths and weaknesses of this strategy, especially over the balance between the aim of adopting a global horizon and sustained Russian presence in the world ocean and the capabilities that reflect a more coastal approach. As one Russian observer put it, there is a "sea of ships, but the ocean is not visible."[36] And the Russian navy faces numerous problems, among them "the complete absence" of modern antitorpedo protection and the obsolescence of antisubmarine capabilities, including in aviation.[37] Western observers also suggest that the current numbers of ships, submarines, and planes are insufficient to carry out bastion-type operations. Moreover, the Russian navy faces difficulties in coordinating strikes against moving naval targets: effective over-the-horizon intelligence, surveillance, and reconnaissance remains a critical challenge.[38]

Nevertheless, two points stand out. First, the Russian navy is, in effect, two tier: although it has substantial capabilities nearer to its shores, it lacks the oceangoing capability to conduct fleet-on-fleet action against Western navies. Second, the Russian navy's purpose has evolved: because of the development of sixth-generation warfare capabilities, the navy has adopted a more central role in Russian military strategy. Moreover, while it retains some defensive tasks, including bastion-type operations, the navy in wartime now also has a more offensive character, especially through fleet-against-shore activities, contributing to a joint campaign against fixed targets to impose cost and manage escalation.

## COMBAT STABILITY: THE RUSSIAN VERSION OF A FLEET IN BEING

The modern Russian navy has reemerged as a serious actor in international affairs. It is smaller than the Soviet navy was, and undoubtedly there are several "inheritances," both conceptual and practical in terms of ships and shipbuilding capacity, that make it tempting to highlight the past in Russian naval activity and even in Moscow's broader national strategy. But Moscow has an ambitious, future-oriented strategy in which the sea and the navy play an important role—and framing the nature of the challenge it poses requires a concerted effort to avoid mirror imaging.

Although the Russian navy faces a series of "universal" problems, which will be widely recognizable—distribution of funding, problems of interoperability and coordination between services, problems in command and control and information management, and so on—it operates according to a distinct strategic construct. This means not only Moscow's different worldview and distinctive Russian geography but also Russian military strategy. The keys to interpreting Russian naval concepts and activity lie here.

The starting point, therefore, for thinking about the Russian navy is an understanding that it is part of a broadly consistent wider grand strategy, one based on foresight through to 2035. This strategy certainly faces problems, but it has been continuously well resourced. The guiding light of this strategy is Moscow's effort to make Russia a leading "seafaring" or "great maritime" power. The navy's role is explicitly linked to wider geoeconomic purposes. Within this, the tasking for the navy has substantially evolved within wider Russian military strategy. This positions the navy within the context of sixth-generation warfare and its evolution using long-range, precision-guided munitions, and it increases the role of the navy within the Russian armed forces as a whole.

The growth of the importance of the sea to Russia, including the expansion of critical infrastructure on or near the Russian coast means that the navy has an important defensive role to protect it. This reflects a traditional defensive task, as does the protection of Russia's nuclear deterrent. Although the Russian navy does not use the fleet-in-being concept, aspects of this can be found in combination of Russian concepts of strategic deterrence, combat stability, (survivability) and active defense, in which the Russian navy's task is not to engage in fleet-on-fleet action in decisive battle but instead to engage in fleet-against-shore action to assist the overall war effort. Equally, though, the navy now has a larger, more forward-leaning, even offensive role in Russian military strategy. The Russian fleet faces a number of ongoing problems and debates about its character and what vessels it needs, but the horizon will remain global and focused on the imposition of costs on an adversary. This reflects an important evolution in the Russian navy's role and a distinctively Russian version of a fleet in being.

## NOTES

1. N. Polmar, "Russian Navy—Putin's Fleet in Being," U.S. Naval Institute *Proceedings* 141, no. 12 (December 2015), https://www.usni.org/magazines/proceedings/2015/december/russian-navy-putins-fleet-being; and L. K. Parnemo, "Russia's Naval Development: Grand Ambitions and Tactical Pragmatism," *Journal of Slavic Military Studies* 32, no. 1 (2019).

2. R. Connolly, "Russia as a Maritime Power: Economic Interests and Capabilities," in *The Sea in Russian Strategy*, edited by A. Monaghan and R. Connolly (Manchester, UK: Manchester University Press, 2023).
3. V. Gerasimov, "Zasedaniye Kollegii Ministerstva Oborony RF po voprosu 'O khode vypolneniya ukazov Prezidenta Rossiiskoi Federatsii ot 7 maya 2012 g, i razvitii Vooruzhonnykh Sil Rossiiskoi Federatsii," website of the Ministry of Defence, 7 November 2017, https://function.mil.ru/news_page/country/more.htm?id=12149743@egNews; "Northern Fleet Task Force Arrives to Kronstadt after Global Circumnavigation," *Tass*, 24 July 2019, https://tass.com/defense/1070077; and "Prezident zaslushal doklad glavkoma VMF Nikolaya Yevmenova o khode kompleksnoi arkticheskoi ekspeditsii," website of the Presidential Administration, 26 March 2021.
4. "Glavny voenno-morskoi parad," website of the Presidential Administration, 26 July 2020, http://kremlin.ru/events/president/transcripts/speeches/63753; and "Priyom po sluchayu Dnya Voenno-Morskovo Flota," website of the Presidential Administration, 28 July 2019, http://kremlin.ru/events/president/news/61177.
5. "NATO: Russian Submarine Activity Equals Cold War Levels," *Independent Barents Observer*, 3 February 2016, https://thebarentsobserver.com/ru/node/396.
6. "Foggo: Fourth 'Battle of the Atlantic' Underway," *Seapower*, 25 June 2020, https://seapowermagazine.org/foggo-fourth-battle-of-the-atlantic-underway/; "UK Military Chief Warns of Russian Threat to Vital Undersea Cables," *Guardian*, 8 January 2022, https://www.theguardian.com/uk-news/2022/jan/08/uk-military-chief-warns-of-russian-threat-to-vital-undersea-cables; and J. Altman, "Russian A2/AD in the Eastern Mediterranean: A Growing Risk," *U.S. Naval War College Review* 69, no. 1 (2016).
7. S. Wills, "These Aren't the SLOCs You're Looking For: Mirror Imaging Battles of the Atlantic Won't Solve Current Atlantic Security Needs," *Defense and Security Analysis* 36, no. 1 (2020); B. Dismukes, "The Return of Great Power Competition: Cold War Lessons about Strategic Anti-Submarine Warfare and the Defense of Sea Lines of Communication," *Naval War College Review* 73, no. 3 (2020).
8. For discussion, see A. Monaghan, *Dealing with the Russians* (Cambridge: Polity, 2019); and M. Kofman, "It's Time to Talk about A2/AD: Rethinking the Russian Military Challenge," *War on the Rocks*, 5 September 2019, https://warontherocks.com/2019/09/its-time-to-talk-about-a2-ad-rethinking-the-russian-military-challenge/.
9. Parnemo, "Russia's Naval Development."
10. "Statya Sekretarya Bezopasnosti Rossiiskoi Federatsii v Rossiiskoi Gazete," website of the Russian National Security Council, 12 November 2019, http://www.scrf.gov.ru/news/allnews/2677/.

11. See A. Monaghan, ed., *Russian Grand Strategy in the Era of Global Power Competition* (Manchester, UK: Manchester University Press, 2022).
12. "Zasedaniye kollegi Ministerstva oborony," website of the Presidential Administration, 21 December 2022, http://kremlin.ru/events/president/news/70159.
13. "Glavnokomanduyushchii Voenno-Morskom Flotom Rossii otrkril organisatstionno-metodicheskii sbor komandnovo sostava VMF," website of the Defence Ministry, 1 February 2023, https://function.mil.ru/news_page/country/more.htm?id=12453190@egNews.
14. "Nachalnik Generalnovo Shtaba VS RF general armii Valeriy Gerasimov provyol brifing dlya voennykh attashe inostrannykh gosudarstv," website of the Ministry of Defence, 22 December 2022, https://function.mil.ru/news_page/person/more.htm?id=12449283@egNews.
15. "Kakie korabli nuzhni na more," *Nezavisimoe voennoye obozrenie*, 2 December 2021, https://nvo.ng.ru/realty/2021-12-02/1_1168_ship.html; "Nuzhen li Rossii silni flot?" *Topwar*, 9 March 2021, https://topwar.ru/178933-chernovik-1.html; and "Shto poleznee: Admiral Nakhimov ili desyat 'Buyanov'?" *Topwar*, 15 March 2021, https://topwar.ru/180862-chto-poleznee-admiral-nahimov-ili-desyat-buyanov.html.
16. A. Lambert, *Seapower States: Maritime Culture, Continental Empires and the Conflict That Made the Modern World* (London: Yale University Press, 2018).
17. S. Gorshkov, *Morskaya moshch gosudarstva* (St. Petersburg: Morskoe Naselenie, 2017). See also B. Watson, *Red Navy at Sea: Soviet Naval Operations on the High Seas, 1956–80* (London: Westview, 1982).
18. I. Kramnik, "Novaya morskaya doktrina: Primenenie ideologia S. G. Gorshkova v XXI veke," IMEMO, 1 August 2022, https://www.imemo.ru/publications/relevant-comments/text/russias-new-naval-doctrine-application-of-the-ideology-of-sg-gorshkov-in-the-xxi-century; and I. Kramnik, *Are Continental Powers Capable of Challenging Supremacy at Sea?*, Valdai Discussion Club, 15 December 2020, https://valdaiclub.com/a/highlights/are-continental-powers-capable/.
19. Gorshkov, *Morskaya moshch gosudarstva*. For useful discussion of Russian and Soviet debate about Russian views of Western concepts and especially "command of the sea" and its rejection as "Mahanist," see P. H. Vigor, "Soviet Understanding of 'Command of the Sea,'" in *Soviet Naval Policy: Objectives and Constraints*, edited by M. McGwire, K. Booth and J. McDonnell (London: Praeger, 1975).
20. M. McGwire, "Command of the Sea in Soviet Naval Strategy," in McGwire et al., *Soviet Naval Policy*, 634.
21. "Boevaya ustoichivost," *Encyclopedia of the Russian Ministry of Defence*, website of the Ministry of Defence, n.d., https://encyclopedia.mil.ru/encyclopedia/dictionary/details.htm?id=12679@morfDictionary.

22. A. Monaghan, *How Moscow Understands War and Military Strategy*, Center for Naval Analyses, 17 November 2020, https://www.cna.org/reports/2020/11/how-moscow-understands-war.
23. "Strategiya voennaya," *Encyclopedia of the Russian Ministry of Defence*, website of the Ministry of Defence, n.d., https://encyclopedia.mil.ru/encyclopedia/dictionary/details.htm?id=14383@morfDictionary.
24. M. Gareev and V. Slipchenko, *Budushchaya voina* (Moscow: Polit.ru, 2005). For discussion, see C. Bartles, "Sixth Generation War and Russia's Global Theatres of Military Activity," in Monaghan, *Russian Grand Strategy*.
25. R. Connolly, *The Kalibrisation of the Russian Navy: Progress and Prospects*, CCW Research Note, February 2019, https://static1.squarespace.com/static/55faab67e4b0914105347194/t/5c62ee054785d35b410281cf/1549987334234/Connolly+Kalibrisation.pdf.
26. "Vykhod na boevuyu sluzhbu fregata Admiral Gorshkov," website of the Presidential Administration, 4 January 2023, http://kremlin.ru/events/president/news/70325.
27. See Michael Kofman, "The Ogarkov Reforms: The Soviet Inheritance behind Russia's Military Transformation," *Russia Military Analysis* (blog), 11 July 2019, https://russianmilitaryanalysis.wordpress.com/2019/07/11/the-ogarkov-reforms-the-soviet-inheritance-behind-russias-military-transformation/.
28. The links to the articles published in *Voenno-promyshlenny kurier* and *Krasnaya zvezda* no longer work, but a detailed summary of the core arguments can be found in Monaghan, *How Moscow Understands War*.
29. V. Gerasimov, "Vektory razvitiya voennoi strategii," *Krasnaya zvezda*, 4 March 2019.
30. "Severniy flot Rossii poluchil status voennovo okruga," *Interfax*, 1 January 2021, https://www.interfax.ru/russia/743819.
31. "Aktivnost oborony," *Encyclopedia of the Russian Ministry of Defence*, website of the Ministry of Defence, n.d. https://encyclopedia.mil.ru/encyclopedia/dictionary/details.htm?id=2750@morfDictionary.
32. There is more to be said about Russian naval (and military) strategy category differences, even down to ship design and purpose, but this goes well beyond the remit of this study. For discussion, see M. Kofman and J. Edmonds, "Why the Russian Navy Is a More Capable Adversary Than It Appears," *National Interest*, 22 August 2017, https://nationalinterest.org/feature/why-the-russian-navy-more-capable-adversary-it-appears-22009.
33. The Maritime Doctrine can be found on the website of the Russian Security Council: Morskaya Doktrina Rossiiskoi Federatsii, http://www.scrf.gov.ru/security/military/document34/. Putin signed Ukaz No. 327, Osnovy gosudarstvennoi politiki Rossiiskoi Federatsii v oblasti voenno-morskoi deyatelnosti na period do 2030 goda on 20 July 2017.

34. The Maritime Doctrine and Foundations documents are thoroughly analyzed in M. Kofman, "Evolution of Russian Naval Strategy," in Monaghan and Connolly, *The Sea in Russian Strategy*; and M. B. Petersen, "Russia's Global Maritime Strategy," in Monaghan, *Russian Grand Strategy*. Kofman focuses more on the military aspects of these documents, while Petersen includes other documents and their economic aspects.
35. "Missions: Navy," website of the Ministry of Defence, n.d., https://eng.mil.ru/en/structure/forces/navy/mission.htm.
36. "More korablei, a okeana ne vidno," *Nezavisimaya Gazeta*, 26 July 2020.
37. "Protivo-torpednaya katastrofa Rossiiskovo flota," *Topwar*, 8 March 2021, https://topwar.ru/180576-protivotorpednaja-katastrofa-rossijskogo-flota.html.
38. Kofman, "Evolution of Russian Naval Strategy"; and M. B. Petersen, "Toward an Understanding of Maritime Conflict with Russia," in Monaghan and Connolly, *The Sea in Russian Strategy*.

# CONCLUSION
## Possibilities and Problems

### S. C. M. Paine

Fleet-in-being strategies have been used in peacetime to deter attack and in wartime to preclude amphibious invasion, enemy naval and merchant transit, and the redeployment of naval assets to other theaters. Whether in peacetime or in wartime, they are a means to mitigate risk to oneself by imposing risk on the enemy, to reduce either the risk of war itself or, failing that, the risk of suffering coastal invasion, losing specific naval assets, or allowing unimpeded enemy merchant and naval traffic. In theory, a fleet in being does so by elevating the risks to the enemy in order to change the enemy's calculations of the costs and benefits of engaging in war or opening a new theater or moving assets. If successful, the strategy deters the attack or denies the seas required for a particular enemy strategy by making the elevated risks not worth the potential reward from pursuing the strategy.

Fleet-in-being strategies, when focused on opposing navies, can either pin or disperse enemy ships; and, when focused on enemy armies, can close friendly shores to amphibious invasion or close seas routes to the transport of enemy armies and supplies. When focused on adjacent merchant traffic, they can shut it down. Fleet-in-being strategies have been used most successfully to prevent amphibious invasions on home shores. In doing so, they remove the coastline as an avenue for invasion. All of the above are high-value objectives. The efficacy of such strategies depends on the geography of the contested seas, the distribution of geographic control among the belligerents, and the coordination of naval and land strategies. In most of the case studies examined here, fleets and armies coordinated minimally, particularly at the operational level. Greater cooperation might have yielded greater benefits.

The preceding chapters have put fleets in being in their historical context. Some chapters have highlighted large fleets in being; others, squadrons in being; and still others, plans for how fleets and squadrons should deter in peacetime and might be deployed in wartime. This concluding chapter organizes the findings into sections on naval theories, geographic realities, operational and strategic possibilities, and purchasing pathologies.

## NAVAL THEORIES

Chapter 5 by Kevin McCranie and chapter 1 by Andrew Lambert delve into naval theory. McCranie's overview of the pre–World War I naval theorists' evaluation of a fleet-in-being strategy reveals their focus on its utility as a tool for weaker navies. He highlights not only Vice Admiral Philip H. Colomb (1831–99), the well-known advocate of the strategy, but also an often-overlooked theorist, James Thursfield (1840–1923), a proponent of an active fleet-in-being strategy, which he considered central to British homeland defense. Captain Alfred T. Mahan (1840–1914) believed that both men overrated the deterrent value of a fleet in being.

Andrew Lambert, whose chapter focuses on the man who coined the term "fleet in being," Admiral Lord Torrington, is partial to Sir Julian Corbett's (1854–1922) favorable evaluation of the strategy. According to Lambert,

> The essence of a fleet in being is the use of a defensive posture to prevent a superior enemy fleet from exploiting command of the sea; it can be used to delay specific offensive operations—notably, an invasion or a commercial blockade—or cover the assembly of additional naval resources to enable the fleet to challenge for command. It is especially important in the wider context of grand strategy, where the power with an inferior fleet may be superior in another aspect of the conflict where it seeks to secure a decision. It is also an effective strategy for a dominant navy to use in a secondary theater, enabling it to concentrate resources to seek a decision in the primary theater.

Milan Vego, who has written voluminously on naval strategy and authored the main text on naval operations long assigned at the U.S.

Naval War College, emphasized the distinction between active and passive fleets in being.[1] Citing Mahan, he called a passive fleet in being a "fortress fleet," whose purpose is to preserve a base (the fortress) but sacrifices the mobility of naval power.[2] Unlike land warfare, where avoiding attack is often impossible, in naval warfare, weaker fleets routinely avoid engaging by declining to deploy or by fleeing the scene.[3] Vego saw no advantages deriving from a passive fleet-in-being strategy since it cedes the initiative to the enemy and elicits a blockade with the blockader in the superior position.[4] Instead, he recommended an active fleet-in-being strategy: "In a war at sea, a weaker side should use every opportunity to inflict losses on the stronger enemy and cause fragmentation of the enemy naval strength."[5]

In chapter 11 Alessio Patalano makes an important qualification. He distinguishes "between a fleet in being as an organizing principle for a peacetime fleet posture design from a fleet in being as a wartime operational preference." He argues: "A fleet in being as a strategic posture is . . . predominantly a passive posture as it emphasizes risk avoidance and force preservation." It is a peacetime strategy, seeking "war avoidance." In contrast, a wartime a fleet in being is an operationally "opportunistic strategy" through fleet action that "puts a premium on the value of a latent threat" in order to contribute to victory in wartime. In both peacetime and wartime, a fleet-in-being strategy is strategically defensive. The peacetime strategy remains so at the operational level. In contrast, the wartime strategy of an active fleet-in-being strategy is operationally offensive.

## OPEN-OCEAN ACCESS

If this is the theory, geography is the reality. No two countries are identically situated. Some countries border on the high seas while others border on narrow seas that must be transited to reach the high sea. Vego, who authored a book on naval operations in narrow seas, defined one as "a body of water that can be controlled from one or both sides in a war," a category that includes "all enclosed and semi-enclosed seas with their exits."[6] Landlocked countries can sail to the seas only by river, if at all. These differences delimit a spectrum of maritime access ranging from secure maritime access (via long oceanic coastlines with multiple deep harbors and no neighboring enemies); to restricted wartime access (for countries with coastlines on narrow seas bordering multiple neighbors, who, if hostile, can close narrow seas); to the restricted peacetime access of landlocked countries, whose ships can reach the seas only by rivers that meander through foreign territory (limiting ship sizes to river depths and their movements to negotiated rights of passage); to no access for the landlocked without waterways connecting the sea. What a country can get out of a fleet depends on its geography, yet remarkably little of the naval literature focuses on these distinctions. A fleet-in-being strategy for whom? And under what geographic, military, and financial conditions? Such factors—and geography above all—should shape each country's naval purchases. Although it is obvious that one size navy cannot fit all, an astounding variety of countries have purchased parity-pursuing prestige fleets.

Back in 1908 Vice Admiral Satō Tetsutarō (1866–1942) noted in his *History of Imperial Defense*, one of the most widely read naval texts in Japan: "Among the Powers in the world, there are only three countries that can defend themselves primarily with navies. They are the UK and the US and Japan."[7] He did not state the obvious: membership to this exclusive club of three depended on unfettered access to the sea, no land border with any hostile state, and thus no vulnerability to landward invasion. All three countries depended on overseas commerce, making naval presence essential in peacetime to keep the trade flowing. For such countries, investment in a navy second to none regionally, if not globally, made economic and military sense.

Such navies have been most reliable (not necessarily most important but most reliable) in what they offer to national defense rather than to military offense. Under the right geographic circumstances, navies serve as strong shields for homeland defense. In the twentieth century, Japan's navy could keep the great continental powers at bay. Only another maritime power such as the United States could reach it—and, initially, in 1942, only with the symbolic Doolittle Raid, and only after Japan had fatally overextended itself for over a decade in China. Britain's neighboring enemies found the narrow English Channel defended by the Royal Navy an insurmountable barrier in the Napoleonic and world wars. The Pacific and Atlantic Oceans in combination with the U.S. Navy present even more formidable barriers to amphibious invasion of the continental United States. However, the same oceanic barrier impedes the maritime power's deployment of troops to distant battlefields. U.S. victory in the world wars depended on large, allied continental armies in Eurasia. Without such allied armies in theater, the United States ultimately found the costs of supporting troops in Vietnam, Iraq, and Afghanistan not worth the benefit. Likewise, Japan ultimately found the costs of occupying China in the 1940s unsupportable. No degree of naval prowess would have enabled Japan to dominate a huge country like China.

Spain and France, like Britain, the United States, and Japan, have unrestricted access to the high sea. However, both historically also bordered on primary enemies: France for Spain in the Napoleonic Wars and Germany for France in the world wars. This made Spain and France highly vulnerable to landward attack. Nevertheless, even though Spain lost much of its navy as a result of Napoleon's invasion, its few surviving ships in the Americas allowed its empire to linger for several additional decades. As Jorge Ortiz-Sotelo shows in chapter 4, the tiny Spanish fleet in being at Callao, Peru, enabled Spanish troop and bullion movements and denied victory to those seeking independence until they finally acquired naval assets late in the war. In other words, Spain got a lot of mileage out of a few ships.

Conversely, as Kenneth Johnson shows in chapter 3, Napoleon Bonaparte's global naval deployments accomplished little at high cost—the ships were expensive to build, and Britain hunted them down. Britain's victory at Trafalgar, won by sinking much of Napoleon's and Spain's fleets, ended the threat to Britain of homeland invasion. This freed Britain's navy to hunt French ships and take over France's overseas possessions. Because Napoleon's security problems were located deep inland and not overseas, a large navy offered him little. Nevertheless, when his forces occupied Spain without any naval assets capable of coastal defense, Britain leveraged naval dominance to support Spanish partisans in what Napoleon called his "Spanish ulcer." The cumulative costs of the Iberian campaign, when combined with the catastrophic costs of his Russian campaign, undermined Napoleon's power.

Yet, fleets in being can greatly constrain a maritime foe. Britain could not reliably take over French colonies until after its destruction of the

French fleet at Trafalgar freed up naval assets from homeland defense for imperial expansion. A fleet in being can also constrain foes by precluding coastal invasion. But a fleet in being cannot protect against invasion across landward borders. Although enemies could not deny Spain and France access to the open ocean, that access could not protect either's long land borders. Landward invasion can eliminate a fleet by sinking it in port with coastal guns or by forcing it to flee from lost home ports, as Napoleon did to Spain.

## NARROW SEA ACCESS

Many countries border on narrow seas. In ascending order of increasingly restricted access are Russia, China, Germany, Italy, and Austria-Hungary. Russia does border on the high seas, but only its least populated and most frozen shores. Its main commercial ports lie on narrow seas (the Baltic and Black Seas). China, Germany, Italy, and Austria-Hungary have no direct high-seas access. China's maritime access is restricted by three concentric island chains largely populated by peoples wary of its rise. Unlike China and Russia, German ports are concentrated on a single network of narrow seas, the Baltic and the North Seas. Likewise, Italy and Austria-Hungary operated within a single network of narrow seas, the Mediterranean and the Adriatic, sharing the latter.

Imperial Russia and Germany, and their follow-on Soviet and Nazi regimes, and China today all tried to build navies equal to, if not superior to, the dominant naval power. As David Stone shows in chapter 7, in the Russo-Japanese War, Russia's Asian naval assets followed a de facto passive fleet-in-being strategy that resulted in their destruction. To prevent this outcome, Russia had deployed the rest of its navy, despite its lack of any intervening basing, to distant Japan to produce one of history's most lopsided naval battles at Tsushima. Japan lost just three torpedo boats but commandeered four battleships, one destroyer, and one auxiliary, for a net gain, whereas Russia lost virtually its entire fleet—European and Asian. Only four cruisers, three destroyers, and two auxiliaries returned home.[8] Recently China has built a prestige fleet surpassing the U.S. Navy in numbers. In light of Germany's difficulty navigating narrow seas in wartime, China's fleet may face similar problems given its own constricted, island-cluttered, and mainly shallow surrounding seas as well as its even more numerous neighbors—fourteen by land and seven by sea. Like Germany in the world wars, China's merchant fleet cannot hope to navigate such waters in wartime if its maritime neighbors are hostile.

As Michael Epkenhans shows in chapter 9, the World War I Battle of Jutland, which Germany won at the operational level by destroying more tonnage, still kept the German fleet in port for the rest of the war, achieving the Royal Navy's strategic objective of barring Germany's High Seas Fleet from the high seas. As Jörg Hillmann shows in chapter 13, in 1943 Adolf Hitler went one step further when he decommissioned the surface fleet that the Navy Ministry had oversold to him and his predecessors. In wartime, a German surface fleet could close but not safely transit narrow seas. Beyond the Norwegian campaign at war's onset, when Germany's surface ships were essential but suffered heavy losses in the narrow North Sea, their inability safety to sortie from home ports undermined their utility. Submarines conducted the commerce raiding, which took place mainly on the oceans that the surface fleet could not easily reach. Hitler's prioritization of submarines over surface ships came far too late in the war to do Germany any good.

Nevertheless, in both world wars, as long as Germany's fleet in being existed, no amphibious landings on its coastline occurred. A far smaller and far less expensive surface fleet could have fulfilled this essential defensive role. The opportunity cost was huge. Had Germany instead invested these resources to double its submarine fleet, its submarine commerce-raiding campaign might have strangled Britain economically before a dilatory United States entered either world war. As it was, German's commerce raiding in both world wars brought Britain perilously close to the brink.[9] Unlike Germany in World War II, for China there is no equivalent to the contiguous French or Norwegian open-ocean coastlines where Germany positioned its submarine pens. The sea separates China from all surrounding island chains, including Taiwan, making China worse off geographically than Nazi Germany in possession of France.

Prior to World War I, both Austria-Hungary and Italy invested in large fleets, Italy more so than Austria-Hungary because Italy had to take French belligerency into consideration. Austria-Hungary had the smallest navy of the great naval powers. Before World War I Italy had incorrectly assumed France would be an enemy not an ally and that France, not Austria-Hungary, would constitute the bigger problem. During the war Austria-Hungary got far more operational mileage out of its fleet than did Italy from its larger fleet. As Lawrence Sondhaus notes, "The [Austria-Hungarian] U-boat threat [to the Allies] from the Adriatic necessitated a convoy system in the Mediterranean . . . including an American force based in Gibraltar and a significant Japanese contribution (one cruiser and fourteen destroyers) at Malta. Thus, Austria-Hungary, by maintaining a classic 'fleet in being,' continued to tie down an enemy force many times larger than its own."[10]

As shown, those on narrow seas can close them in wartime, provided that in peacetime they have bought the appropriate naval assets to do so. So even if their surface ships cannot get out, others cannot get in. It turns out that Austria-Hungarian submarines did get out, while Allied submarines dared not enter, and surface ships based in the Adriatic mostly stuck to port. There is a case to be made for a minimalist fleet in being for those bordering on narrow seas that minimizes opportunity costs but that can lock down coastlines to invasion and seas to enemy transport.

## DETERRENCE AT THE STRATEGIC LEVEL

At the strategic level, fleets in being have been used to deter attack in peacetime or in wartime at the operational level to deny the seas necessary for amphibious attack or for naval and merchant transit, or to prevent redeployments by pinning assets. Although deterrence of war or sea denial to preclude attack on the homeland are national goals of the highest value, one can never know what size navy is necessary to deter or whether any sized navy can deter nuclear attack. Negative objectives (objectives to prevent a contingency) do not lend themselves to definitive answers. Nevertheless, geography can shed some light on the problem.

Great Britain used its dominant navy to deter attacks on the homeland or, at a minimum, prevent an invasion. With the advent of submarines, commerce raiding gravely threatened British trade in the world wars and, with the development of airpower, the sea no longer presented an insurmountable barrier against attack. Nevertheless, no invasion beyond small landings occurred after 1688.[11] Since the U.S.

Civil War and the possibility of British intervention, the United States, separated by vast oceans from all enemies, save Cuba (population 11 million), has suffered no external attacks let alone armed landings on its home territory, beyond ineffective Japanese armed balloons in World War II and the 9/11 attacks using four passenger planes. Neither posed the threat of invasion or even sustained aerial attack.

Bordering hostile powers, however, posed problems for a deterrence strategy based on a fleet in being. Spain and Italy developed naval plans to deter or prevent such invasions based on a credible navy—a peacetime fleet in being to dissuade others from attacking. Chapter 2 by Iván Valdez-Bubnov details Spain's long-term deterrence strategy, while chapters 8 and 10 by Francesco Zampieri and Fabio De Ninno, respectively, lay out Italy's analogous plans. In the Napoleonic Wars and World War I, the strategy worked against their immediate neighbors for their maritime but not their land borders. Napoleon invaded Spain overland while Italy fought twelve battles of Isonzo against Austria-Hungary at a cost of over half a million lives for both sides in World War I. With a different set of allies, World War II did not work out nearly as well for Italy, which the Allies, with dominant fleets, conquered from the sea via amphibious landings on Sicily and the Italian peninsula. While Britain, an island with no bordering hostile powers, did not suffer invasion despite facing hostile coastlines across narrow seas, Italy succumbed to such an invasion. Unlike Britain, Italy faced landward enemies and lacked direct access to the high seas and so could be cut off from oceanic trade. Efficient resupply by sea was essential for Britain but impossible for Italy. In narrow seas, like the North Sea or the Mediterranean, insurmountable problems arose when the enemy controlled the opposing shore (as Germany did vis-à-vis Britain in the world wars, and as the Allies eventually did in North Africa vis-à-vis Italy), in combination with a lack of direct high-seas access (Italy's, not Britain's, predicament) or other reliable supply lines. Only the high seas afford access to the resources of the world and the possibility of a global alliance system.

The British and U.S. attempts to deter Japanese expansion with fleets in being stationed far from home at Singapore and Pearl Harbor, respectively, failed upon belligerency as described by John Kuehn in chapter 12. The fleets were not long in being but soon at ocean's bottom. The

Russian fleet suffered a similar fate in the Russo-Japanese War when deployed far from the home industrial and population centers but near to those of its enemy. Thus, fleets located far from home and tied to a single base without maneuver space among bases may invite rather than deter attacks not on the homeland but on the fleets themselves.

Even dominant naval powers must deploy their fleets prudently. Deployments intended to deter can boomerang by eliciting the very response ostensibly being forestalled. The United States deployed its fleet at Pearl Harbor to deter escalation of Japan's war in China. Instead the ships became a lucrative target, which Japan sank or heavily damaged. Conversely, although Japan's naval superiority precluded any Chinese attack on the home islands during the Second Sino-Japanese War (1931–45), its operationally successful attack on Pearl Harbor did not deter further U.S. intervention in Asia. Quite the contrary, it elicited U.S. intervention in Asia unprecedented in scale and duration. Deterrence turns out to be tricky; the enemy may react to an intended deterrent as an accelerant.

With the advent of nuclear weapons, strategists believed nuclear-armed and -powered submarines would provide the most reliable second-strike capability and therefore the ultimate deterrent to an enemy first strike. We can hypothesize, but we will never know what exactly was deterred. We do know that neither side in the Cold War invaded into opposing NATO or Warsaw Pact territory, despite multiple Berlin crises, Soviet invasions of its satellites, proxy wars across the globe, plus hot wars for the United States in Korea and Vietnam and for the Soviet Union in Afghanistan. We also know that with the advent of Polaris submarines, the Soviet Union had ever less confidence in the survivability of its own submarines and therefore doubted their deterrent value. The Soviets entertained no such doubts about the survivability of U.S. submarines with their nuclear payloads. Perhaps this contributed to Soviet willingness to call off the Cold War. We will never know since Soviet decision-making was secretive and involved numerous people, presumably with varying perceptions. Likewise, we can also speculate that navy and coast guard fleets in being probably deter piracy. If pirates could operate at will, surely they would do so since much money could be made by pirating vulnerable cargo ships, which at scale would make international trade unsustainable.

This lack of clarity arises from negative objectives that concern preventing something from happening, such as deterring a nuclear attack or preventing attacks on commerce. While the failure to deter is obvious—the Pacific Fleet at the bottom in Pearl Harbor—successful deterrence is unknowable. Perhaps no attack was ever contemplated. Therefore, conclusions about deterrence are only definitive when deterrence fails, with proof in the form of a very visible attack, whereas the continuation of peace provides no conclusive proof that deterrence succeeded even though it may well have. This does not make negative objectives any less consequential than positive ones, but it does make discussions about them inconclusive.

## DENIAL AT THE OPERATIONAL LEVEL

Fleet-in-being strategies have contributed to the success of military operations in the main theater not through deterrence but through denial. An operationally successful fleet in being may simply deny merchant or naval transport, or it may not only make amphibious attacks on the homeland impossible but may tie up disproportionate numbers of enemy ships, denying their use in more promising theaters or making certain enemy military operations too risky to contemplate.

This was Admiral Lord Torrington's plan in 1690. If the Crown had followed Torrington's advice, he could have retained his ships while still forestalling a French invasion that did not happen in any case. In the Russo-Japanese War, as long as the Russian fleet held out at Port Arthur, Japan could not concentrate its armies to win an annihilating land battle deep in Manchuria but instead suffered terrible attrition from its repeated assaults on the fortress that made its plans for an annihilating battle in Manchuria ever less probable. As long as Port Arthur held, the siege tied up one Japanese army out of four—a major operational effect for a passive fleet in being. One can only speculate about the possibilities had Russia deployed and lost that fleet, not in port as it did but in an active fleet-in-being strategy imposing costs on Japan by sinking troop transports, eliminating supply ships, and elevating commercial insurance rates to disrupt Japan's essential battlefield supply lines, trade, and war loans.

As shown in chapter 14, during the Cold War, once the Soviet Union established naval basing on the Mediterranean, it assumed an active role in all Arab–Israeli Wars. The U.S. Navy could no longer deploy as it pleased in the Mediterranean because it had to account for the risk of a clash with the Soviet navy. This entailed keeping its distance, no longer dropping off Marines at will as it had done in the 1958 Lebanon crisis. As long as the Soviet Union remained involved, there was no peace on Western terms. Such Soviet naval deployments, while not necessarily realizing the Soviets' own strategic goals, could deny those of its enemies, gaining a veto-player role by vetoing the plans of others—a successful victory-denial strategy. This left frozen conflicts with costs borne mainly by the local populations.

Even a comparatively small fleet in being with the right force structure can shut down enemy merchant traffic, constrain the enemy fleet's freedom of action, close narrow seas, and preclude amphibious invasion, thereby foreclosing promising military possibilities for a stronger enemy navy. The Central Powers' fleet in being shut down Russian oceanic trade during World War I with terminal consequences for the Romanov dynasty, which its allies could not supply, producing defeats on the battlefield and food riots in the capital that removed Russia from the war. Austria-Hungarian and Italian belligerence in World War I closed the Adriatic, preventing either from invading across it. In chapter 6, focusing on Austria-Hungary, Lawrence Sondhaus shows how a small navy can have outsized influence in a narrow sea. Austria-Hungary's navy closed the Adriatic, protected those shores, and deployed submarines from the Adriatic that forced its enemies to convoy in the Mediterranean, pinning enemy naval assets to that defensive mission rather than to offensive missions. Francesco Zampieri's chapter 8 demonstrates that in the Mediterranean, a larger sea than the Adriatic, Italy required ships, basing, and allies as well as deployments combining a fleet in being with aggressive patrols. In chapter 10 Fabio De Ninno emphasizes Italy's failure to develop the naval attrition arms—submarines and naval air—necessary for a successful active fleet-in-being strategy. Degrading enemy commerce, troop transports, and ships in order to shift the naval balance required such submarine and naval air assets. The narrower the sea, the more a country can potentially achieve from a small fleet in being with the correct force structure based on a high sub-to-surface ratio and with adequate air cover.

German and British belligerence likewise shut down the North Sea in both world wars; neither could invade the other by sea. Yet naval presence on one side elicited naval presence on the other, pinning naval assets to watching each other's ports. They closed these seas to commercial traffic and made naval traffic perilous. Britain had alternate maritime supply lines; Germany did not, so Germany lost access to the world with major growth-depressing and inflationary consequences.

For Britain, with direct access to the open ocean, these pinned assets engaged in blockade or convoy were unavailable for other missions. Similarly, Napoleon at various times diverted British ships to or from various theaters but with no major strategic impact on Britain. It is unclear whether the opportunity costs to France of investing in ships rather than armies were greater than the costs imposed on Britain with the diverted deployments. For a country like Germany with no direct access to the open ocean, there were no wartime opportunity costs for a pinned ship that had no ability to transit a closed narrow sea. But Germany overinvested in the surface fleet necessary for this mission at the huge opportunity cost of inadequate submarines. Thus, excess procurement carries the important opportunity costs of underinvestment in something else.

Opening up operational possibilities for oneself, denying promising strategies for one's enemy, closing a narrow sea, severing commercial maritime access, precluding enemy amphibious invasion, or pinning an opposing navy are all high-value wartime naval missions but ones that do not necessarily require a full range of naval platforms. For example, during the waning years of empire in the Americas, despite occupation by France, Spain's small squadron of ships kept territory Spanish for decades until those seeking independence finally built their own navy to destroy Spain's. In World War I, a small squadron of Austria-Hungarian submarines imperiled Allied Mediterranean supply lines; to protect them, the Allies diverted numerous naval assets from other missions to conduct convoys in the Mediterranean. Meanwhile, the Ottoman Empire locked up the tsarist navy in the Black Sea with the assistance of only two German cruisers—closing Russia's primary trade route for the war's duration. Without access to trade through the Baltic or Black Seas, Russia's Romanov dynasty fell to bread riots in the capital—an enormous strategic consequence. Thus, with constricted geography, even a tiny fleet in being can have an outsized impact. More recently, as Bruce Elleman shows in chapter 15, PRC naval presence in the Paracels precluded Soviet aid to Vietnam in the 1979 Sino-Vietnamese War, a war in which China suffered huge casualties. Without the fleet in being, Soviet aid to Vietnam might have elevated China's casualties.

## PROCUREMENT PATHOLOGIES

A careful calculation of precisely what is necessary to achieve such denial missions can produce a lower-cost but still high-reward navy that few countries have purchased in practice. Instead, the rich but imperfectly located too often have bought vanity navies with extravagant high-end platforms—the choices of Napoleon, tsarist Russia, Germany and Italy in the world wars, the Soviet Union, and perhaps China today. Yet the utility of a fleet in being depends on the geography of the battlespace—which side has more reliable access, when, and to what?

As an analogy, buying an automobile fleet with cars capable of two hundred miles per hour for a road system adequate only for thirty miles per hour is not only pointless but comes with steep opportunity costs, particularly since the high-end cars are more expensive to purchase and maintain than the more basic models. A recent example to illustrate the problem, not of constrained access but of the operational consequences of opportunity costs: the United States has numerous high-end ships and planes, but apparently the West collectively does not produce enough artillery shells for the ongoing Ukraine war let alone a Taiwan contingency. The tradeoff for one deferred plane purchase must be a huge number of shells. Yet platforms without adequate ordnance are useless and, if in theater, become targets.

Given that navies are costly and potentially bankrupting, buying more navy than needed can weaken rather than strengthen national security, as the Soviet Union belatedly discovered and as China has yet to realize. Symmetric strategies have often seduced rising powers into seeking navies second to none or at least equal to some. These strategies have often proven wasteful both economically and militarily. A fleet that cannot reliably deploy in wartime for lack of high-sea access is not worth nearly as much as one that can. Moreover, buying a fleet that can reliably deploy only in peacetime entails the opportunity costs of foregoing investments in other assets more dependably useful in wartime, ranging from the railways that Russia should have built for flexible deployments in World War I instead of the prestige fleet coveted by royal relatives that went to the bottom in the Russo-Japanese War, to the submarines that should have been the focus of German naval procurements prior to both world wars rather than the undeployable large surface ships it purchased. Both Tsarist Russia and the Soviet Union had a palate for prestige fleets, whose exorbitant costs helped overextend a country famous for its weak economy. Since the 1990s China has followed suit, albeit with stronger economic foundations. Yet China, like Russia, is surrounded by narrow seas and numerous potentially hostile neighbors.

The disastrous deployments of fleets in being are worth listing: In the First Sino-Japanese War of 1894–95, China tried to preserve its fleet in being at Weihaiwei. Japan imposed a close blockade on the port, landed troops on the Shandong Peninsula where Weihaiwei is located, marched to the port, took it by land, and trained the Chinese guns intended to defend the port on the Chinese ships in the harbor to sink them. Japan replayed the strategy in the Russo-Japanese War, likewise taking the Liaodong Peninsula by land to sink the Russian fleet in being in Port Arthur with large land-based guns. Italy at Taranto (1940), Britain at Singapore (1941), and the United States at Pearl Harbor (1941) all lost their fleets in being, which—far from deterring—became tempting targets. Passive fleet-in-being strategies have a catastrophic track record. These examples make the case, highlighted by Vego, that a passive wartime fleet-in-being strategy ultimately loses the naval assets, so it is far wiser to risk them earlier in an active strategy to inflict as much damage as possible while the ships last. This was Germany's conclusion in World War II when it risked and lost much of its fleet in the Norway campaign but soon set up submarine pens there that made the shortest Lend-Lease convoy route to Russia (via Murmansk) the most perilous convoy route.

These examples suggest effective counter-fleet-in-being strategies: the immediate elimination of the fleet in being by preemptive attack (Taranto, Pearl Harbor, Singapore), or a naval blockade coordinated with an amphibious landing to destroy the fleet by land (Weihaiwei,

Port Arthur). In other words, a fleet in being deployed within reach of an enemy navy, or deployed without landward protection by an army, or lacking alternative basing may invite destruction.

In chapter 16 Joel Wuthnow highlights the problem of precision strike for a current-day fleet-in-being strategy. If the location of the fleet is known, there are missiles to sink it. He recommends a peacetime fleet-in-being deterrence strategy, with forward-based U.S. ships scattered across allied ports. Given that their destruction by China would expand China's list of enemy belligerents, perhaps this would be sufficient to deter such attacks. Such a strategy would also force China to disperse its naval assets to prepare for all contingencies, particularly a distant blockade if such a scattered fleets-in-being strategy by the United States failed to deter. Scattered U.S. fleets in being would also divert Chinese naval assets away from Taiwan contingencies. In chapter 17 Toshi Yoshihara shows China trying to prepare for these many contingencies but at great cost. Like Germany's prewar naval planners, Chinese planners apparently assume that their navy will be able to execute far seas missions in wartime despite the difficulty of exiting narrow seas and despite the absence of a global network of naval bases. Historical experience does not support these assumptions.

Likewise, in chapter 18 Andrew Monaghan shows how the tyranny of geography has constrained Russian naval strategy. In the Ukraine war, precision strike struck Russia's Black Sea Fleet in being in 2023, a fleet no longer homeported in Sevastopol, Russia's only defensible natural harbor on the Black Sea but subsequently redeployed to Novorossiysk, a coastal breakwater at the sea's eastern extremity. Building artillery shell factories rather than surface ships would have better prepared Russia for the Ukraine war or a future China war, should China decide Russia is sufficiently weakened to reclaim resource-rich territories lost to the tsars.

Ukraine demonstrates daily what platforms to buy for a continental power with coastal borders on a narrow sea essential for its exports and with land borders facing both its primary enemy and its many partners. This should be sobering for China, which has invested in a prestige fleet that cannot avoid narrow seas. It also should be a wake-up call for the United States, with its penchant to purchase exorbitantly expensive naval platforms that it cannot afford to lose in wartime and that even have trouble operating in peacetime—most notoriously, the technology-challenged and budget-busting USS *Gerald R. Ford* (CVN 78) and the *Zumwalt*-class destroyers, whose guns never worked. Their opportunity costs sponged up resources for far more numerous and far more economical, deployable, and replaceable alternatives. Naval assets can do a lot, but not extravagant purchases potentially deployed in constrained locations.

In wartime in the right geographic context (narrow seas, near home, multiple ports), a no-frills fleet in being can impose a world of hurt on an expansionist neighbor. It can deny amphibious invasion, or invasion via a closed sea, or access to overseas theaters. The costs it can impose include hunting merchant ships or dispersed warships; denying seas to enemy traffic; pinning enemy warships to blockade or convoy duty, precluding their deployment on offensive missions; overtaxing the opposing navy with too many missions, preventing adequate maintenance; and making the most costly ships a wartime liability when their owners focus on their protection rather than on their useful deployment in military operations.

Comparatively small navies with the right mix of platforms can close narrow seas not only to merchant traffic but also to warships—a fact that China and its many small neighbors should ponder deeply. In peacetime, if China's neighbors buy enough submarines and land-based air assets and, in wartime, if they coordinate, neither Chinese surface ships let alone its vital merchant traffic can safely transit its surrounding narrow seas. In contrast, many of China's neighbors either border directly on the open ocean or have dual coastlines—one on the narrow seas shared with China and another on their far side that China cannot close off. For China to attack them all would invite overextension.

Far better for China to return to the Deng Xiaoping model of compounded economic growth through cooperation with the rules-based global trading system that has fostered China's prosperity rather than attempting to overturn it as Xi Jinping seems intent on doing. While China's leaders mull over their choices, its neighbors can purchase the combined assets as a deterrent to war and to make the wartime closure of China's near seas highly likely. And, should peacetime deterrence fail, these assets will deny China's navy freedom of movement and strangle its maritime trade. Such a fleet-in-being strategy is their best bet to deter war or, failing that, to position themselves to weather the onslaught. This is the purpose, versatility, and practicality of a fleet in being: deterrence in peacetime and, failing that, denial in wartime.

## NOTES

1. Milan Vego has written a series of naval books published by Routledge: *Exercising Control of the Sea: Theory and Practice* (2021); *Maritime Strategy and Sea Denial: Theory and Practice* (2019); *Operational Warfare at Sea: Theory and Practice* (2017); *Maritime Strategy and Sea Control: Theory and Practice* (2016); and *Naval Strategy and Operations in Narrow Seas* (2003). In addition, the Naval Institute Press has published his *General Naval Tactics: Theory and Practice* (2020); and *Soviet Naval Tactics* (1992). The Naval War College Press published his text assigned for many years by the Joint Military Operations Department: *Joint Operational Warfare: Theory and Practice* (2009).
2. Vego, *Maritime Strategy and Sea Denial*, 124–25.
3. Vego, 125–26.
4. Vego, 148.
5. Vego, 60.
6. Vego, 105; and Vego, *Naval Strategy and Operations in Narrow Seas*.
7. Cited in Tadokoro Masayuki, "Why Did Japan Fail to Become the 'Britain' of Asia?" in *The Russo-Japanese War in Global Perspective: World War Zero*, edited by John W. Steinberg, Bruce W. Menning, David Schimmelpenninck van der Oye, David Wolff, and Shinji Yokote (Leiden: Brill, 2005), 2:301–2.
8. Tanaka Kenichi [田中健一] and Himuro Chiharu [氷室千春], 東郷平八郎目でみる明治の海軍 [The Meiji navy in the eyes of Tōgō Heihachirō] (Tokyo: 東郷神社, 1996), 142, 170.
9. Paul G. Halpern, "'*Handelskrieg mit U-Booten*': The German Submarine Offensive in World War I," in *Commerce Raiding*, edited by Bruce A. Elleman and S. C. M. Paine, *Newport Papers 40* (2013): 143–48; and Werner Rahn, "The German U-Boat Campaign in World War II," in Elleman and Paine, *Commerce Raiding*, 193–99.
10. Lawrence Sondhaus, *The Great War at Sea: A Naval History of the First World War* (Cambridge: Cambridge University Press, 2014), 268.
11. That year the Dutch invasion contributed to the Glorious Revolution that replaced Catholic King James II of England with his Protestant daughter Queen Mary II and her Dutch husband, William of Orange.

# CONTRIBUTORS

**Fabio De Ninno**, an associate professor of contemporary history at the University of Siena, is a military and naval historian. He has extensively researched the Italian navy in the world wars. His works include *Fascisti sul mare: La marina e gli ammiragli di Mussolini* (2017).

**Bruce A. Elleman** is the author of nearly forty books. Recent publications include *Navies and Soft Power: Historical Case Studies of Naval Power and the Nonuse of Military Force* (2015), edited with S. C. M. Paine; *A History of the Modern Chinese Navy: 1840–2020* (2021); and *Principles of Maritime Power* (2022).

**Michael Epkenhans** was the director of research at the Center for Military History and Social Sciences of the Bundeswehr at Potsdam, Germany (2009–21), and a professor of modern history at Hamburg University.

**Jörg Hillmann** (1963–2023) joined the German navy in 1982 and served as commander of the Center for Military History and Social Sciences of the Bundeswehr at Potsdam from 2017 to 2021. He held the rank of captain at sea from 2009 until his death in 2023.

**Kenneth Johnson** is an associate professor of Military and Security Studies at the Air Command and Staff College. His specialty is French naval and colonial strategy and operations during the French Revolutionary and Napoleonic Wars. He previously taught for the Naval War College and West Point and served as a research coordinator for Air University.

**John T. Kuehn** is a professor of military history at the Army Command and General Staff College. He has authored or coauthored seven books and was awarded a Vandervort Prize from the Society for Military History in 2023. His latest book is *Strategy in Crisis: The Pacific War, 1937–1945* (Naval Institute Press, 2023).

**Andrew Lambert** is the Laughton Professor of Naval History at King's College London. His books include *The Crimean War: British Grand Strategy against Russia 1853–1856* (2nd ed., 2011); *The Challenge: The Naval War of 1812* (2012); *Seapower States: Maritime Culture, Continental Empires and the Conflict That Made the Modern World* (2018), winner of the Gilder Lehrman Prize; and *The British Way of War: Julian Corbett and the Battle for a National Strategy* (2021).

**Kevin D. McCranie** is the Philip A. Crowl Professor of Comparative Strategy at the U.S. Naval War College, where he is a member of the Strategy and Policy Department. He is the author of *Mahan, Corbett, and the Foundations of Naval Strategic Thought* (Naval Institute Press, 2021).

**Andrew Monaghan** is a senior associate fellow at the NATO Defense College in Rome and a senior associate fellow at the Royal United Services Institute in London. He is the author of *Blitzkrieg and the Russian Art of War* (2025) and coeditor of *The Sea in Russian Strategy* (2023).

**Jorge Ortiz-Sotelo** retired as a commander from the Peruvian navy; earned a PhD in maritime history, St. Andrews University, Scotland; and is a professor at the Peruvian Naval College and at the Universidad Nacional Mayor de San Marcos and former Head of the Peruvian National Archive.

**S. C. M. Paine**, William S. Sims University Professor of History and Grand Strategy (emerita), U.S. Naval War College, has coedited, with Bruce A. Elleman, books on naval blockades, commerce raiding, and expeditionary warfare; and authored *The Wars for Asia, 1911–1949* (2012) and *The Japanese Empire: Grand Strategy from the Meiji Restoration to the Pacific War* (2017).

**Alessio Patalano** is a professor of war and strategy in East Asia and co-director of the Centre for Grand Strategy at King's College London. His latest book is *The New Age of Naval Power in the Indo-Pacific: Strategy, Order, and Regional Security* (2023), coedited with Catherine Grant and James Russell from Naval Postgraduate School, Monterey.

**Lawrence Sondhaus** is the Gerald and Marjorie Morgan Professor of History at the University of Indianapolis. He is author of fourteen books, including *World War I: The Global Revolution* (2nd Ed., 2021), *The Great War at Sea: A Naval History of the First World War* (2014), *Naval Warfare, 1815–1914* (2001), and *The Naval Policy of Austria-Hungary: Navalism, Industrial Development, and the Politics of Dualism* (1994).

**David R. Stone** is the William E. Odom Professor of Russian Studies at the U.S. Naval War College. He received a BA from Wabash College and a PhD in history from Yale. He is the author of numerous books and several dozen articles on Russian military history.

**Iván Valdez-Bubnov** is a full-time research fellow at the Institute for Historical Research of the National Autonomous University of Mexico (Intituto de Investigaciones Históricas / Universidad Nacional Autónoma de México). He specializes on the history of the Spanish shipbuilding industry during the Age of Sail.

**Joel Wuthnow** is a senior research fellow in the Institute for National Strategic Studies at the U.S. National Defense University in Washington, DC, and an adjunct professor of security studies at Georgetown University. His research focuses on Chinese foreign and security affairs, the Chinese military, U.S.-China relations, and strategic developments in Asia.

**Toshi Yoshihara** is a senior fellow at the Center for Strategic and Budgetary Assessments (CSBA). He was the inaugural John A. van Buren Chair of Asia-Pacific Studies at the Naval War College. His latest book is *Mao's Army Goes to Sea: The Island Campaigns and the Founding of China's Navy* (2023).

**Francesco Zampieri** is a specialist in Italian naval history and strategy of the nineteenth and twentieth centuries. He is a lecturer of strategy and naval strategy at the Italian Naval Staff College (ISMM) in Venice and senior researcher at the Centre for Military Maritime Studies of the Italian Navy.

# INDEX

*Note*: page numbers with *n* or *t* indicate notes or tables respectively. Many subheadings reference specific countries or wars and are too numerous to cross reference under each country or war.

Abarca de Bolea, Pedro Pablo, 36
Acton, Ferdinando, 155
active defense, 2, 3, 9, 28, 35, 48, 55, 104, 159, 337–39, 346, 365, 367, 369, 376
Adams, Charles F., 241
Adriatic Sea, in Austro-Hungarian strategy, 110–12, 115, 119–23, 125, 380, 382, 386; in French strategy, 57, 60, 64–66; in German strategy, 181; in Italian strategy, 5, 147–148, 150–52, 154, 159–64, 380; in Russian strategy, 276–78
*Admiral* class (Britain), 156
*Admiral Gorshkov* (Russia), 355, 364
*Admiral Graf Spee* (Germany), 262–63
*Admiral Scheer* (Germany), 266
Aegean Sea, 194, 200, 277–78
Akhromeyev, Sergei F., 289
aircraft carrier: 265, 285–86, 360; British, 192*t*, 197–98, 200; Chinese, 319, 322, 327, 343, 345, 348; French, 190*t*; German, 255, 258, 261, 266; Italian, 190*t*, 192*t*, 192–93, 195*t*, 197; Japanese, 222–23, 235, 242; Russian, 288–89; U.S., 240–241, 243–45, 297, 301–2, 317, 320–21, 323, 329. *See also* Taranto, Battle of; Pearl Harbor attack
Alekseev, Evgenii Ivanovich, 136–38, 140–41, 142–44

Algeciras, Battle of, 142
*Alejandro* (Spain), 84
*Alejandro I* (Spain), 78
*Almirantas* (Spain), 33
Alston, Beilby, 216–17
*Altmark* (Germany), 263
*Amagi* (Japan), 220
American Revolution, 36, 103
Amiens, Treaty of, 42, 45, 52–54
Anglo–Dutch Fleet, 13–14, 16–20, 22, 27–29, 91, 212
Anglo-Dutch Wars 2, 23–26
Anglo-German Naval Agreement, 231, 239, 259, 260–61
Anglo-French War. *See* Napoleonic Wars
Anglo-Japanese Alliance, 217–18, 231
anti-access / area denial (A2/AD), 356
*Aquiles* (Spain), 84
Arab–Israeli wars, 279–82, 386
*Aranzazu* (Spain), 77, 81–82
*Araucano* (Chile), 77
Armitage, Richard, 304–5
*Asia* (Spain), 85
*Athenia* (Britain), 262
Aston, George, 4, 101, 105,
Atlantic Ocean: 45, 54, 78, 286, 364, 378; basing, 73, 264; Euro-Atlantic community, 354–55, 357–59, 367; ports, 55, 58–59, 65, 76, 149, 264; sea control, 224; sea lines of communication, 33, 35–36, 41, 75, 176; war plans, 255, 257–60, 356; warfare, 36, 182–83, 185, 262–65, 267–68
Aube, Hyacinthe Laurent Théophile, 153–55
*Audacious* (Britain), 182

Australia, 217, 247, 321, 324, 326, 330–31, 344, 349, 359
Austria, 46, 52–53, 57, 64, 111–12, 260, 280
Austria-Hungary: 4–5, 111, 380–81; naval strategy, 111–18; in World War I, 117–27, 381–83, 386–87; in German war planning, 181; in Italian naval strategy, 147–52, 156, 159–64; 189, 381–82; revolution in 184
aviation: 196, 368, 280, 282, 284, 286, 289, 301, 310, 368, 383, 388; land-based, 196–97, 201, 247, 285–86, 345, 347, 349, 391. *See also* naval aviation

Balkan Pact, 278
Balkan Wars, 152, 161
Baltic Sea, 55, 6, 342, 380; in wartime, 170, 178–80, 185; in Russian naval thinking, 134–35, 275–276, 288, 360–61; in German naval thinking, 251–53, 255–60, 264. *See also* Russian Navy, Baltic Fleet
Barents Sea, 276, 286, 288
basing. *See* naval basing
bastion strategy, 286–90, 361, 368
battleships: 201, 240; in Austro-Hungarian strategy, 112, 114–15, 119, 121–23; in British strategy, 197, 246; in French strategy, 153*t,* 154–54, 189–91; in German strategy, 7, 169, 171–173, 180, 183–84, 191, 252, 256–58, 260–63, 265–66, 269; in Italian strategy, 147, 149, 153*t,* 153–57, 163, 189–93, 195*t,* 195–200, 202; in Japanese strategy, 221, 242–44, 380; in Russian strategy, 135–37, 140–41, 143; in U.S. strategy, 241–42, 244–45
Beachy Head, Battle of, 13–15, 18–19, 21, 25–27, 29, 32, 91, 95–96, 100, 133, 212, 385
Beatty, David, 175, 185, 232
Belli, Vladimir Aleksandrovich, 2
*Berlin* (Germany), 182
Bernotti, Romeo, 190, 193

*Bismarck* (Germany), 264, 267
Black Sea, 119–20; in Russian strategy, 134–35, 150, 275–78, 280, 288, 356, 360, 380, 387, 390. *See also* Russian Navy, Black Sea Fleet
Blanco Encalada, Manuel, 77
blockade, 1–2, 13, 120, 387, 391; in British strategy, 41–42, 49, 53, 59–65, 67, 94, 99, 123, 170–73, 176, 184–85, 264, 269, 376; in Chinese strategy, 300, 303, 308–9, 311, 330–31, 349; in French strategy, 16, 28, 59, 121, 148, 387; in German strategy, 252, 269; in Italian strategy, 158, 161–63, 197; in Japanese strategy, 223, 389–90; in Russian strategy, 282, 356; in Spanish strategy, 4, 36, 46–47, 72, 77–79, 82–85; in U.S. strategy, 8, 99, 231, 318, 312, 325, 328, 376–77. *See also* counterblockade
*Blücher* (Germany), 178
Bonamico, Domenico, 154–55, 157–59
Bonaparte, Joseph, 47, 73
Bonaparte, Louis, 56, 65
Bonaparte, Napoleon, 42, 44, 46–47, 52–68, 72–73, 102–3, 379–80, 383, 387–88. *See also* Napoleonic Wars
Bosphorus. *See* Turkish straits
*Breslau* (Germany), 118–20, 181
brig, 55, 58, 64, 75–77, 84–85
Brin, Bendetto, 155–56
Brindisi, 119, 122, 159, 160, 162, 164, 194
Brion, Luis, 76
Brown, William, 76
Burgues de Missiessy, Édouard Thomas, 65
Brzezinski, Zbigniew, 306

Cai Xihong, 311
Callao squadron, 4, 72–73, 76–78, 80–86, 379
Callwell, Charles, 4, 102–3
Campbell, John, 26
*Canton* (Spain), 77
Cape of Teulada, Battle of, 200

Cape St. Vincent, Battle of, 41
*Capitana* (Spain), 33
Carlos IV, 50
Caribbean Sea: in British strategy, 42–43; in French strategy, 40, 44, 46, 54, 58, 61, 66; in Spanish strategy, 33–35, 37, 40–43, 46, 73–75.
Carter, Jimmy, 306–7
Castex, Raoul, 28–29, 212
Cavagnari, Domenico, 193–94, 196–200
*Cavour* class (Italy). *See Conti di Cavour* class (Italy)
Cervera y Topete, Pascual, 98
*Chacabuco* (Chile), 77
Chamoun, Camille, 279
Charles III, 35–36
Charles, Emperor, 124
Chen Shuibian, 310
Chernavin, Vladimir, 290
Chile, 46, 74–77, 182; Chilean squadron, 3–4, 72–73, 77–86
Chiang, Kai-shek, 235
China. *See also* Sino-Japanese War
China, People's Republic of (PRC): narrow seas, 380–81, 391; naval competition with U.S., 7–9, 317–31, 389–90; relations with Vietnam, 8, 297–313, 337–50, 388; relations with Russia, 255, 276, 279–80, 320, 328, 355, 357; Sino-Soviet split, 276, 279, 290, 308
China, Republic of: in China, 135, 214, 217–17, 220–23, 225, 234–36, 243, 246 378–79, 384; on Taiwan, 8, 299–300, 310, 317–18, 320–22, 324–27, 330–31, 338–39, 345, 347, 349, 359, 388, 390
chokepoints. *See* British Channel; Danish Straits; Gallipoli; Kattegat; Malacca Strait; Otranto, Strait of; Scapa Flow; Skagerrak; Suez Canal; Turkish straits; Tsushima Strait
Churchill, Winston S., 118, 120, 170–71, 236, 245
Churruca, Cosme Damián, 47

Clausewitz, Carl von, 27–28, 131
*Cleopatra* (Spain), 77
Clowes, William Laird, 4, 99–100, 102
Cochrane, Thomas Alexander, 73, 77–79, 82
Coig, Luis, 80
Colby, Franny, 238
Cold War, 1, 7, 276, 278, 280, 288, 290, 304, 356–57, 361, 384–85
Collingwood, Cuthbert, 60
Collins, Gabriel, 328
Colomb, Phillip H., 2, 4, 26–28, 91–100, 102–103, 105, 128–129, 212–213, 376. *See also* fleet in being theorists, Colomb
commerce raiding, 1, 5, 196; diversionary effects, 6; in Chinese strategy, 312, 349; in French strategy, 59–60, 62, 154; in German strategy, 176, 181–84, 246, 268–69, 381–82; in Russian strategy, 133; in Spanish strategy, 34–35, 47
Committee of Imperial Defence (CID), 236–37
*Constante* (Spain), 85
*Conti di Cavour* class (Italy), 191, 199
Conversion Plan, 251, 254, 255*t*, 256
convoys, 5, 391; Allies, 389, Axis, 202; British, 6, 15, 36, 62, 197, 201–3, 266–67, 387; Entente, 122, 177, 184, 382, 386; Italian, 197; Japanese, 224; Russian, 282; Spanish, 41, 75–76
convoys, attacks on: by Axis, 201; by Austria-Hungary, 382, 386; by Germany, 265–67; by Italy, 198, 203*t*; by Russia, 133; by Spain, 38–39
Corbett, Julian, 2, 4, 27–29, 102–104, 129, 213, 376; *Some Principles of Maritime Strategy*, 27, 29, 103–4, 129. *See also* fleet in being theorists, Corbett
Córdoba, José de, 41
Cornwallis, William, 59
Coronel, Battle of, 182
corvette, 58, 64–66, 77, 84–85, 319, 327*t*, 345

counterblockade, 118, 121, 142, 152, 322, 328–29, 342, 349, 387
Cradock, Christopher, 182
cruiser: 62, Austro-Hungarian, 112, 118–19, 123–24; British, 117, 120, 171–72, 191, 192*t*, 233, 238–39, 241, 245–46, 263; Chinese, 319, 327*t*, 345; French, 121, 153–54; German, 123, 163, 169, 173–75, 177, 179, 181–83, 252–54, 255*t*, 256–58, 260, 261*t*, 262, 266, 387; Italian, 118, 122, 153, 156, 158, 189, 190*t*, 192*t*, 195*t*, 197, 200; Japanese, 137, 141, 218, 220–22, 233–34, 242, 382; Russian, 123, 130, 133, 135–36, 138, 140, 144, 302, 360, 380; Spanish, 33–36, 41, 45; U.S., 233–34, 238, 240–44
cryptography, 265, 267–68
Cuba: in Spanish empire, 37, 39, 41, 44, 46, 48, 74, 98–99; in Cold War, 284, 306, 355, 383
Cuban Missile Crisis, 283, 285, 290

d'Estrées, Jean, 24–25
Dardanelles. *See* Turkish straits
Danish Straits, 179, 275
de Álava, José María, 41
de Ruyter, Michiel, 23–26
Decrès, Denis, 54, 59–61, 63–64, 66,
Delaval, Ralph, 22–23
Deng Xiaoping, 303, 306–7, 391
denial. *See* sea denial
destroyer, 197, 245; Astro-Hungarian, 123; British, 192*t*, 201, 246, 265, 267; Chinese, 307, 320, 327*t*, 345, 348; French, 121, 190*t*; German, 123, 252*t*, 255*t*, 255–56, 258, 261*t*, 266*t*; Italian, 154, 189–190*t*, 191, 192*t*, 195*t*, 200; Japanese, 136–37, 140–41, 233, 380, 382; Russian, 123, 140, 143–44, 302, 380; U.S., 241–44, 317, 323, 391; Taiwanese, 299
deterrence, 1–2, 10, 375, 382, 391–92; by Austria-Hungary, 4, 126, 383; by Britain, 246, 382–83, 389; by

China, 308, 319, 326, 344–46, 391; by Germany, 170, 251, 269; by Italy, 5–6, 163, 204, 383, 389; by Japan, 7, 210–11, 224, 226; by Russia, 8, 280, 287, 290, 361, 364, 366–67, 369, 384; by Spain, 3, 33–35, 49, 383; by USA, 8–9, 318, 322, 325–26, 328, 330, 383–85, 389–90; theories of, 103, 215, 376
*Deutschland* class (Germany), 191
dockyards, 46; British, 17, 21, 33, 53; Cuban, 37; French, 55, 58; Italian, 159, 194; Japan, 220; Spanish, 42; U.S., 241
doctrine, 214–15; British, 27, 95, 102; Chinese, 318, 322, 325, 329, 350; Italian, 6, 188, 192, 198, 200; Japanese, 210, 218, 220, 222, 224–25; Russian, 286, 288, 356–57, 366; Spanish, 32, 47; U.S., 324, 330
Dogger Bank, Battle of, 120, 175, 184
Dönitz, Karl, 251, 260, 263–68
*Dreadnought* (Britain), 115–25, 156, 172, 179, 182, 189–190*t*, 255*t*
*Dresden* (Germany), 182
Ducci, Gino, 193
*Duilio* class (Italy), 155–56, 195, 200
*Dunkerque* class (Germany), 191
Dutch East Indies, 247
Dutch Republic. *See* Netherlands, Dutch Republic
Dutton, Peter, 312

*E-11* class (Russia), 302
East China Sea, 319–20, 326, 338, 345
Egypt, 42, 57, 60, 63–66, 150, 197–98, 279–83
*Emanuele Filiberto* class (Italy), 156
*Emden* (Germany), 182
Engel'man, Lieutenant, 130–32
English Channel, 14–16, 20–21, 26–27, 39, 46, 58–60, 65, 97, 123, 212, 378
Entente Cordiale, 115, 150, 156
Entente, Triple 115, 117–18, 121, 125,162, 169, 239

*Enterprise* (USA), 244
*Erzherzog Karl* class (Austria-Hungary), 112
*Esmeralda* (Spain), 76–77, 79–83
*Essex* class (USA), 245
Ethiopia: Italian invasion of, 191–92, 194, 239; Russian bases in, 281, 283–84
Evertsen, Cornelius, 18, 20
Excess, Operation, 200

Ferdinando VII, 47
Ferdinand Max, 111
Ferdinand of Naples, 57
Finch, Daniel (Earl of Nottingham), 15–16, 18–21
Fioravanzo, Giuseppe, 191–92
Firth, Charles, 27
Fiske, Bradley, 233
fleet-against-shore engagement, 9, 362–63, 367–69
fleet in being, in Austro-Hungarian strategy, 4, 120–21, 123, 125; in British strategy, 3, 7, 18, 21, 25, 29, 231, 236, 245–47; in Chinese strategy, 8–9, 297–98, 300–1, 303, 305, 308–10, 312, 337, 346–50; in Dutch strategy, 23–24; in French strategy, 3, 52, 59–61, 63, 67, 379–80; in German strategy, 5–7, 251, 264, 269, 381; in Italian strategy, 5–6, 147, 152, 154, 157, 159–61, 163–64, 188, 191–93, 202–4, 383, 386; in Japanese strategy, 6, 210–11, 218–19, 224–25, 234; in Russian strategy, 5, 8–9, 101, 103–4, 137–39, 144–45, 275, 279–84, 286–90, 362–63, 365, 369, 380, 385–86, 390; in Spanish strategy, 3–4, 72–73, 86, 379, 383; in U.S. strategy, 7–8, 242, 245, 247, 317–18, 322, 325–26, 328–29, 384, 391-92
fleet-in-being theorists: Aston, 105; Callwell, 102; Castex, 28–29; Clowes, 99–100; Colomb, 27–28, 91–95, 97–99, 103, 105, 128–29, 212–213, 376; Corbett, 27–29, 102, 104, 129,
376; Hannay, 95; Kipling, 97–98, 105; Mahan, 26–28, 96–98, 103–4, 128, 376; Maurice, 97; Thursfield, 92, 96–97, 102–3; Till, 214; Vego, 213, 376–77; Wainright, 100–1; Wilkinson, 93–95; Wylie, 213–13
fleet in being, theory: 1–2, 4, 13, 130–31, 133–34, 210–16, 226, 375–77, 385; definition, 1–2, 18; term origin, 3, 13–14, 22, 32, 91, 212, 376
fleet in being, typology: active, 2, 9, 35, 48–49, 132–33, 213–14, 337, 346, 350; by default, 170, 172, 175, 177, 185, 191; passive, 2, 114, 123–24, 125-26, 141, 213, 380, 389; fortified, 231, 245; forward-based, 245, 383–84, 390
fleet in efficiency (*efficienza*), 6, 188, 192, 200, 204
fleet-on-fleet engagement, 1, 3, 6, 9, 154, 159, 170, 197, 236, 257, 361, 368, 385
Floridablanca, Count of, 35–40, 42–43, 48–49
Ford, Henry, 114
Fouché, Joseph, 64
Four-Power Pact, 235
France, 40, 150, 379–81, 237; navy, 154t, 190t, 195t, 239, 344; relations with Britain, 44, 112, 117, 169, 239–40, 245; relations with Germany, 181, 188, 251–53, 256–60, 262; relations with Russia, 112, 169; relations with Southeast Asia, 298–99; relations with Spain, 35–42, 48, 75; relations with U.S., 43–44, 279. *See also* Beachy Head, Battle of; Italy, relations with France; Napoleonic Wars; World War I, World War II
Franz Ferdinand, 111–112, 115, 118
Franz Joseph, 111–112, 124
French Revolution, 32, 40, 42, 96, 128
Frigates, 33–34, 36, 42, 46, 48, 53–54, 57–66, 73, 75–86, 301, 327t, 345, 355, 364
*Furutaka* class (Japan), 222
Fushimi, Hiroyasu, 219

*Galvariño* (Chile), 77
Ganteaume, Joseph Antoine, 59–60, 63
Gardner, Alan, 60
Genet, Edmond Charles, 42–43
Geneva Naval Conference, 189, 219, 232
George K. *MacKenzie* (USA), 301
*Gerald R. Ford* class (USA), 320, 391
Gerasimov, Valery, 357, 264–65
German Air Force. *See* Luftwaffe
German Navy. *See* Kaiserliche Marine (Imperial German Navy); Kriegsmarine (1935–45) (German Navy); Reichsmarine (Weimar Republic navy)
German-Polish nonaggression pact, 257, 260
Germany, 129, 144, 149, 191, 217, 380, 384, 390; naval buildup, 111, 116, 169–70, 214, 251–62, 388–89; rearmament, 231, 237; rivalry with Britain, 117, 149–51, 171–72; in World War I, 5–6, 110, 118–126, 162, 173–185, 189, 379, 381, 387; in World War II, 5, 7, 263, 197–98, 200, 203, 224, 246, 262–69, 287, 379, 381, 387. *See also* Anglo-German Naval Agreement; Triple Alliance
Gibraltar, 14–15, 36, 38–39, 42, 53, 157–158, 188, 193, 197–98, 203, 280, 382
Glorious Revolution (1688), 15, 133, 292*n*11
*Gneisenau* (Germany), 263, 265–266
Godoy, Manuel, 40, 43–44, 46–47
*Goeben* (Germany), 118–20, 181
Göring, Hermann, 264
Gorshkov, Sergey G., 285, 287–88, 290, 355, 361–62,
*Graf Zeppelin* (German), 266
Grand Fleet, 171–77, 179, 184–85, 191
Great Britain, 259–61, 383; in Americas, 37–38, 41–44, 73, 78–79; in Cold War, 277, 279, 283; interwar diplomacy, 231–33, 235–43, 245–47, 256–57; naval

dominance, 115–17, 119, 133, 156, 169–71, 192*t*, 192–93, 196, 210, 219, 233, 382; naval theory on, 91–97, 103–5, 376; pre-World War I diplomacy, 148–52, 162; shipbuilding, 114, 170, 214. *See also* Anglo-; Beachy Head, Battle of; Grand Fleet; London Naval Treaty; Napoleonic Wars; Royal Navy; World War I; World War II
Greece, 150, 160–62, 194, 199–200, 277–78
Groener, Wilhelm, 253–54
Gromyko, Andrei, 281
Guam, 219, 222, 242, 317, 323*t*, 324
*guerre de course. See* commerce raiding
gunboats, 55, 57, 82, 84–85, 266*t*
Guruceta, Roque, 85

*Habsburg* class (Austria-Hungary), 112, 117
Haig, Alexander, 301
Hamaguchi, Osachi, 234
Hannay, David, 4, 95
Haus, Anton, 113, 116–23
Hayward, Thomas B., 289
Heeringen, August von, 172
Henry, Prince, 179
Herbert, Arthur (Lord Torrington), 3–4, 13–23, 25–29, 91–93, 95–96, 98–100, 106*n*2, 133, 212–13, 376, 385
*Heroina* (Buenos Aires), 84
Herrick, Robert Waring, 1
High Seas Fleet, 120, 169, 171–77, 179, 184–185
Hipper, Franz Ritter von, 175
Hitler, Adolf, 237, 255–57, 259–68, 381
Hoover, Herbert, 232–33, 241–42
Hu Bo, 340–41, 347–49
Huang Hua, 301
Hussein, King, 282
*Hyperion* (Britain), 82

Iachino, Angelo, 198–200
Iberian Campaign. *See* Peninsular War

*Illustrious* (Britain), 198, 200
Imperial Japanese Navy (IJN), 7, 141–42, 210–11, 217–26, 232, 234, 247; factions, 210, 219, 232–34
Indian Ocean, in British strategy, 35, 53, 58, 63, 217, 239; in Chinese strategy, 8, 318, 339, 342, 344, 348–49; in German strategy, 182–83; in French strategy, 54, 60, 62–65; in Italian strategy, 191; in Russian strategy, 283–284, 364; in Spanish strategy, 36, 38, 40, 45; in U.S. strategy, 321, 328–29, 331, 347
Ingenohl, Friedrich von, 172–75, 184–85
intelligence, 21, 122–23, 174, 197, 200–1, 226, 243, 268, 280, 288, 301, 342, 345, 368. *See also* cryptography
Inukai, Tsuyoshi, 235
Ionian Sea, 154, 159–60
Israel, 8, 275, 278–84, 386
*Italia* class (Italy), 155–56
Italo-Turkish War, 117, 151
Italy, 110–11, 116, 132–33, 181, 380–83, 386, 388; in Napoleonic Wars, 56–57, 65–66; in Spanish strategy, 33, 44; relations with Austria-Hungary, 5, 112, 115, 147–52, 156, 159–64, 189, 381–82; relations with Britain, 238–40, 245–46; relations with France, 5–6, 112, 115, 147–60, 162–163, 188–89, 190*t*, 191, 193–94, 195*t*, 196–97, 382. *See also* Taranto, Battle of; World War I; Regia Aeronautica (air force); Regio Esercito (army); Regia Marina (navy); World War II
Itu Aba Island. *See* Spratly Islands

Japan, 8, 112, 321, 323–26, 330–31, 338, 344, 378; disputed islands, 298–99, 320, 327; in Cold War, 289; in World War I, 217, 382; in World War II, 246–47, 383; U.S. basing in, 317–18, 323*t*, 323–25; war planning 1930s, 6–7, 210–11, 216–26, 231–47. *See also* Pearl Harbor attack; Russo-Japanese War; Sino-Japanese War

Japanese navy. *See* Imperial Japanese Navy (IJN)
Java Sea, Battle of, 247
*Jean Bart* (France), 121
Jellicoe, John, 172, 176, 185
Jervis, John, 41–42, 53
Jeune École, 153, 156–57, 163
joint operations, 101, 155, 161, 180, 236, 253, 261, 319, 322, 339, 341, 356, 365, 368
Jones, Hilary, 233
*Justiniano* (Spain), 77
Jutland, Battle of, 6, 176–77, 185, 191, 258, 381

Kadlčák, Josef, 113
*Kaiserin Elisabeth* (Austria-Hungary), 112
Kaiserliche Marine (Imperial German Navy), 115–16, 118–19, 122–24, 149–50, 152, 163. 169–85, 189, 191, 214, 239, 251–260, 356, 381, 387. *See also* High Seas Fleet
*Kashin* class (Russia), 301
Kato, Kanji, 219, 233–34, 240
Kato, Tomosaburo, 219, 233
Kattegat, 179, 277
Kavkaz, Operation, 282
Kempenfelt, Richard, 28
Keyes, Roger, 233, 238
Khrushchev, Nikita S., 285
Killigrew, Francis, 14–16, 19
Kinkaid, Thomas C., 242
Kipling, Rudyard, 97–98, 105
*Kirk* (USA), 305
Kissinger, Henry, 302
*Königsberg* (Germany), 182
Krepinevich, Andrew, 343
Kriegsmarine (1935–45), 7, 200–1, 203*t*, 245, 255, 258, 260–69, 287, 356, 381
Krupp, 112
*Kursk* (Russia), 356
*Kursograf* (Russia), 302

La Maddalena, 154, 157–59, 194
La Spezia, 56, 154, 157–58, 194

La Serna, José de, 84
Laird, Melvin R., 286
Laughton, John, 26–27
*Lautaro* (Chile), 77
Le Duc Tho, 302
League of Nations, 192, 216, 235, 237, 256
Lebanon, 279, 282, 284, 290, 386
Lehman, John, 289
*Leningrad* (Russia), 285
*Léon Gambetta* (France) 121
*Leonardo da Vinci* (Italy), 123
Levetzow, Magnus von, 256
*Lexington* (USA), 244
*Liberté* class (France), 156
*Littorio* class (Italy), 191, 196–99
Liu Huaqing, 321, 338, 340
Liu Jin, 346–48
Liu Zhenmin, 312
Locarno Pact, 237–39
London Naval Treaty (1930), 219, 231–34, 237–38, 240–43, 254
London Naval Treaty (1936), 237, 240, 244
Louis XIV, 13, 15
Louis XVI, 40, 43, 56
Luftwaffe, 200–1, 203*t*, 239, 246, 259, 161, 264, 268
*Lützow*, 266

MacDonald, Ramsay, 232
MacDonnell de Gondé, Enrique Reynaldo, 45–48
*Macedonian* (USA), 82
*Magdeburg* (Germany), 179
*Magenta* class (France), 153
Makarov, Stepan Osipovich, 129–30, 137–41
Mahan, Alfred Thayer, 4, 28, 96–98, 100, 102–3, 128, 163, 212–13, 287, 371*n*19, 376; Battle of Beachy Head, 25–27, 95; fleet-on-fleet battle, 7, 170, 181, 183, 231, 257, 322; fortress fleet, 18, 377; *Influence of Sea Power upon History, 1660-1783*, 25, 96, 128; *Influence of Sea Power upon the French Revolution and Empire*, 96, 128; *Life of Nelson*, 97–98, 100; Russo-Japanese War, 103–5. See also fleet in being theorists, Mahan
Malacca, Strait of, 311, 321, 328, 331
Maldini, Galeazzo Giacomo, 157
Mao, Zedong, 277, 303, 307, 338, 346
Mar, José de la, 84
Marcos, Ferdinand, 305
Martinson, Ryan, 342, 344
Masaryk, Tomáš, 113
Maurice, John Frederick, 97
*Mayak* class (Russia), 301
*Maypu* (Spain), 80–84
Mazarredo, Joseph de, 42, 47
McDevitt, Michael, 342, 347, 349
Mediterranean Sea, 286, 342, 347, 380, 383; in Battle of Beachy Head, 14–16, 29; in Austro-Hungarian strategy, 112, 116–17; in British strategy, 238, 245; in Italian strategy, 147–52, 156–59, 163, 188–94; in Napoleonic Wars, 53, 55–57, 59–61, 63, 65; in Russian strategy, 276–81, 284, 360, 364, 385–86; in Spanish strategy, 33–36, 39, 41–42, 45, 195*t*; in World War I, 5, 118, 120, 122, 180–83, 217, 382, 387; in World War II, 6, 194–203, 267;
merchant ships, 14, 18–19, 29, 33, 36, 41, 44–45, 48, 53, 63, 76–77, 79–80, 82, 84–85, 121, 177, 180–83, 189, 198, 203*t*, 263–64, 282, 310–11, 375, 381–82, 386, 391
Messina, 118–19, 154, 157–59 180, 194
*Michigan* (USA), 116
Mikoyan, Anastas, 281
Milne, Berkeley, 120
mine warfare, 171, 192, 278; in German strategy, 252*t*, 256, 261*t*; in Italian strategy 193, 201; in Russo-Japanese War, 130–31, 140–42; in World War I, 6, 123, 173, 177–80, 184, 191; in World War II, 201, 263, 266*t*

minesweeper, 252*t*, 256, 261*t*, 266*t*
missiles, 282, 301, 306–7, 311, 317–18, 322–323*t*, 324, 326, 327*t*, 327–29, 331, 340, 344, 347, 349–50, 356, 360, 364, 390; Polaris missile, 285–87, 384; Poseidon missile, 385–86; submarine-launched ballistic missile (SLBM), 285–89, 323*t*, 301–2, 319, 323*t*, 323–24, 327*t*, 345, 361, 367; Trident missile, 285–86. *See also* Cuban Missile Crisis
*Missouri* class (USA), 245
*Mogami* class (Japan), 218, 222
*Monarch* class (Austria-Hungary), 117
Monsell, Bolton, 237–38
Montecuccoli, Rudolf, 115–17
Montreux Convention, 277, 280
*Moltke* (Germany), 177
Monsell, Bolton, 237–38
*Morskoi sboornik*, 129–30, 132, 134
*Moskva* (Russia), 285, 360
*Moyano* (Spain), 85
*Möwe* (Germany), 183
Mühlwerth, Albert von, 117
Murat, Joachim, 58, 64–65
Mussolini, Benito, 188–89, 191–93, 196, 200, 203
mutiny, 114, 123–25, 177
*Myoko* class (Japan), 222

Nagano, Osami, 240
Nansha Islands. *See* Spratly Islands
Napoleon. *See* Bonaparte, Napoleon
Napoleonic Wars, 3, 32, 39–42, 44, 46, 52–68, 75, 128, 378–80, 383, 393. *See also* Bonaparte, Napoleon
narrow seas. *See* Adriatic; Aegean; Baltic; Barents; Black Sea; Caribbean Sea; East China; Ionian, Mediterranean; North; Norwegian; Red Sea; South China; Tyrrhenian; Yellow Sea
*Nassau* (Germany), 116
Nasser, Gamal Abdel, 279–82
NATO. *See* North Atlantic Treaty Organization (NATO)

naval aviation, 164, 218, 220, 223, 232, 237, 247
naval basing: 10, 24, 192, 213, 256, 377, 384, 389–90; Austro-Hungarian, 111, 119, 121, 123, 382; British, 7, 14, 16, 19, 60, 117, 197, 231, 236–38, 245; *see also* Singapore; Chinese, 297–300, 303–4, 308, 310–12, 319–20, 34–44, 347–49, 390; French, 57, 149, 162; German, 123, 171, 174, 177, 180–82, 258, 264–65; Italian, 5–6, 124, 147–49, 154, 157–62, 191, 193–94, 198–99, 382, 386; Russian, 8, 135, 139, 141, 144, 275–77, 279–81, 283–84, 287, 306, 360, 380, 385, 390; Spanish, 4, 37, 41, 45, 72–73, 75–78, 86; U.S., 7, 242, 244–46, 318, 322, 323–25, 329–30, 382, 390. *See also* Brindisi; Guam; La Maddalena; La Spezia; Messina; Pola; Taranto; Venice; Vladivostok
naval presence, 7, 37, 41–42, 58, 60, 62, 65, 122, 131–32, 185, 208*n*67, 211, 279–84, 287–88, 308, 321–26, 329–30, 342, 344, 347–48, 355–56, 358, 360–62, 367, 378, 387–88
Navarro, Juan Joseph, 34–35
Nelson, Horatio, 95, 97–98, 100, 102–3
Netherlands, 245; Dutch Republic, 37–38, 40, 56, 392*n*11; Napoleonic rule, 59, 61–62, 64–65, 67; World War II, 245–46. *See also* Anglo-Dutch Fleet, Anglo-Dutch Wars, Dutch East Indies.
neutrals, 34, 39–40, 43, 46, 48, 61, 82, 84, 118, 121–22, 139, 141, 144, 150, 152, 181, 204, 267, 280–81, 325, 330
Nicholas II, 136, 143
Nine-Power Pact, 235, 243
Nine Years' War, 91
Njegovan, Maximillian, 123–24
Nixon, Richard, 297, 300–2, 315*n*36
North Atlantic Treaty Organization (NATO), 8, 276–80, 287, 290, 356, 359, 364, 384

North Sea, 115, 120, 123, 150, 169, 171–79, 181, 183–85, 191–192, 251–53, 255–57, 259–60, 263–65, 276–78, 280, 381, 383, 387
Norwegian Sea, 267, 286
Nottingham, Earl of. *See* Finch, Daniel
*Novik* (Russia), 144

O'*Higgins* (Chile), 77. *See* Reina Maria Isabel (Spain)
O'Higgins, Bernardo, 73, 75, 77–78
Objectives: negative, 1, 10, 131, 382, 385; positive, 1
Orlov, N. A., 129
Ogarkov, Nikolai, 364
Osumi, Mineo, 219–220, 234
Otranto Straits, 121–24, 278
Ottoman Empire, 33, 40, 57, 60, 117–19, 150–51, 160–62, 181, 387

Pacific Ocean: in British strategy, 41, 236, 245–46; in Chinese strategy, 324–25, 329, 338–39, 342, 348; in German strategy, 182–83; in Japanese strategy, 217, 219, 222, 224, 231, 233–34, 243–46; in Russian strategy, 134–35, 137, 141, 144, 276–77, 283, 288–89, 302, 354, 359–61; in Spanish strategy, 35, 38, 41, 46, 73, 75–78, 85; in U.S. strategy, 244–46, 278, 317, 322, 323*t*, 331, 347, 349–50, 378–79, 385; *See also* Japan; Pearl Harbor attack; Russian Navy Pacific Fleet; Russo-Japanese War; U.S. Navy, Pacific Fleet
*Palafox* (Spain), 77
Papen, Franz von, 254
Paracel Islands, 7–8, 297–304, 307–13, 388.
Pearl Harbor attack, 7, 246, 329, 383–85, 389
Peninsular War, 48, 64, 74, 379
People's Liberation Army (PLA), 303, 307–8, 317–18, 321–323*t*, 324–327*t*, 328–31, 337–39, 335*n*41, 335*n*46 336*n*54, 341, 343, 345, 349–50

People's Liberation Army Navy (PLAN), 300, 302–4, 307–8, 311, 318–22, 325–31, 337–50
*Peresvet* (Russia), 140
Peru. *See* Callao squadron
Perez del Camino, Meliton, 79
*Petropavlovsk* (Russia), 130, 140–41
*Pezuela* (Spain), 77, 82
Pezuela, Joachin de la, 78–81, 84
Pham Van Dong, 300
Philip V, 33
Philippines, 34, 38–39, 42, 219, 222, 242, 245, 298, 305, 308, 311–12, 317, 321, 323–24, 326–27, 338, 342, 347, 350
Phillips, Tom, 246–47
piracy, 33, 48, 319–20, 342, 384
Pohl, Hugo von, 129, 175
Pola, 111–12, 117–25, 194
Polaris missile. *See* missiles
Porlier, Rosendo, 78
Port Arthur Squadron, 5, 101, 103–4, 128–45, 361, 385, 389–90
Poseidon missile. *See* missiles
*Potrillo* (Spain), 77
Pratas Islands, 298, 310
Pratt, William
*Presidenta* (Spain), 77
*Prince of Wales* (Britain), 246–47
*Prinz Eugen* (Austria-Hungary), 116, 121
*Prinz Eugen* (Germany), 264–66
privateering, 34–36, 41, 43–44, 48–49, 80–81, 85
*Provence* class (France), 153
*Prueba* (Spain), 78–81, 83–84
Pu Yi, Henry, 235
Putin, Vladimir, 355, 357–58, 362
Puttkamer, Karl-Jesko von, 268

Quasi-War, 44, 48
Quintanilla, Antonio, 85

*Radetsky* class (Austria-Hungary), 112, 114–17, 120
Raeder, Erich, 182, 251, 253–64, 266–68
Rahn, Werner, 185

*Rawaldpindi* (Britain), 263
*Re Umberto* class (Italy), 155
Reagan, Ronald, 289
*Real Phelipe* (Spain), 24
Red Sea, 192*t*, 278, 283–84
Regia Aeronautica, 190*t*, 196–98, 203*t*
Regia Marina, 147–64, 188–190*t*, 191–192t, 193, 195*t*, 197–203*t*
*Regina Margherita*, 156
Regio Esercito, 152, 155, 161, 164, 190*t*
Reichsmarine, 251–60, 264, 268
*Reina Maria Isabel* (Spain), 76–78
Republic of China: *See* Taiwan
*République* class (France), 156
*Repulse* (Britain), 246
*Resolución* (Spain), 77
*Rheinland* (Germany), 180
Riccardi, Arturo, 200–1
Rodil, José Ramon, 85
Rommel, Erwin, 201
*Rosa de los Andes* (Chile), 81
Roosevelt, Franklin D., 238, 240, 242–44
Rousselet de Châteaurenault, François Louis, 16
Royal Naval War College, 26–27
Royal Navy (RN), 23, 44, 47, 53, 63, 78, 175, 191–92*t*, 195*t*, 233, 238, 245, 252, 262, 378, 38; French strategy for 3, 52, 62, 67; German arms race with 6, 169–70, 182, 234, 239, 241; German war plans for 171–72, 181, 214, 264; theorists' advice for, 28, 92–93, 95, 100, 104
*Ruggiero di Lauria* class (Italy), 155
Ruiz de Apodaca, Sebastián, 41
Rupert, Prince, 24
Russell, Edward, 14–16, 18, 20
Russia, 37, 39–40, 48, 76, 110, 115, 124, 152, 160, 223; alliance with France, 112, 149–51, 162–63; constricted geography, 170, 275–79, 380, 386–87, 390; in German war plans, 260, 262; in Middle East, 279–84, 290; in Napoleonic Wars, 46, 52–53,

57, 60, 66–67, 379. *See also* bastion strategy; China, People's Republic, relations with Russia; China, People's Republic, Sino-Soviet split; Entente, Triple; Gorshkov, Sergey; naval basing, Russian; submarines, Russian; World War I, Russia
Russian naval buildup, 388; tsarist, 149, 389; Soviet, 287, 290, 389; under Putin, 7, 9, 355
Russian naval theory, 2, 18, 128–34, 359–66, 369; sixth-generation warfare, 363–64, 367–69
Russian Navy, 114, 354–69: Baltic Fleet, 135, 178–80, 275, 288, 360; Black Sea Fleet, Russian, 135, 275, 277, 280, 288, 360, 390; Northern Fleet, 275–77, 280, 355, 360, 365. *See also* Gorshkov, Sergey G.
Russian Navy Pacific Fleet, tsarist, 137–45, 361; Soviet, 276–78, 283, 288–89, 302; post-Soviet, 360, 276.
Russo-Japanese War, 4–5, 92, 101–105, 128–45, 178, 361–62, 380, 384–85, 389; Vladivostok Squadron, 135, 138–39. *See also* Port Arthur Squadron

Sa Zhenbing, 298
Sadat, Anwar, 282
Saint-Bon, Simone Antonio Pacoret de, 155
Salazar, Francisco, 84
*Sampson* (USA), 317
Sampson, William, 98
*San Martín* (Chile), 77
San Martín, José de, 75, 77, 81–82, 84, 86
*San Telmo* (Spain), 78, 80
*Saratoga* (USA), 244
Satō Tetsutarō, 378
Scapa Flow, 171, 184, 268, 277
*Scharnhorst* (Germany), 263, 265–66, 269
Scheer, Reinhard, 175–177, 185
Schleicher, Kurt von, 254–55, 259
Schooenveldt, Battles of, 24, 26
Schooner, 76, 81–82

## 408  INDEX

*Schlesien* class (Germany), 252
*Science of Military Strategy*, 328, 338, 348
sea denial, 10, 382, 388–92; in Austo-Hungarian strategy, 385; in British strategy, 202, 385, 387; in Central Power strategy, 385; in Chinese strategy, 297, 307, 309–13, 349; in German strategy, 387; in Italian strategy, 154, 163, 385; in Russian strategy, 278, 290, 356, 385–86; in Spanish strategy, 37; in U.S. strategy, 278, 287, 289, 356
sea lines of communication (SLOC), 36, 92, 191–92, 257–58, 263; of Axis, 6; of Britain, 7, 14, 28, 34–35, 188, 239, 263, 269; of China, 341–42; of France, 62, 154, 158–59, 163, 188–89; of Germany, 171, 253, 264; of Italy, 157–58, 188–90, 193, 198, 202; of Japan, 136, 138; of NATO, 356; of Philippines, 40; of Spain, 4, 41–42, 72, 76–77; of USA, 289
*Sebastiana* (Spain), 77, 84
Sechi, Giovanni, 132–33
*Seeadler* (Germany), 183
Sevastopol, 123, 275, 360, 390
*Sevastopol'* (Russia), 143
Seven Years' War, 35–36, 39
Shen Jinlong, 343–44
Shipbuilding, Austro-Hungarian, 112, 114–15; British, 169; Chinese, 319, 337, 344–45, 350; French, 54, 56, 58; German, 169–70, 174, 177, 184, 214, 251, 252*t*, 254, 255*t*, 256, 259, 262; Italian, 147, 152, 154–55; Japanese, 7, 234–35, 242–43; Russian, 149, 287, 290, 358, 366, 368; Spanish, 34–36, 42; U.S., 247. *See also* Germany, naval buildup; London Naval Treaty; Russian naval buildup; Vinson–Tramel Naval Bill; Washington Naval Treaty
Shiozawa, Koichi, 235
Shoigu, Sergei, 357
Shovell, Cloudesley, 15–16
Shtal', A., 132

Singapore, 7, 231–32, 236–39, 245–47, 278, 324, 383
Singapore, Battle of, 7, 246–247, 389
Sino-French War, 298–99
Sino-Japanese War: First, 4, 92, 94, 96, 298, 389; Second, 221–23, 234–37, 243, 379
Sino-Soviet split, 276, 279, 290, 308
Sino-Vietnamese War, 8, 297–98, 303–5, 307, 310, 312
Six-Day War. *See* Arab-Israeli wars
Skagerrak, 277
Skoda Works, 112–15
Slipchenko, Vladimir, 364
Somalia, 281, 283–84
Somodevilla, Zenón de, 34
Soroa, Joachín, 83
Souchon, Wilhelm, 118–19
South China Sea, 297–99, 301–5, 308–12, 319–23*t*, 326–27, 329, 331, 338, 343, 345, 347, 350
Soviet Union: *See* Russia
Spain, 157, 194, 264, 379–80,
Spanish Civil War, 196, 239
Spanish Empire, 2–4, 13–14, 26, 33–40, 42–44, 48–49, 383; in Napoleonic Wars, 32, 40–48, 53, 56, 61–62, 64, 67, 72–75, 379–80; wars for independence from, 3–4, 73–86, 379, 387. *See also* Peninsular War; Spanish-American War
Spanish-American War, 4, 92, 97–99, 104, 128
Spaun, Hermann von, 114
Spee, Maximilian von, 182
Spratly Islands, 298–300, 309–11, 327, 338–39, 347; Itu Aba Island, 299, 310,
Spragge, Edward, 25
Stabilimento Tecnico Triestino, 112, 114–15, 117
Standley, William, 242
Stark, Oskar Viktorovich, 137–38
Stessel', Anatolii Mikhailovich, 142
submarine-launched ballistic missiles (SLBM). *See* missiles.

submarines, 2, 5–6, 104, 171, 178, 277, 311, 391; Austro-Hungarian, 121–23, 382, 386–87; British, 177, 180, 192*t*, 195*t*, 239; Chinese, 307, 319, 321–223*t*, 324–25, 327*t*, 344–45, 347–48; Dutch, 245; French, 189, 190*t*, 195*t*; German: *see* U-boat; Italian, 125, 162, 190*t*, 190–92, 192*t*, 193–95, 195*t*, 196–203, 386; Japanese, 218, 220, 222, 233, 299; nuclear-powered submarines (SSBN), 285–88, 327*t;* Russian, 7–8, 275, 279–80, 284–90, 301–2, 356, 361, 367–68, 384; Taiwanese, 310; U.S, 241–43, 285–89, 317, 322, 384

Suetsugu, Nobumasa, 219

Suez Canal, 150, 188–89, 191, 193, 198, 203, 276, 278–79, 281, 283–84, 355

Suez Crisis, 279, 284, 290

Supermarina, 194–95, 197–201

Syria, 280–3, 356, 364

*Szent István* (Austria-Hungary), 116, 122, 124–25

*Tagle* (Spain), 77

Taiwan. *See* China, Republic of

Takahashi, Sankichi, 219

*Takao* class (Japan), 222

Taranto, 57, 122–24, 149, 154, 157, 159–60, 164, 194, 198–99

Taranto, Battle of, 6, 198–200, 204, 389

*Tegetthoff* (Austria-Hungary), 116–17, 121

Tegetthoff, Wilhelm von, 111

*Terrible* (Chile), 61

Texel, Battle of the, 24–25

Thursfield, James, 4, 92–93, 96–97, 101–3, 376

Till, Geoffrey, 214

*Tirpitz* (Germany), 266, 269

Tirpitz, Alfred von, 115, 117, 169–70, 172, 174, 181–82, 185, 214, 252–53, 257, 268

Tito, Josip Broz, 377

torpedo, 102, 131, 139, 171, 177, 196–97, 199–200, 222–23, 262–63, 368

torpedo boat, 104, 124–25, 132, 136–37, 140, 143, 153–54, 158, 161, 163–64, 169, 173, 179–80, 189–190*t*, 192*t*, 194, 195*t*, 252*t*, 255, 261*t*, 266*t*, 380

Torrington, Lord. *See* Herbert, Arthur

Tourville, Anne-Hilarion de, 14–17, 219–21, 27–29

trade. *See* commerce raiding

Trafalgar, Battle of, 46, 56–57, 185, 379–80; Trafalgar-like battle, 95, 171, 184

Trident missile. *See* missiles

Triple Alliance, 112–13, 117–18, 148–52, 157, 159–60, 162–63, 180

Triple Entente. *See* Entente, Triple

Trost, Carlisle A. H., 289

Troubridge, Ernest, 120

Truguet, Jean François, 59

Truman, Harry, 277, 317

*Tsesarevich* (Russia), 144

Tsushima, Battle of, 5, 361, 380

Tsushima Strait, 135, 141, 302

Turkey, 277–78. *See also* Ottoman Empire

Turkish straits, 151, 277: Bosphorus, 277, 181; Dardanelles, 60, 119, 181 ; Sea of Marmora, 277

Turner, Stansfield, 287

Two-Ocean Navy Act, 245, 247. *See also* Vinson–Trammel bills

Tyrrhenian Sea, 147–49, 154, 156–60, 163, 202

U-boat, 169, 239, 387, in World War I, 7, 122–23, 170, 172–74, 176–79, 181, 183–85, 382, 389; in World War II, 246, 151, 252*t*, 252–55, 255*t*, 258–69, 287, 381, 389. *See also* submarines

*U5* (Germany), 121

*U9* (Germany), 183

*U12* (Germany), 121

*U30* (Germany), 262

*U48* (Germany), 263

Udržal, František, 113
Ukraine, 278, 356, 358–60, 390
United States, 260, 269, 317, 381–82, 388; geography, 3, 5, 32, 49, 378–79, 383; in British strategy, 43, 218, 232; in Chinese strategy, 7, 9, 306, 317–327t, 328–30, 337–38, 343, 345, 347, 349–50, 380; in German strategy, 183, 257; in French strategy, 43–44, 67; in Japanese strategy, 211, 217, 220–21, 225–26, 232–34, 238, 246, 378, 389; in Russian strategy, 7, 275, 279–82, 284–86, 288–89, 306, 359, 366, 386; in Spanish strategy, 37, 42, 45–46, 48–49, 82, 98–99; naval superiority over Japan, 210–11, 219, 232–34, 238, 240–44, 247; strategy for China, 8, 235, 299—301, 306, 308, 311, 317, 320–22, 323t, 323–26, 328–31, 347, 349–50, 390; strategy for Japan, 7, 221, 224, 231–33, 235–36, 245–47, 383–84; strategy for Middle East, 279, 281–82; strategy for Russia, 289, 298, 356, 386; strategy for Spain, 98; strategy for Taiwan, 299; strategy for Vietnam, 297–98, 301–2, 304–5. *See also* Pacific Fleet; Washington Naval Treaty
U.S. Naval War College, 241, 312, 376–77. *See also* Mahan, Alfred Thayer
U.S. Navy (USN): General Board ; Pacific Fleet, 317–31, 334n35, 345.
USSR. *See* Russia
Uztárez, Gerónimo de, 32–36, 48

Vacaro, Antonio, 73, 78–84
Vázquez de Figueroa, José, 48
Vego, Milan, 203, 213, 376–77, 389
*Veloz Pasajena* (Spain), 77
Venice, 57, 64, 125, 157, 160, 194
*Venganza* (Spain), 76–77, 79–81, 83–84
Versailles, Treaty of, 216, 238–39, 251–55, 258
*Victoria de Ica* (Spain), 81

Vietnam: Democratic Republic of, 7–8, 278, 297–98, 300–13, 323–24, 379, 384, 388; Republic of (South Vietnam), 278, 297, 299–300, 303–5. *See also* Sino-Vietnamese War
Villaret de Joyeuse, Louis Thomas, 58
Villegas, José, 83–84
Vinson–Trammel bills, 240, 243–44. *See also* Two-Ocean Navy Act
*Viribus Unitis* (Austria-Hungary), 116, 121, 125
Vitgeft, Wilgelm Karlovich, 140–44, 361–62
*Vittorio Veneto*, 198, 200
Vivero, José Pacual de, 80
Vladivostok, 135, 138–39, 141–44, 276

Wainwright, Richard, 4, 100–1
War of Jenkins's Ear, 34
War of the League of Augsburg, 3, 13. *See also* Beachy Head, Battle of
War Plan Orange, 236, 241–42
Warsaw Pact, 278, 280, 290, 384
Washington, George, 42–43
Washington Naval Treaty, 189, 191, 218–19, 231, 232, 238–41, 243–44, 254, 257
Watkins, James D., 289
Watson, Bruce W., 278
Weichold, Eberhard, 197
Weihaiwei, Battle of, 389
Weserübung, operation, 264
Wilhelm II, 149, 171, 174–76
Wilkinson, Spenser, 4, 93–95
William III, 13–16, 18, 20–21, 23, 25, 28
William V, 56
Witkowitz foundry, 112, 114–15
*Wolf* (Germany), 183
Work, Robert, 343
World War I, 4–5, 164; Austria-Hungary, 110, 112, 117–26, 181, 184, 382, 386–87; Britain, 118, 120, 122–23, 129, 175–77, 180–85, 217, 264, 378, 381, 382–83, 387; Germany, 118–24, 169–85, 264,

268, 379, 381, 383, 386–89; France 118–19, 120–22, 181, 189, 379, 382, 387; Italy, 121–23, 125, 152, 162, 189, 382–83, 386, 388; Japan, 216–17, 382; Russia, 118–19, 123–24, 178–80, 265, 386–89; Turkey, 119, 181; USA, 379, 382–84. *See also* Dogger Bank, Battle of; Germany, in World War I; Japan in World War I; Jutland, Battle of; U-boat

World War II, 4–6; Britain, 195*t*, 197, 199–202, 203*t*, 245–47, 262–65, 267, 269, 287, 378, 381–82; France, 195*t*, 196–97, 223, 245–46, 264–65, 379; Germany, 201, 203*t*, 262–69, 379, 381, 387–89; Italy, 192, 195*t*, 195–204, 287–88; Japan, 383; Russia, 277; USA, 245–47, 265, 287, 379, 383. *See also* Germany, in World War II; Japan, in World War II; Pearl Harbor attack; Taranto, Battle of; U-boat
Wylie, Joseph C., 213–14

*Xaviera* (Spain), 80
Xi Jinping, 343, 391
Xisha Islands. *See* Paracel Islands

Yamamoto Isoroku, 232, 243
*Yamato* class (Japan), 219, 224, 244
Yellow Sea, 5, 103, 128, 135–36, 143–44, 319, 321, 329, 338, 361
Yellow Sea, Battle of, 144, 361
Yemen, 281–84, 342

Zenker, Hans, 251
Zhou Enlai, 300; 315*n*36
Zhukov, Georgy, 279
*Zumwalt* class (USA) 391

THE NAVAL INSTITUTE PRESS is the book-publishing arm of the U.S. Naval Institute, a private, nonprofit, membership society for sea service professionals and others who share an interest in naval and maritime affairs. Established in 1873 at the U.S. Naval Academy in Annapolis, Maryland, where its offices remain today, the Naval Institute has members worldwide.

Members of the Naval Institute support the education programs of the society and receive the influential monthly magazine *Proceedings* or the colorful bimonthly magazine *Naval History* and discounts on fine nautical prints and on ship and aircraft photos. They also have access to the transcripts of the Institute's Oral History Program and get discounted admission to any of the Institute-sponsored seminars offered around the country.

The Naval Institute's book-publishing program, begun in 1898 with basic guides to naval practices, has broadened its scope to include books of more general interest. Now the Naval Institute Press publishes about seventy titles each year, ranging from how-to books on boating and navigation to battle histories, biographies, ship and aircraft guides, and novels. Institute members receive significant discounts on the Press' more than eight hundred books in print.

Full-time students are eligible for special half-price membership rates. Life memberships are also available.

For more information about Naval Institute Press books that are currently available, visit www.usni.org/press/books. To learn about joining the U.S. Naval Institute, please write to:

Member Services
**U.S. NAVAL INSTITUTE**
291 Wood Road
Annapolis, MD 21402-5034

Telephone: (800) 233-8764
Fax: (410) 571-1703
Web address: www.usni.org